# BUILDING THINKING SKILLS®
## PRIMARY

**SERIES TITLES**
BUILDING THINKING SKILLS®—PRIMARY
BUILDING THINKING SKILLS®—BOOK 1
BUILDING THINKING SKILLS®—BOOK 2
BUILDING THINKING SKILLS®—BOOK 3 FIGURAL
BUILDING THINKING SKILLS®—BOOK 3 VERBAL

**WARREN HILL & RONALD EDWARDS**

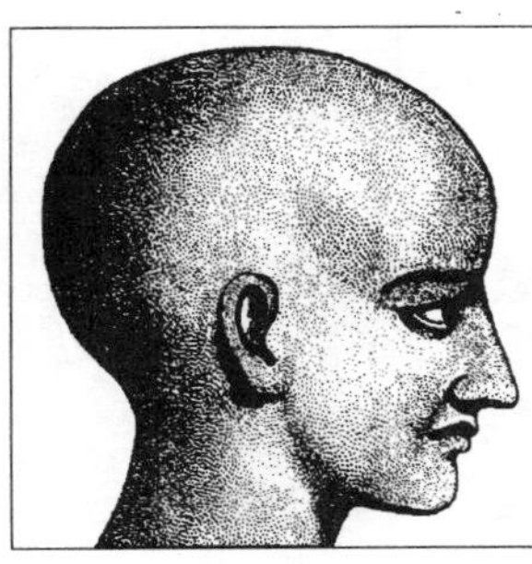


CRITICAL THINKING BOOKS & SOFTWARE
(formerly Midwest Publications)
P.O. Box 448 • Pacific Grove • CA 93950-0448
Phone 800-458-4849 • FAX 831-393-3277 • www.criticalthinking.com
ISBN 0-89455-332-1
Printed in the United States of America

# TABLE OF CONTENTS

# TEACHER SUGGESTIONS AND INSTRUCTIONS

BUILDING THINKING SKILLS—PRIMARY promotes the development of analytic thinking skills for primary-level children. The complete series includes Activity Sheets, detailed Lesson Plans, and necessary manipulative materials. The Activity Sheets in this book are designed to be used in conjunction with the correlated lesson plans and the manipulative materials to present an activity-based approach to analytic reasoning.

## The Activity Book

Activity Sheets, a basis for the BUILDING THINKING SKILLS—PRIMARY series, are used in conjunction with sets of manipulative materials to encourage development of four specific analytic thinking skills:

- identifying similarities and differences
- forming sequences and patterns
- classifying objects by their attributes, and
- creating analogies by organizing objects according to their characteristics.

Directions written at the top of each Activity Sheet provide the teacher with a brief summary of each activity. More detailed activity development, as well as preliminary teacher-led classroom lessons, are presented in the Lesson Plans.

> It is important to realize that the Activity Sheets are not meant to be used as paper-and-pencil activities or traditional worksheets. They are intended to serve as a vehicle to promote classroom discussion. The series is based upon the premise that the ability to analyze, verbalize, and communicate is the keystone of analytic thinking. Often, the student's rationale for a particular response is more important than the response itself.

## The Lesson Plans

Development rationale and detailed lesson plans for each Activity Sheet are found in the Teacher's Manual to BUILDING THINKING SKILLS—PRIMARY. Each plan: (1) states the objectives of the activity and the thinking skill addressed; (2) describes the manipulative materials and the Activity Sheets required for the lesson; (3) provides insights regarding the concepts underlying the activity; and (4) details a step-by-step description of a typical classroom presentation promoting the objectives of the activity.

Each lesson plan focuses on using a particular set of manipulative materials to introduce analytic reasoning in conjunction with the Activity Sheets. A detailed description is provided for a sequence of activities that allows student interaction with the manipulative materials prior to introduction of the Activity Sheets. A typical lesson plan from the Teacher's Manual is presented on the next page.

## The Manipulative Materials

Manipulative materials used in BUILDING THINKING SKILLS—PRIMARY are commercially available through Midwest Publications or many distributors of mathematical learning materials. The series utilizes three types of materials—*PATTERN BLOCKS, ATTRIBUTE BLOCKS,* and *INTERLOCKING CUBES*—to present an activity based approach to analytic reasoning. The lessons incorporate these materials in problem-solving situations that stress the ability to analyze relationships between objects and sets of figures.

*PATTERN BLOCKS* are manufactured in standard sizes. A set consists of 250 wooden blocks: 50 green triangles, 50 red trapezoids, 50 blue rhombuses, 50 tan rhombuses, 25 orange squares, and 25 yellow hexagons. Thick figure outlines on the Activity Sheets compensate for any irregularities in the blocks. Outlines of the five pattern-block shapes can be found on Activity Sheets 1–2.

*INTERLOCKING CUBES* are plastic linking cubes. A set consists of 100 cubes: 10 cubes each of 10 different colors. Each cube edge is 2 centimeters in length. The ability to link cubes to form three-dimensional figures permits construction of figures using the attributes of both color and shape. Illustrations of interlocking-cube figures are found on Activity Sheets 5–6.

*ATTRIBUTE BLOCKS* are commercially available in several different formats. Sets differ in the sizes of blocks, in the shapes used, and in the number of shapes in the set. The set referred to in this series consists of 60 molded plastic pieces: 5 shapes (triangle, square, rectangle, circle, hexagon), 3 colors (red, blue, yellow), 2 sizes (large, small), and 2 thicknesses (thick, thin). Attribute block shapes outlined on the Activity Sheets match the "desktop set" manufactured by *Invicta Plastics Ltd*, available from many educational distributors. Outlines for the small shapes are found on Activity Sheets 3–4; outlines for the large shapes are on Activity Sheets 159–164.

## Supplementary Materials

The solution to many problems presented in BUILDING THINKING SKILLS—PRIMARY includes the tasks of tracing blocks and coloring the resulting pictures. Since most solutions give rise to figures or patterns based on shape or color, these drawings provide students with visual verifications of the appropriateness of their responses and assist the teacher in evaluating the students' progress.

A variety of supplemental manipulative materials for use with the Activity Sheets are commercially available, including rubber stamps for pattern blocks, templates for attribute and pattern blocks, and templates with two-centimeter squares suitable for reproducing interlocking cube outlines. These materials provide alternatives to tracing the actual blocks. In addition, transparent pattern block shapes are available for use with an overhead projector. These materials, combined with teacher-made transparencies of Activity Sheets, provide the teacher with numerous classroom instructional strategies.

*Sample Lesson Plan*

# Matching Shapes (Activity 17–18)

**Objectives:**

Using INTERLOCKING CUBES:

1. construct matching figures
2. match figures with pictures

**Materials:**

| | |
|---|---|
| For each group of six students | • One set of INTERLOCKING CUBES |
| For each student | • Activity Sheets 17–18<br>• Crayons |

**Teacher Instructions:**

This activity extends the previous lesson, with INTERLOCKING CUBES replacing ATTRIBUTE BLOCKS, and continues the tasks of comparing and matching figures. Students should again be encouraged to verbalize why some figures do not match the shaded figures. Discussions that focus on the number of cubes used or their position in the figure are appropriate. Since some figures require more than five cubes, judicious color selection might be necessary for some constructions. Students may need to pool or exchange cubes to complete the activities.

**Classroom Activity:**

Ask the students to select five INTERLOCKING CUBES of the same color from their set of cubes. Begin by constructing a length of five cubes, then ask each student to construct a different figure using the same five cubes. Students should compare figures to determine which students constructed matching figures. Repeat this activity using four and six cubes as time permits.

After distributing Activity Sheet 17, ask the students to use one color from their cubes to construct a figure to match the shaded figure at the top of the sheet. Work with the students to find another picture that matches their figure. (There are three correct choices.) Students should verify their choice by moving the cubes to the picture they selected. After students color their selection, ask them to find another matching figure on the sheet. Stress that turning and/or flipping the figure does not change its shape. After students verify and color the second picture, continue until they have located all figures that match the shaded figure. Encourage students to explain why the other pictures do not match the figure. After completing the sheet, distribute Activity Sheet 18 and continue the task of locating all the figures that match the shaded figure. Continue emphasizing the geometric motions of turning and flipping. Verify student responses by comparing the color of their construction to the appropriate figures.

## MATCHING SHAPES

Find a PATTERN BLOCK to match each shape.
Place the block on the matching shape.
Color the pictures to match the blocks.

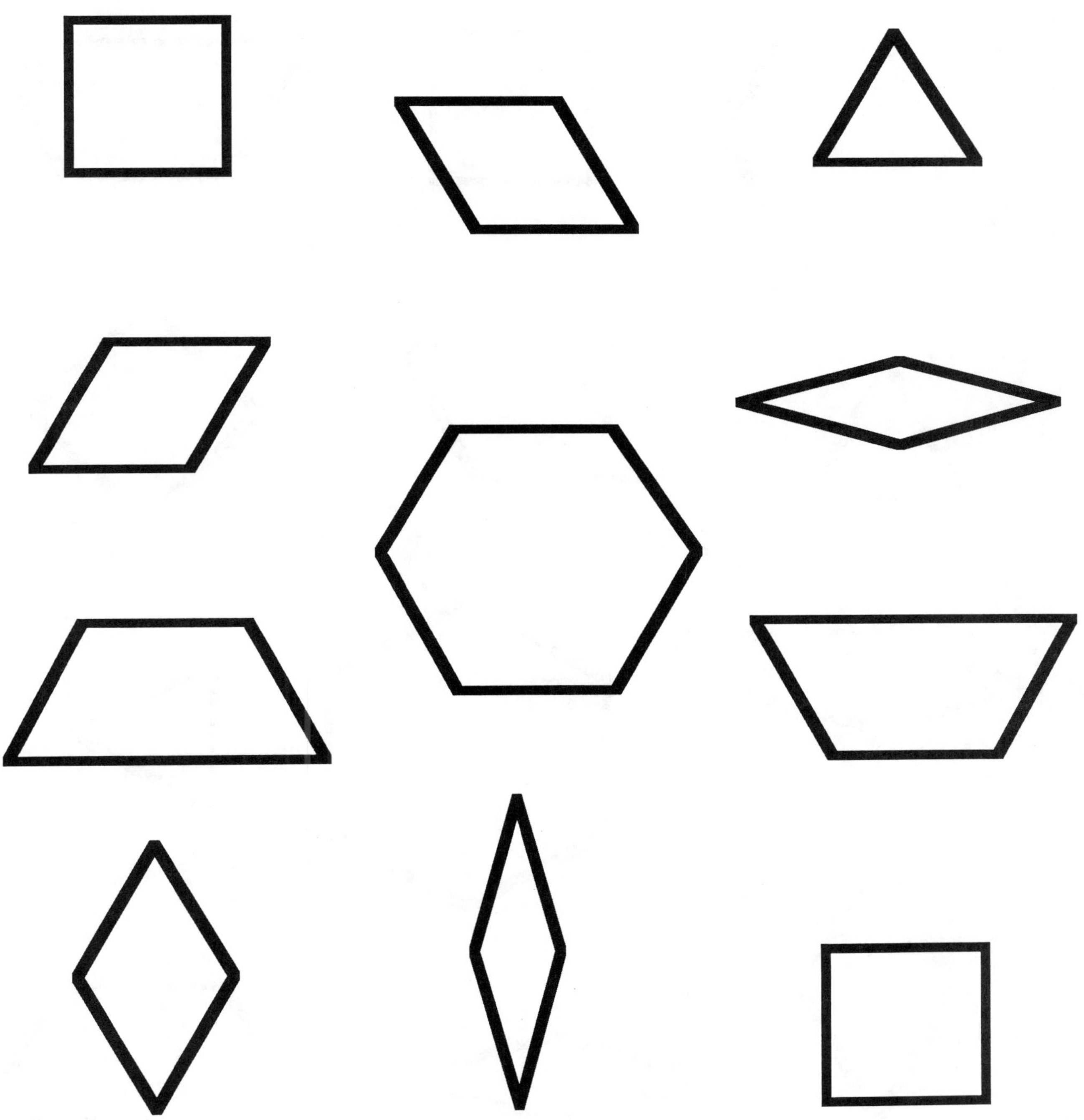

## MATCHING SHAPES

Find a PATTERN BLOCK to match each shape.
Place the block on the matching shape.
Color the pictures to match the blocks.

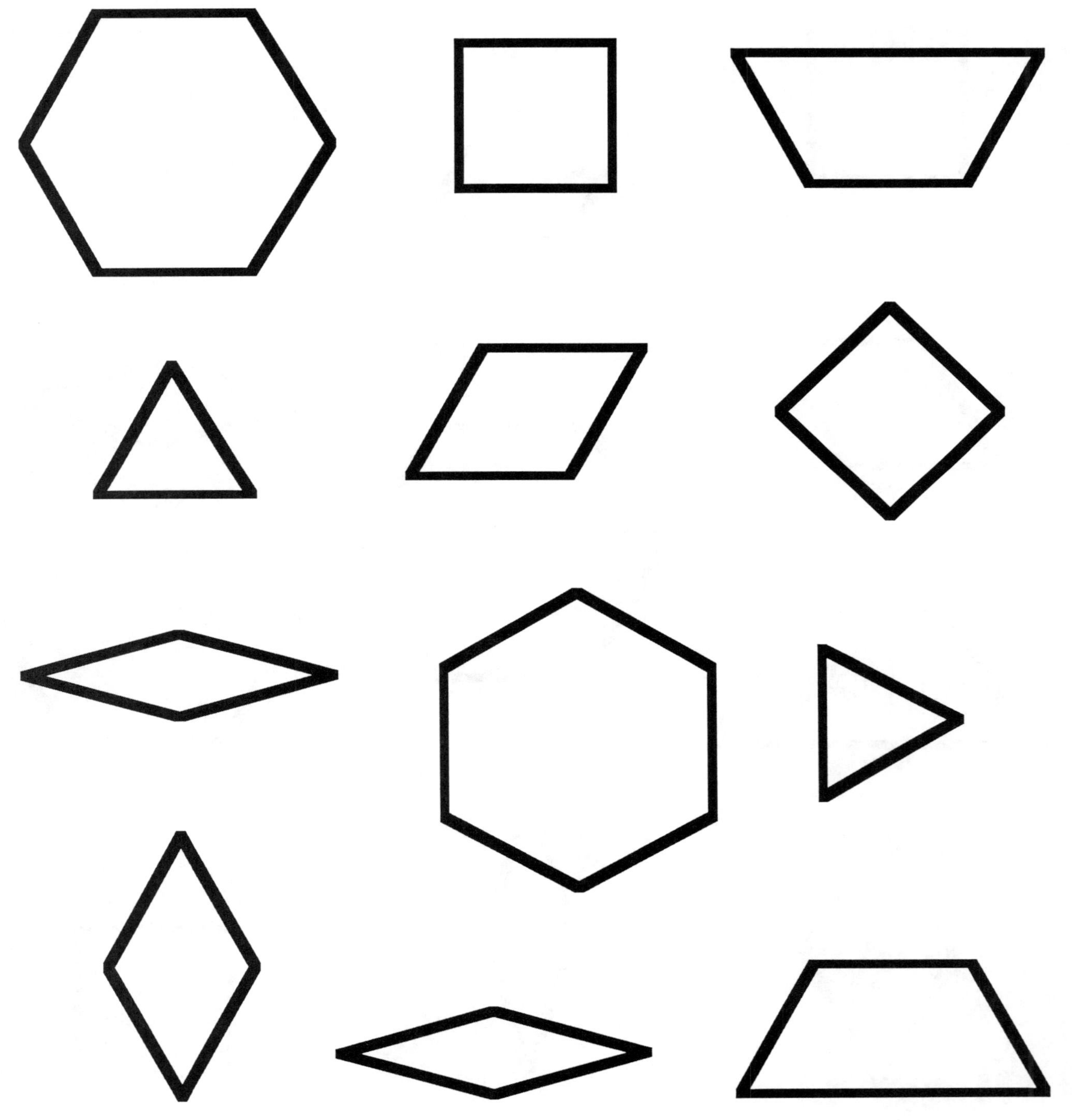

## MATCHING SHAPES

Find an ATTRIBUTE BLOCK to match each shape.
Place the block on the matching shape.
Color the pictures to match the blocks.

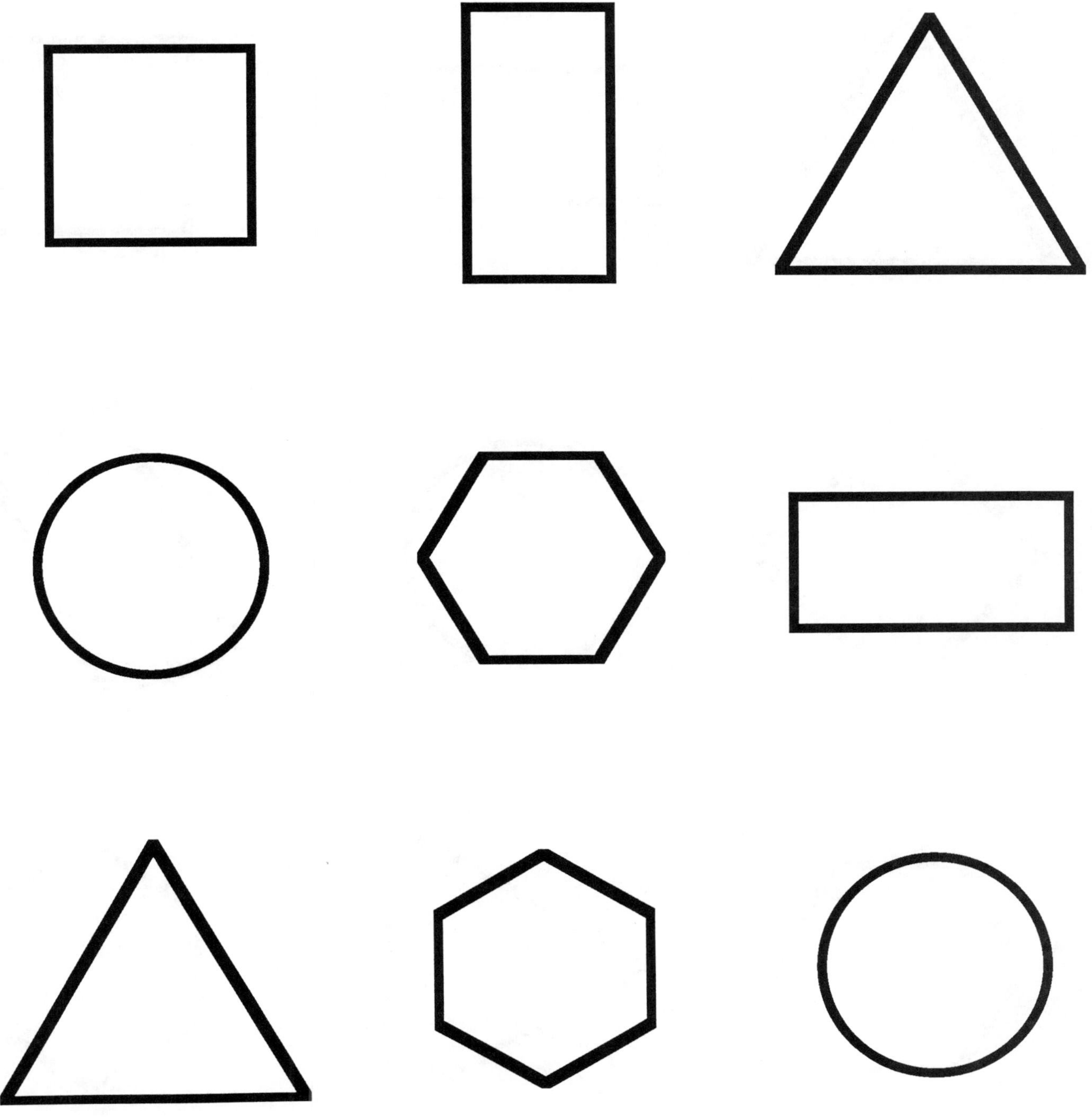

## MATCHING SHAPES

Find an ATTRIBUTE BLOCK to match each shape.
Place the block on the matching shape.
Color the pictures to match the blocks.

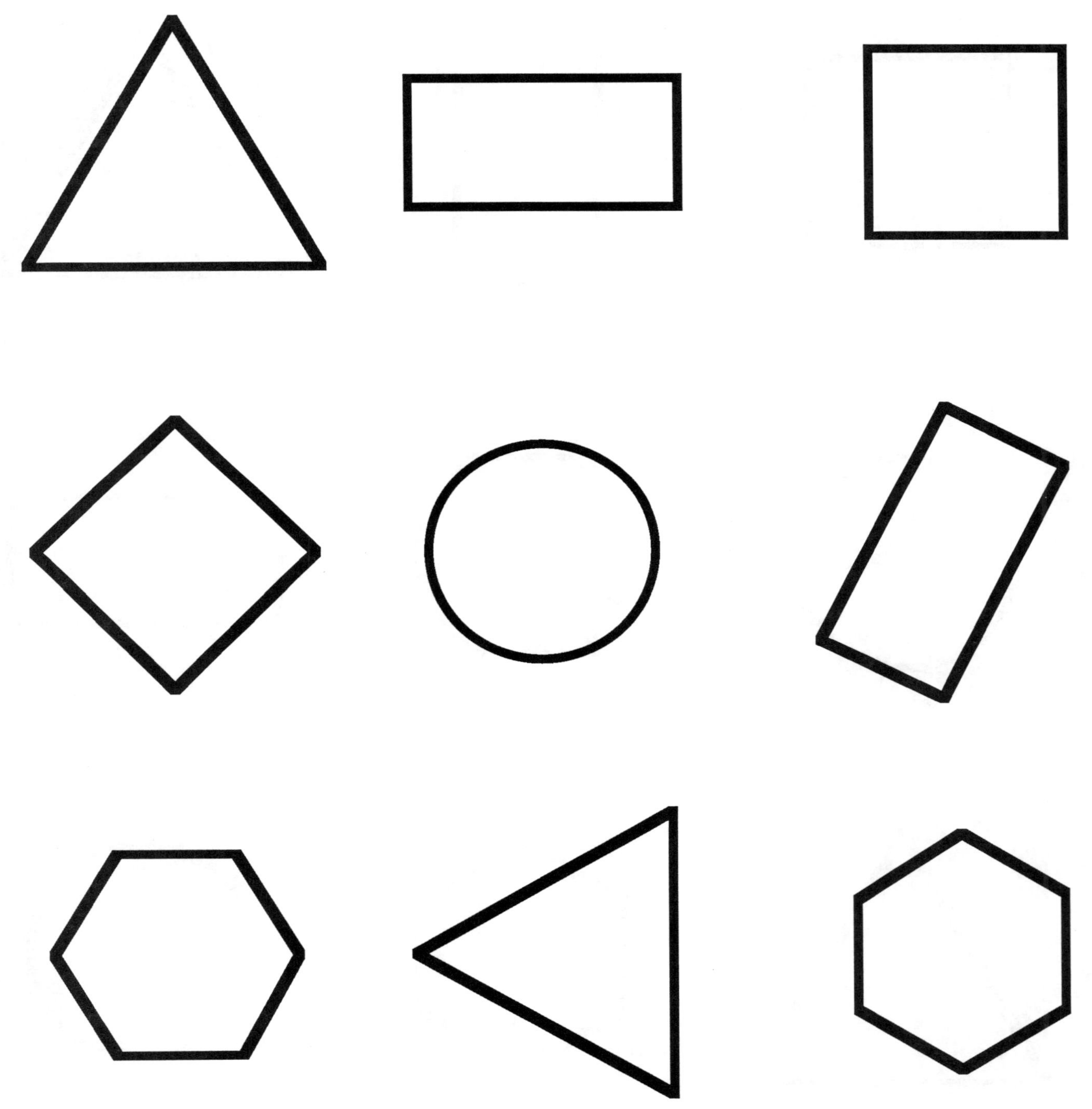

## MATCHING SHAPES

Use a different color of INTERLOCKING CUBES to make each figure below.
Place your constructed figures on the matching pictures.
Color each picture to match the cubes.

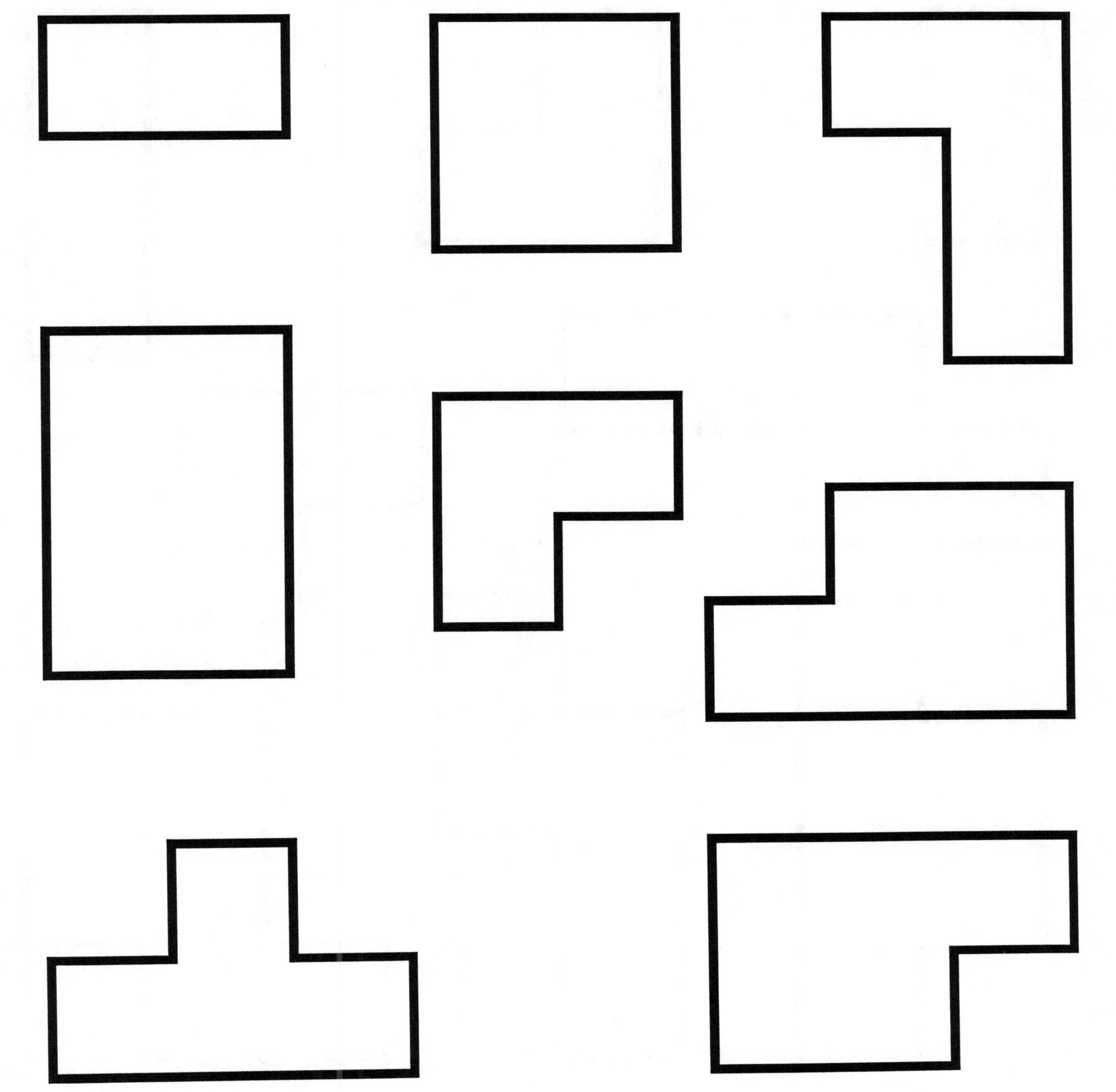

## MATCHING SHAPES

Use a different color of INTERLOCKING CUBES to make each figure below.
Place your constructed figures on the matching pictures.
Color each picture to match the cubes.

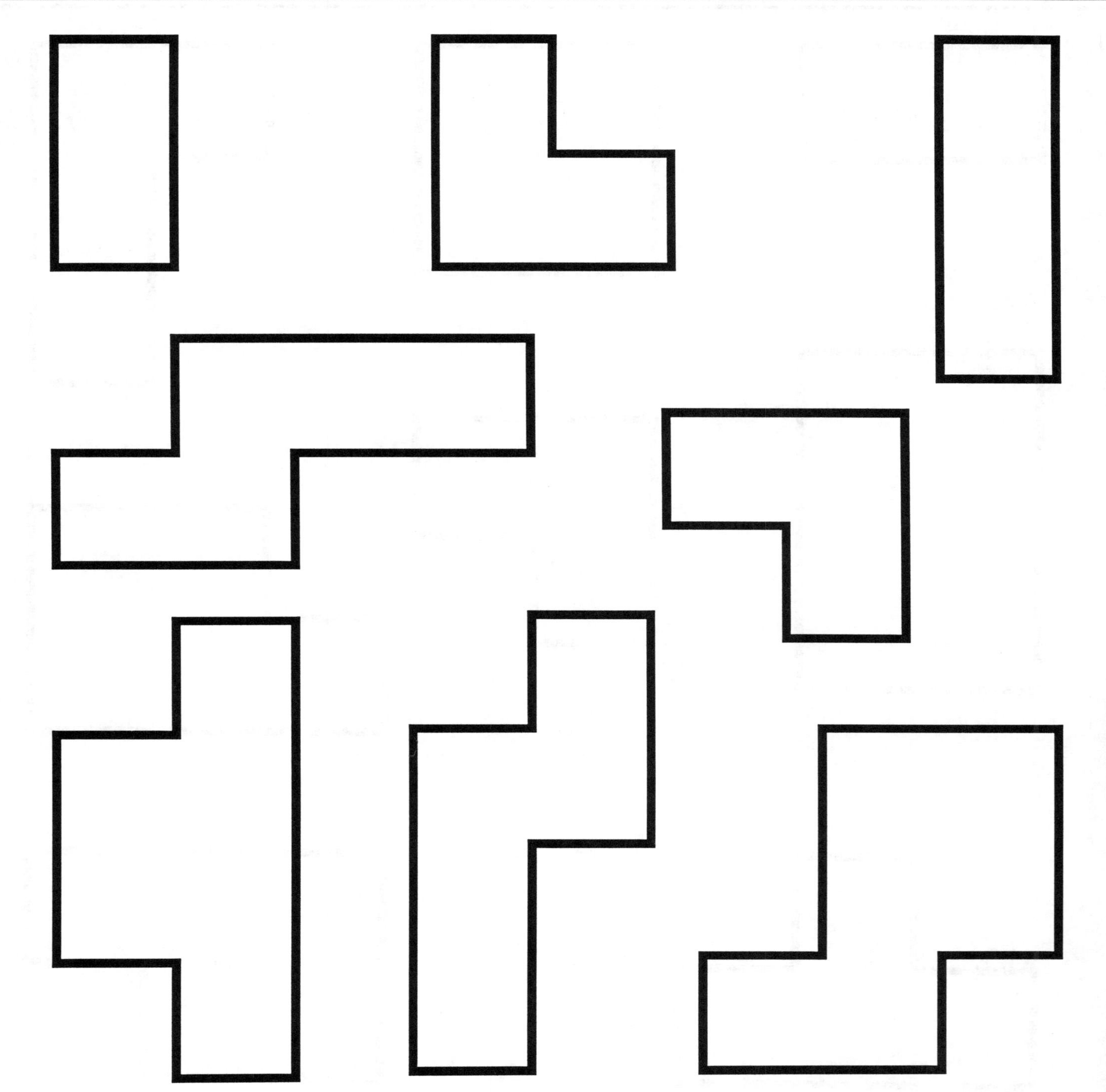

## MATCHING SHAPES

Place a PATTERN BLOCK on each shaded shape below.
Move each block to the matching shape in the same row.
Color the matching shapes the same color as the block.

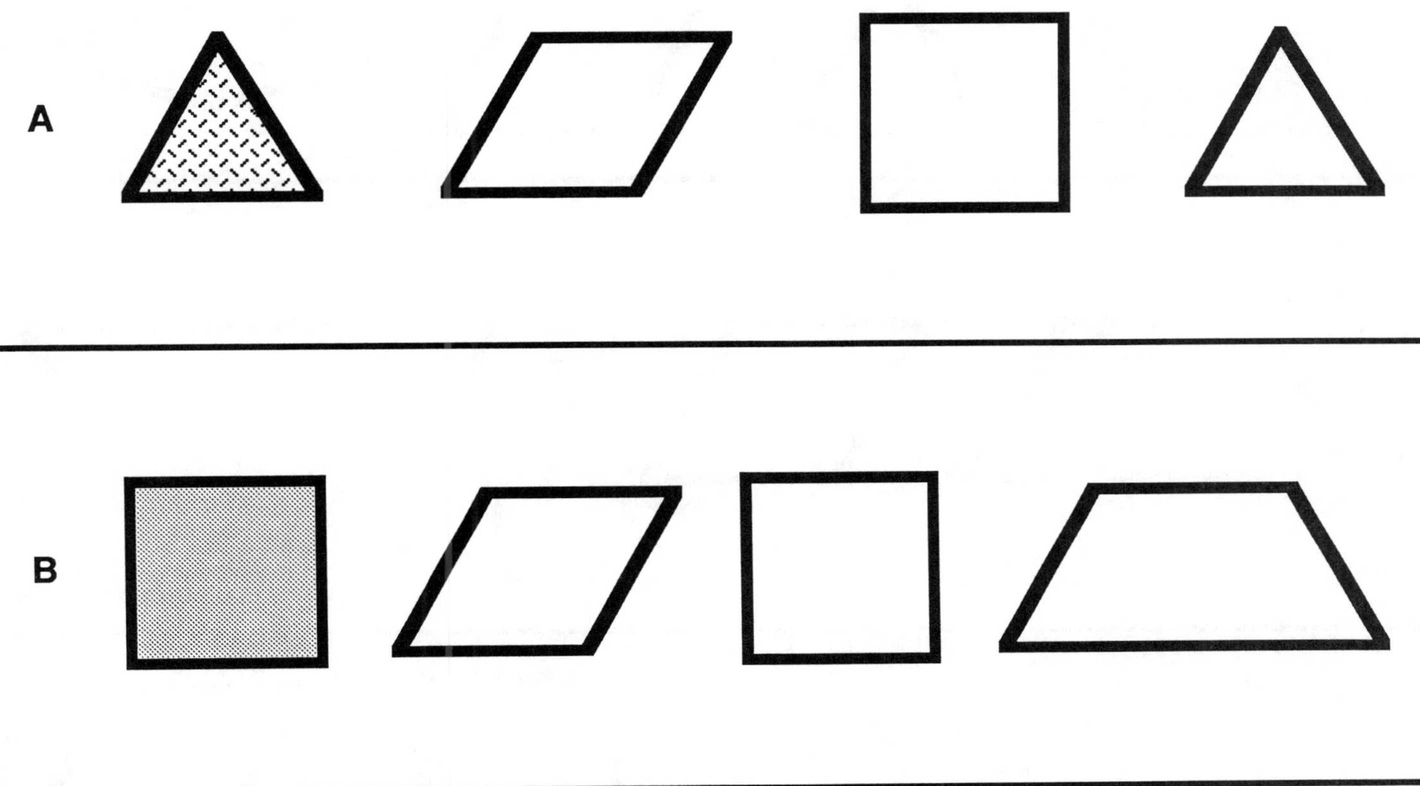


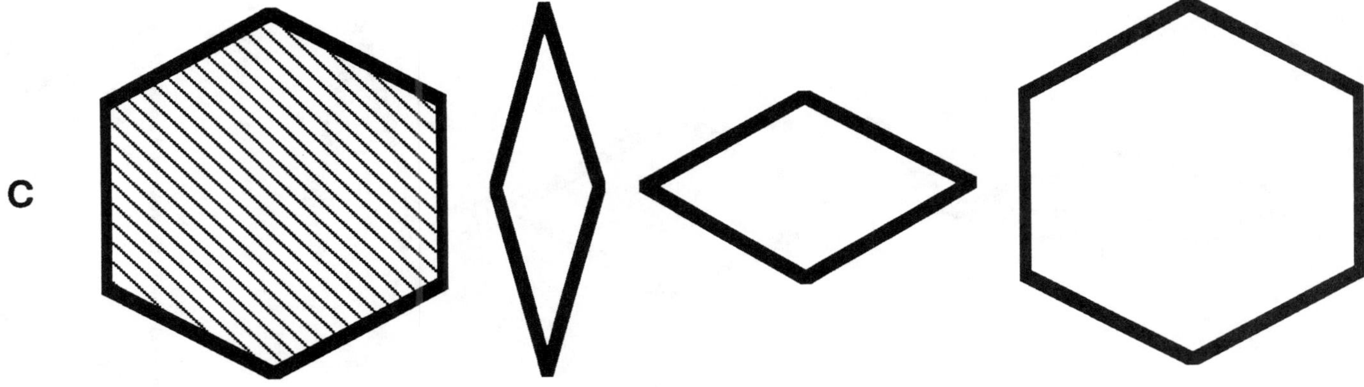

## MATCHING SHAPES

Place a PATTERN BLOCK on each shaded shape below.
Move each block to the matching shape in the same row.
Color the matching shapes the same color as the block.

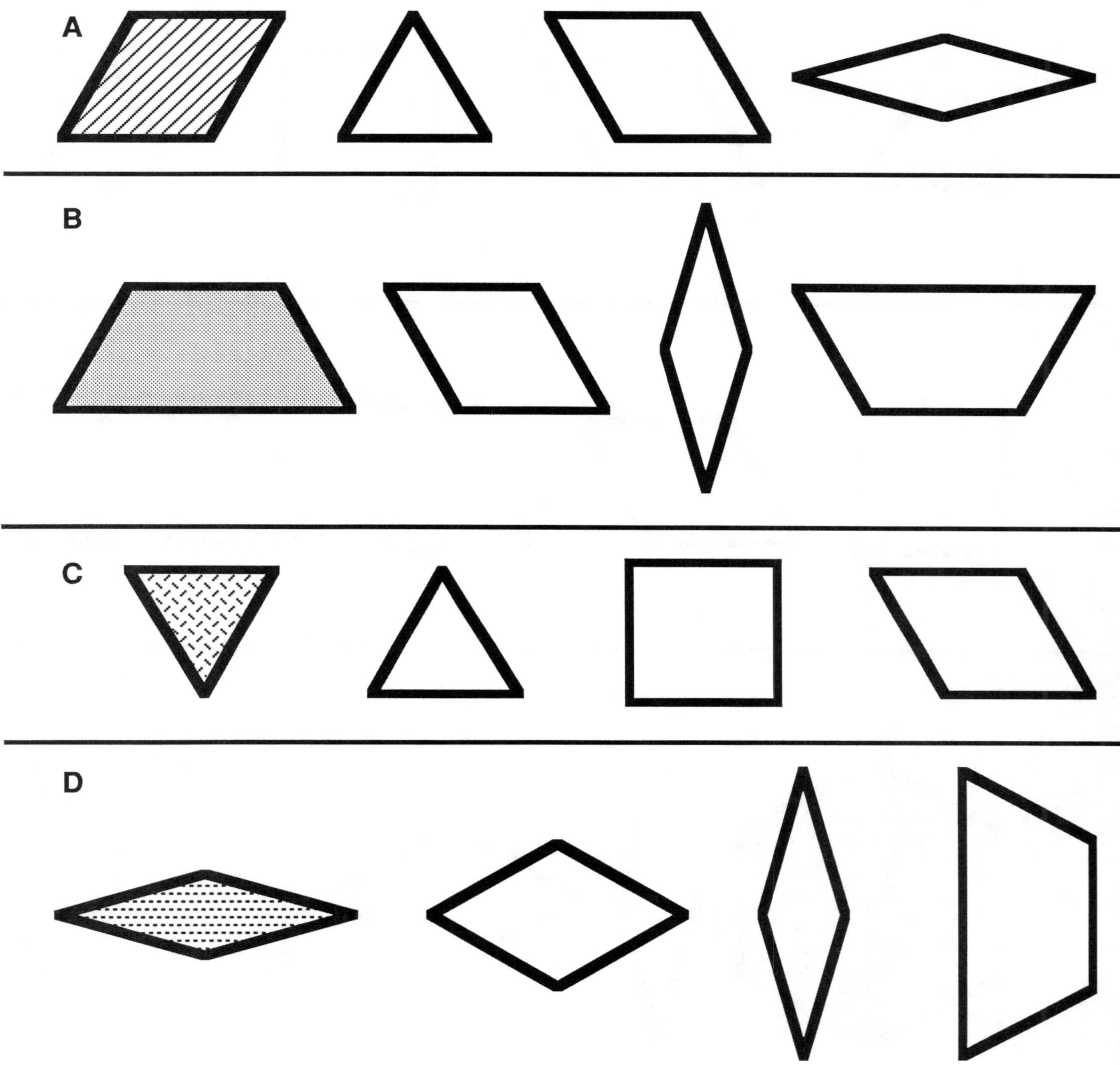

## MATCHING SHAPES

Place an ATTRIBUTE BLOCK on each shaded shape below.
Move each block to the matching shape in the same row.
Color the matching shapes the same color as the block.

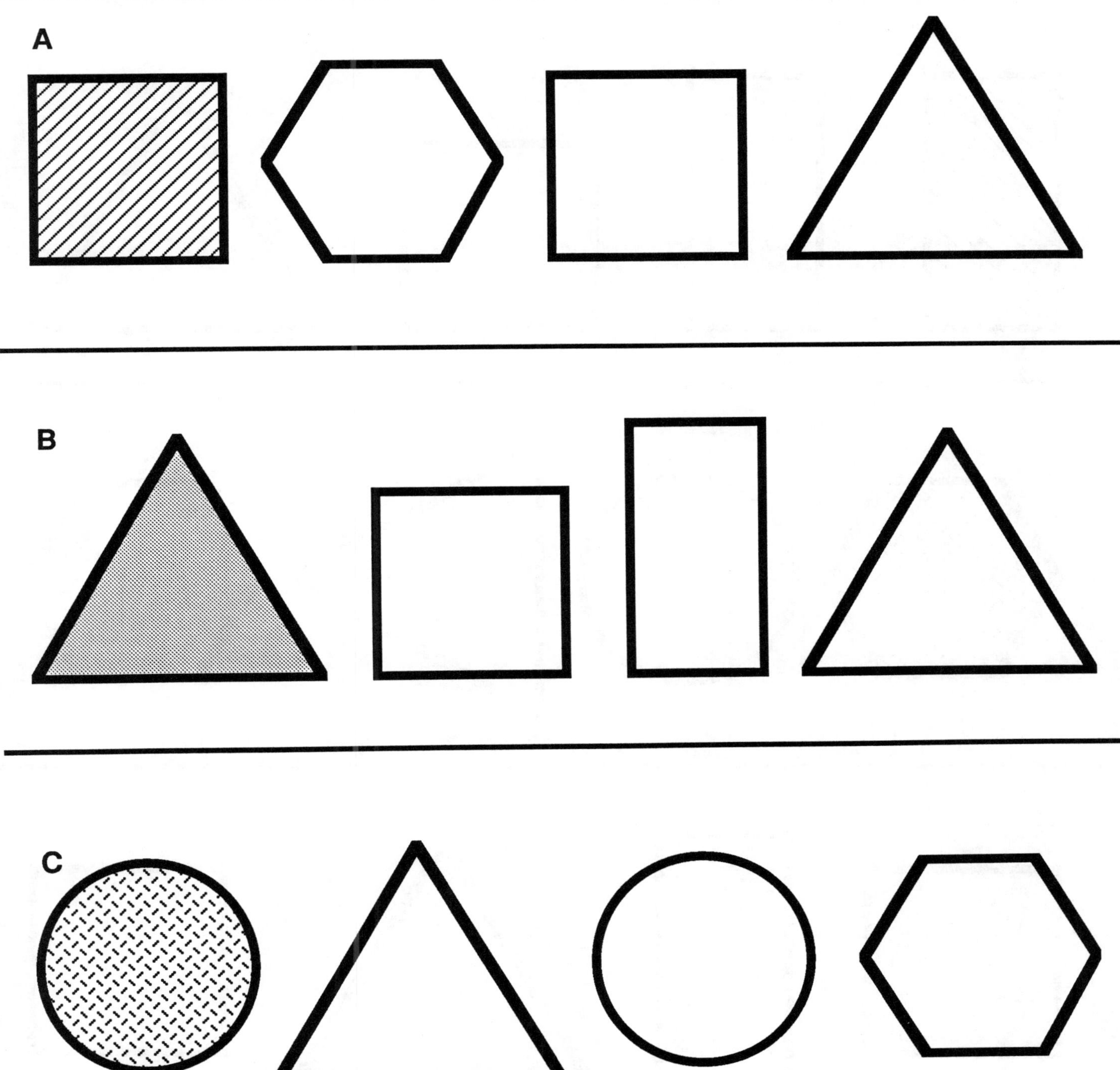

## MATCHING SHAPES

Place an ATTRIBUTE BLOCK on each shaded shape below.
Move each block to the matching shape in the same row.
Color the matching shapes the same color as the block.

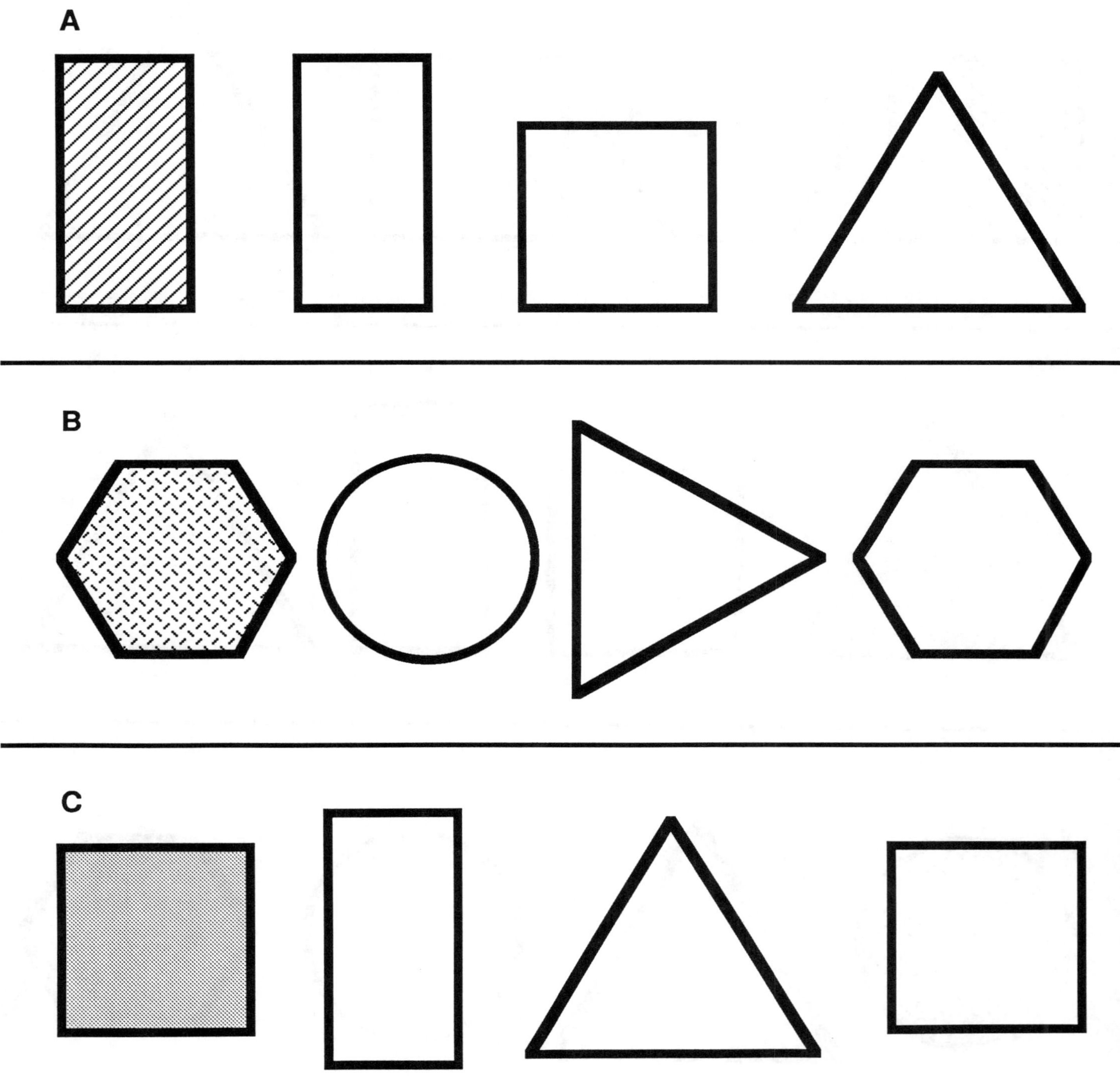

# MATCHING SHAPES

Place a PATTERN BLOCK on the shaded shape.

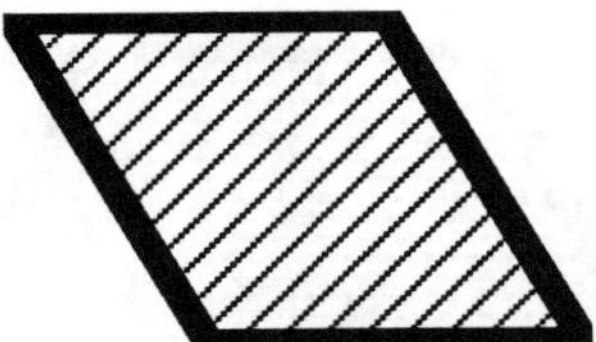

Move the block to the matching shapes on the page.
Color the matching shapes the same color as the block.

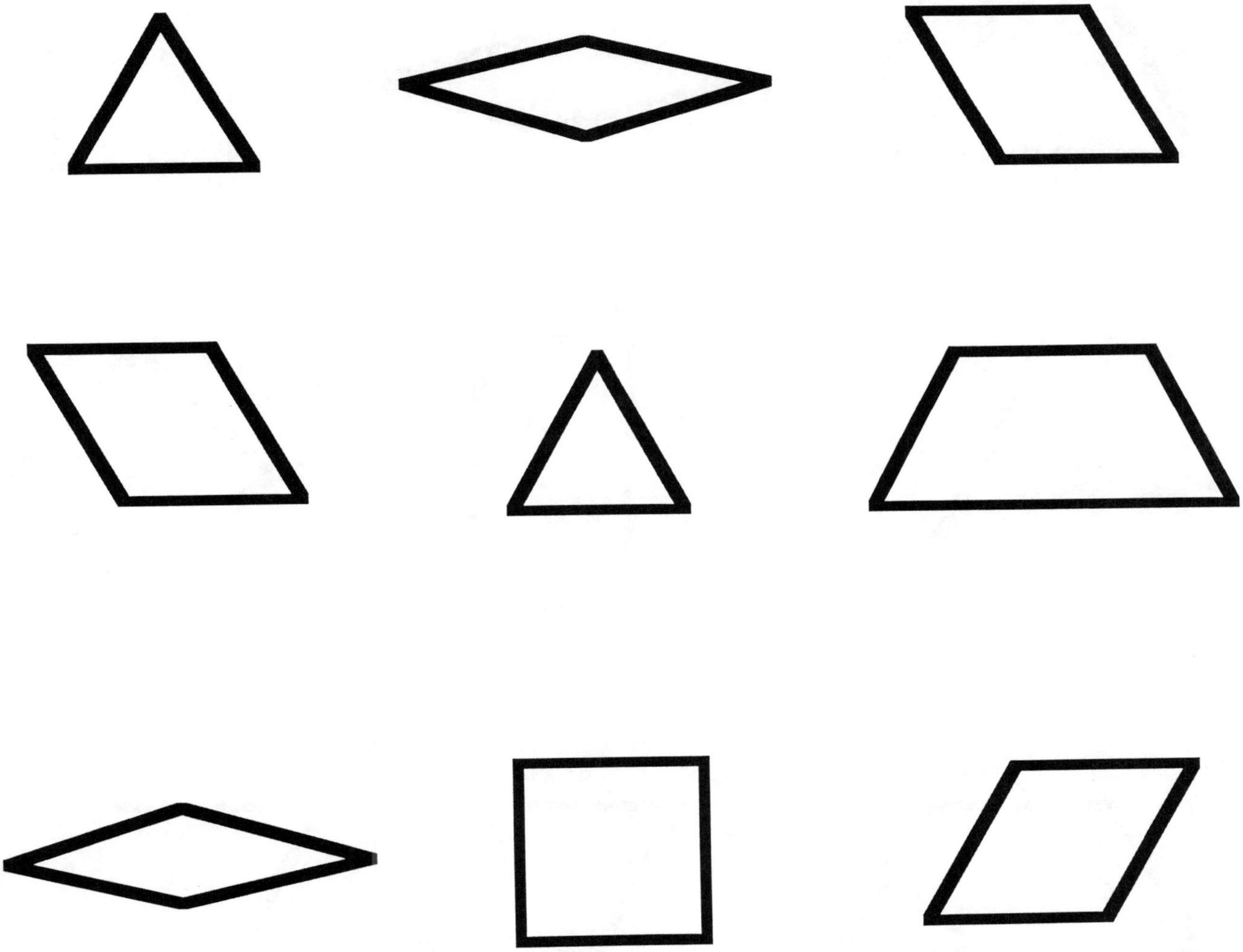

## MATCHING SHAPES

Place a PATTERN BLOCK on the shaded shape.

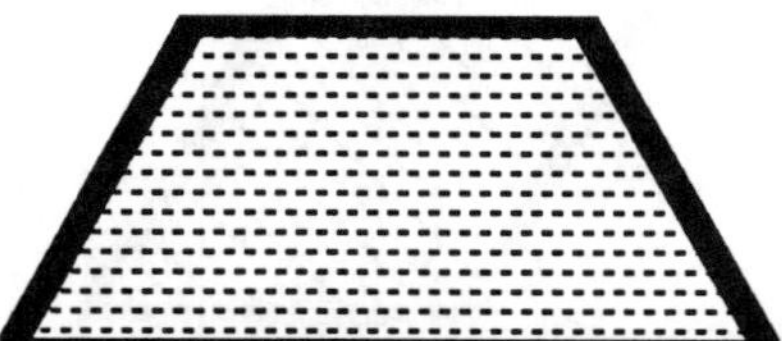

---

Move the block to the matching shapes on the page.
Color the matching shapes the same color as the block.

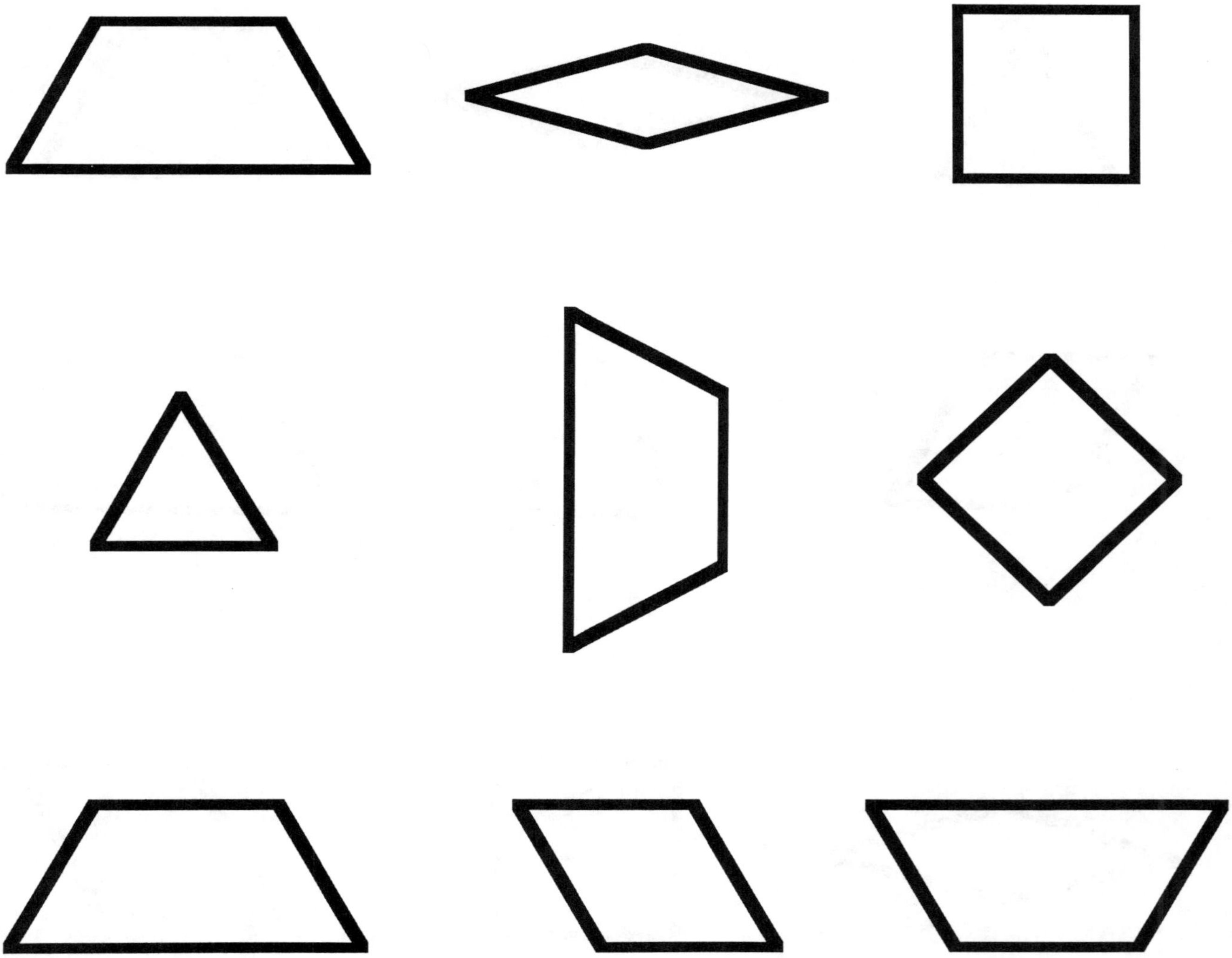

## MATCHING SHAPES

Place a PATTERN BLOCK on the shaded shape.

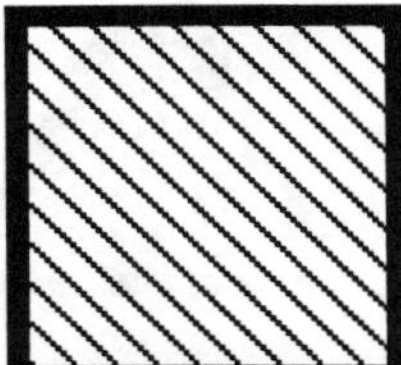

Move the block to the matching shapes on the page.
Color the matching shapes the same color as the block.

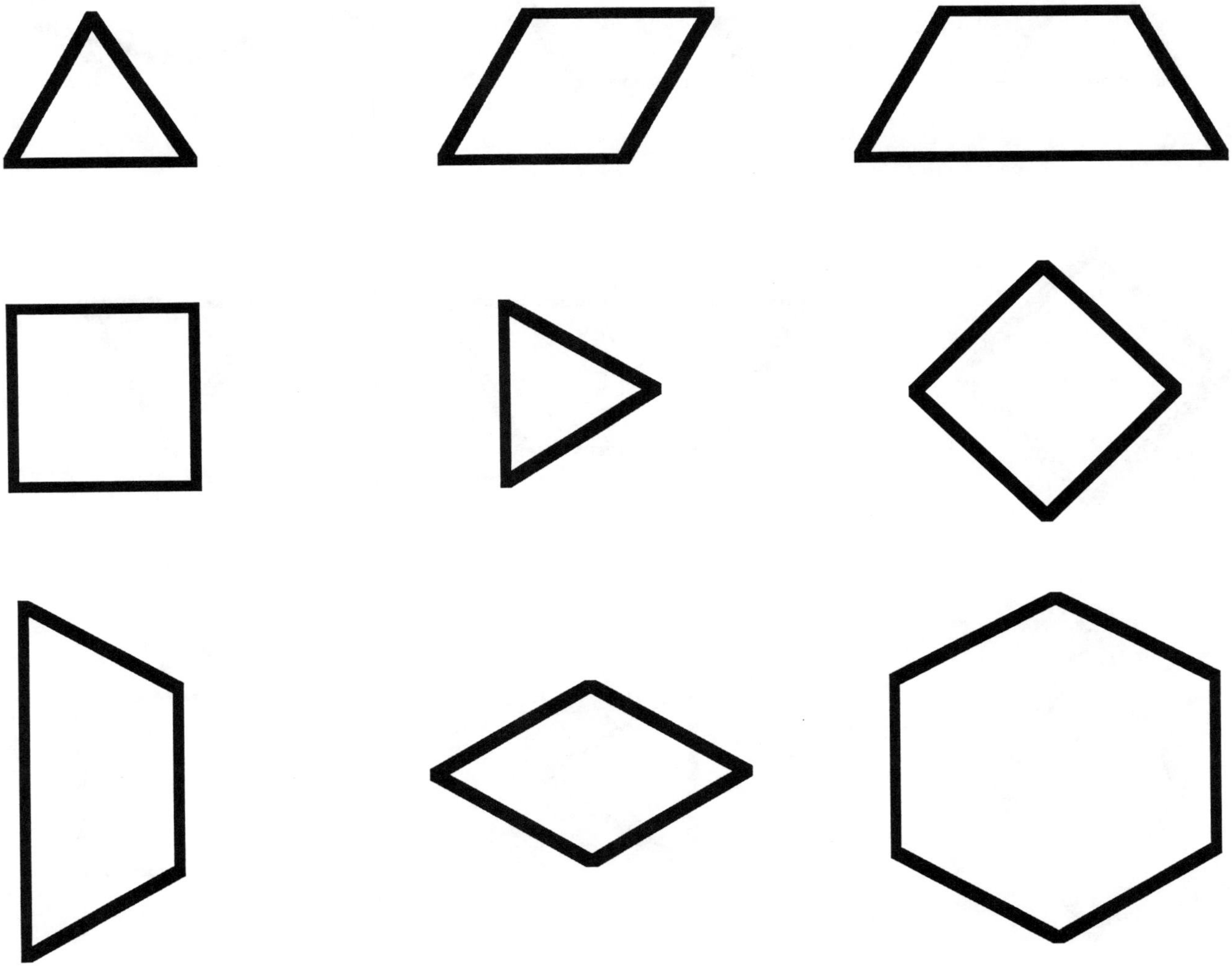

# MATCHING SHAPES

Place a PATTERN BLOCK on the shaded shape.

Move the block to the matching shapes on the page.
Color the matching shapes the same color as the block.

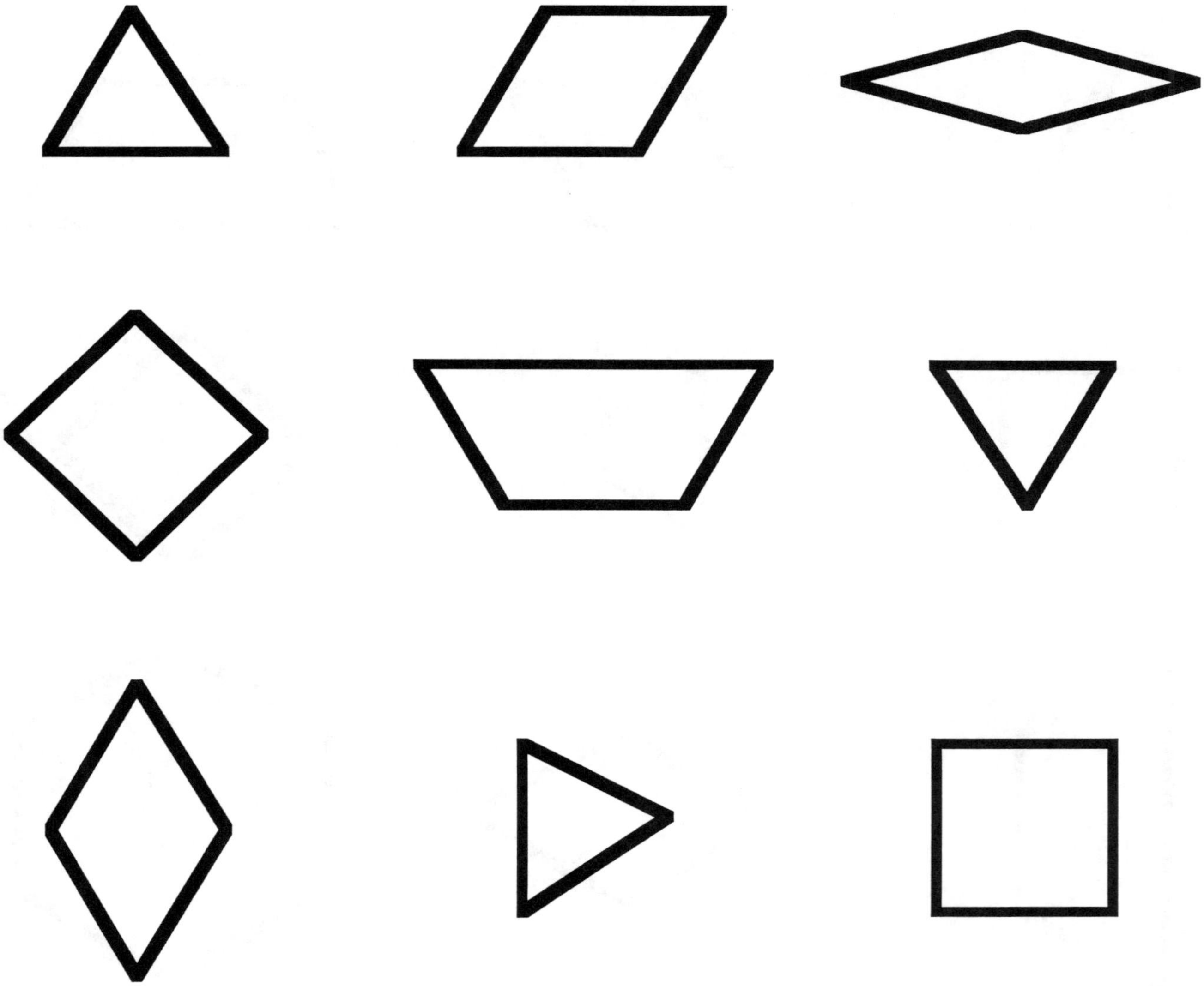

## MATCHING SHAPES

Place an ATTRIBUTE BLOCK on the shaded shape.

Move the block to the matching shapes on the page.
Color the matching shapes the same color as the block.

## MATCHING SHAPES

Place an ATTRIBUTE BLOCK on the shaded shape.

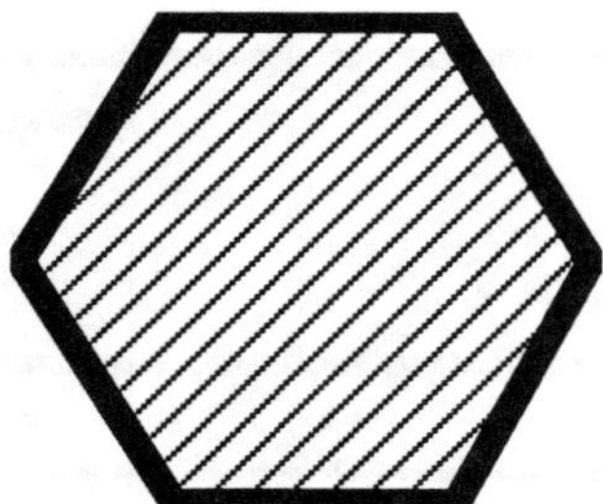

---

Move the block to the matching shapes on the page.
Color the matching shapes the same color as the block.

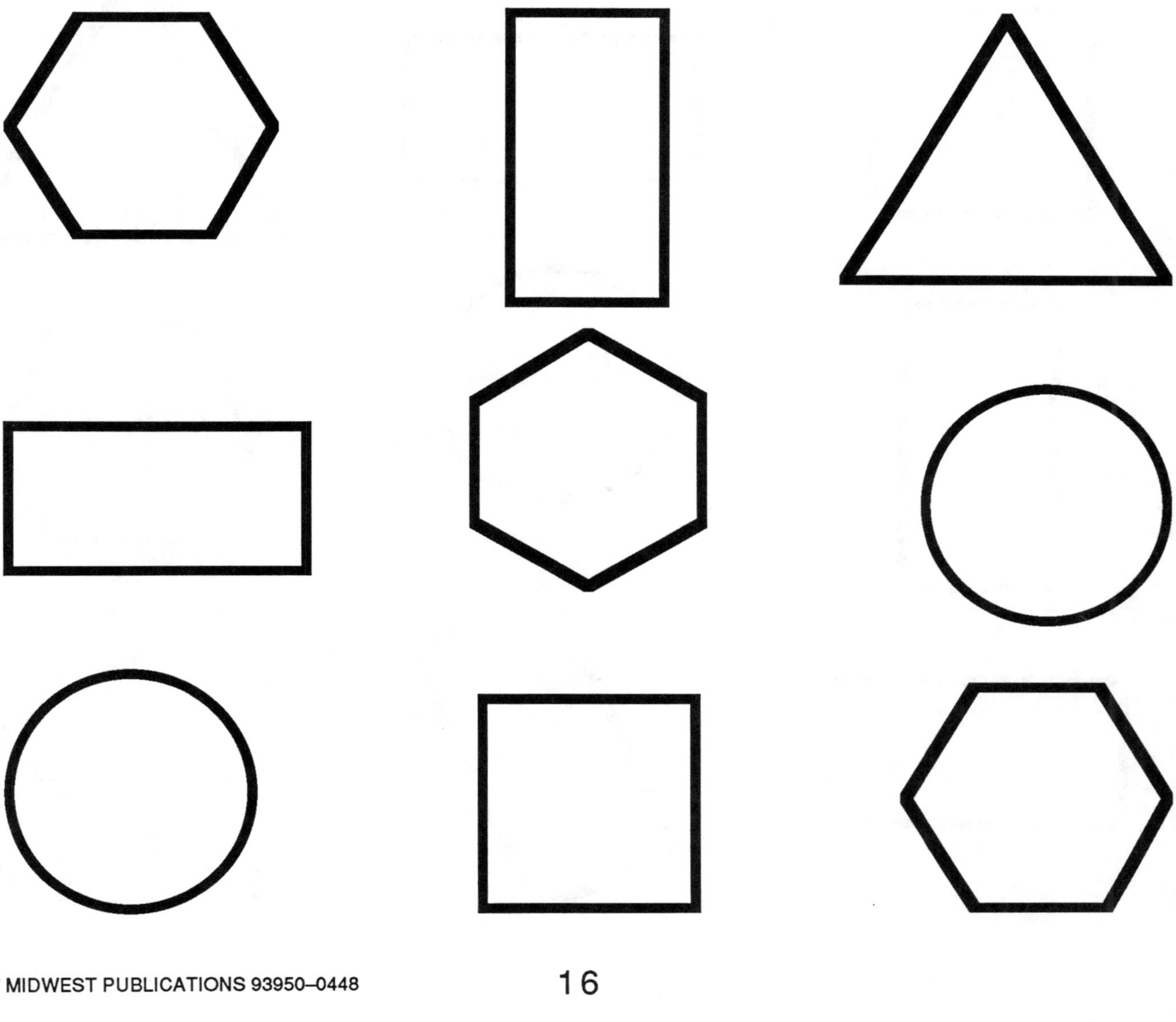

## MATCHING SHAPES

Make the shaded figure using INTERLOCKING CUBES.

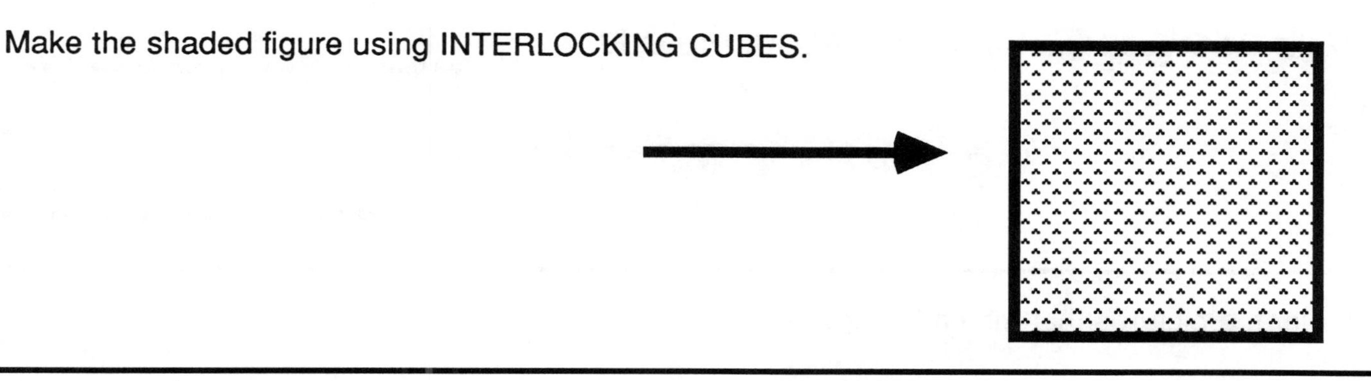

Color the pictures that match the figure.

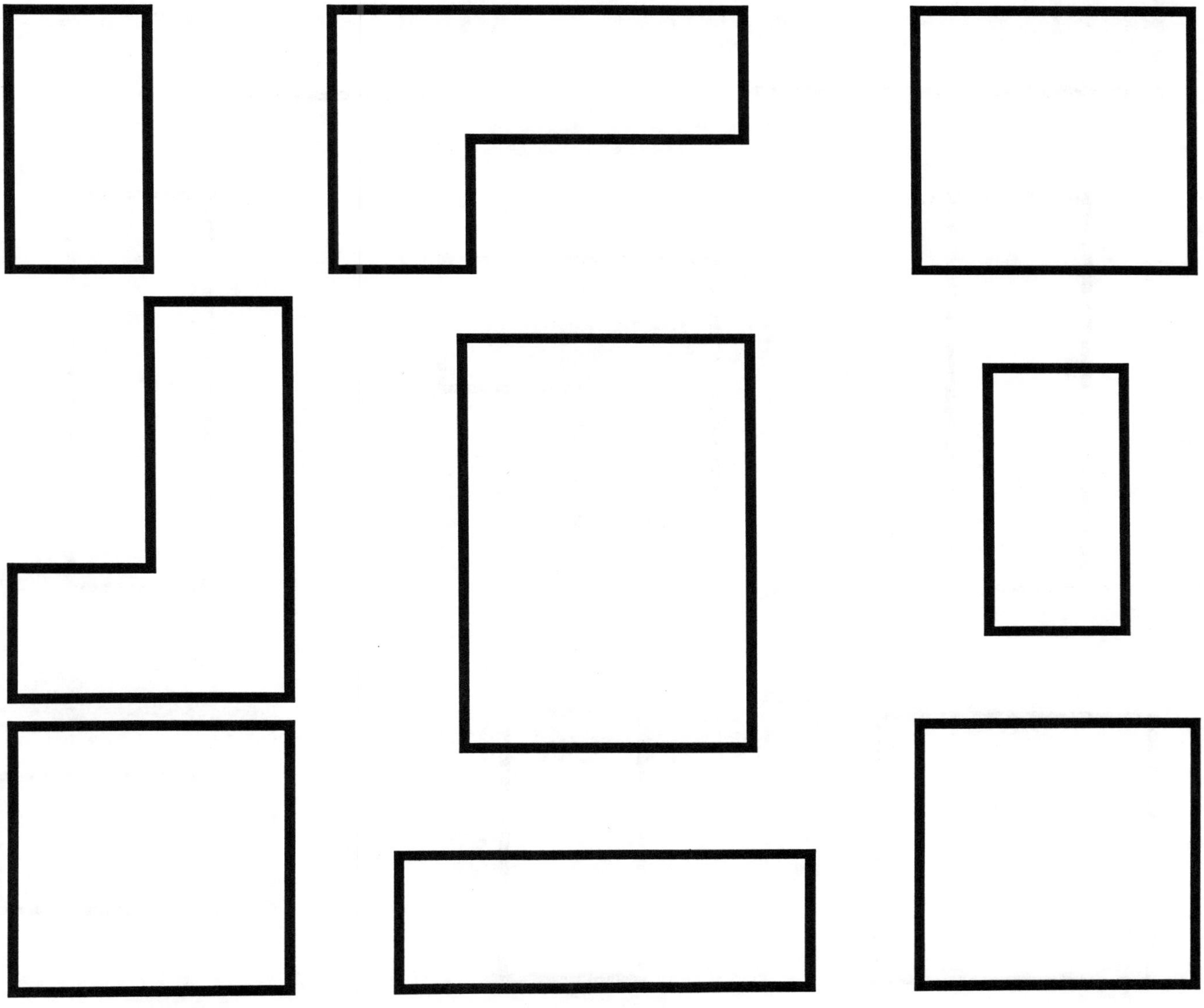

## MATCHING SHAPES

Make the shaded figure using INTERLOCKING CUBES.

Color the pictures that match the figure.

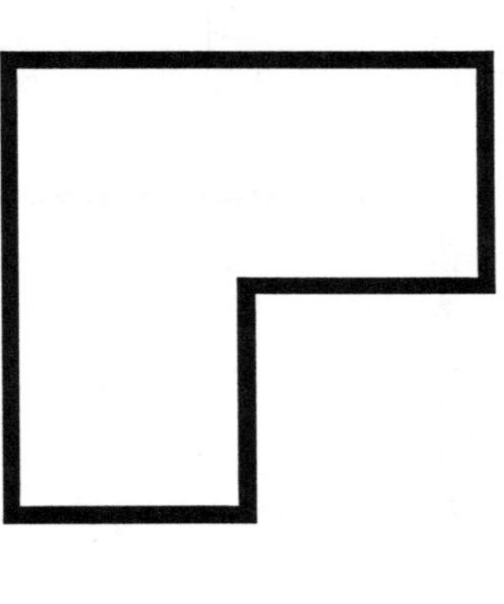

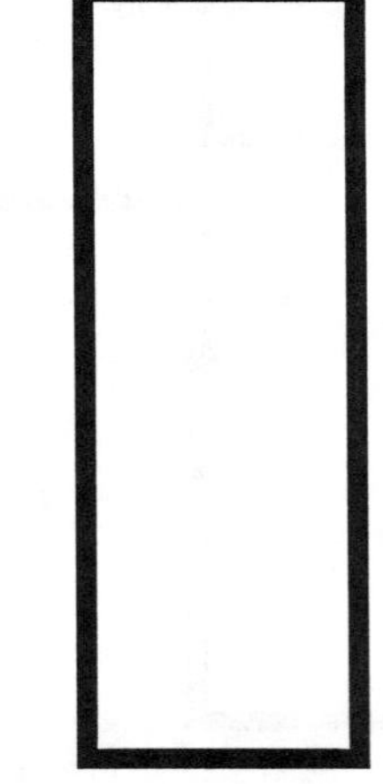

## SHAPES THAT DO NOT MATCH

Place a PATTERN BLOCK on each shaded shape.
In each box, find the shape that DOES NOT match the block.
Color the shape that DOES NOT match.

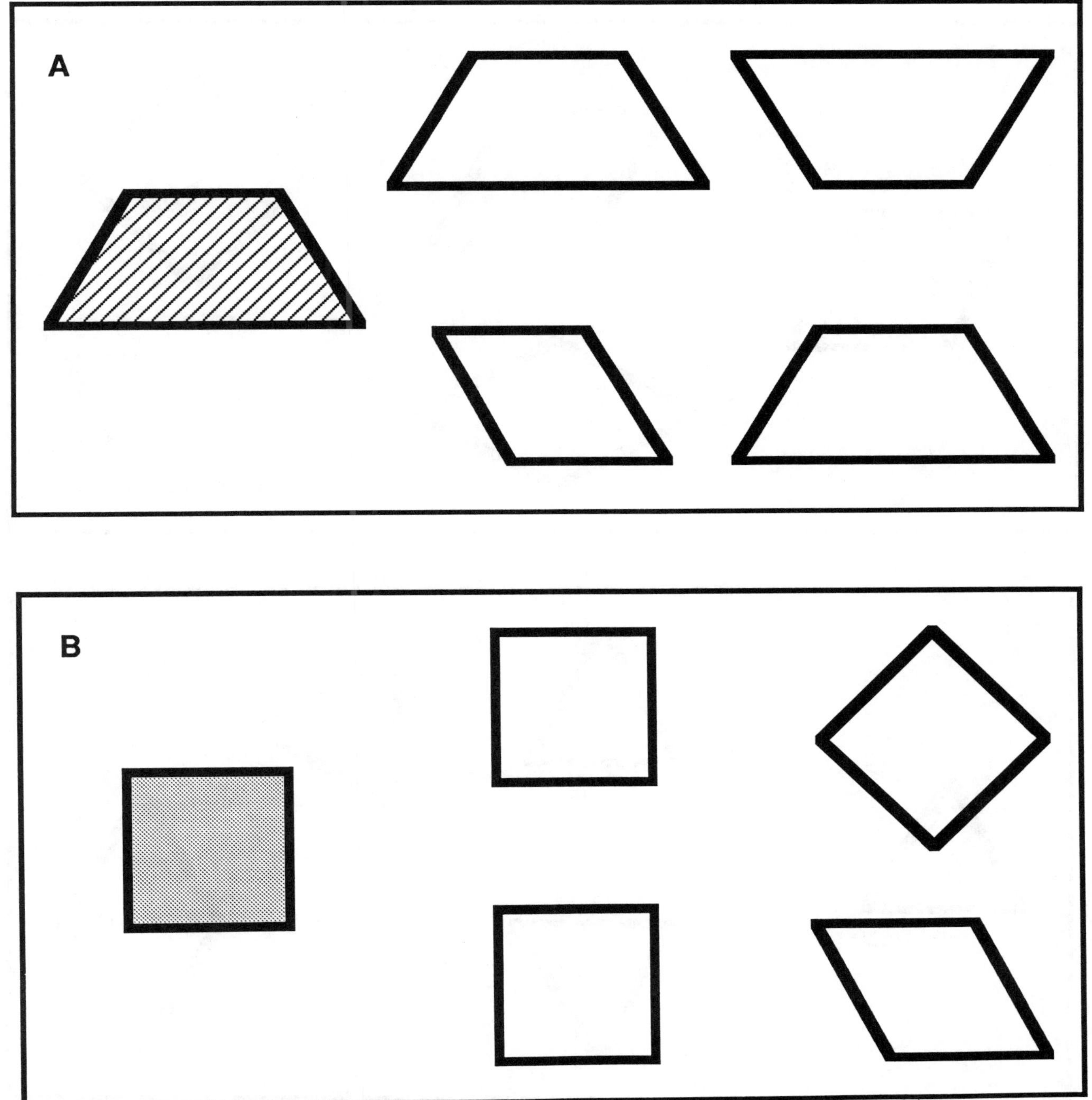

## SHAPES THAT DO NOT MATCH

Place a PATTERN BLOCK on each shaded shape.
In each box, find the shape that DOES NOT match the block.
Color the shape that DOES NOT match.

---

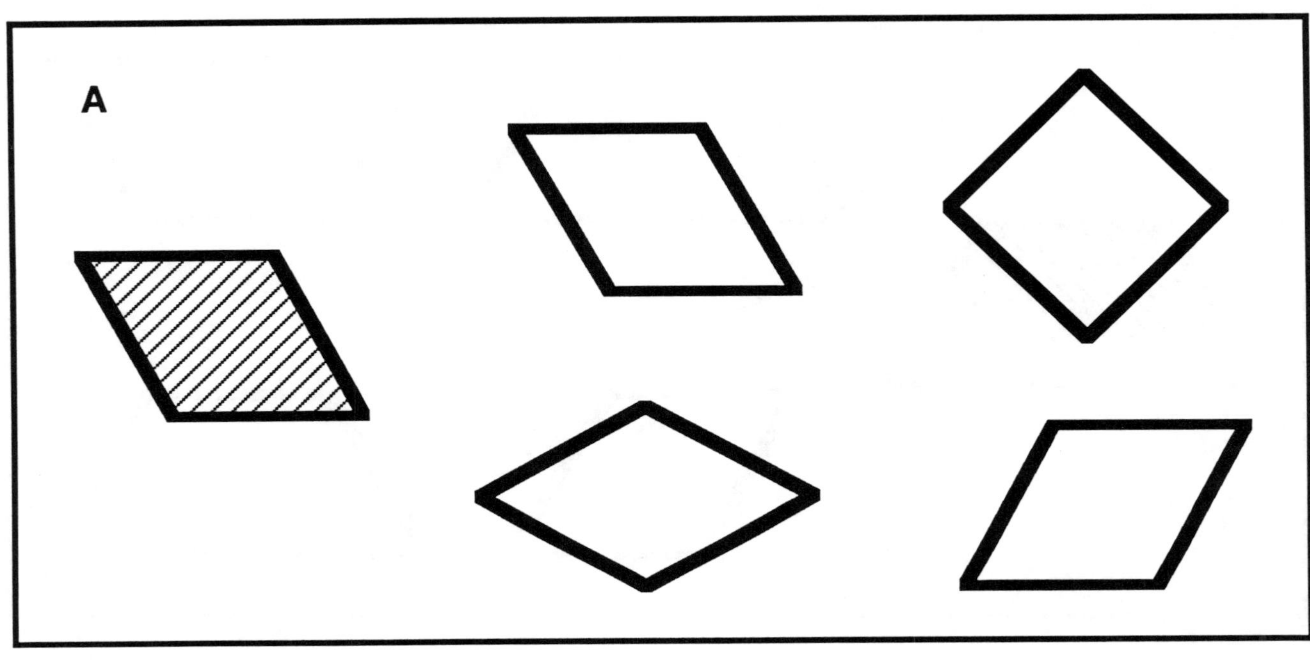


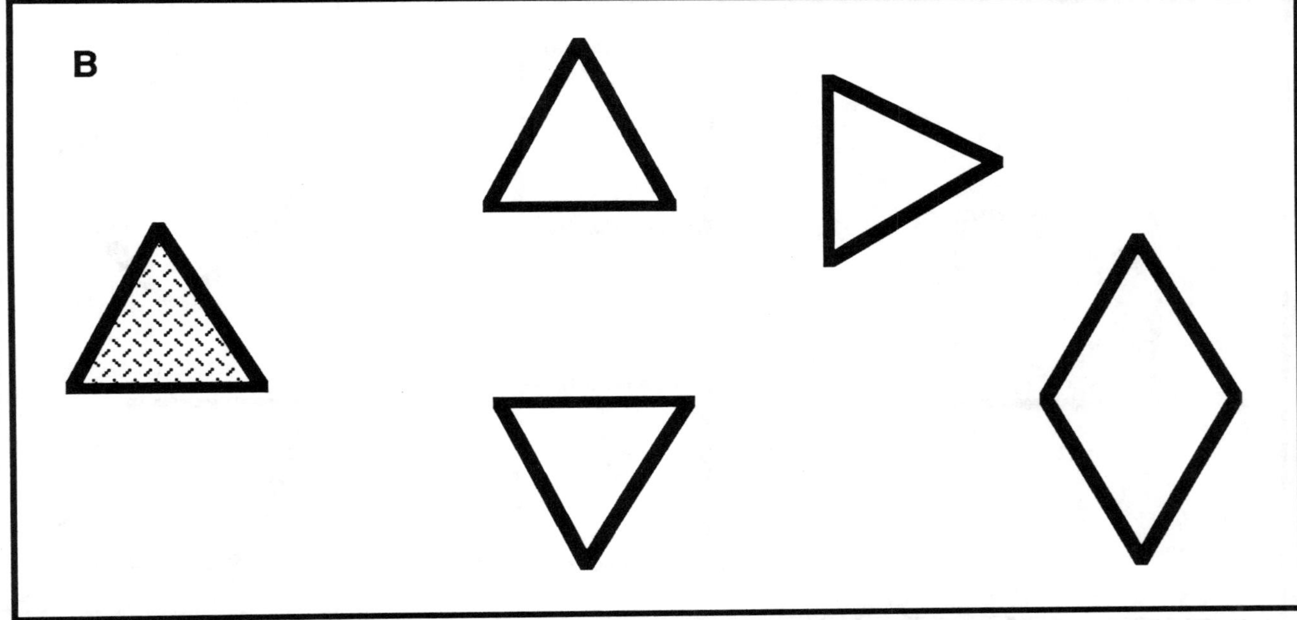

## SHAPES THAT DO NOT MATCH

Place an ATTRIBUTE BLOCK on each shaded shape.
In each box, find the shape that DOES NOT match the block.
Color the shape that DOES NOT match.

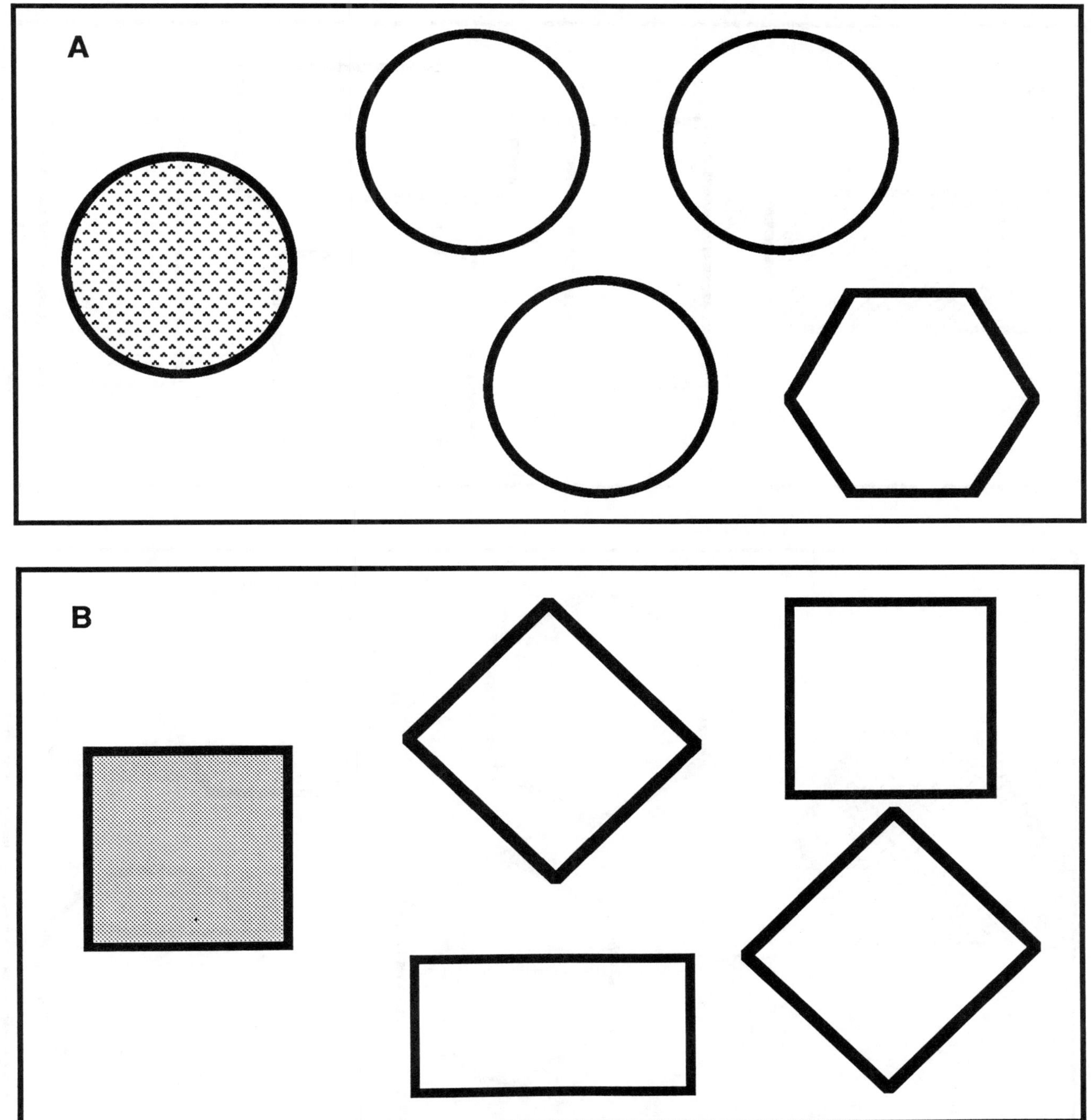

## SHAPES THAT DO NOT MATCH

Place an ATTRIBUTE BLOCK on each shaded shape.
In each box, find the shape that DOES NOT match the block.
Color the shape that DOES NOT match.

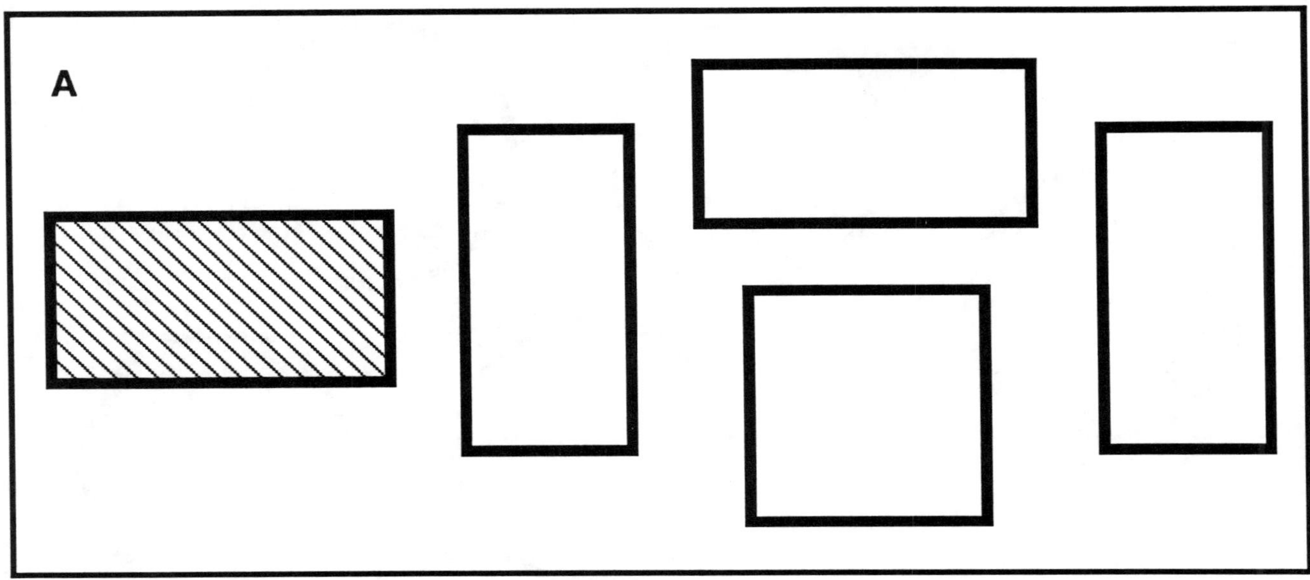


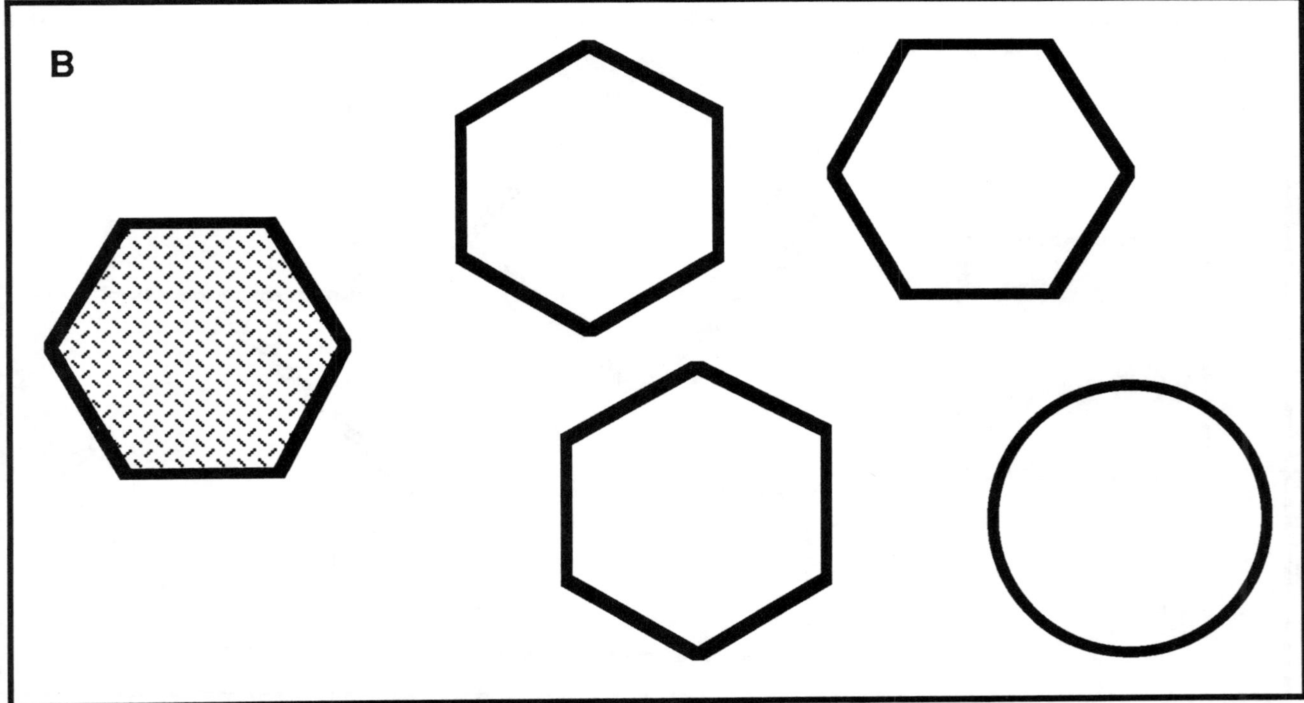

## SHAPES THAT DO NOT MATCH

Place a PATTERN BLOCK on the shaded shape.

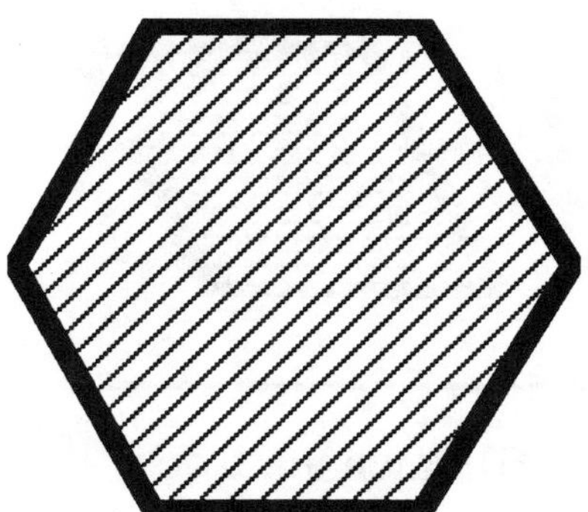

Find the shape below that DOES NOT match the block.
Color the shape that DOES NOT match.

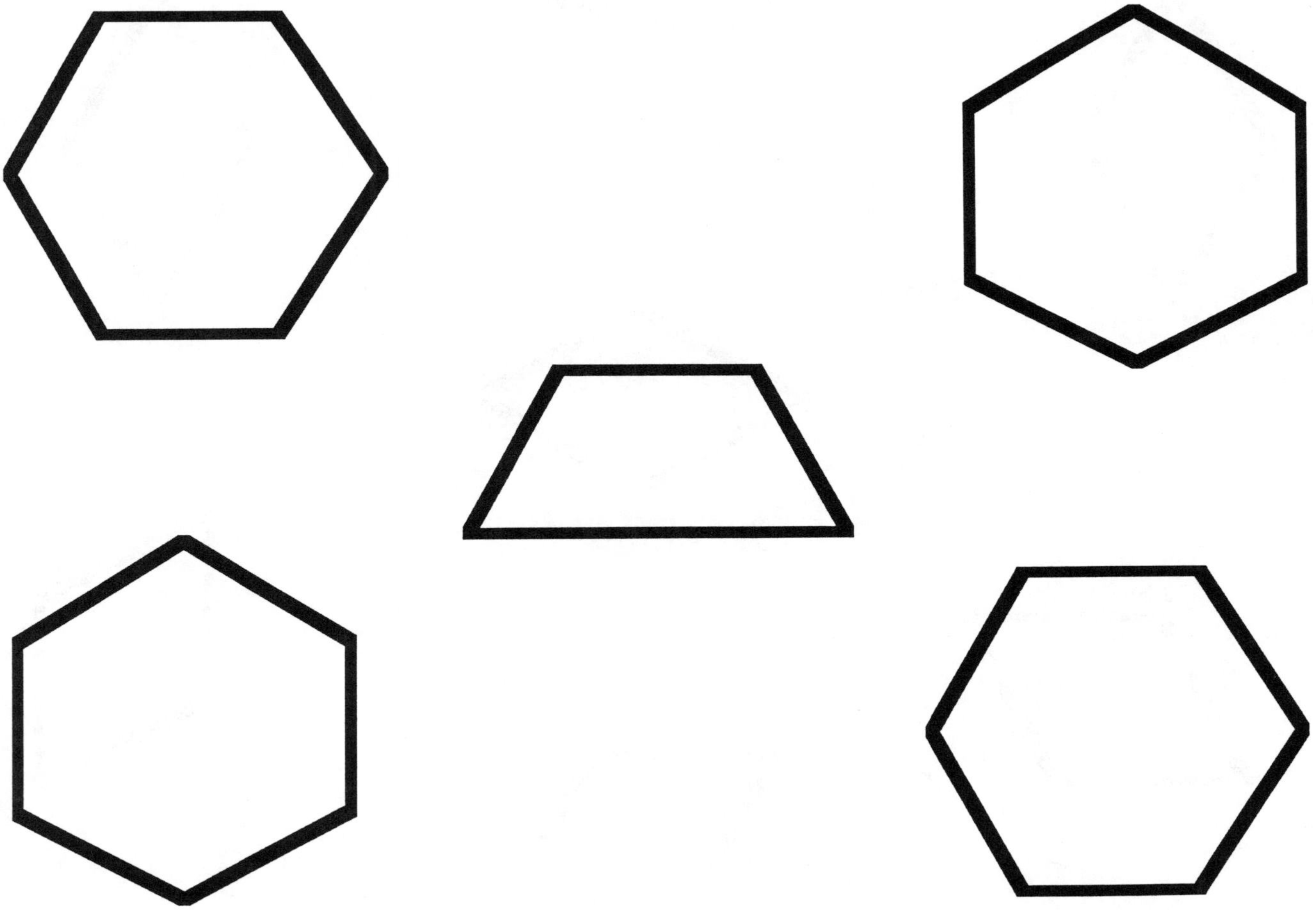

## SHAPES THAT DO NOT MATCH

Place a PATTERN BLOCK on the shaded shape.

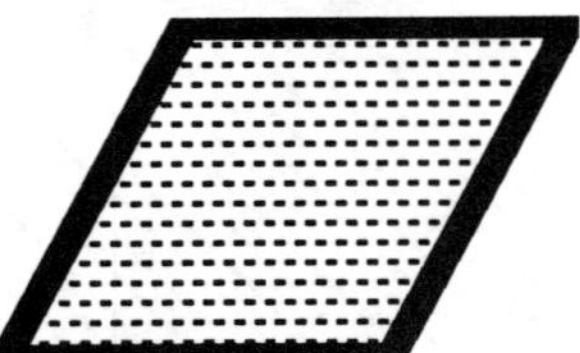

Find the shape below that DOES NOT match the block.
Color the shape that DOES NOT match.

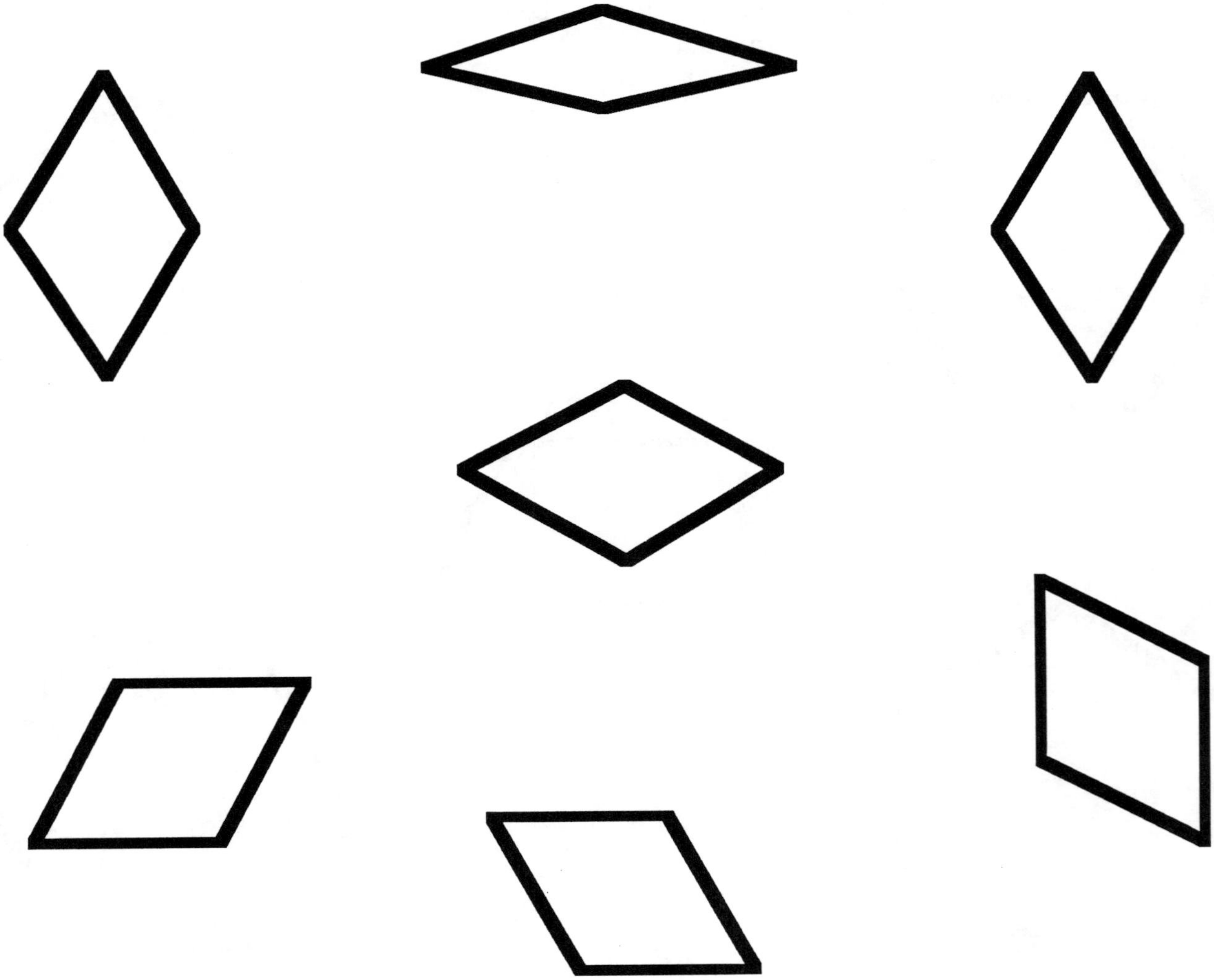

## SHAPES THAT DO NOT MATCH

Place an ATTRIBUTE BLOCK on the shaded shape.

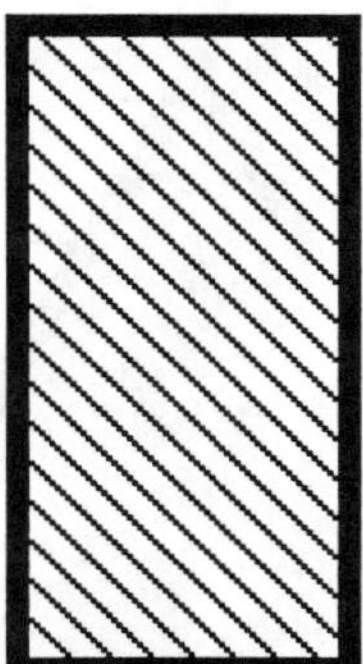

Find the shape below that DOES NOT match the block.
Color the shape that DOES NOT match.

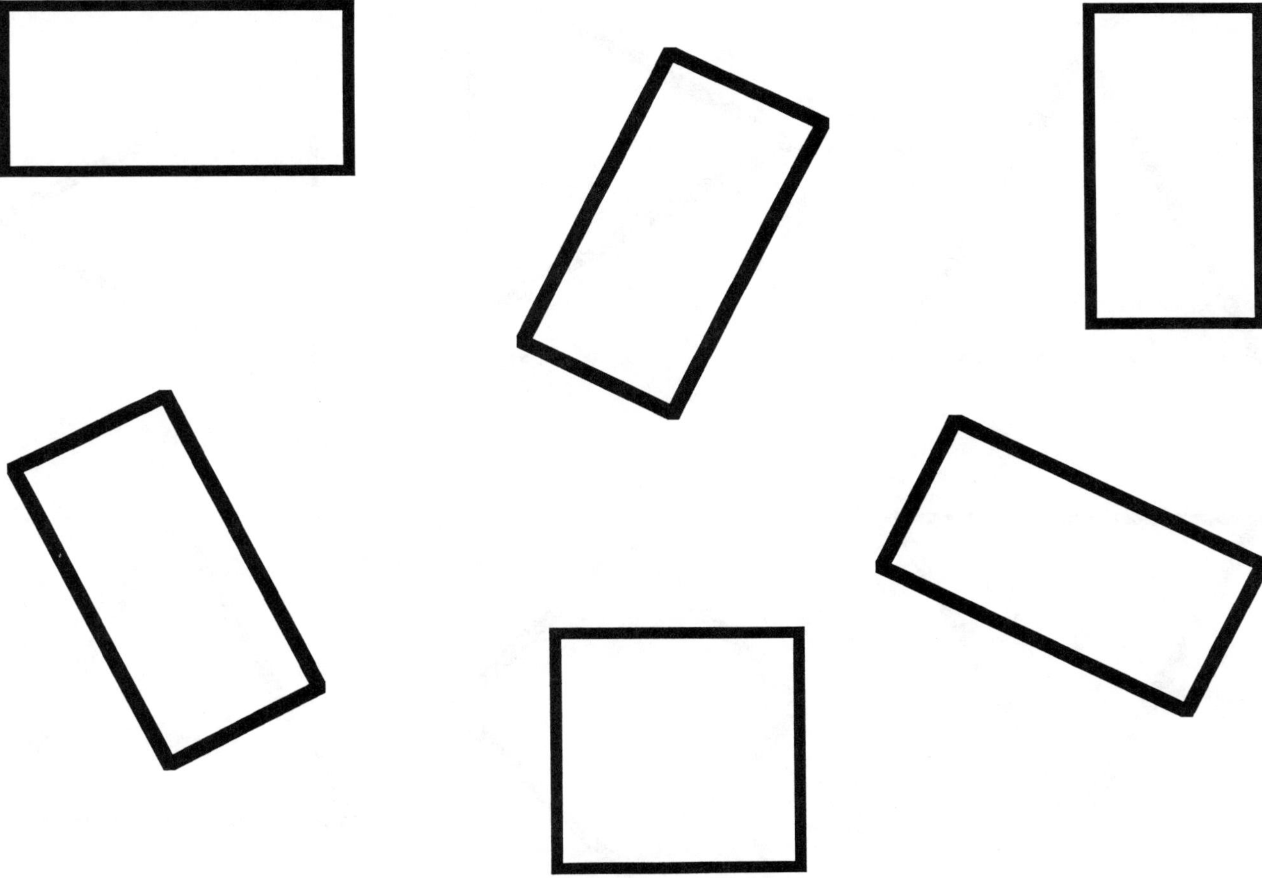

## SHAPES THAT DO NOT MATCH

Place an ATTRIBUTE BLOCK on the shaded shape.

Find the shape below that DOES NOT match the block.
Color the shape that DOES NOT match.

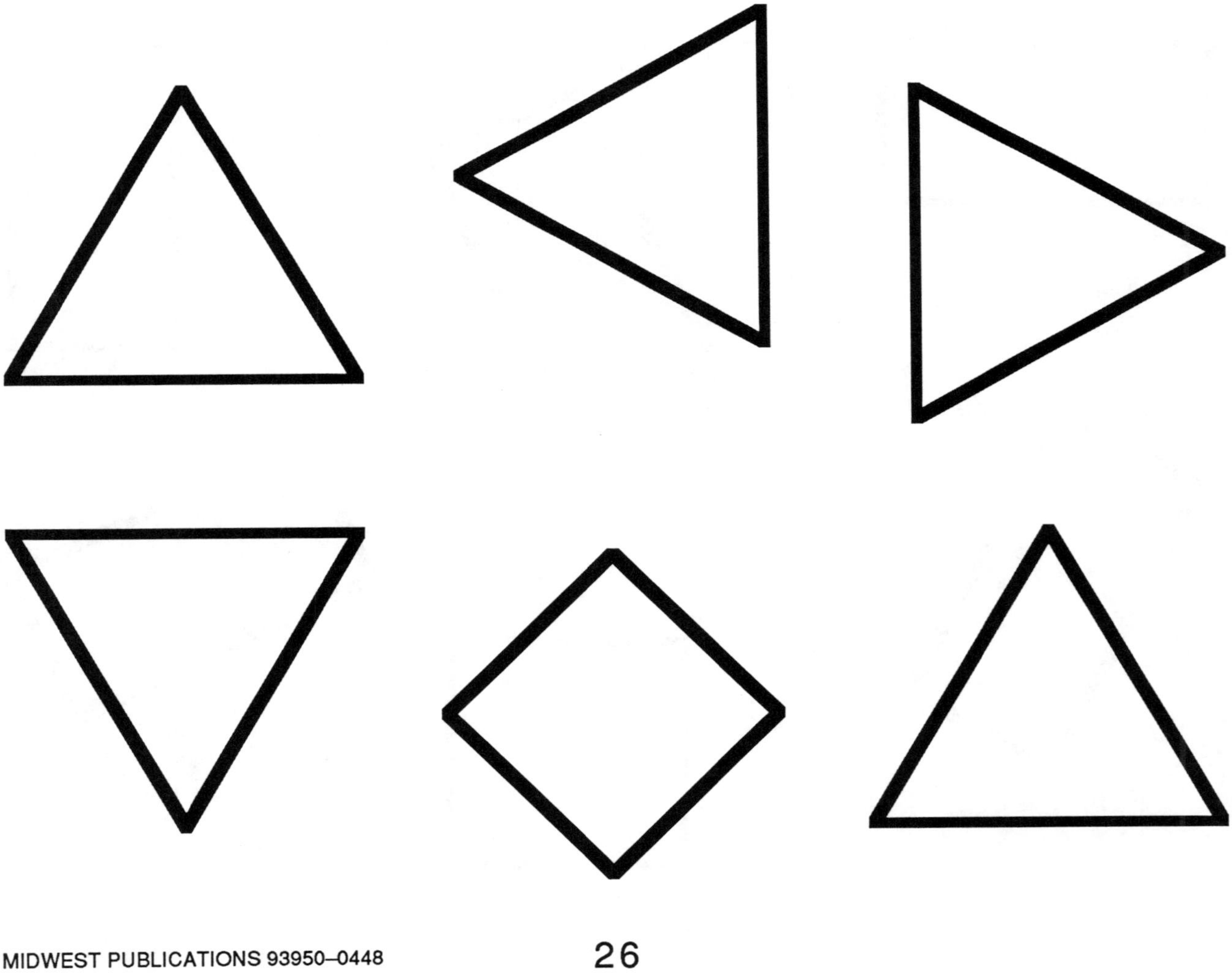

# SHAPES THAT DO NOT MATCH

Make the shaded figure using INTERLOCKING CUBES.

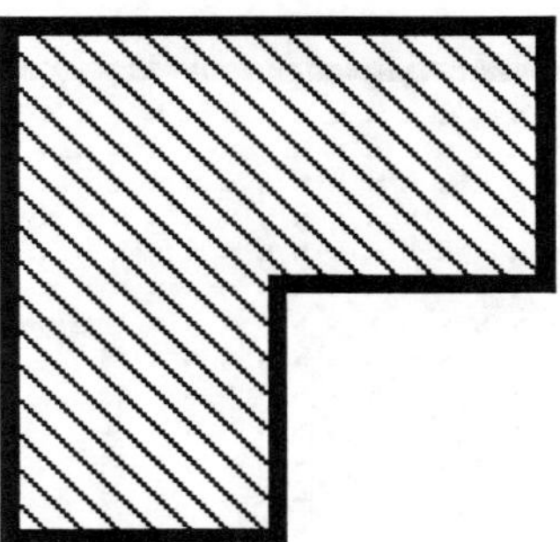

Find the figure below that DOES NOT match the construction.
Color the figure that DOES NOT match.

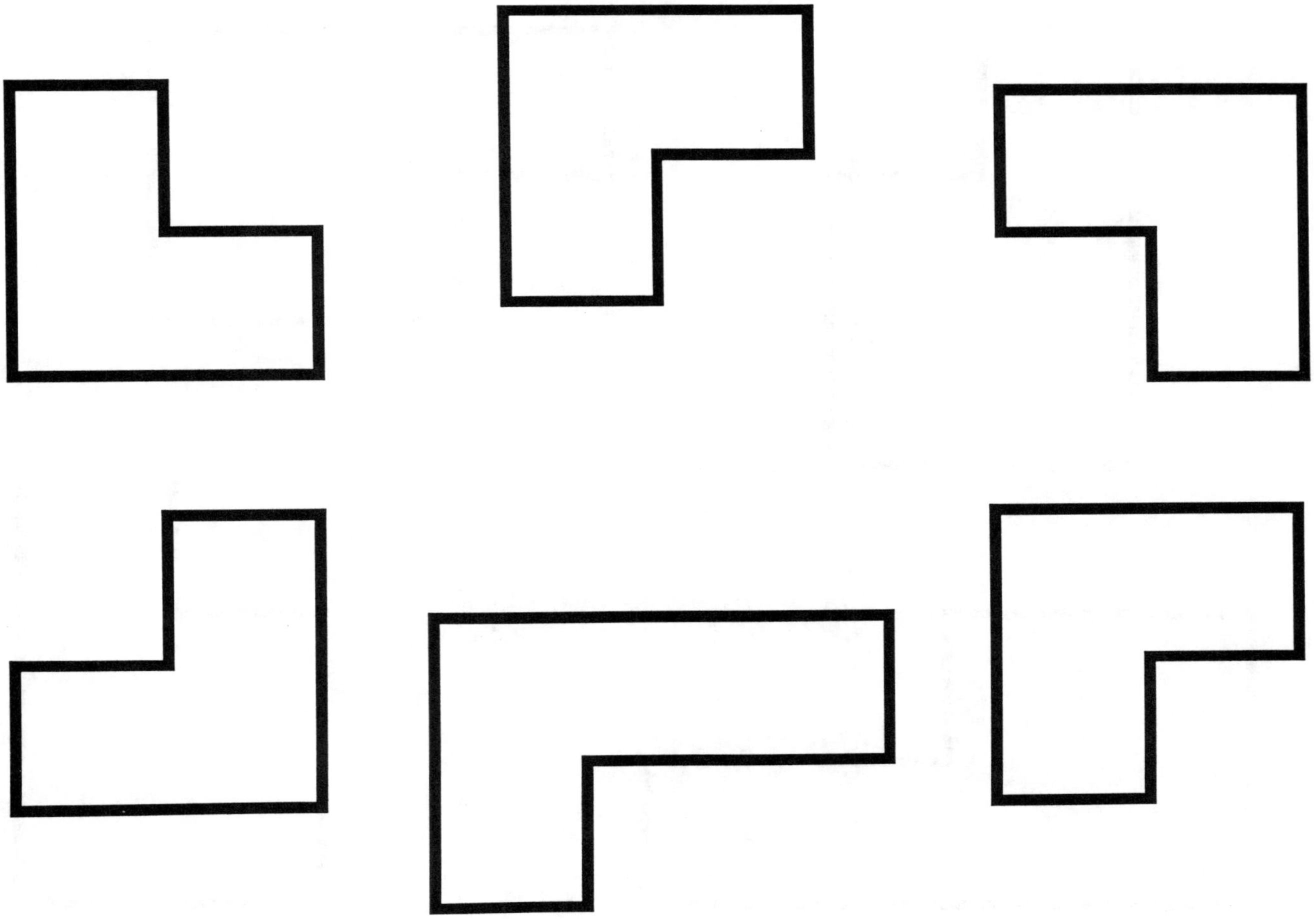

## SHAPES THAT DO NOT MATCH

Make the shaded figure using INTERLOCKING CUBES.

Find the figure below that DOES NOT match the construction.
Color the figure that DOES NOT match.

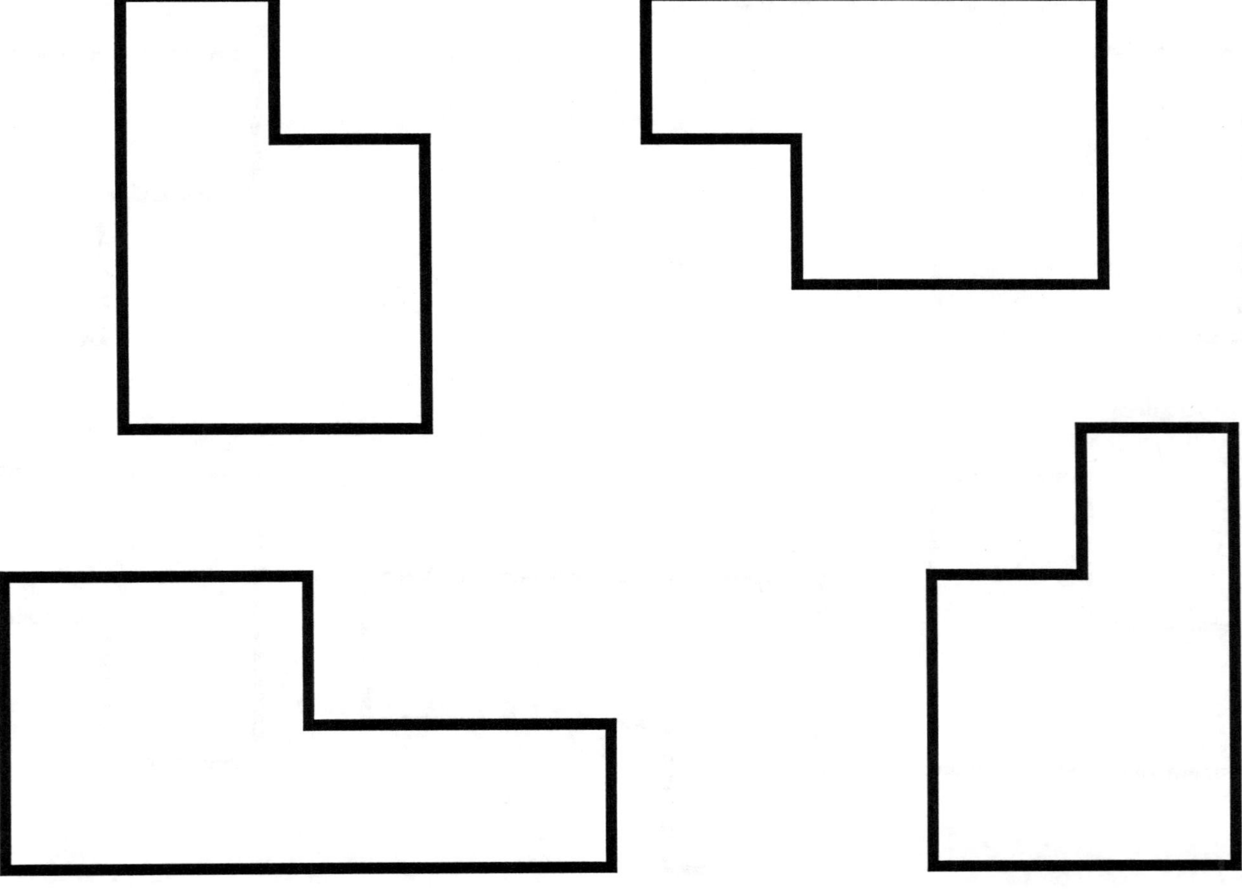

## SHAPES THAT DO NOT MATCH

Make the shaded figure using INTERLOCKING CUBES.

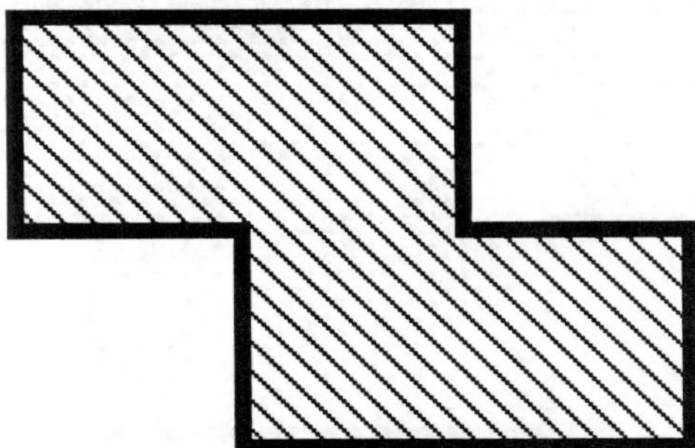

Find the figure below that DOES NOT match the construction.
Color the figure that DOES NOT match.

# SHAPES THAT DO NOT MATCH

Make the shaded figure using INTERLOCKING CUBES.

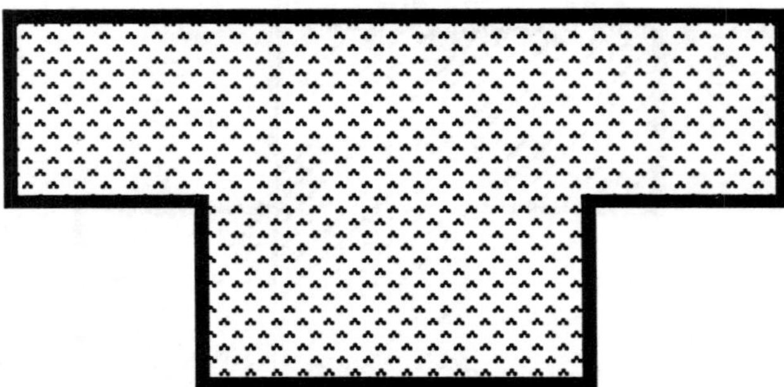

Find the figure below that DOES NOT match the construction.
Color the figure that DOES NOT match.

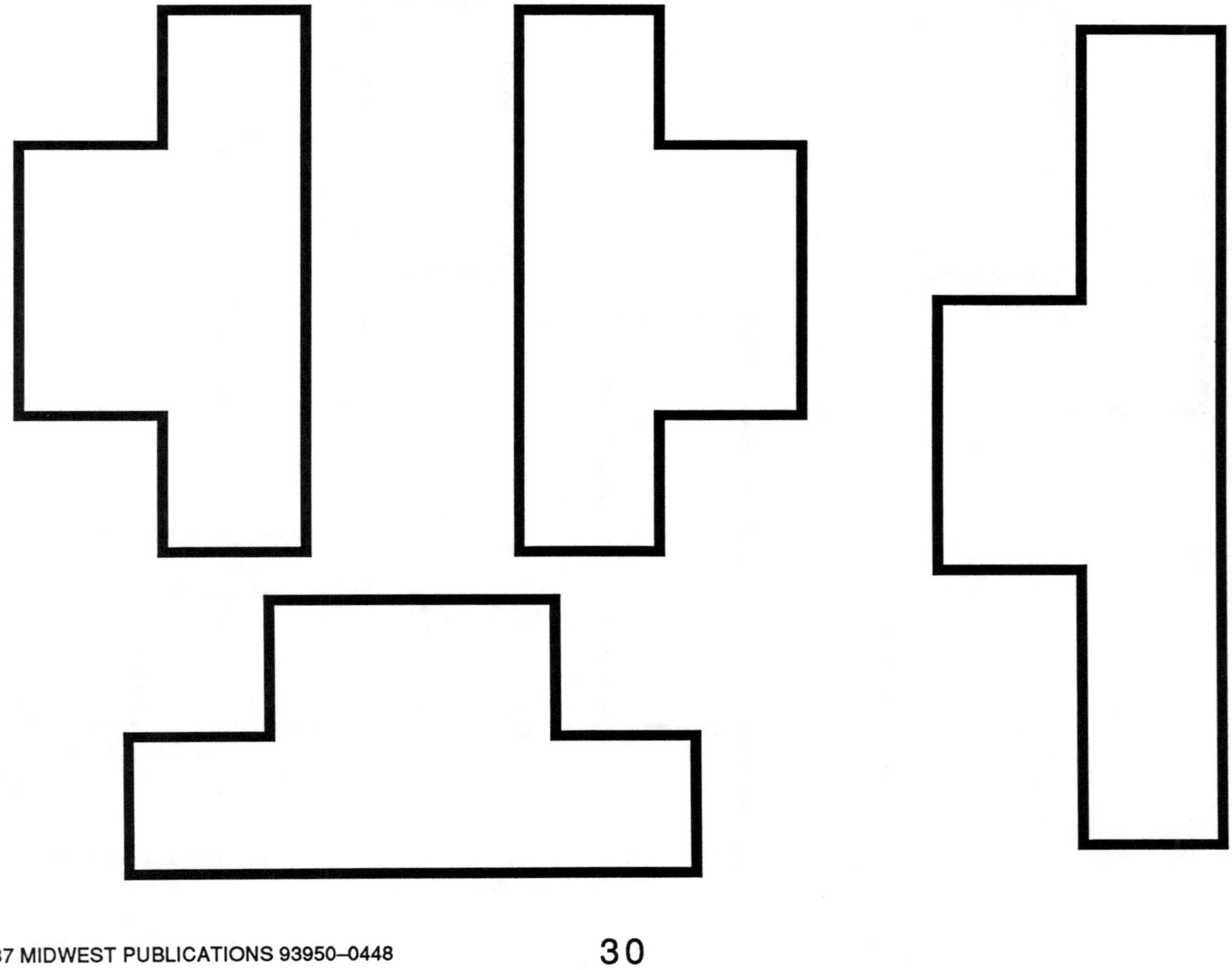

## COMBINING SHAPES

Place an ATTRIBUTE BLOCK on each shaded shape.

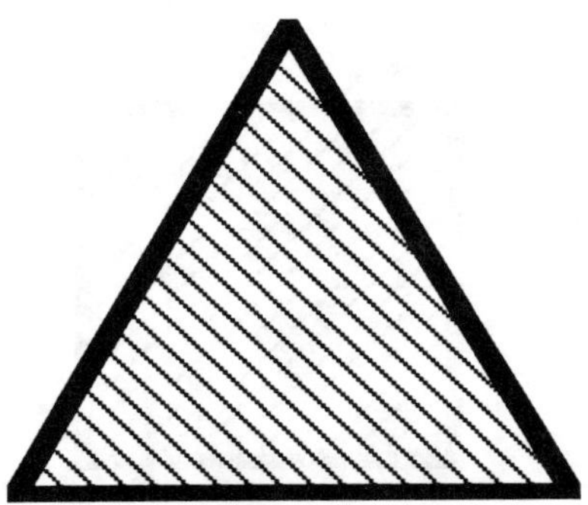

---

Find the figures below that can be made by combining the two blocks.
Color the figures you can make.

**A**

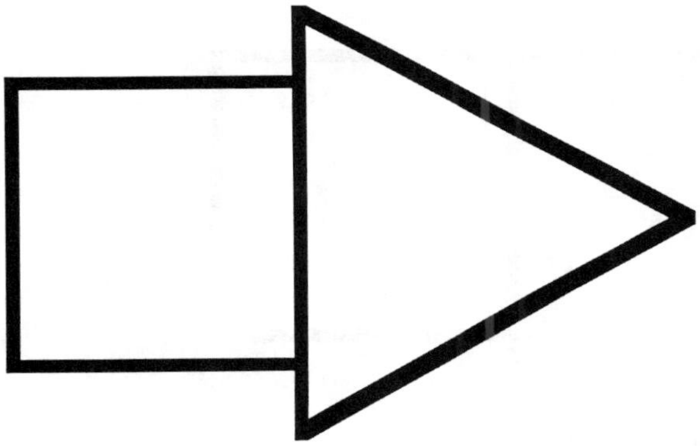

**B**

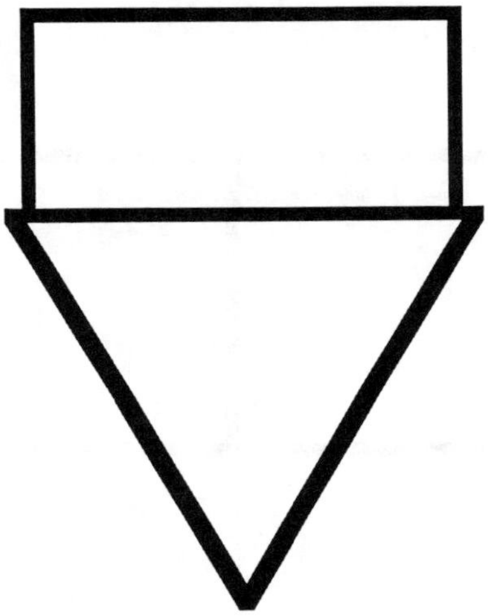

**C**

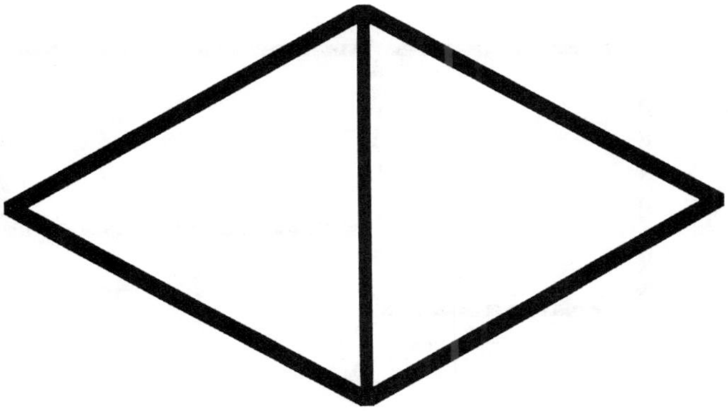

**D**

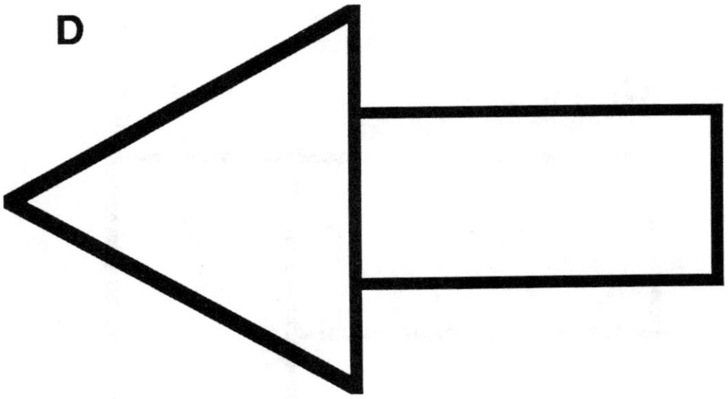

# COMBINING SHAPES

Place an ATTRIBUTE BLOCK on each shaded shape.

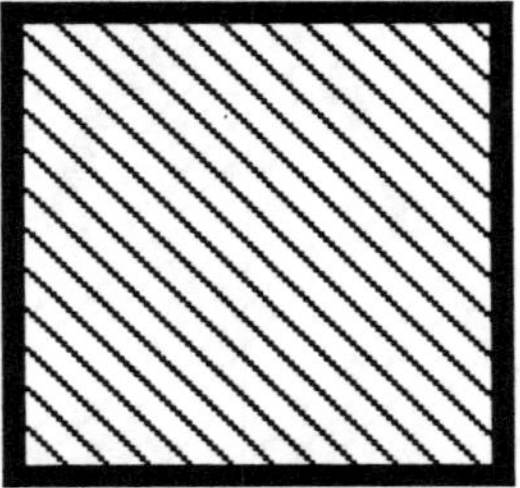

Find the figures below that can be made by combining the two blocks.
Color the figures you can make.

**A**

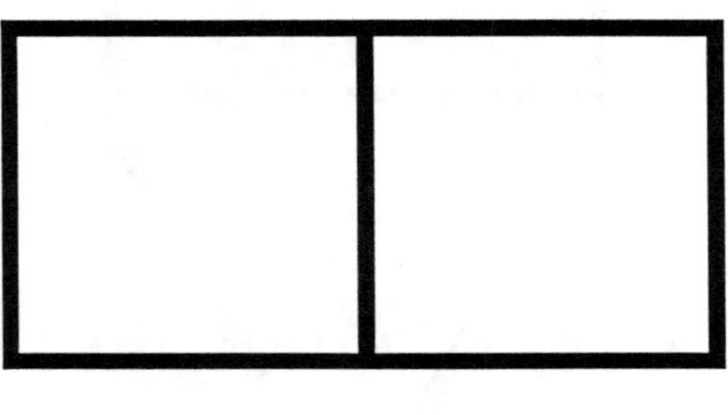

**B**

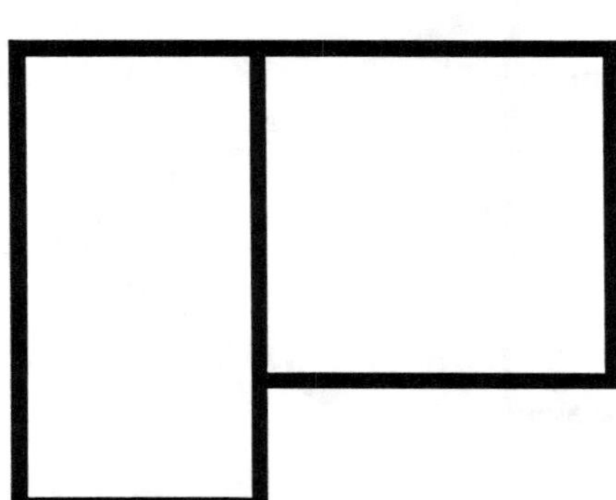

**C**

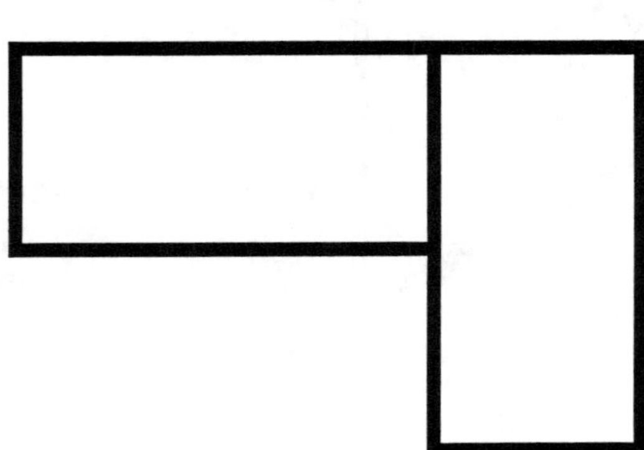

**D**

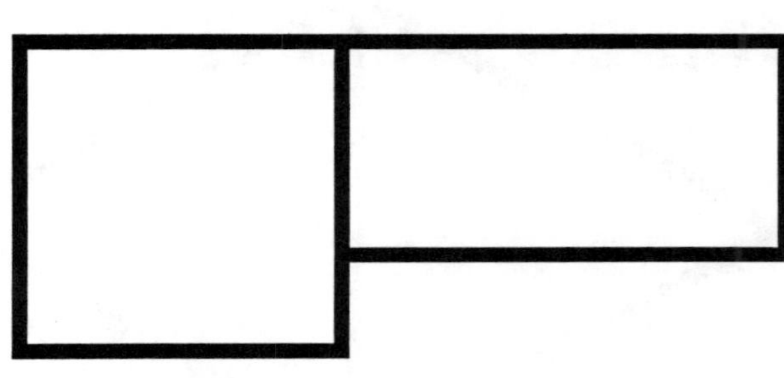

## COMBINING SHAPES

Make each shaded figure using INTERLOCKING CUBES.
Use a different color for each construction.

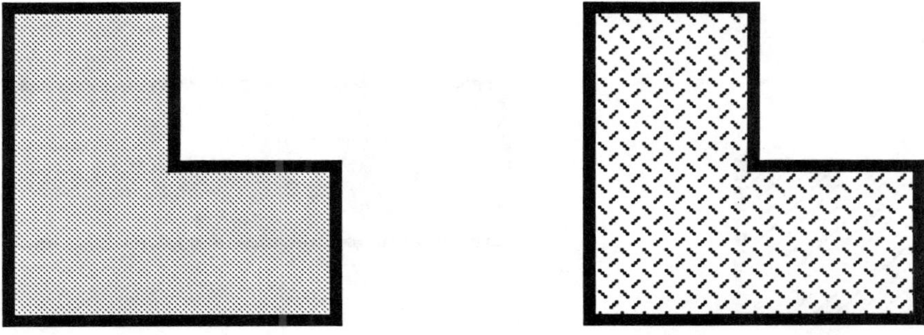

---

Find the figures below that can be made by combining the two constructed figures.
Color the figures you can make.

**A**

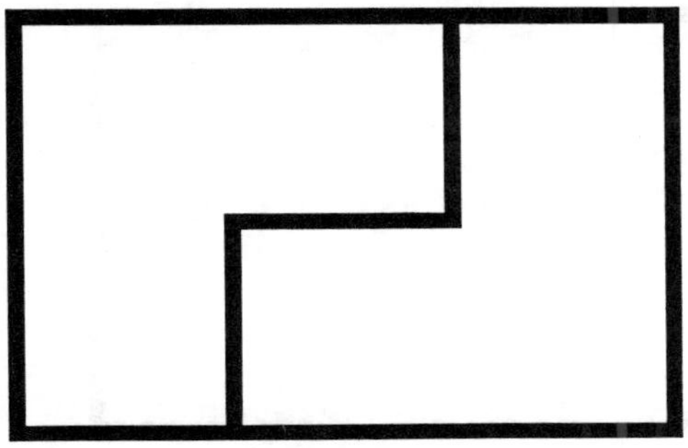

**B**

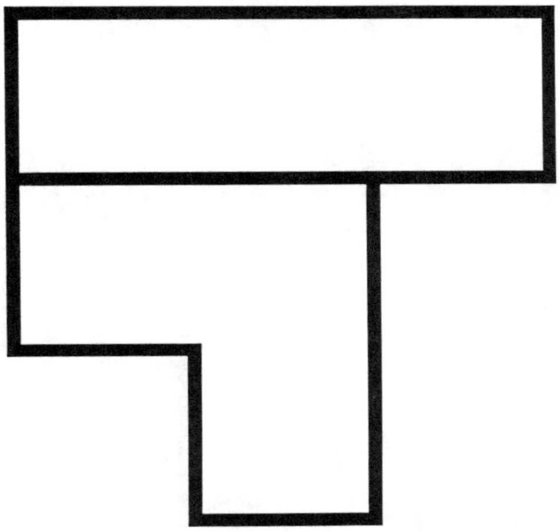

**C**

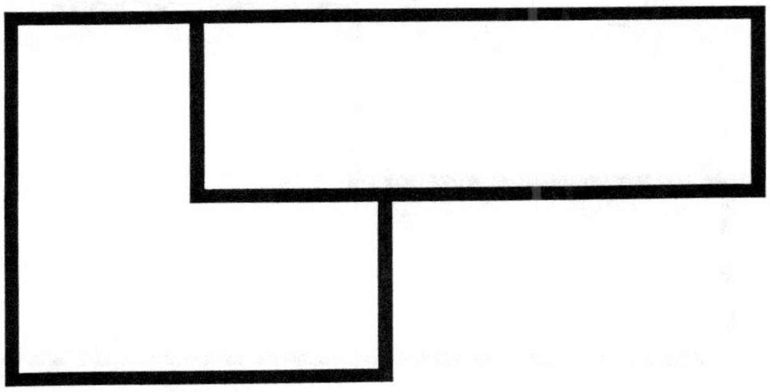

**D**

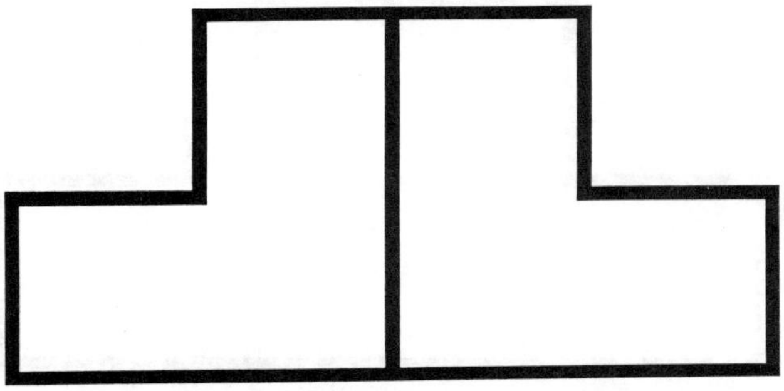

## COMBINING SHAPES

Make each shaded figure using INTERLOCKING CUBES.
Use a different color for each construction.

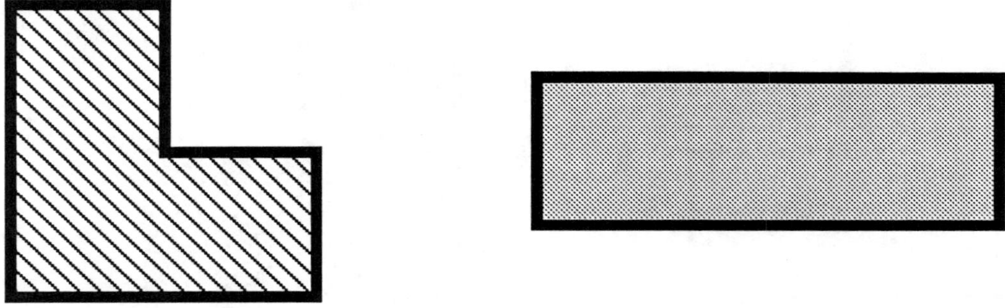

---

Find the figures below that can be made by combining the two constructed figures.
Color the figures you can make.

A

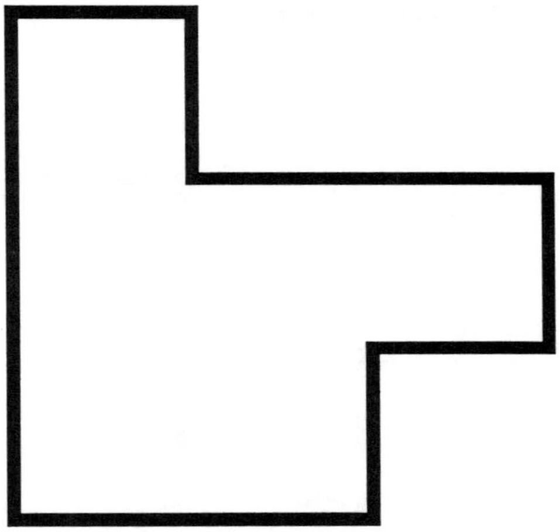

B

C

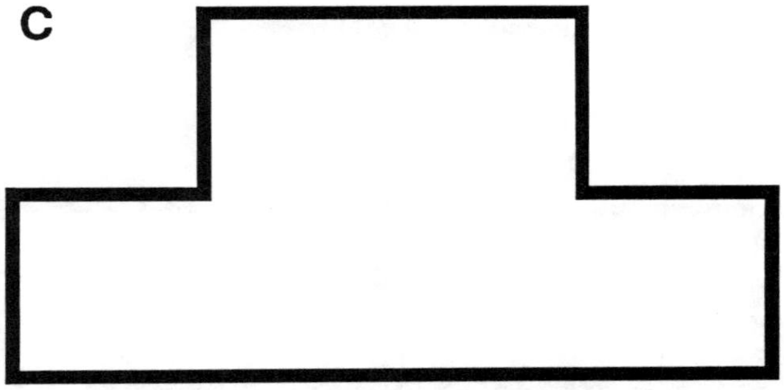

D

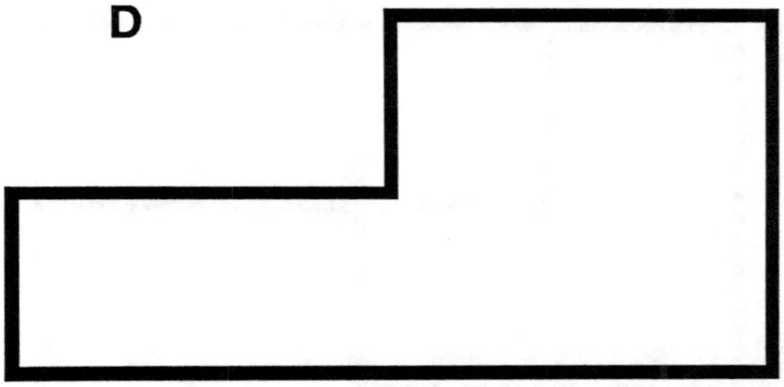

## COMBINING SHAPES

Place a different colored ATTRIBUTE BLOCK on each shaded shape.

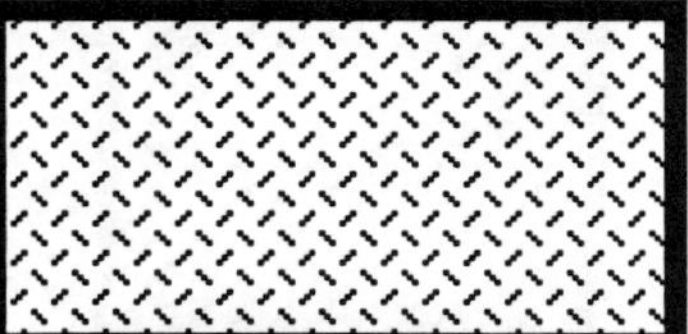

---

Find the figures below that can be made by combining the two blocks.
Color the figures you can make.

**A**

**B**

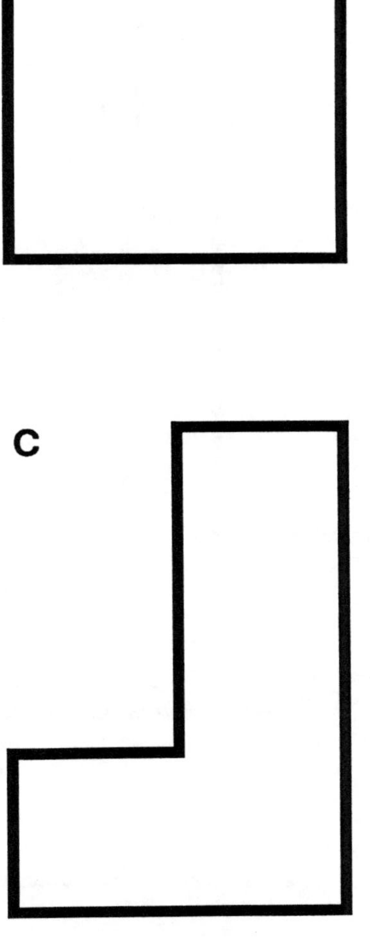

**C**

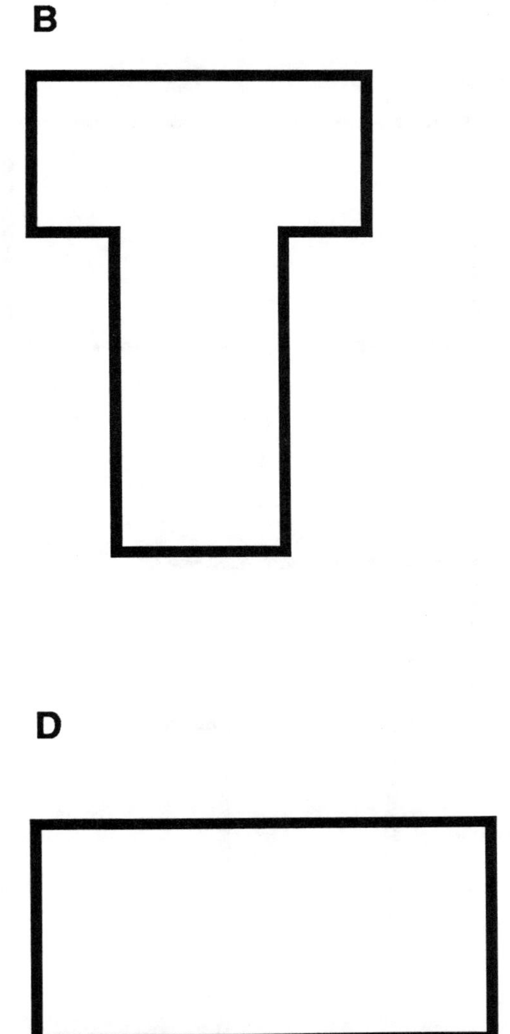

**D**

## COMBINING SHAPES

Place a different colored ATTRIBUTE BLOCK on each shaded shape.

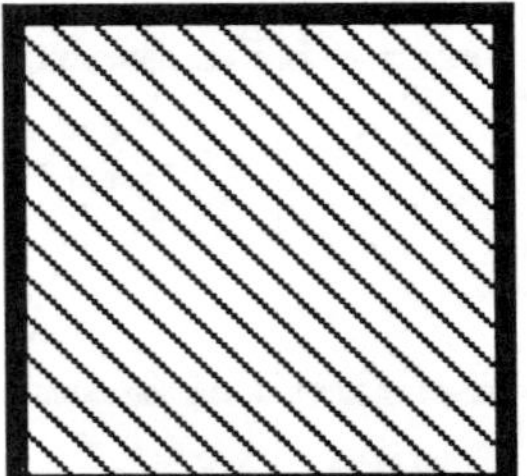

---

Find the figures below that can be made by combining the two blocks.
Color the figures you can make.

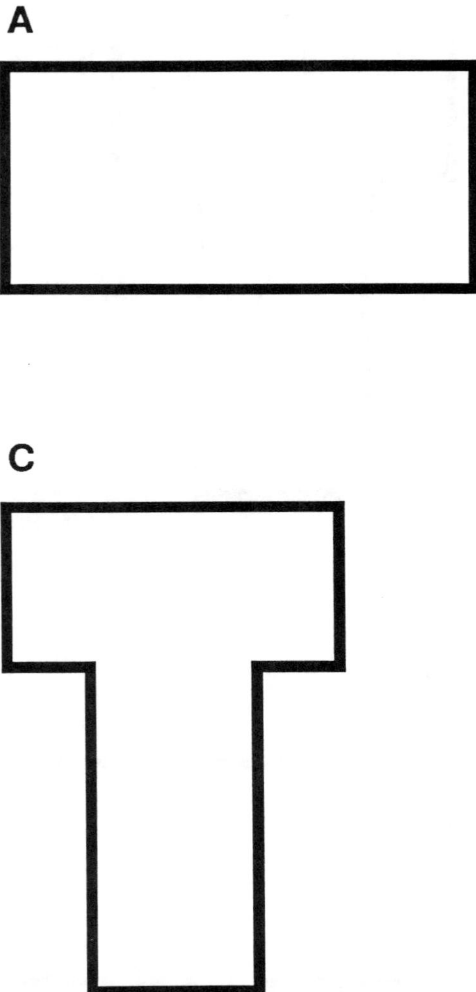


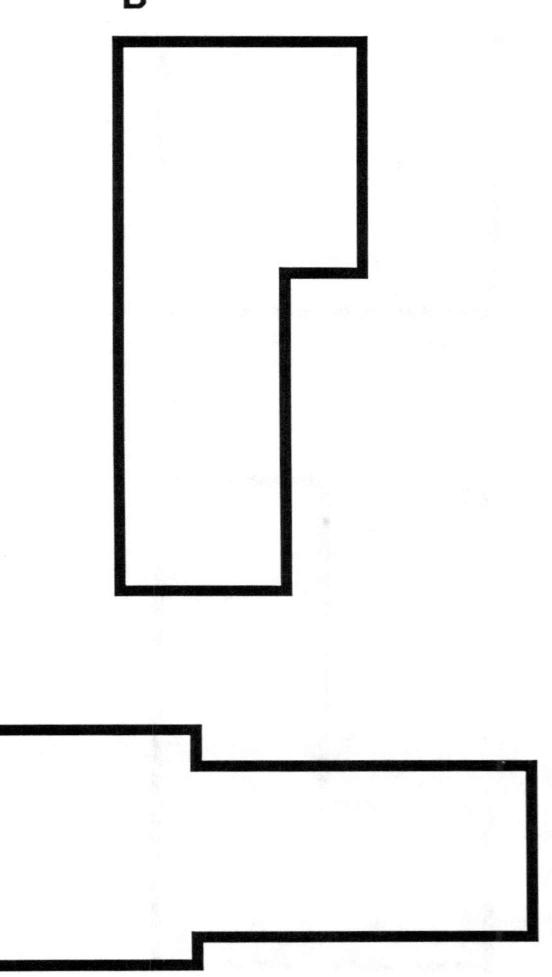

## COMBINING SHAPES

Place a PATTERN BLOCK on each shaded shape.

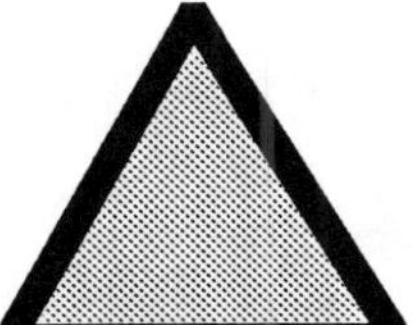
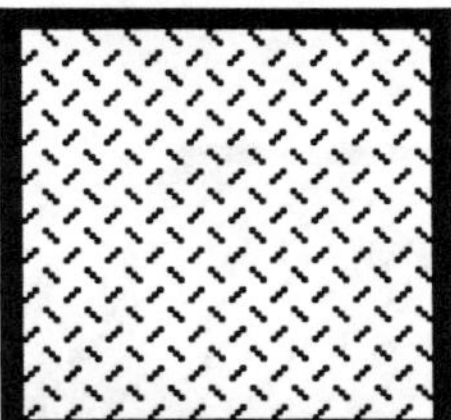

---

Find the figures below that can be made by combining the two blocks.
Color the figures you can make.

A

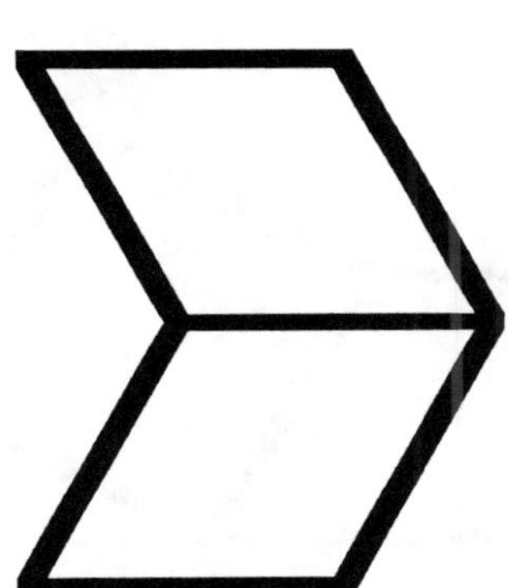

B

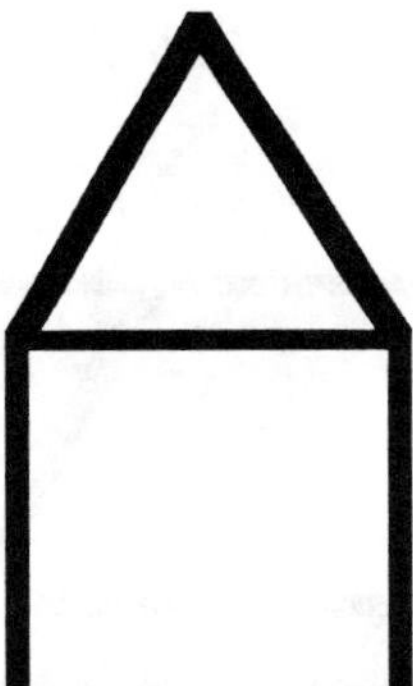

C

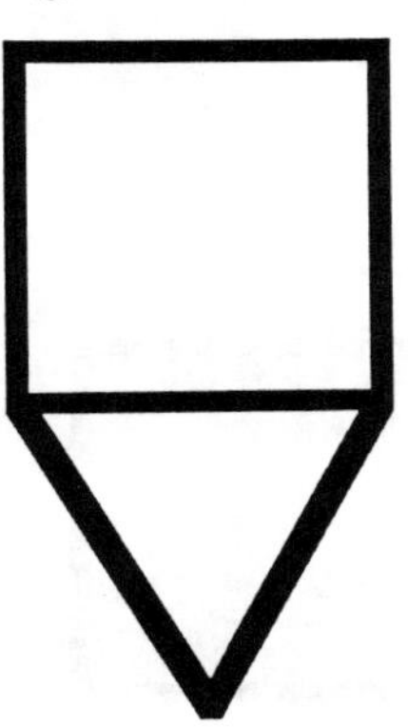

D

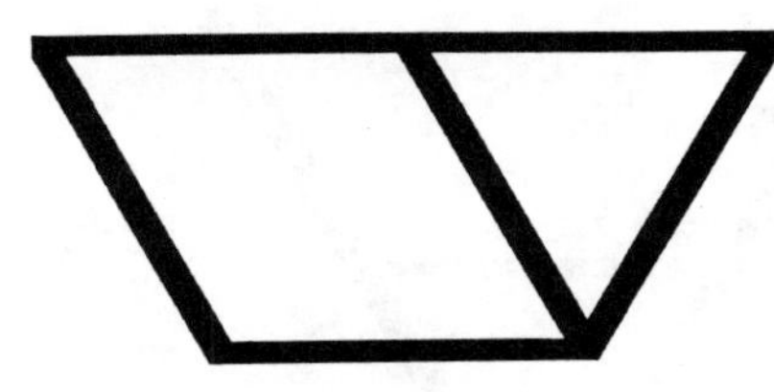

## COMBINING SHAPES

Place a PATTERN BLOCK on each shaded shape.

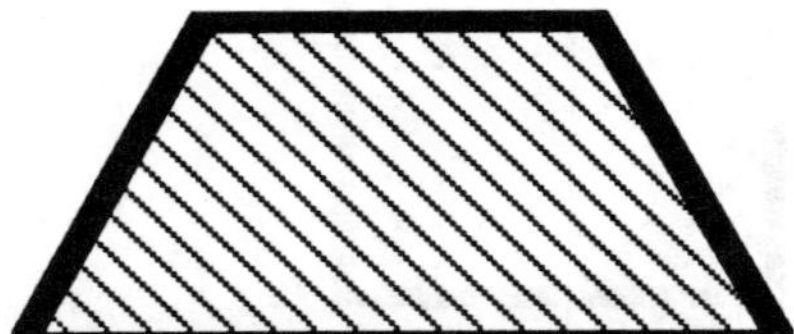

---

Find the figures below that can be made by combining the two blocks.
Color the figures you can make.

**A**

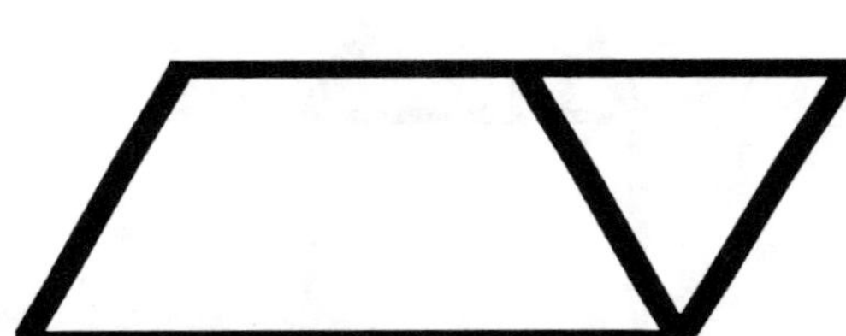

**B**

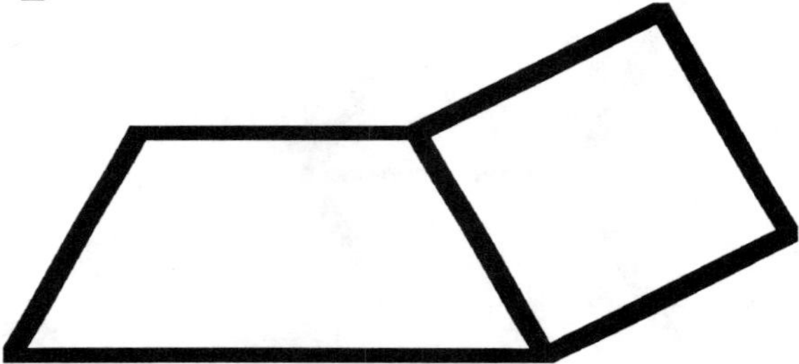

**C**

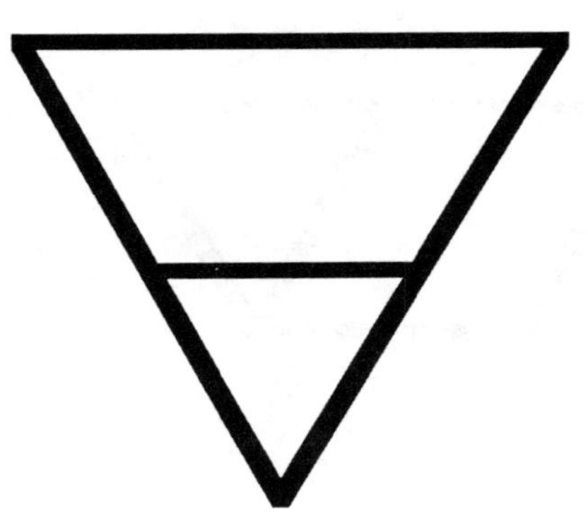

**D**

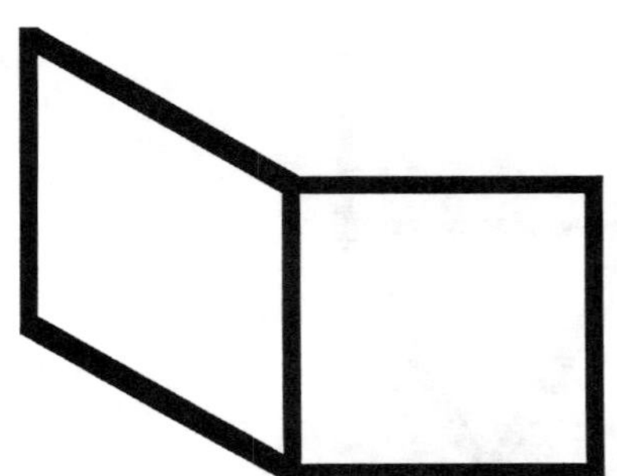

# COMBINING SHAPES

Place a PATTERN BLOCK on each shaded shape.

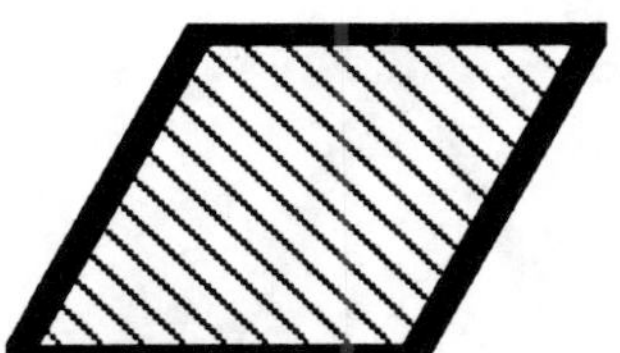

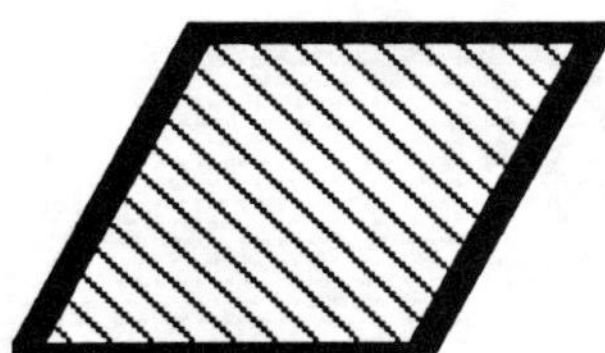

---

Find the figures below that can be made by combining the two blocks.
Color the figures you can make.

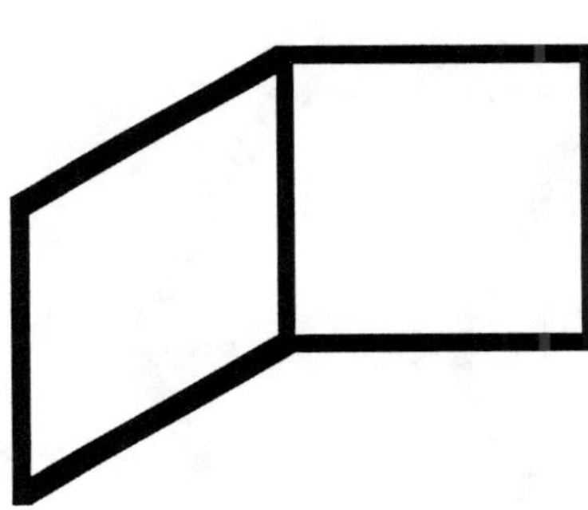

**C**

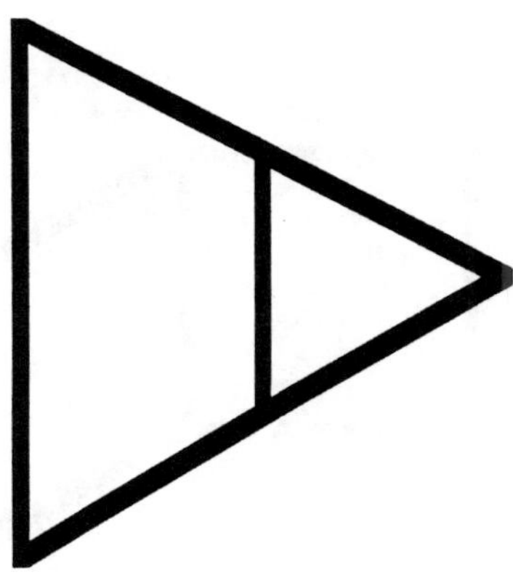

**D**

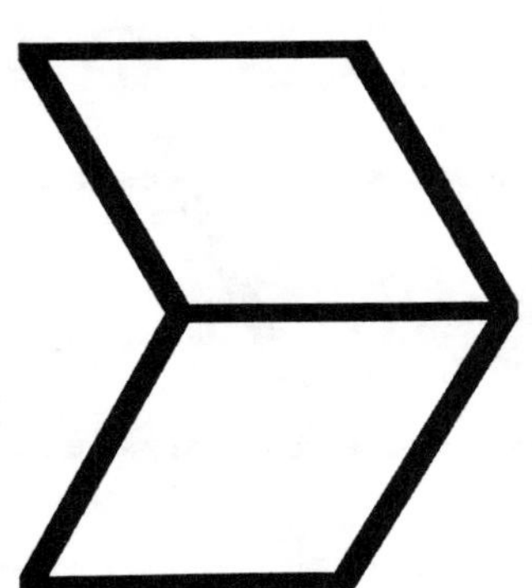

# COMBINING SHAPES

Place a PATTERN BLOCK on each shaded shape.

---

Find the figures below that can be made by combining the two blocks.
Color the figures you can make.

**A**

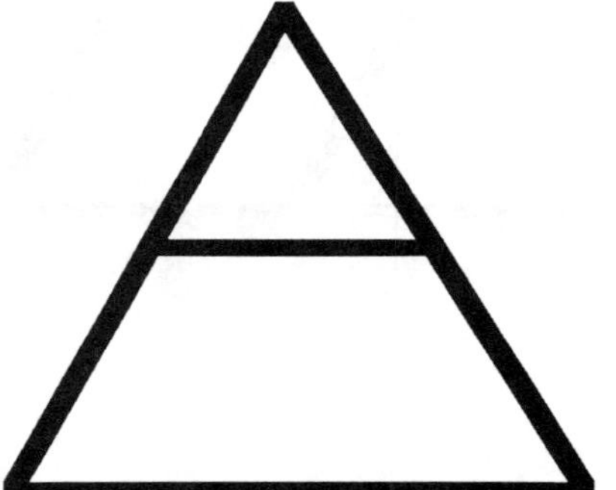

**B**

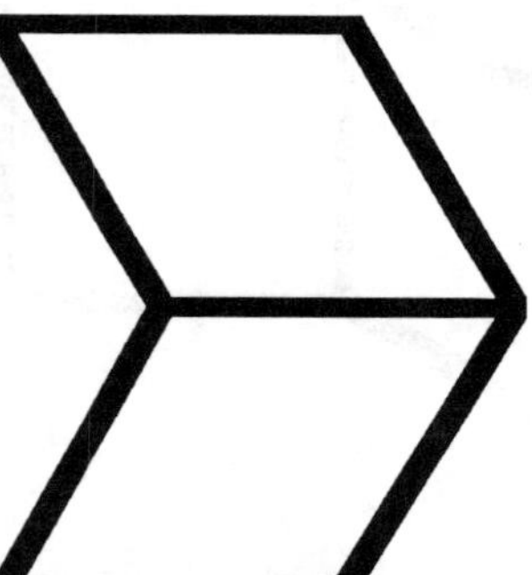

**C**

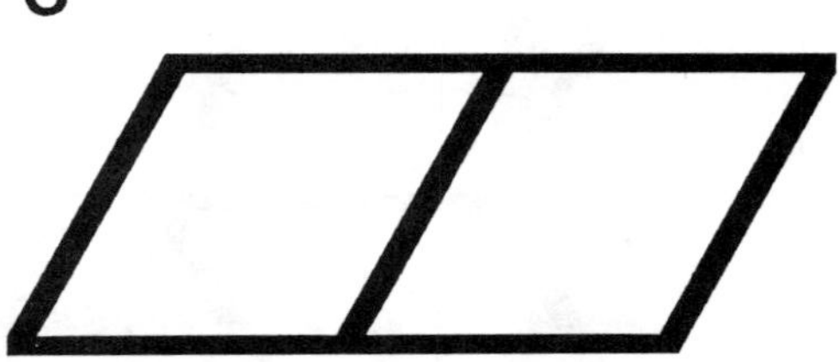

**D**

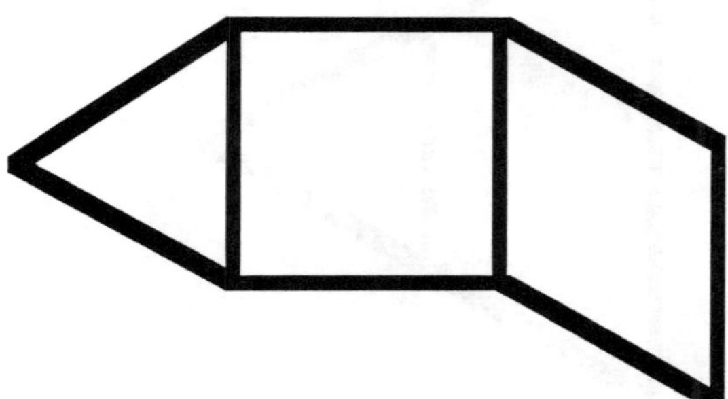

## COMBINING SHAPES

Place a PATTERN BLOCK on each shaded shape.

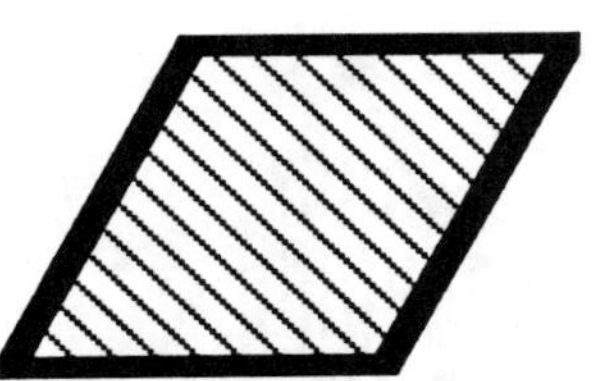
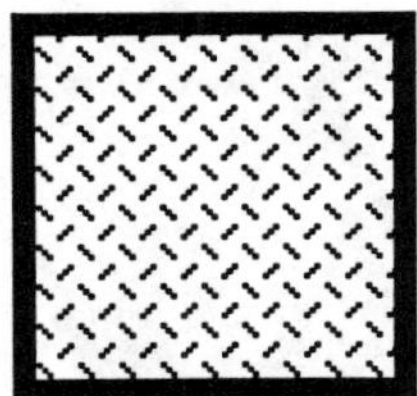
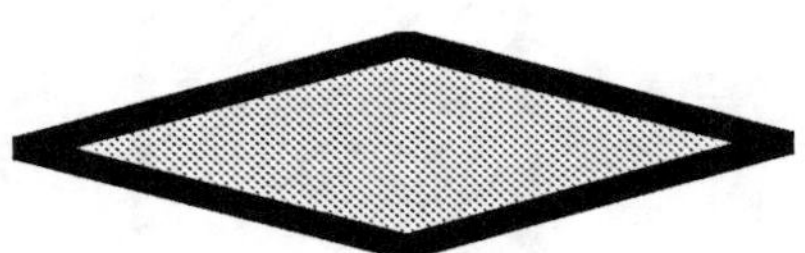

Find the figures below that can be made by combining the three blocks.
Color the figures you can make.

A

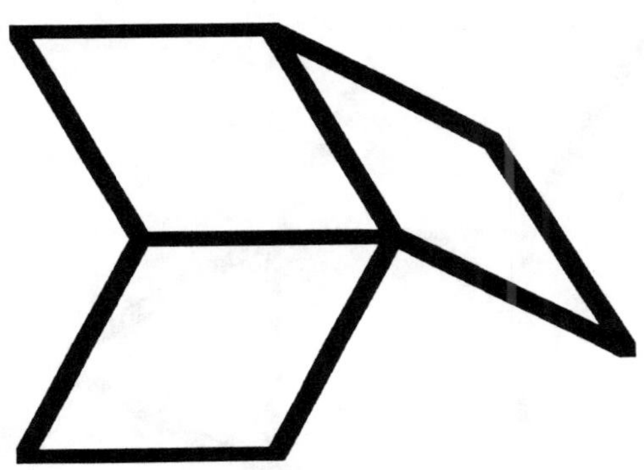

B

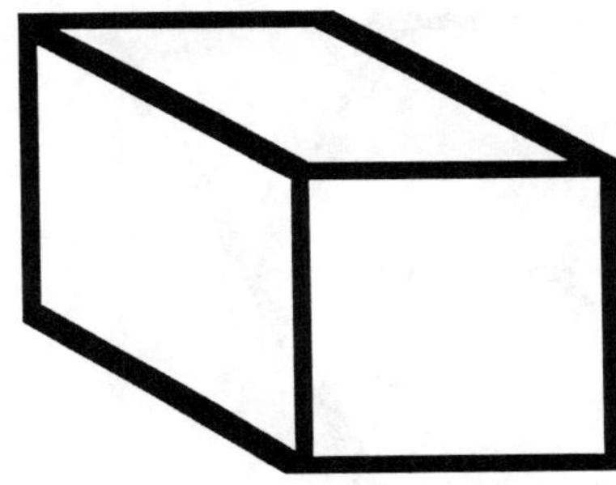

C

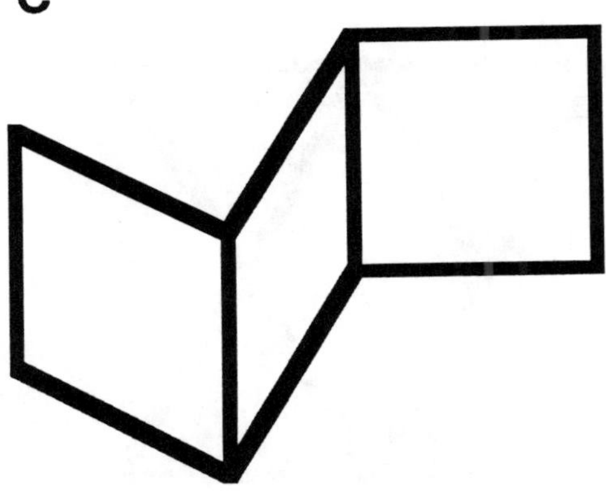

D

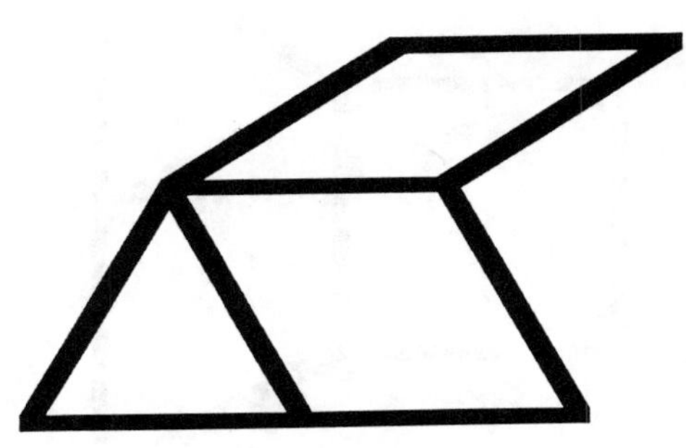

## COMBINING SHAPES

Place a PATTERN BLOCK on each shaded shape.

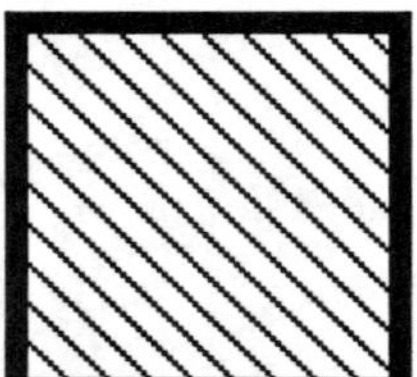
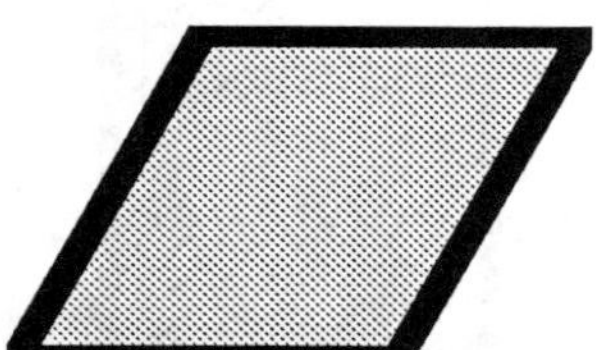
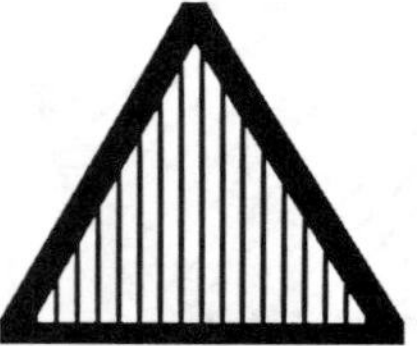

---

Find the figures below that can be made by combining the three blocks.
Color the figures you can make.

**A**

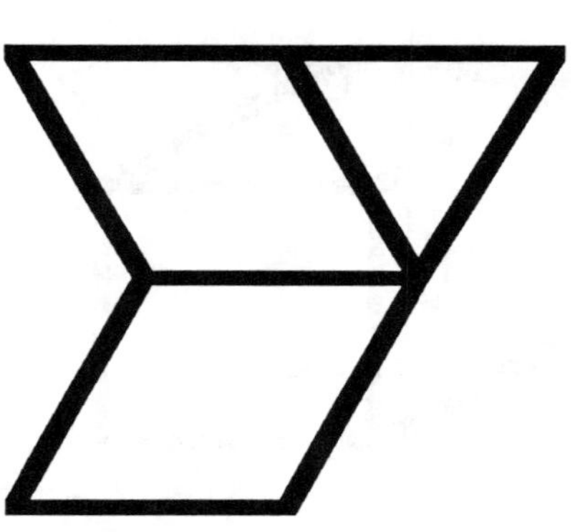

**B**

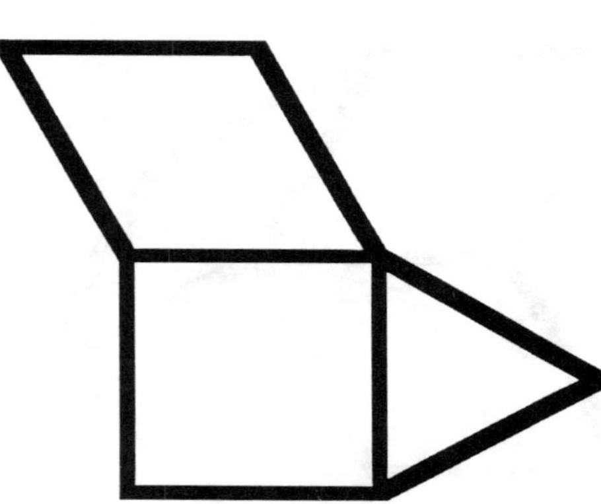

**C**

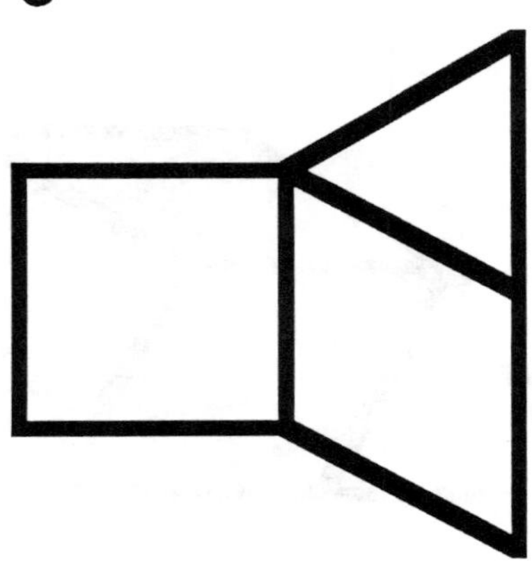

**D**

# COMBINING SHAPES

Place a PATTERN BLOCK on each shaded shape.

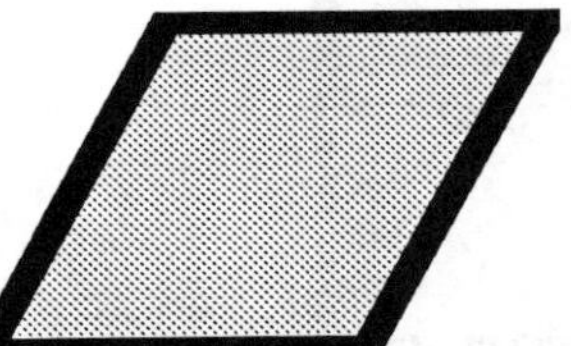

---

Find the figures below that can be made by combining the two blocks.
Color the figures you can make.

**A**

**B**

**C**

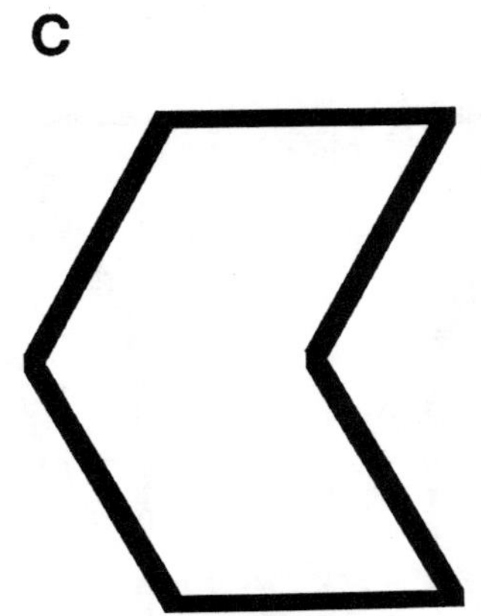

**D**

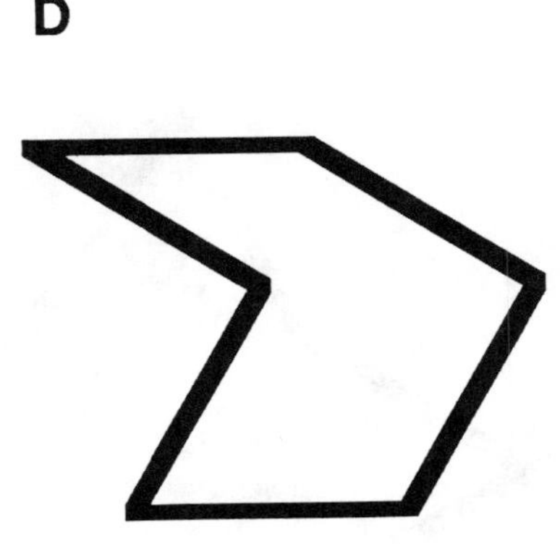

## COMBINING SHAPES

Place a PATTERN BLOCK on each shaded shape.

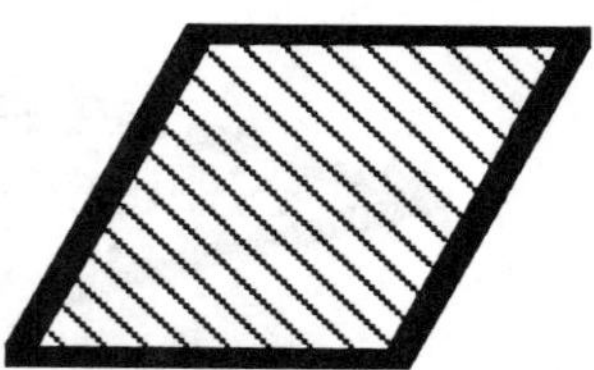

Find the figures below that can be made by combining the three blocks.
Color the figures you can make.

**A**

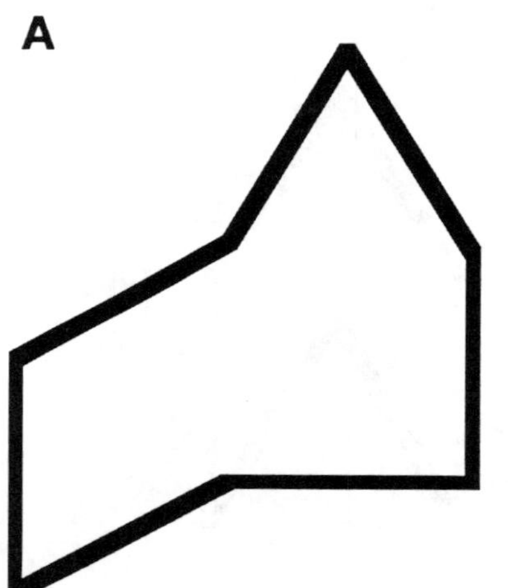

**B**

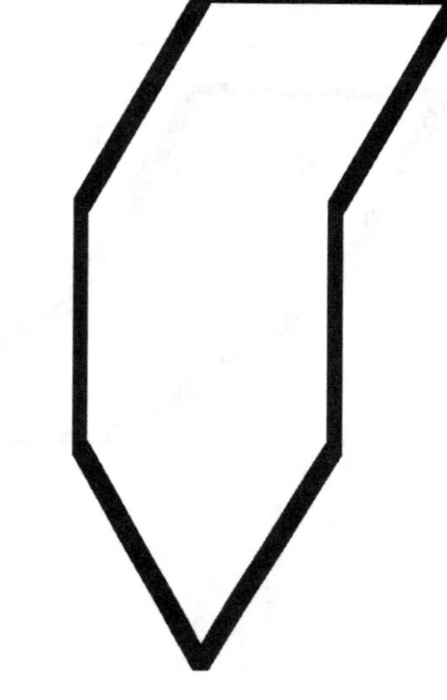

**C**

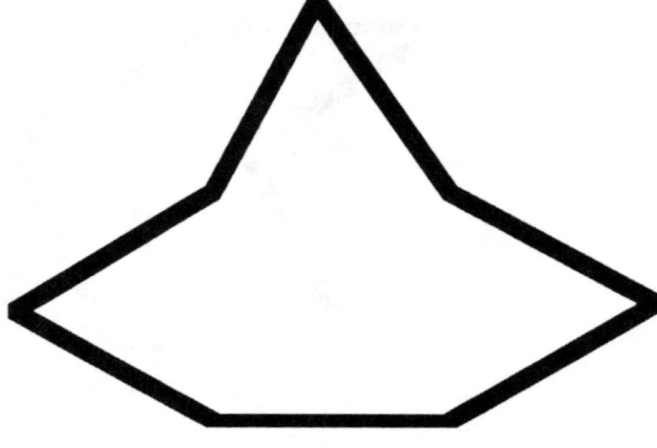

**D**

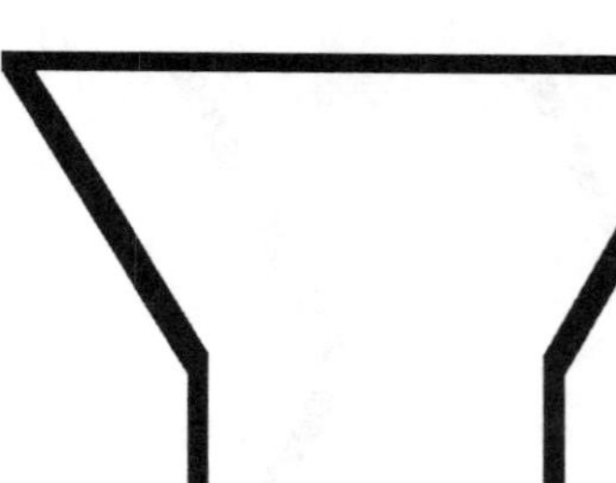

## FINDING SHAPES

Place a PATTERN BLOCK on the shaded shape.

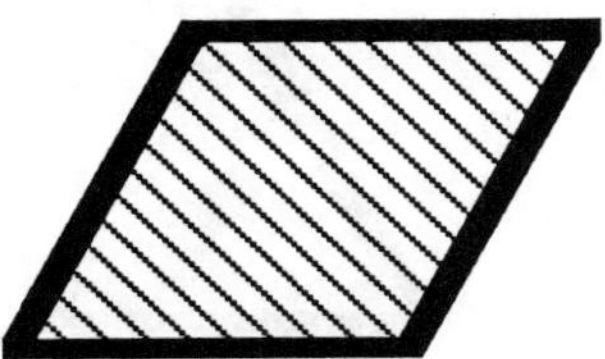

---

Find the shape in each figure below.
Color the shapes you find.

**A**

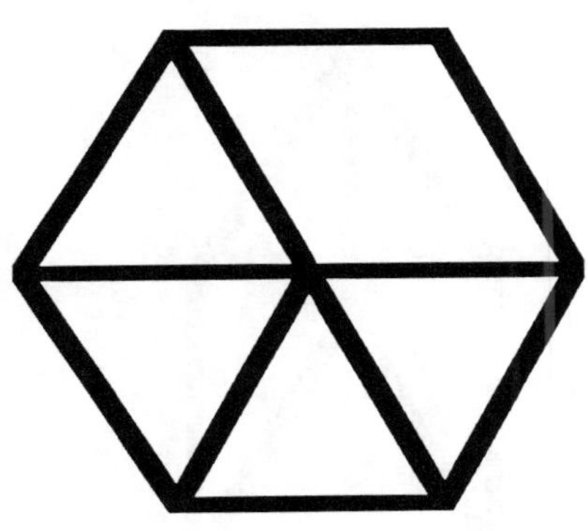

**B**

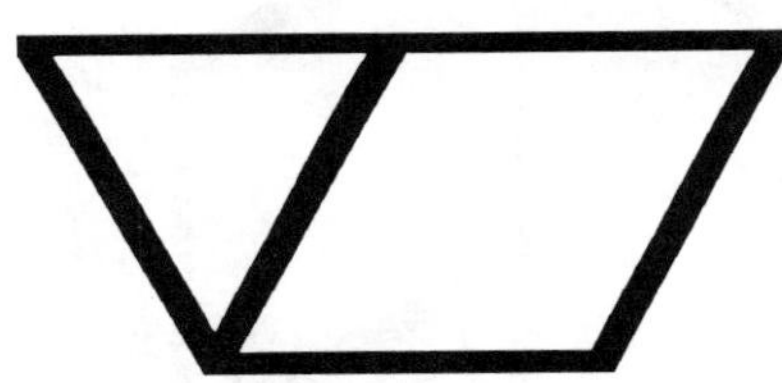

**C**

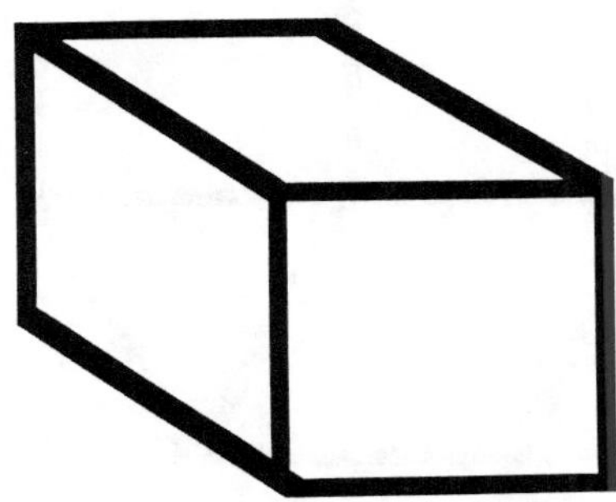

**D**

# FINDING SHAPES

Place a PATTERN BLOCK on the shaded shape.

---

Find the shape in each figure below.
Color the shapes you find.

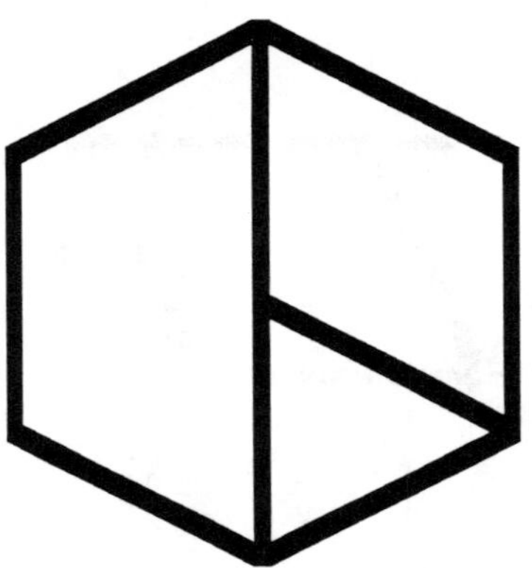

B

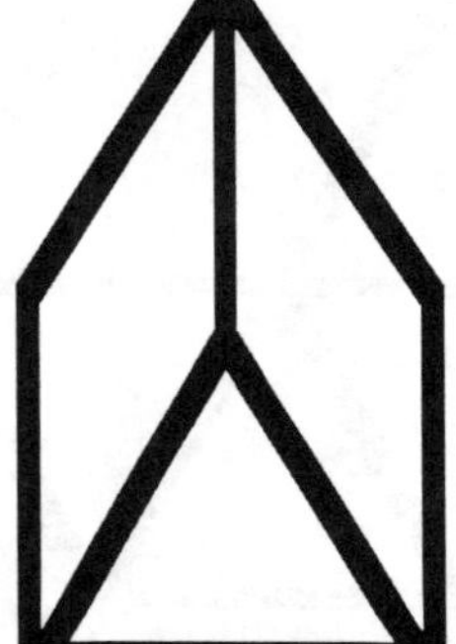

C

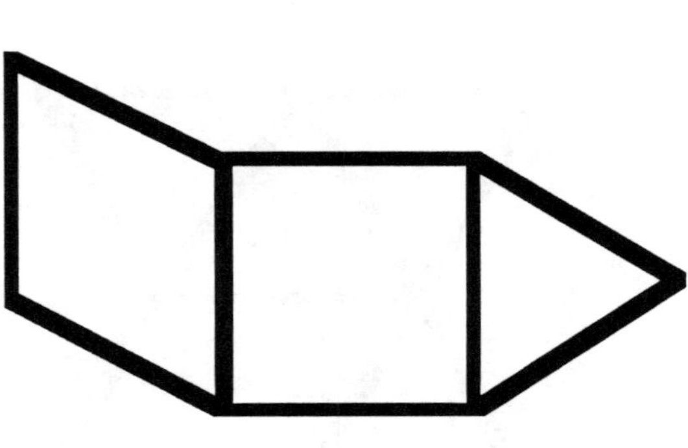

D

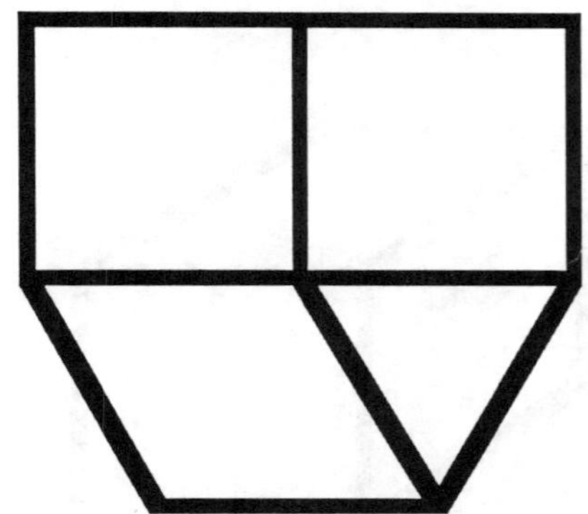

# FINDING SHAPES

Make the shaded figure using INTERLOCKING CUBES.

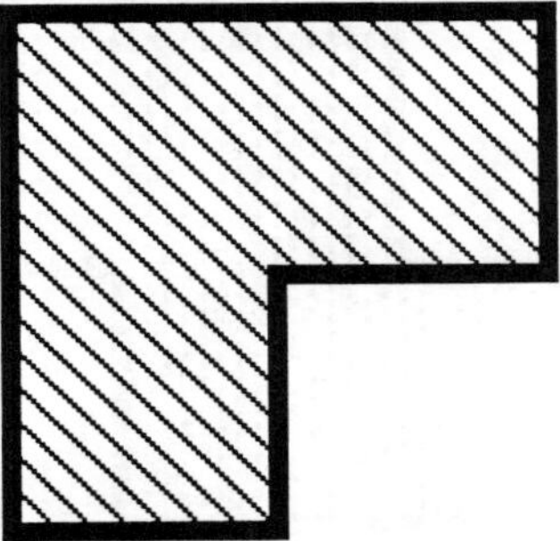

In the picture below, find all the pieces that match the figure.
Color the pieces that match the figure.

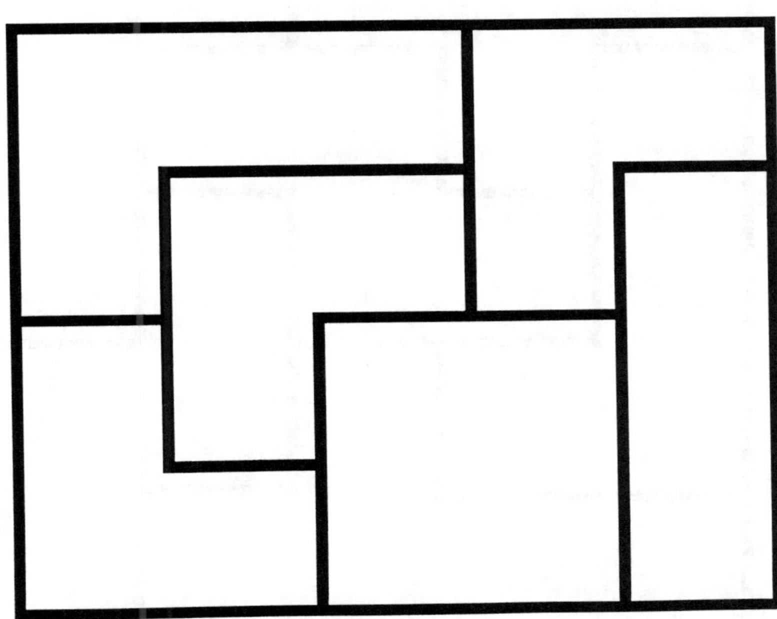

# FINDING SHAPES

Make the shaded figure using INTERLOCKING CUBES.

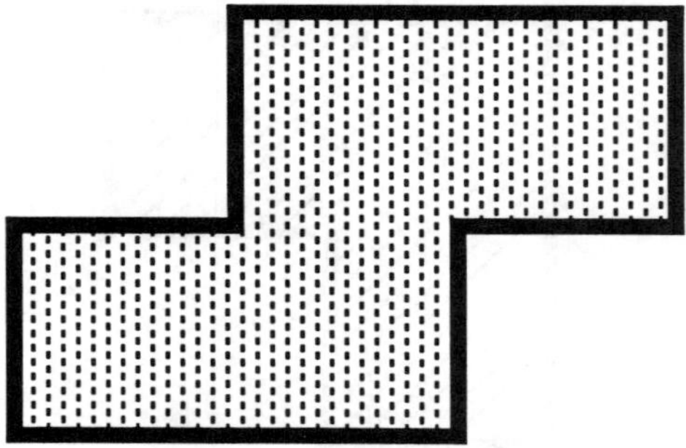

In the picture below, find all the pieces that match the figure.
Color the pieces that match the figure.

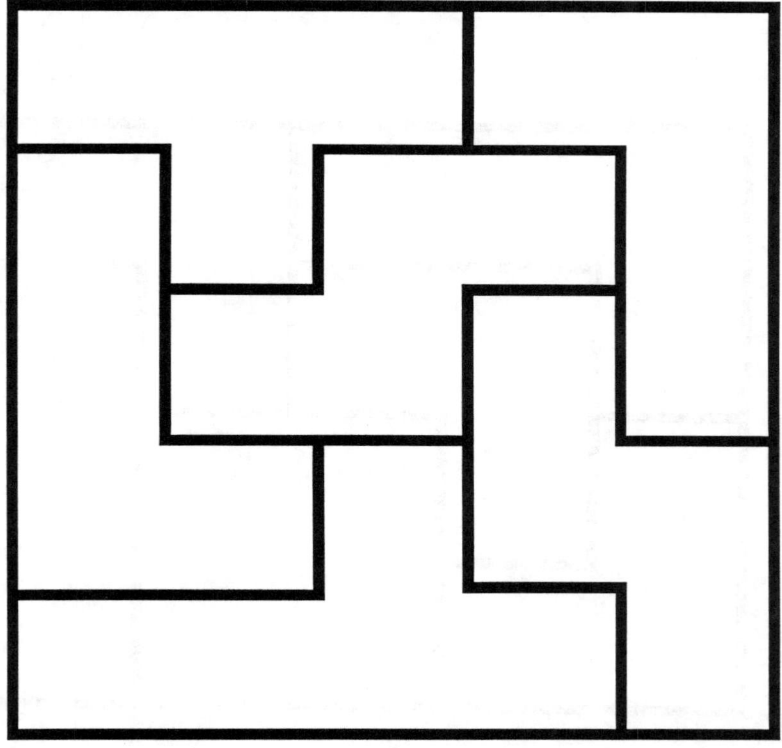

# FINDING SHAPES

In each box, color all the PATTERN BLOCK shapes you can find in the figure to the left.

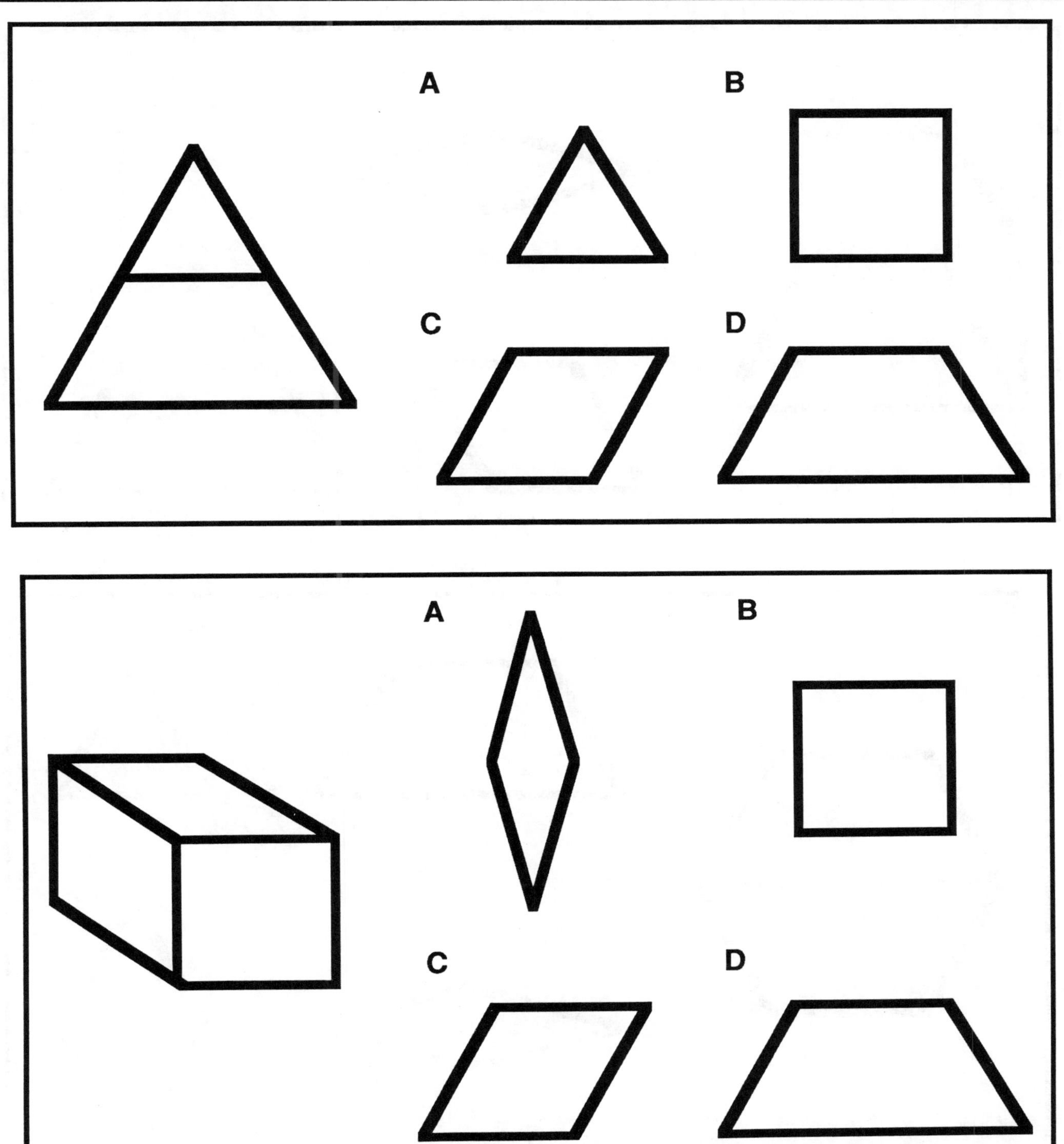

## FINDING SHAPES

In each box, color all the PATTERN BLOCK shapes you can find in the figure to the left.

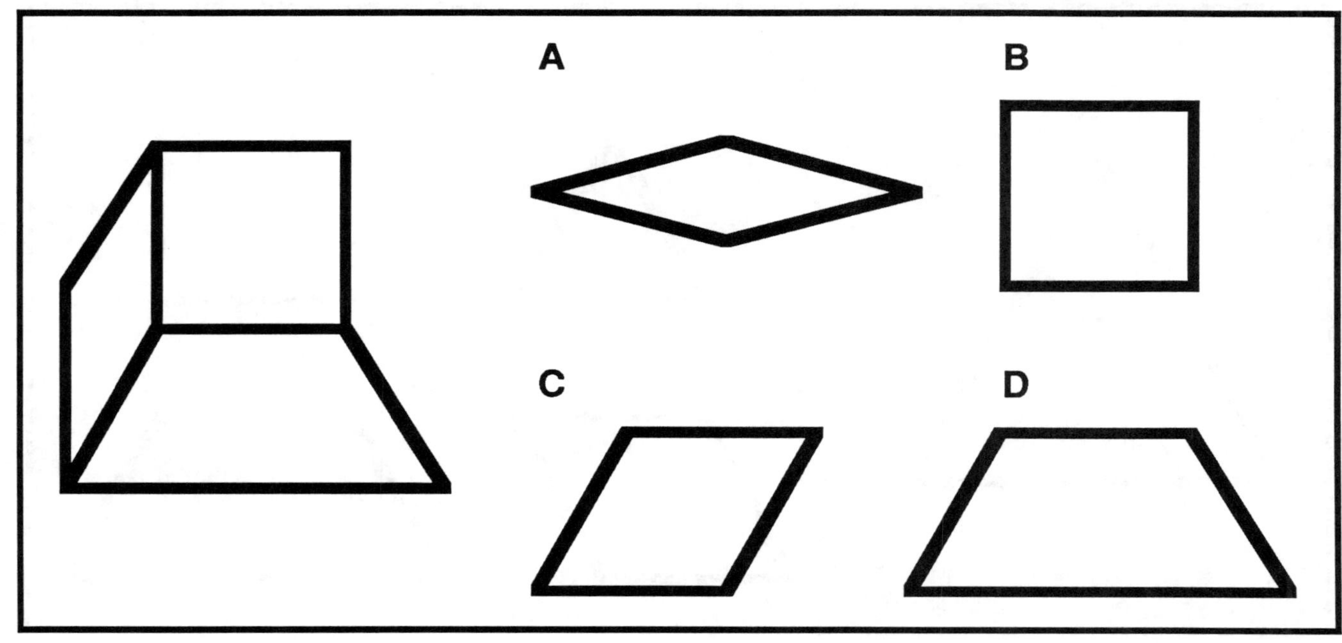


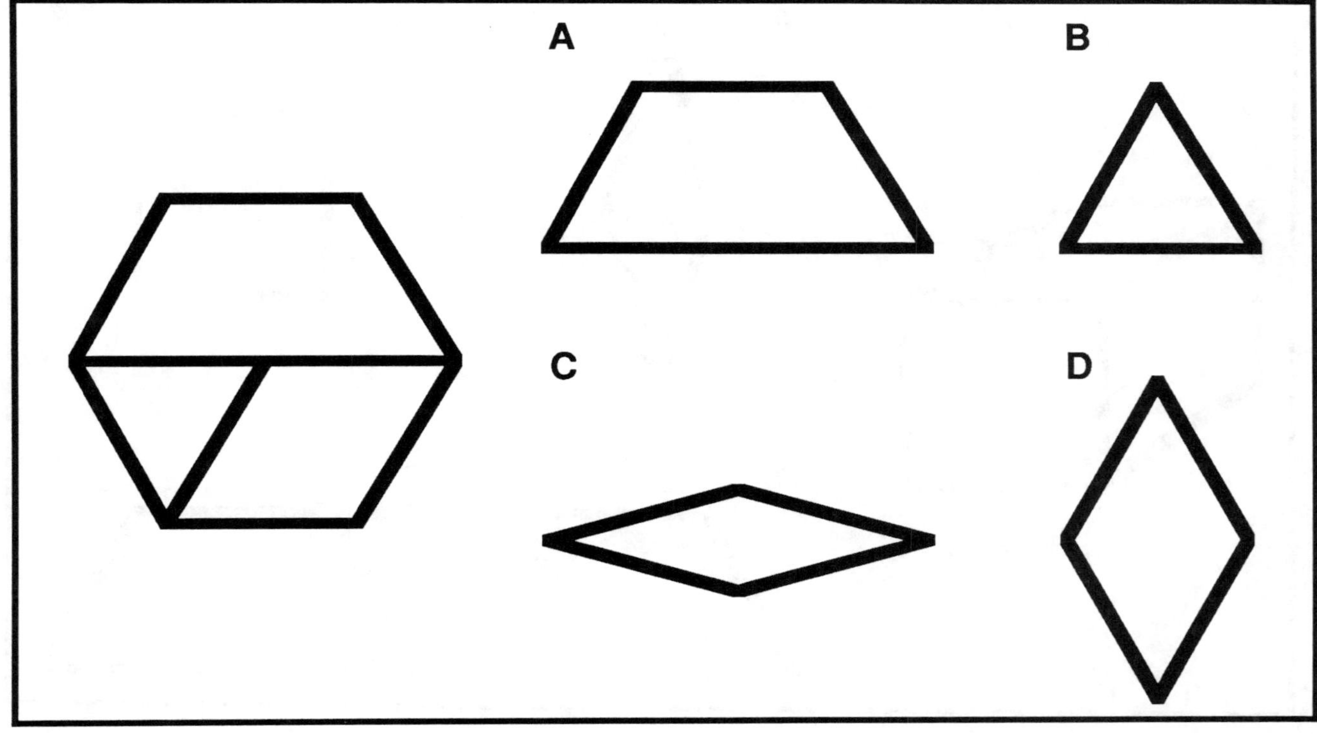

# DIVIDING SHAPES INTO EQUAL PARTS

Place a PATTERN BLOCK on each shaded shape.
Use the two blocks to cover the figure to the right.
Draw a line in the figure to outline the two shapes.
Color the figure to match the blocks.

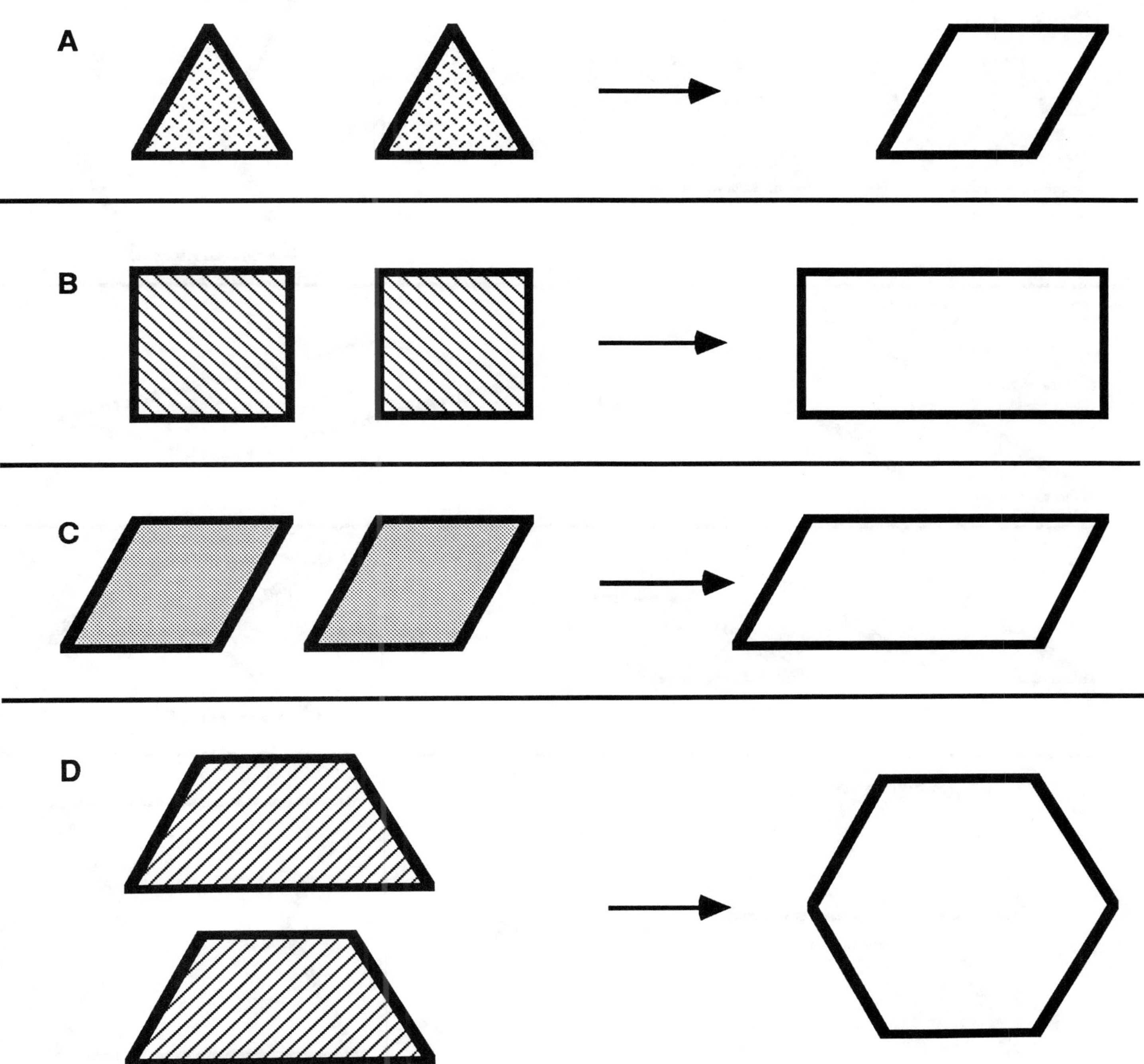

# DIVIDING SHAPES INTO EQUAL PARTS

Place a PATTERN BLOCK on each shaded shape.
Use the two blocks to cover the figure to the right.
Draw a line in the figure to outline the two shapes.
Color the figure to match the blocks.

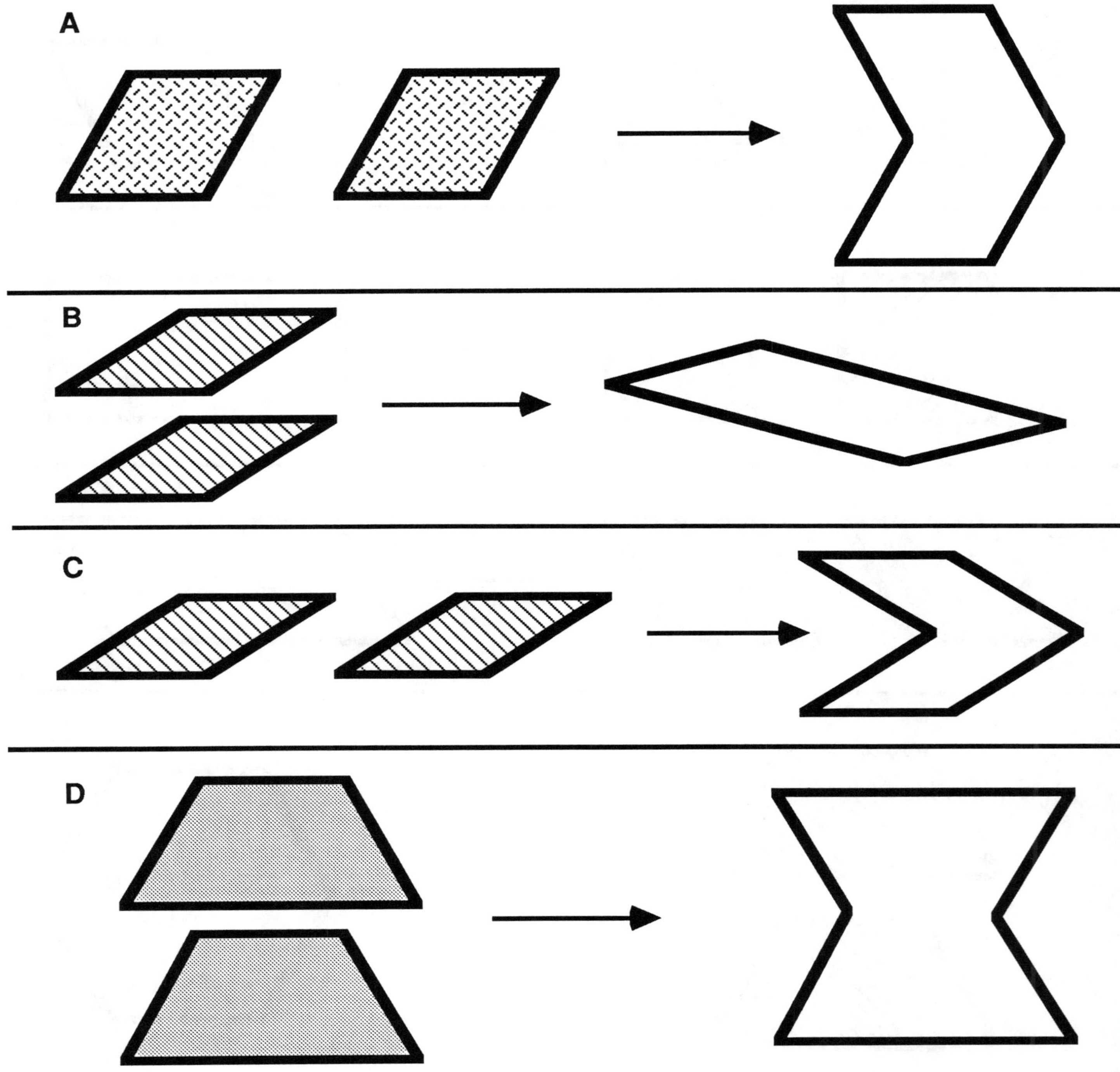

## DIVIDING SHAPES INTO EQUAL PARTS

Place an ATTRIBUTE BLOCK on each shaded shape.
Use the two blocks to cover the figure to the right.
Draw a line in the figure to outline the two shapes.
Color the figure to match the blocks.

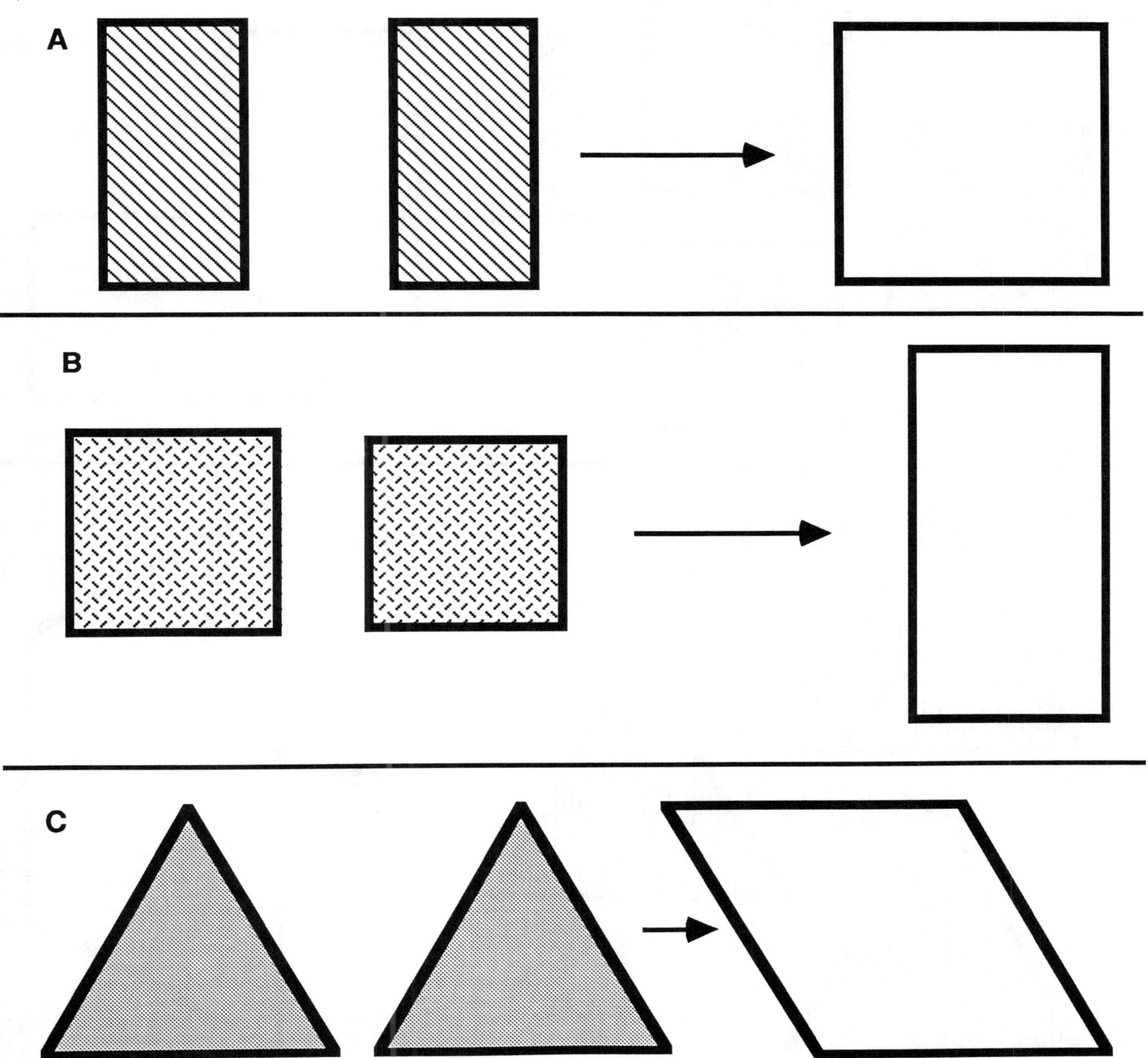

## DIVIDING SHAPES INTO EQUAL PARTS

Place an ATTRIBUTE BLOCK on each shaded shape.
Use the three blocks to cover the figure to the right.
Draw lines in the figure to outline the three shapes.
Color the figure to match the blocks.

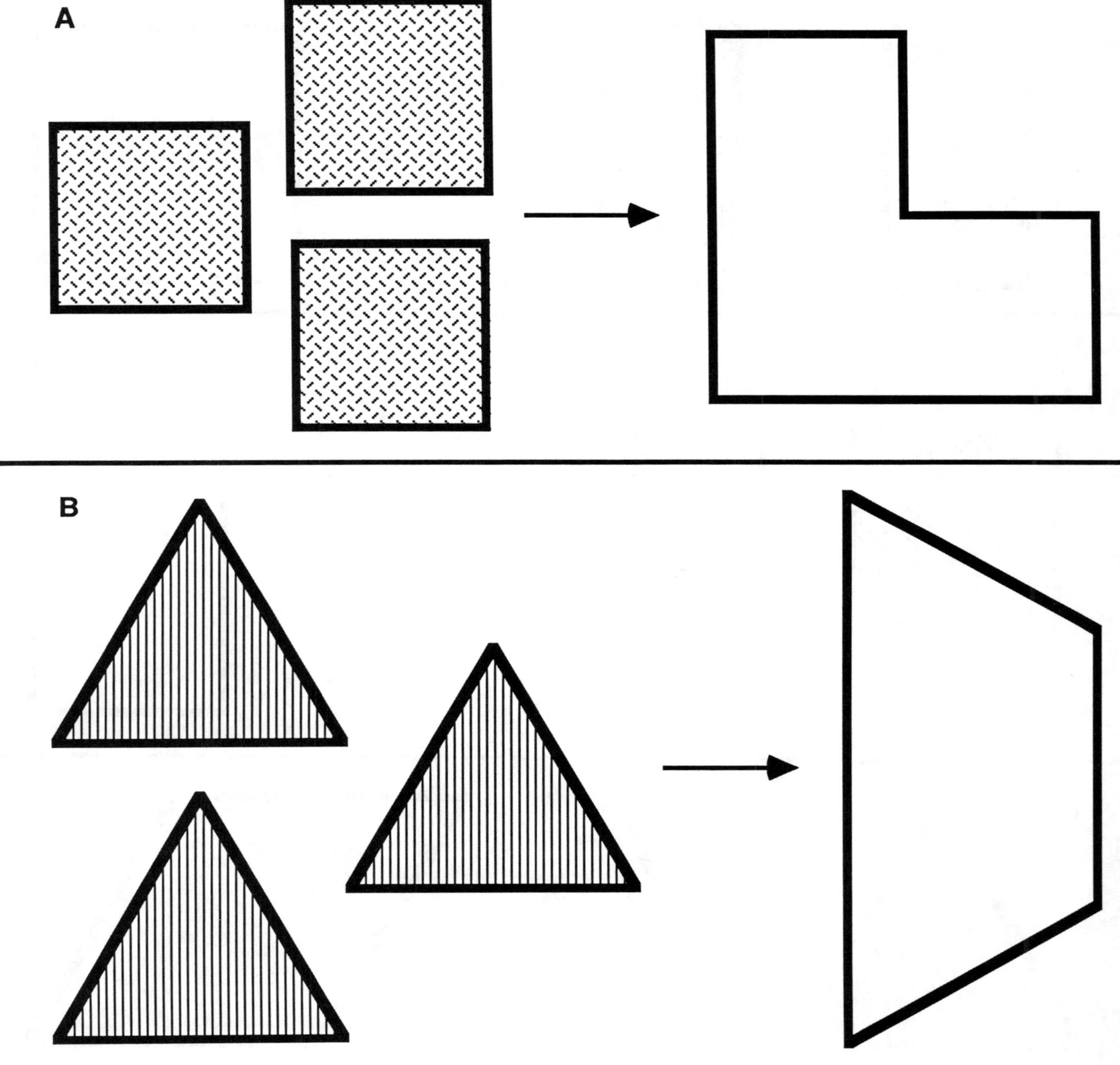

## DIVIDING SHAPES INTO EQUAL PARTS

Make each shaded figure using MULTILINK CUBES.
Use a different color for each construction.

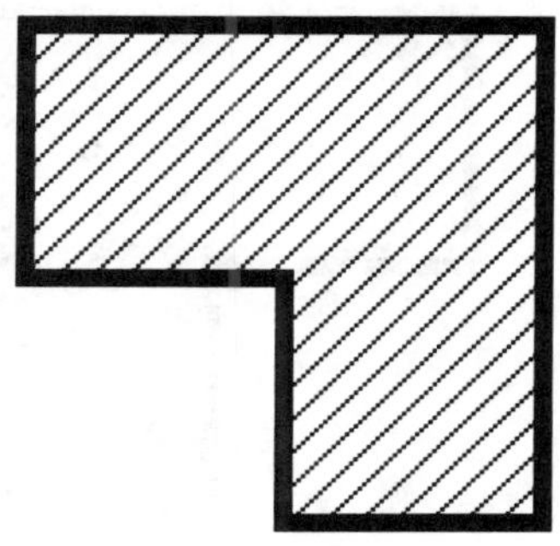

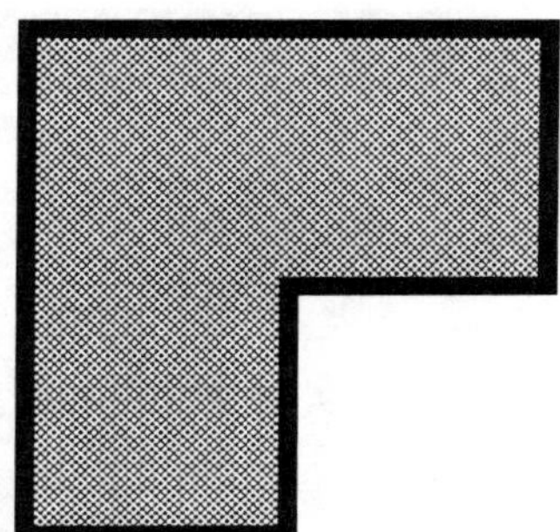

Cover each figure below using the two MULTILINK constructions.
Draw lines to outline the two figures.
Color the pictures to match the cubes.

A

B

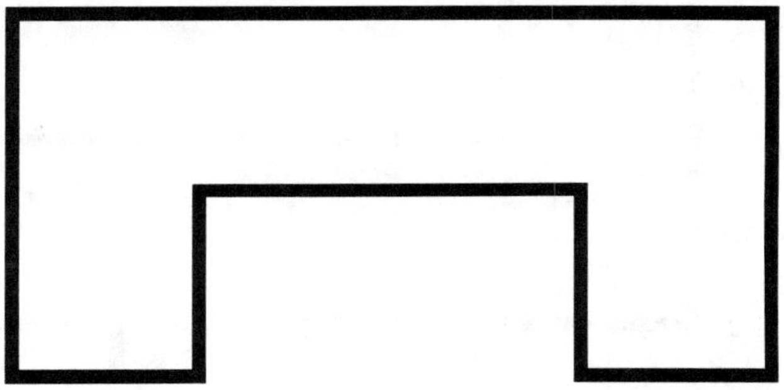

C

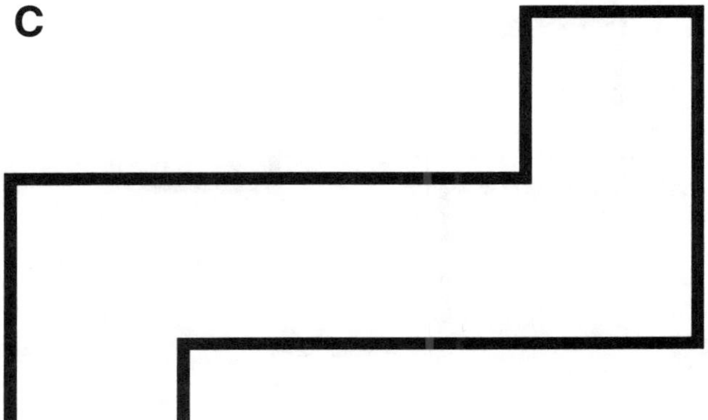

D

## DIVIDING SHAPES INTO EQUAL PARTS

Make each shaded figure using INTERLOCKING CUBES.
Use a different color for each construction.

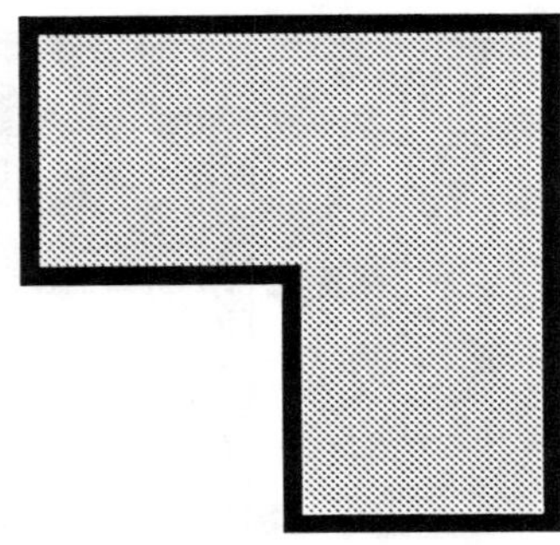

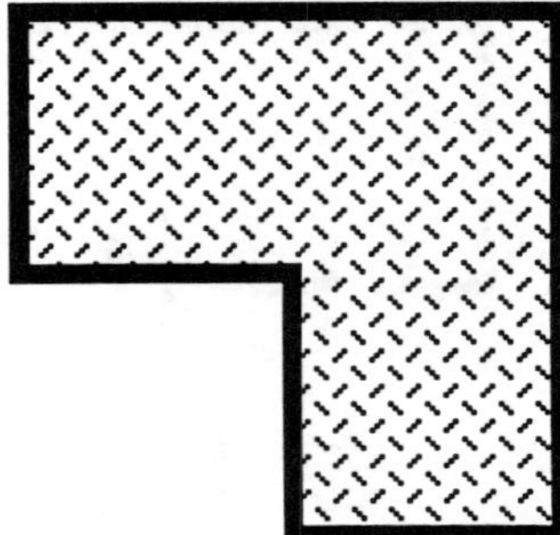

---

Cover each figure below using the two figures you made.
Draw lines to outline the two figures.
Color the pictures to match the cubes.

A

B

C

D

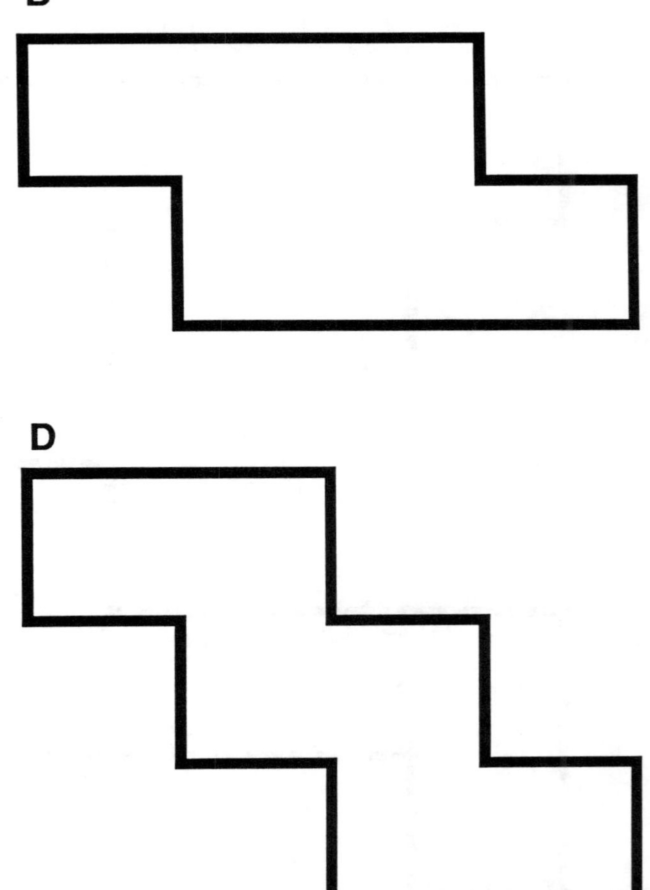

## DIVIDING SHAPES INTO EQUAL PARTS

Make each shaded figure using INTERLOCKING CUBES.
Use a different color for each construction.

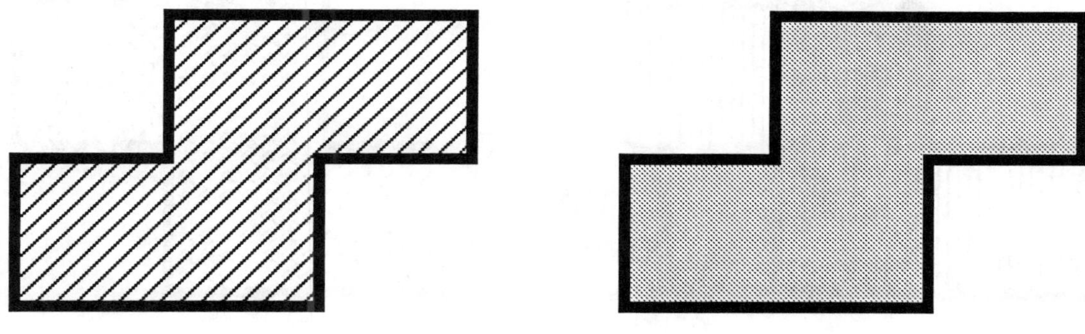

Cover each figure below using the two figures you made.
Draw lines to outline the two figures.
Color the pictures to match the cubes.

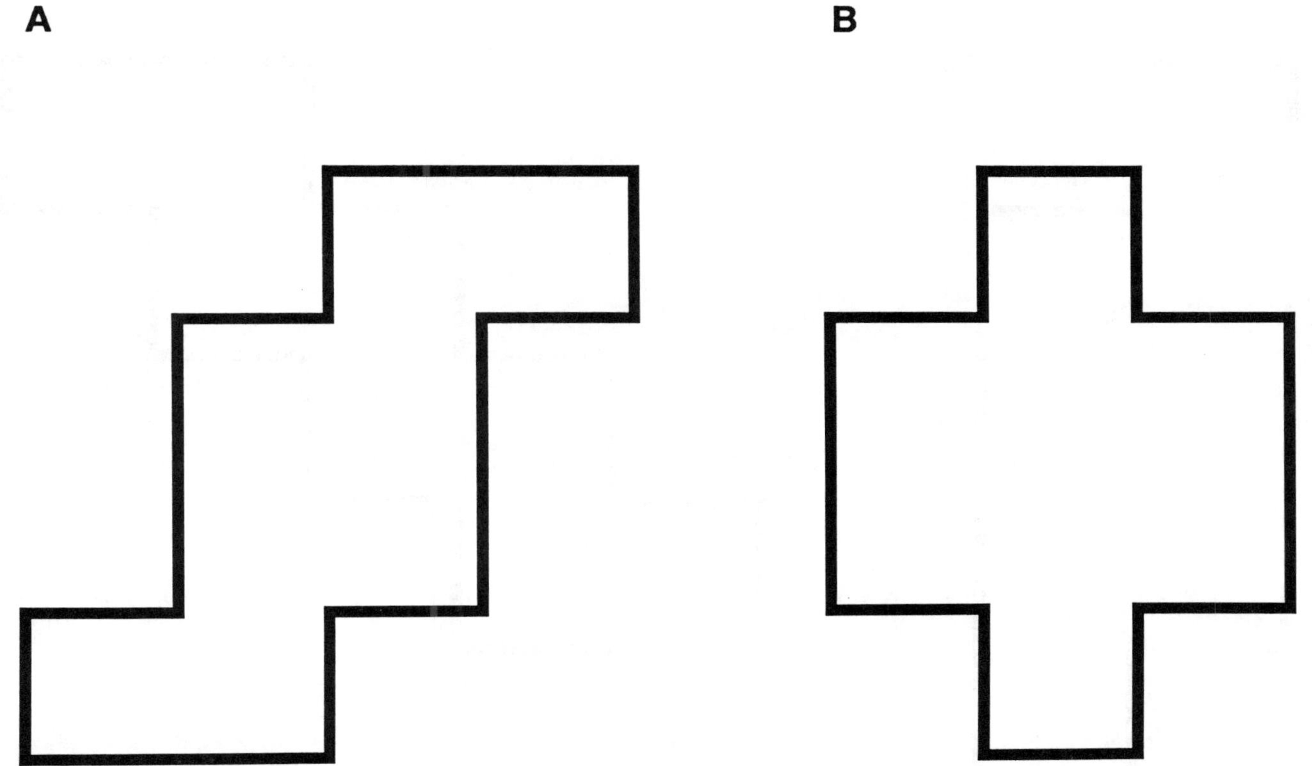

## DIVIDING SHAPES INTO EQUAL PARTS

Make each shaded figure using INTERLOCKING CUBES.
Use a different color for each construction.

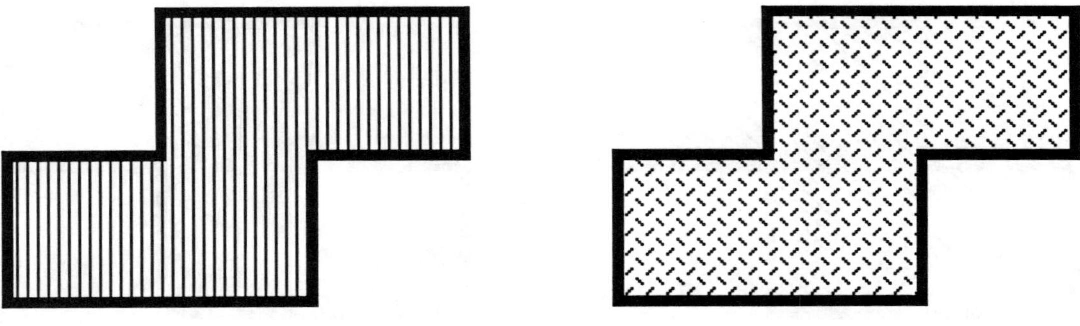

Cover each figure below using the two figures you made.
Draw lines to outline the two figures.
Color the pictures to match the cubes.

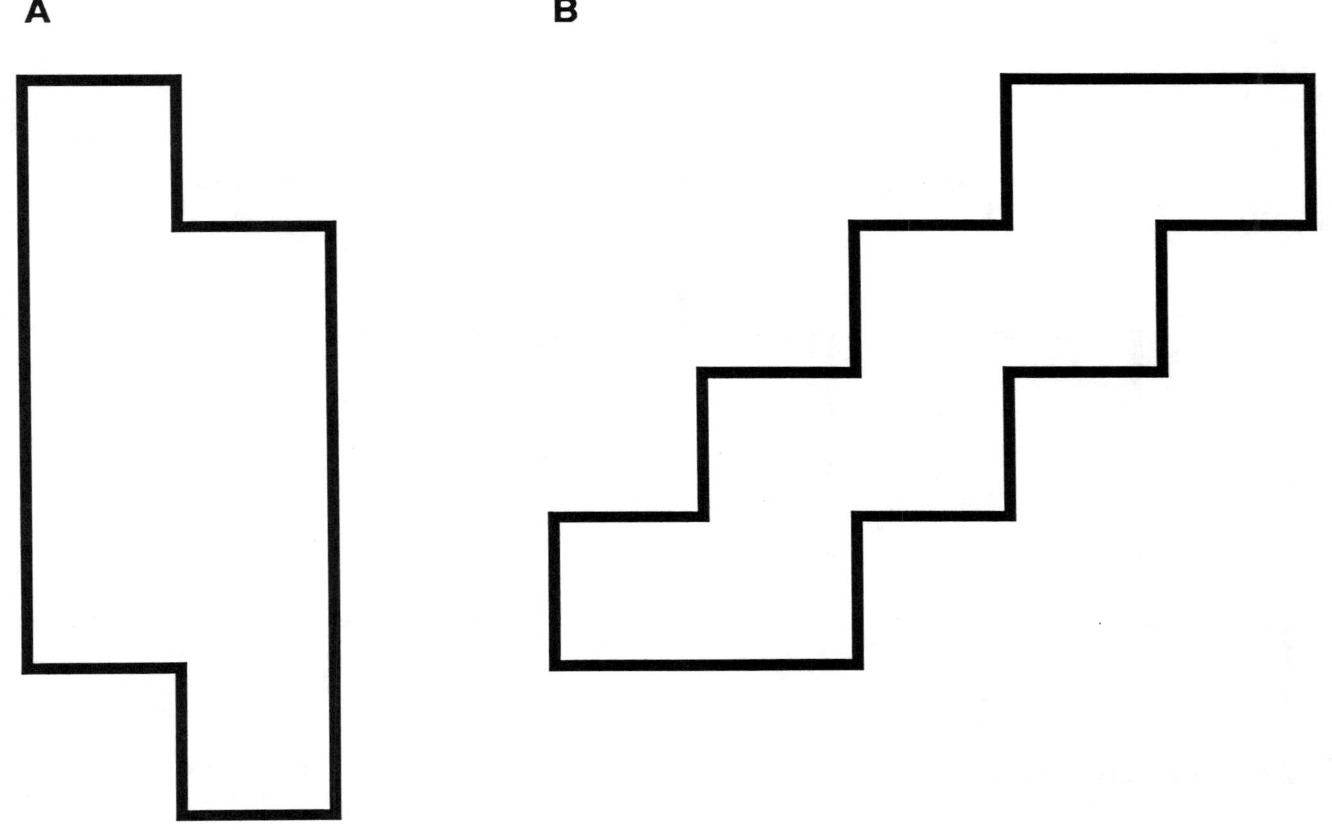

## DIVIDING SHAPES INTO EQUAL PARTS

Make each shaded figure using INTERLOCKING CUBES.
Use a different color for each construction.

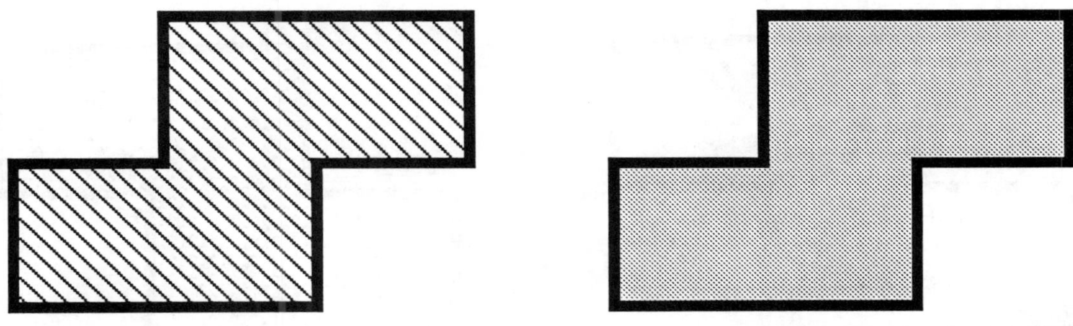

Cover each figure below using the two figures you made.
Draw lines to outline the two figures.
Color the pictures to match the cubes.

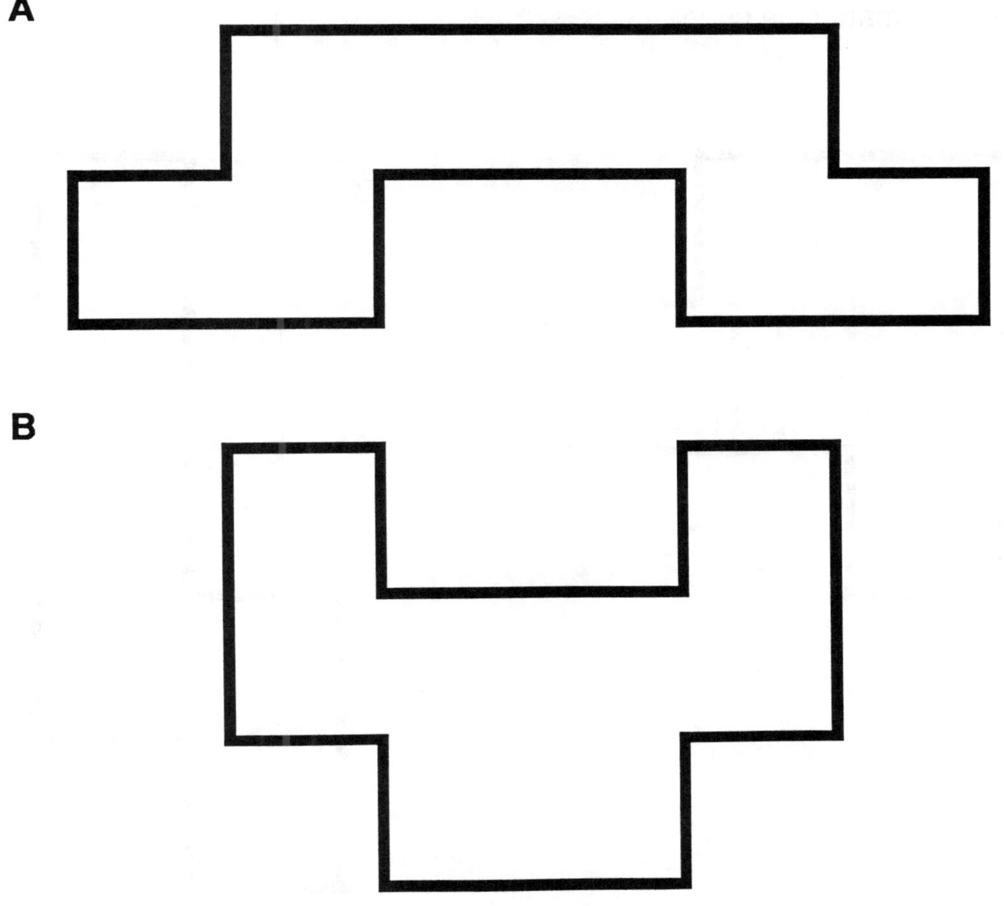

## DIVIDING SHAPES INTO EQUAL PARTS

Make each shaded figure using INTERLOCKING CUBES.
Use a different color for each construction.

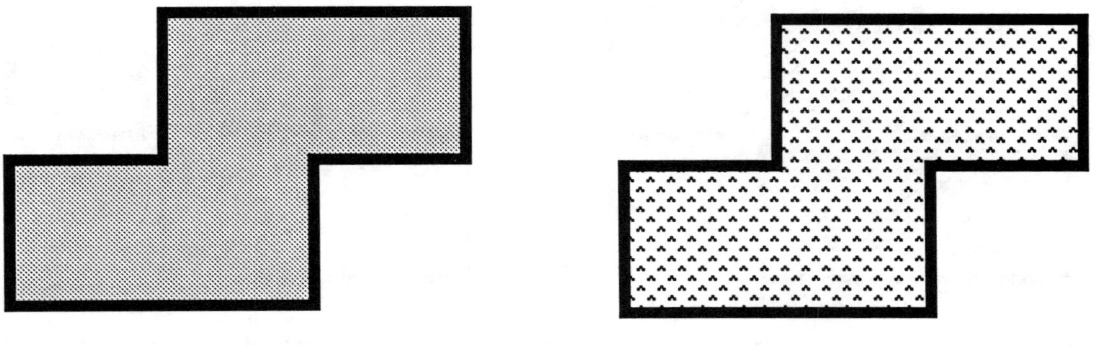

Cover each figure below using the two figures you made.
Draw lines to outline the two figures.
Color the pictures to match the cubes.

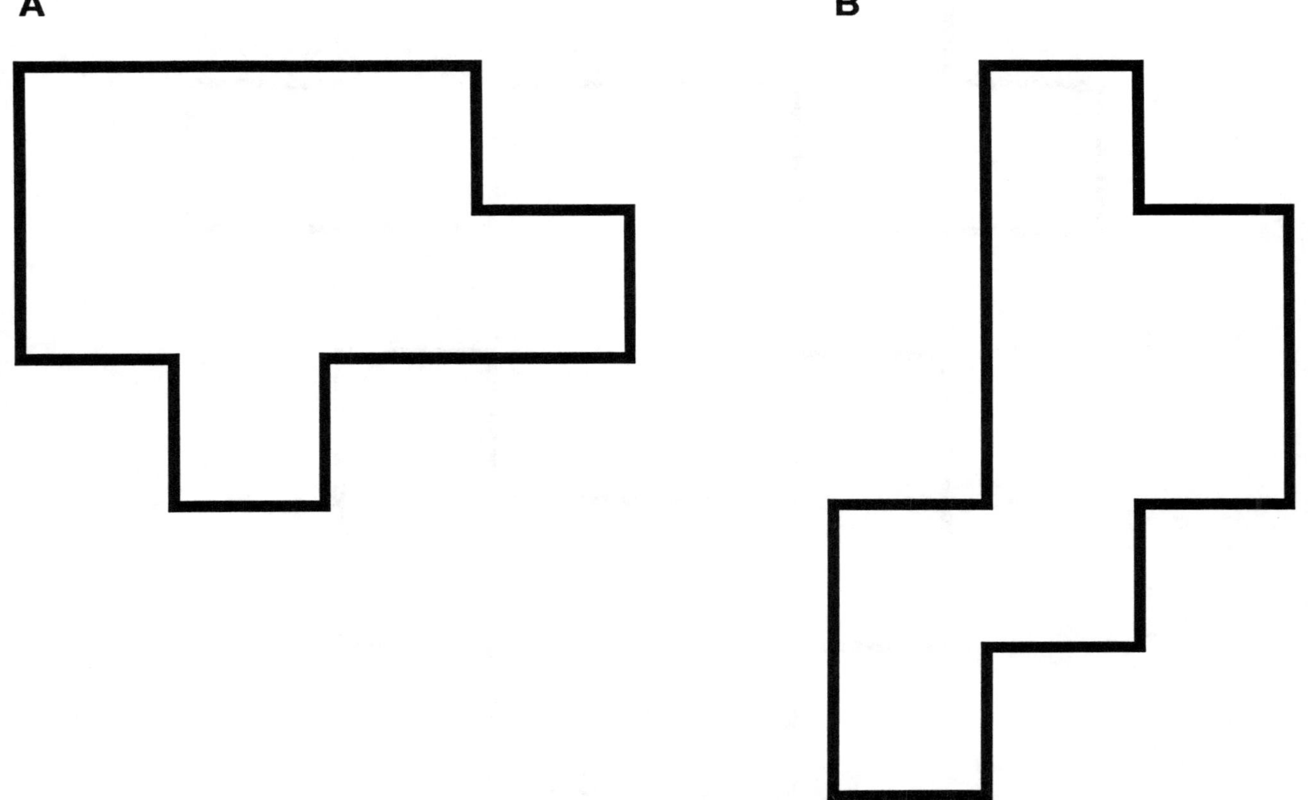

# COMPLETING THE SHAPE

The shaded shape is covering part of a small ATTRIBUTE BLOCK.
Find the block that is under the shape.
Draw in the covered part of the block and color it.

---

**A**

**B**

**C**

**D**

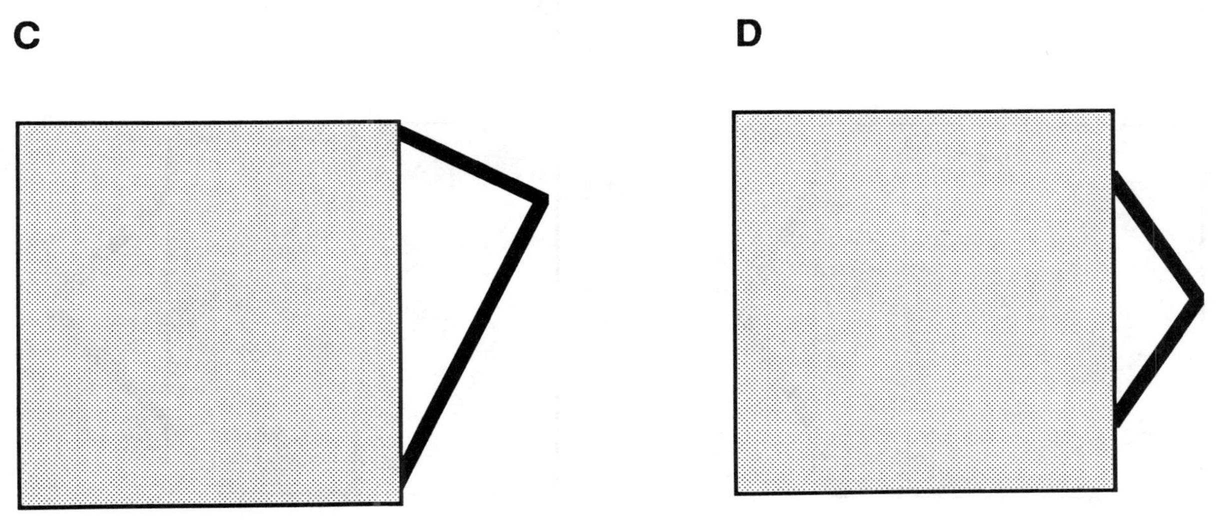

# COMPLETING THE SHAPE

The shaded shape is covering part of a small ATTRIBUTE BLOCK.
Find the block that is under the shape.
Draw in the covered part of the block and color it.

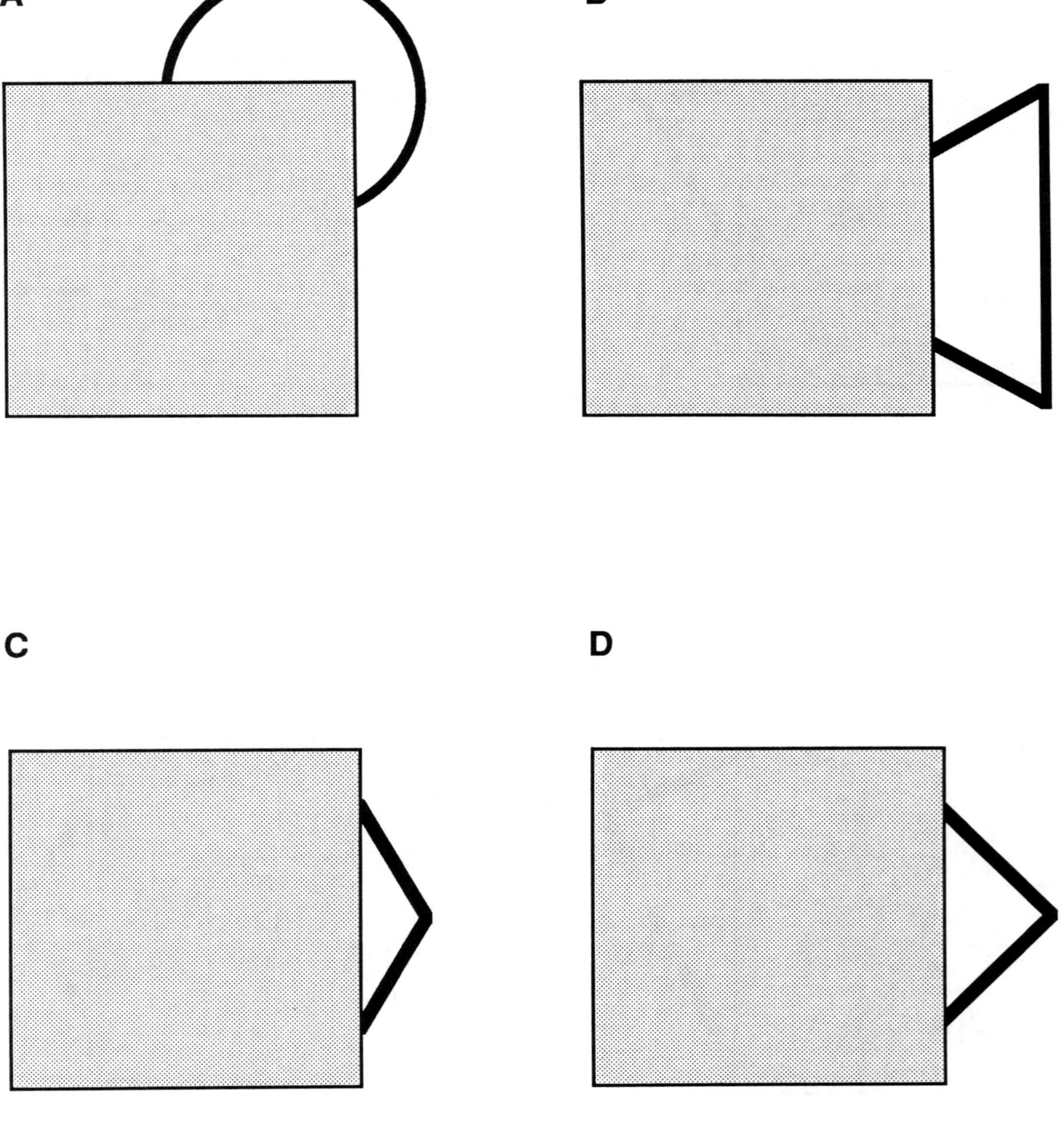

## COMPLETING THE SHAPE

The shaded shape is covering part of a PATTERN BLOCK.
Find the block that is under the shape.
Draw in the covered part of the block and color it.

---

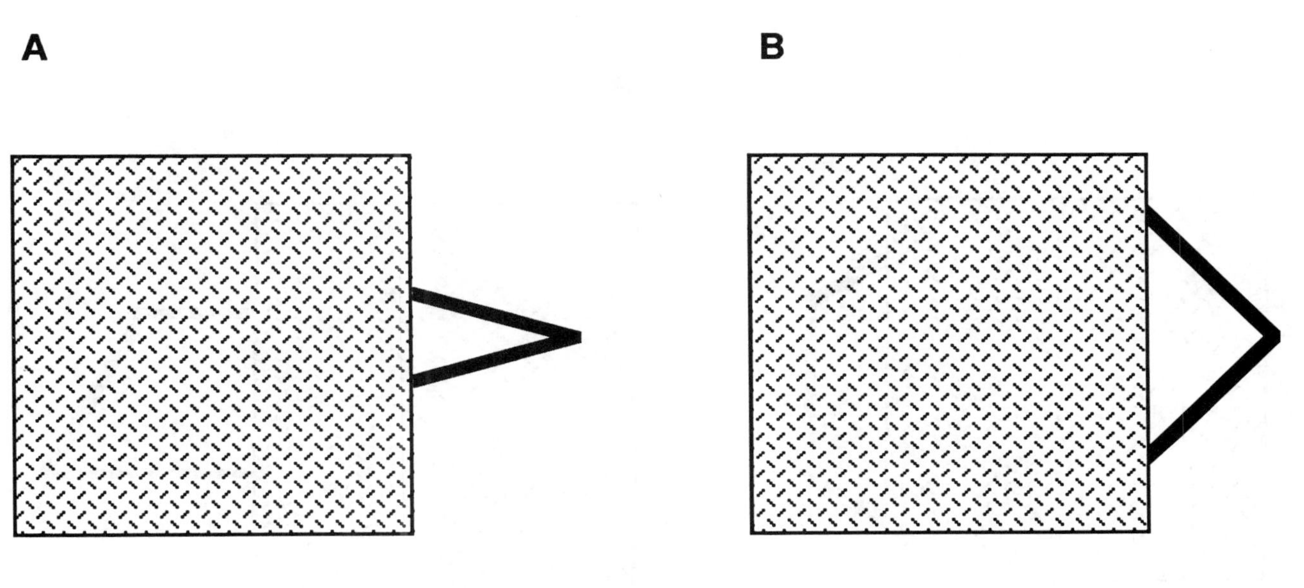


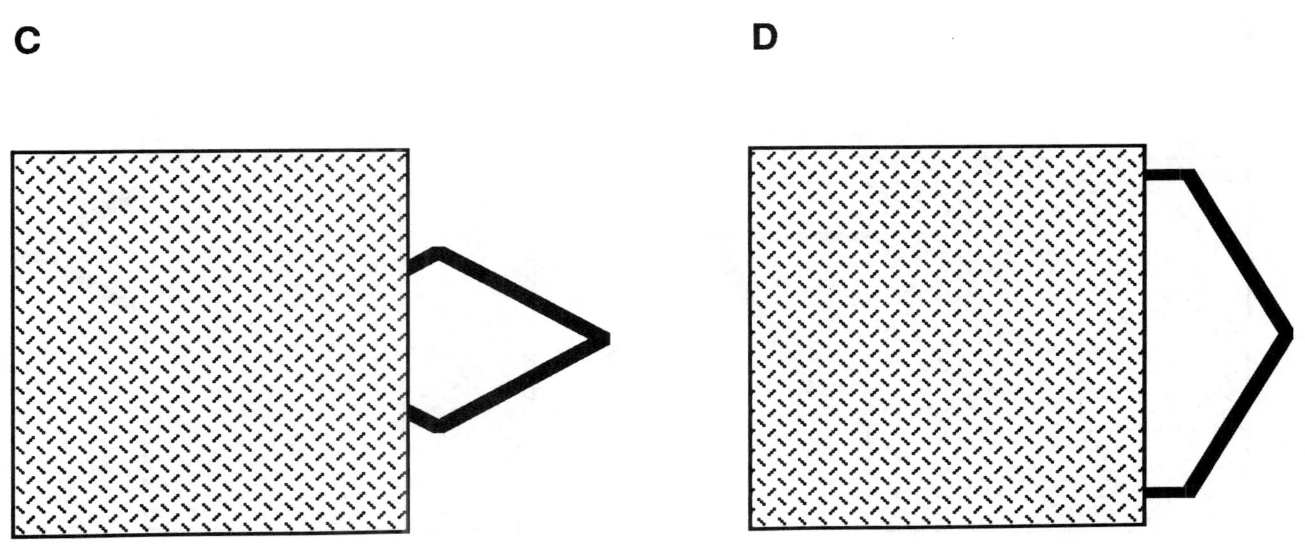

## COMPLETING THE SHAPE

The shaded shape is covering part of a PATTERN BLOCK.
Find the block that is under the shape.
Draw in the covered part of the block and color it.

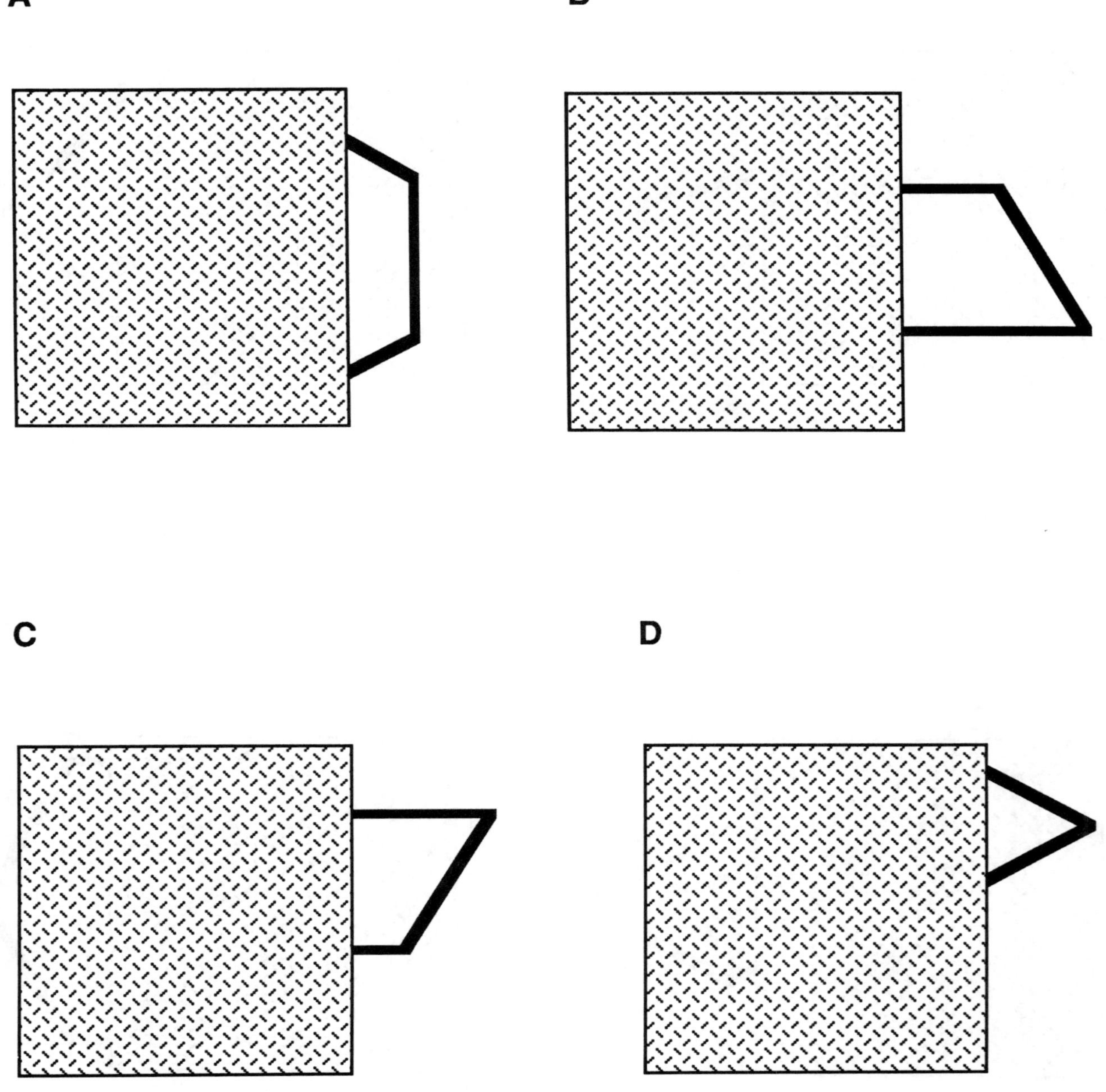

## COMPLETING THE SHAPE

Make each shaded figure using INTERLOCKING CUBES.
Use a different color for each construction.

The large white rectangle is covering part of each CUBE figure.
Match the figures you made to those covered by the white rectangle.
Draw in the covered part of each figure and color the figure to match the cubes.

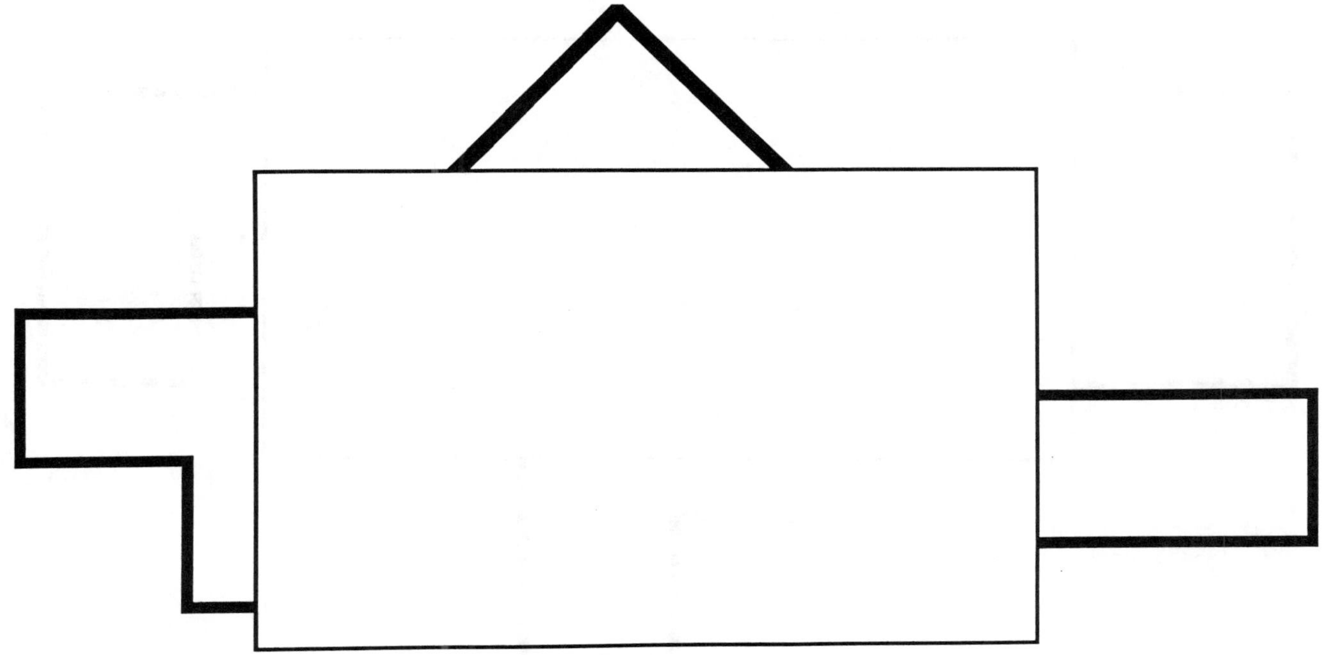

## COMPLETING THE SHAPE

Make each shaded figure using INTERLOCKING CUBES.
Use a different color for each construction.

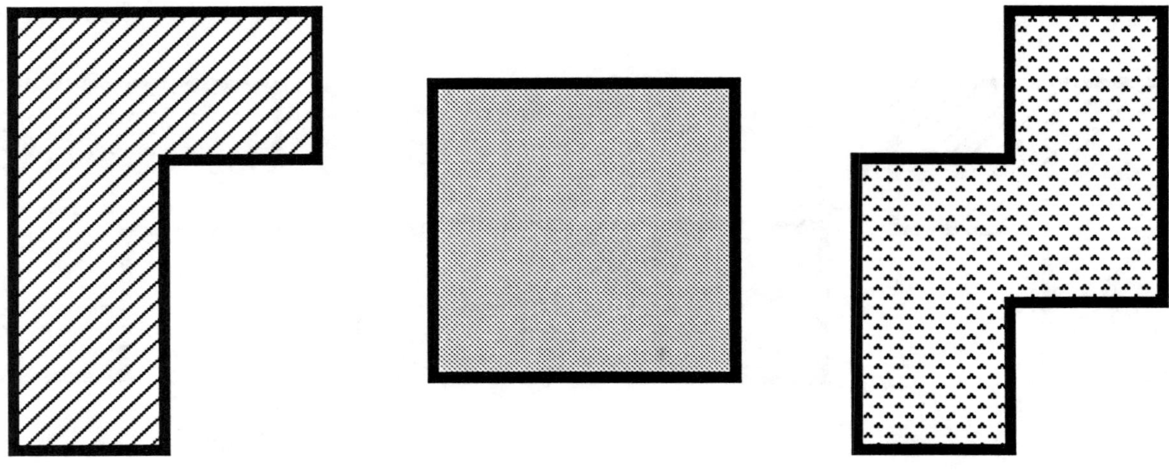

The large white rectangle is covering part of each CUBE figure.
Match the figures you made to those covered by the white rectangle.
Draw in the covered part of each figure and color the figure to match the cubes.

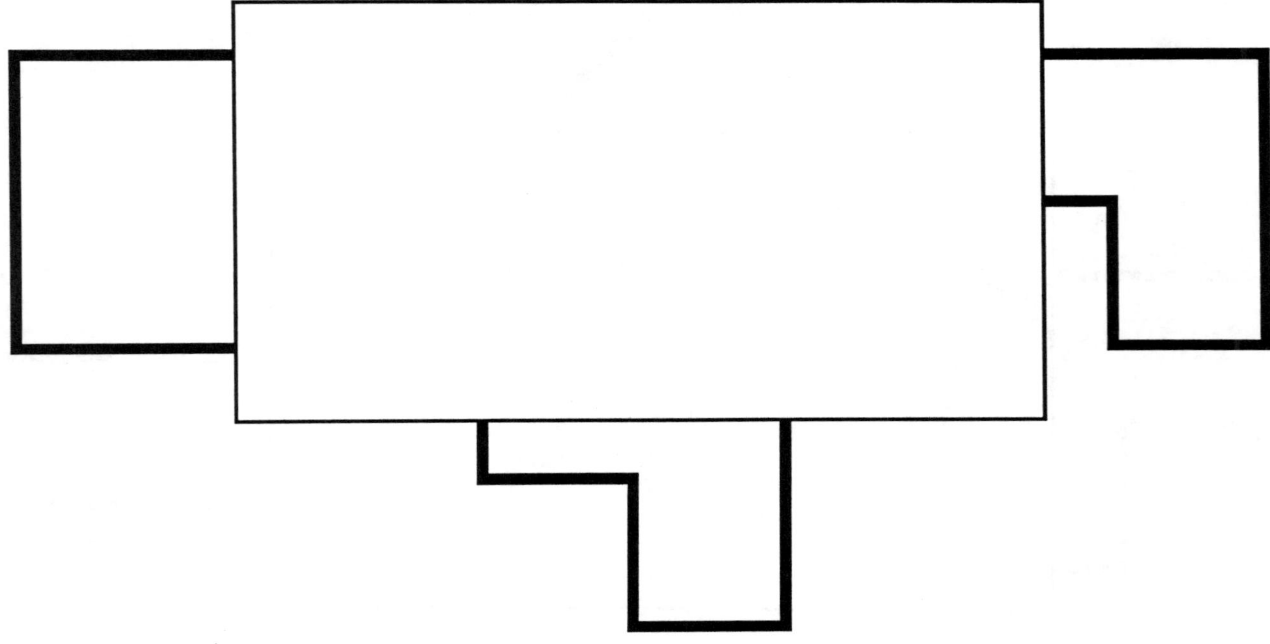

## COPYING A FIGURE

Cover each figure with ATTRIBUTE BLOCKS.
Color the pictures to match the blocks.

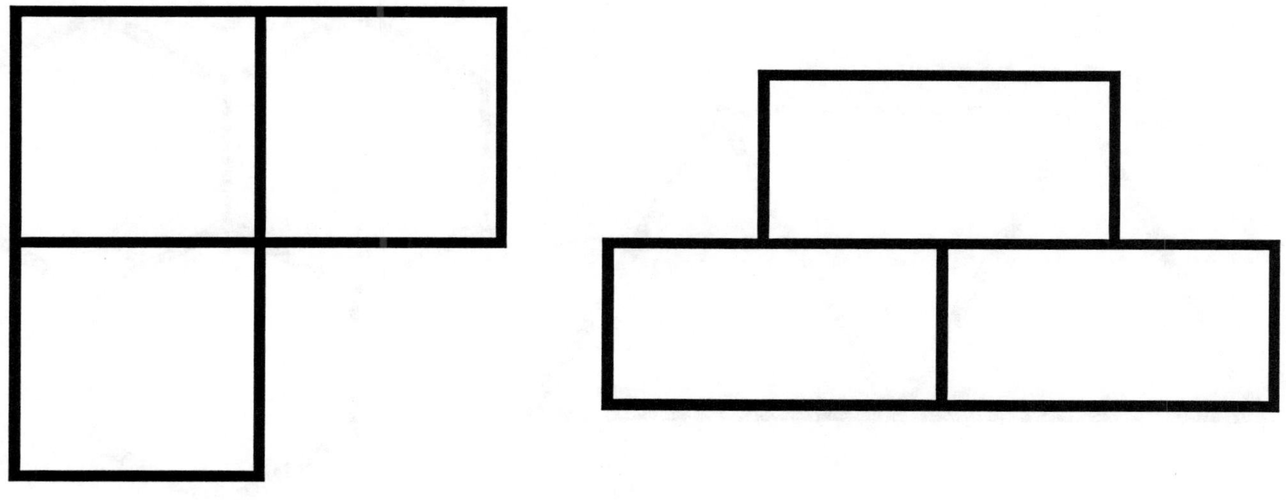

In the space below, build an exact copy of each figure using the same ATTRIBUTE BLOCKS.

# COPYING A FIGURE

Cover each figure with ATTRIBUTE BLOCKS.
Color the pictures to match the blocks.

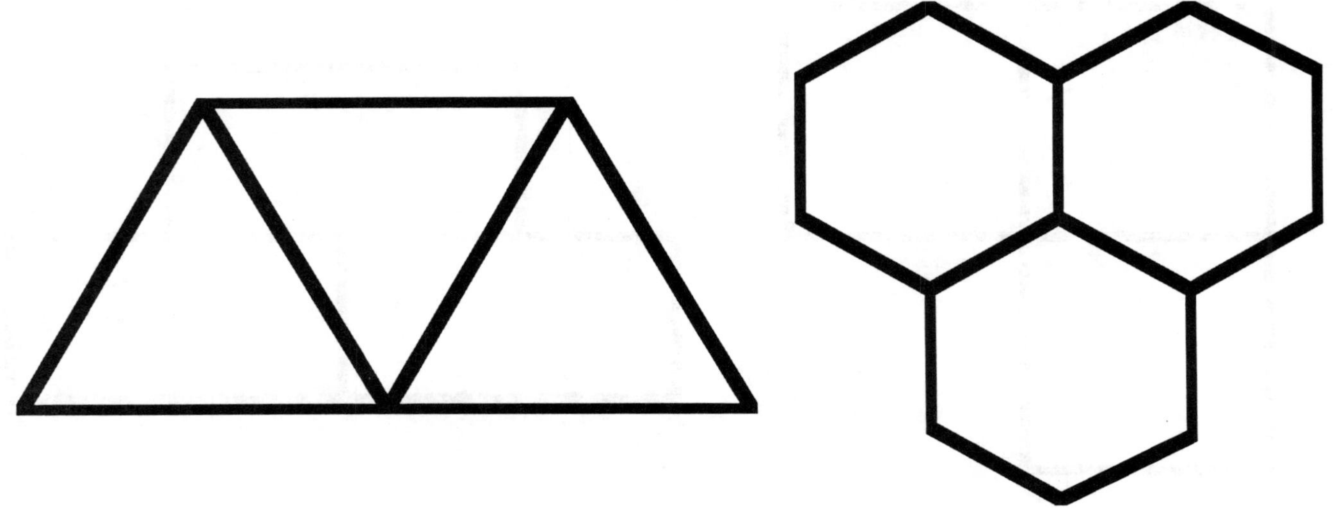

In the space below, build an exact copy of each figure using the same ATTRIBUTE BLOCKS.

## COPYING A FIGURE

Use INTERLOCKING CUBES to make and cover each shaded figure in the box.
Use a different color for each construction you make.
Color the picture to match the cubes.

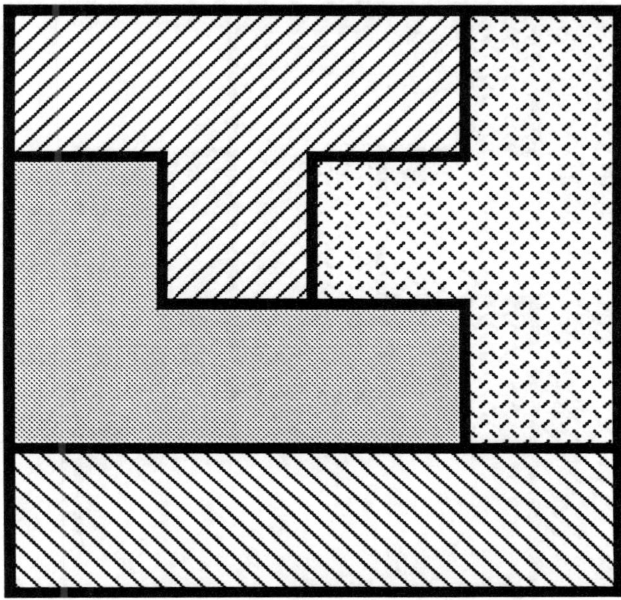

In the box below, build an exact copy of the figure using the same CUBE constructions.

# COPYING A FIGURE

Use INTERLOCKING CUBES to make and cover each shaded figure in the box.
Use a different color for each construction you make.
Color the picture to match the cubes.

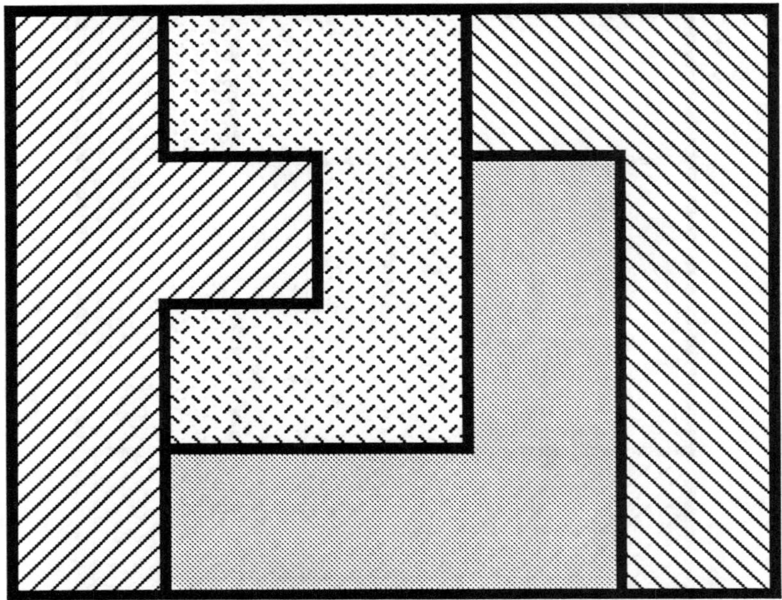

In the box below, build an exact copy of the figure using the same CUBE constructions.

# COPYING A FIGURE

Cover the figure with PATTERN BLOCKS.
Color the picture to match the blocks.

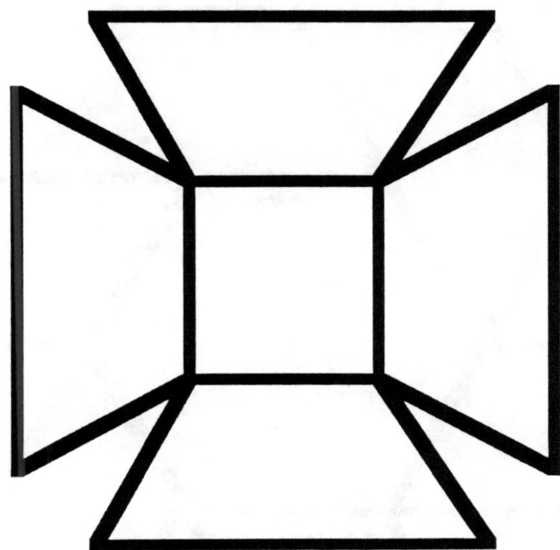

---

In the space below, build an exact copy of the figure using the same PATTERN BLOCKS.

## COPYING A FIGURE

Cover the figure with PATTERN BLOCKS.
Color the picture to match the blocks.

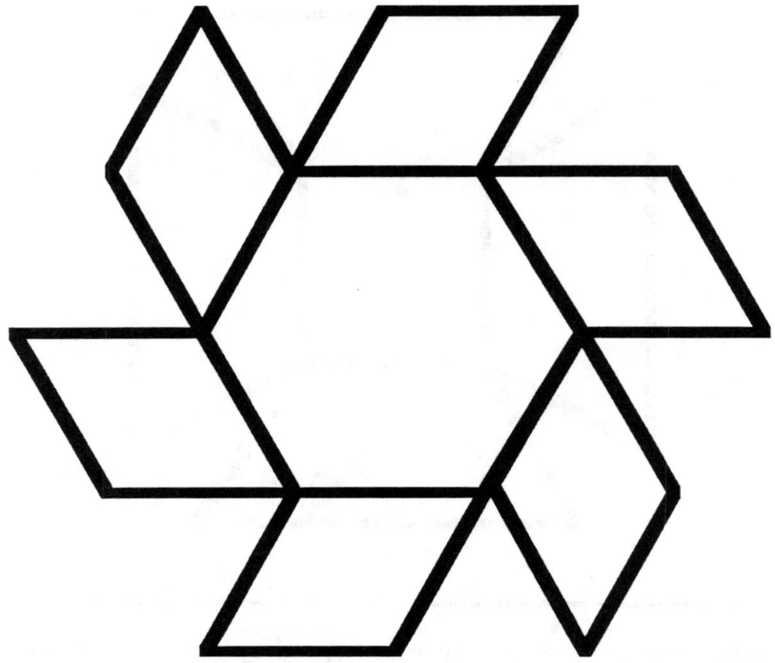

---

In the space below, build an exact copy of the figure using the same PATTERN BLOCKS.

# COPYING A FIGURE

Cover the figure with PATTERN BLOCKS.
Color the picture to match the blocks.

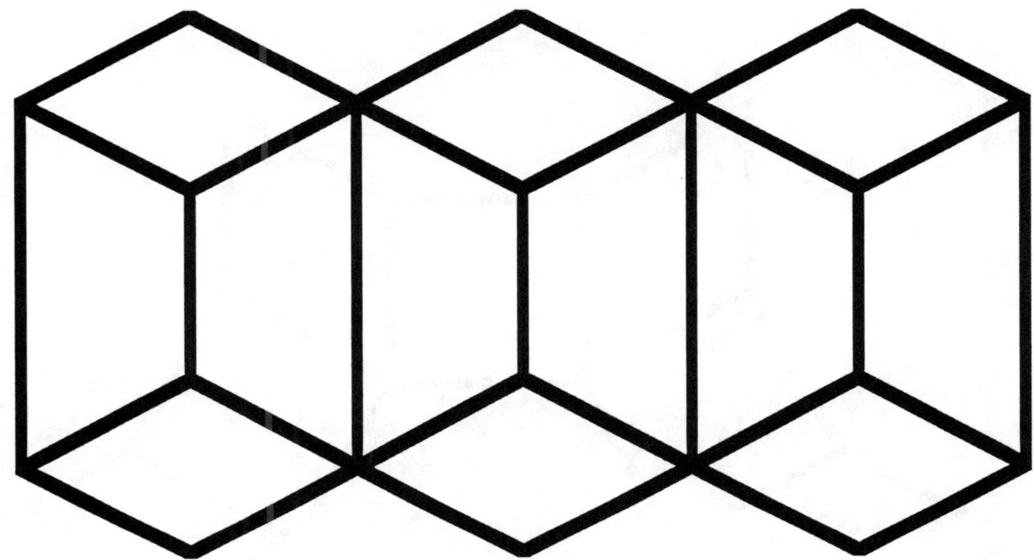

---

In the space below, build an exact copy of the figure using the same PATTERN BLOCKS.

## COPYING A FIGURE

Cover the figure below with PATTERN BLOCKS.
Color the picture to match the blocks.

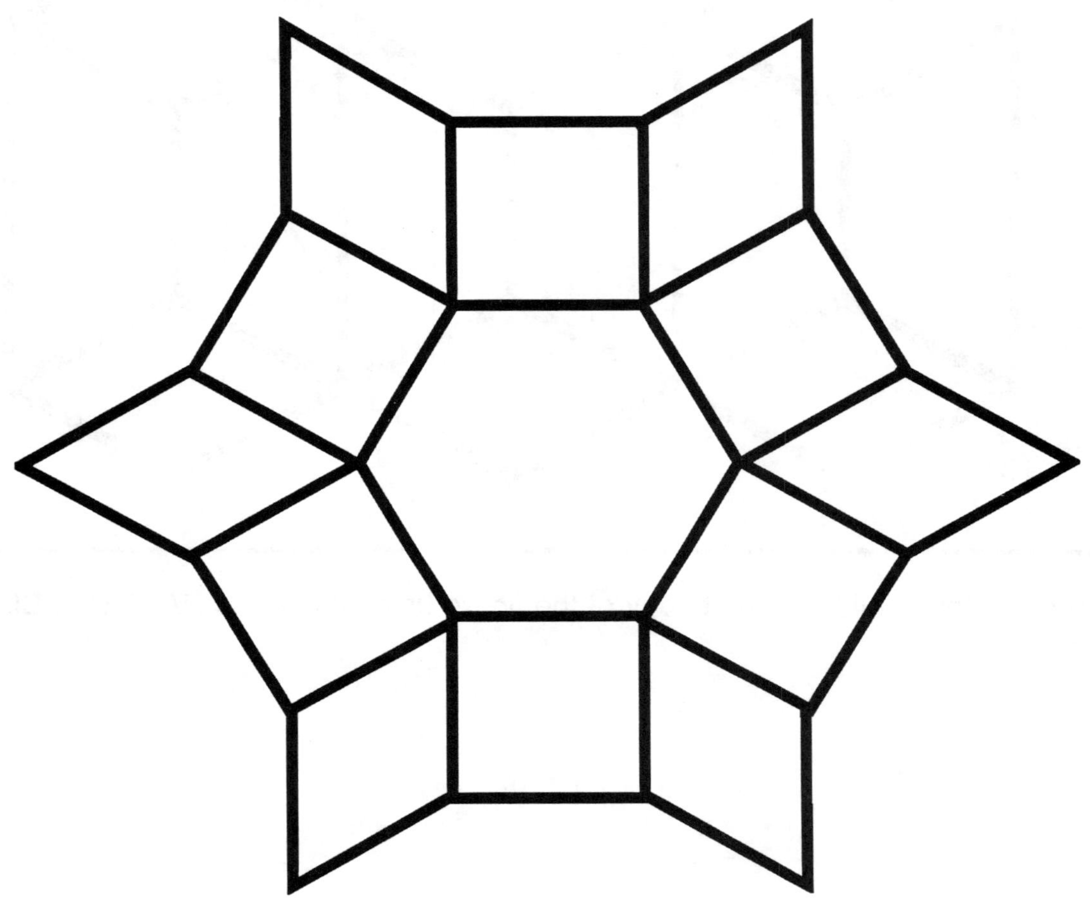

On a separate sheet of paper, build an exact copy of the figure using the same PATTERN BLOCKS.

## COVERING A FIGURE

Cover the figure below using only yellow PATTERN BLOCKS.

---

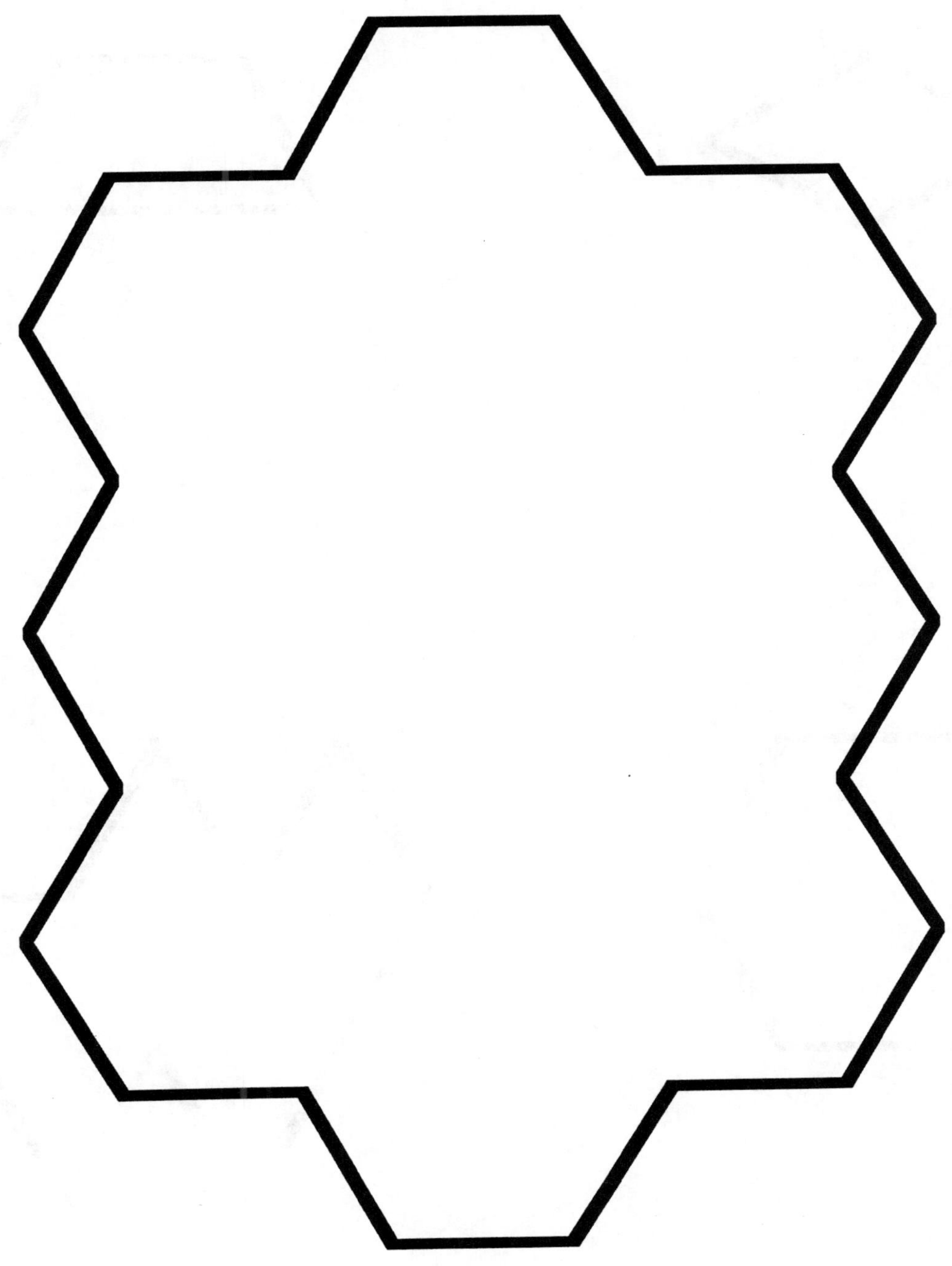

## COVERING A FIGURE

Cover each figure below using only green PATTERN BLOCKS.

---

**A**

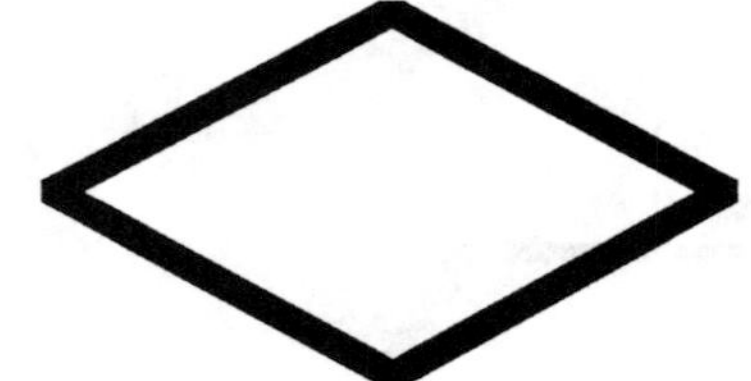

**B**

**C**

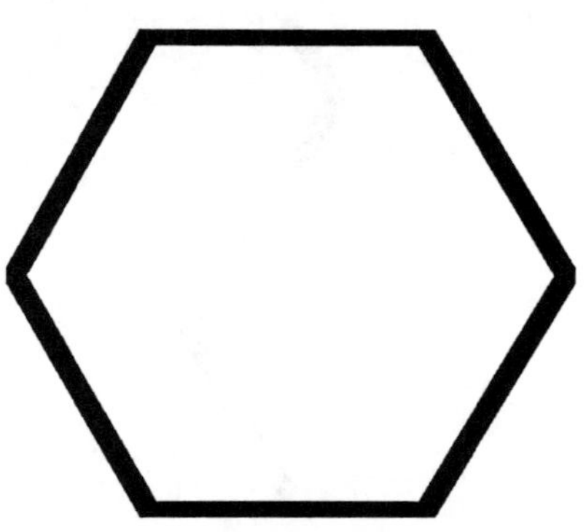

**D**

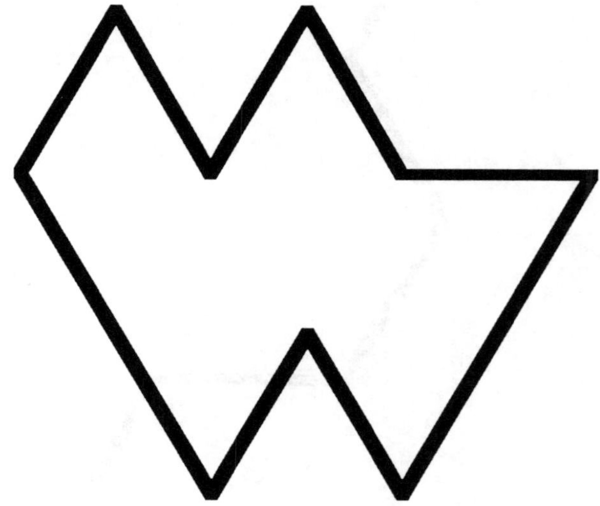

## COVERING A FIGURE

Cover each figure below using only blue PATTERN BLOCKS.

---

**A**

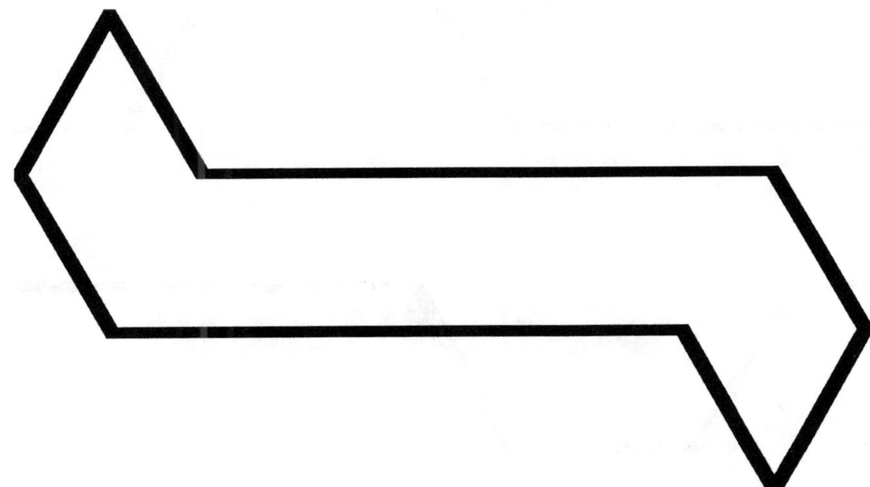

**B**

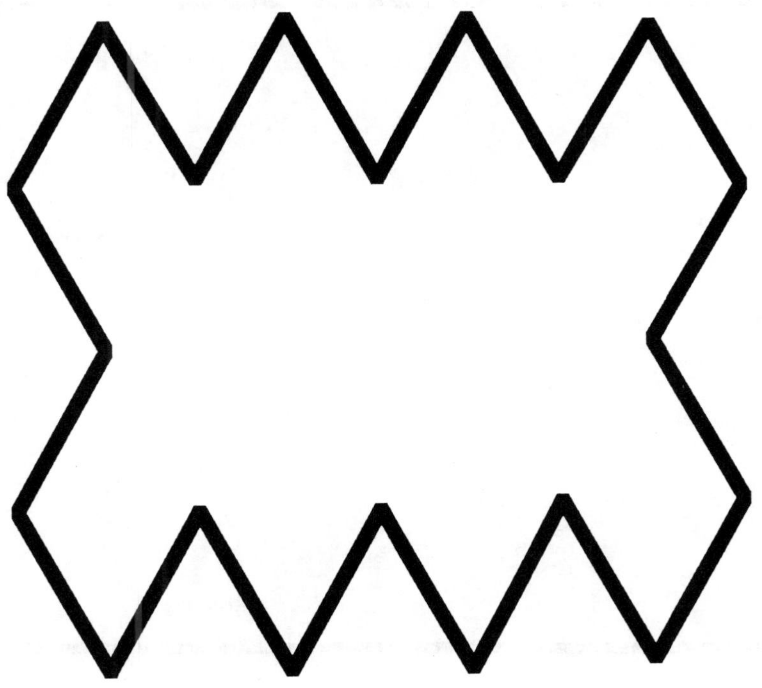

## COVERING A FIGURE

Cover each figure below using only red PATTERN BLOCKS.

---

A

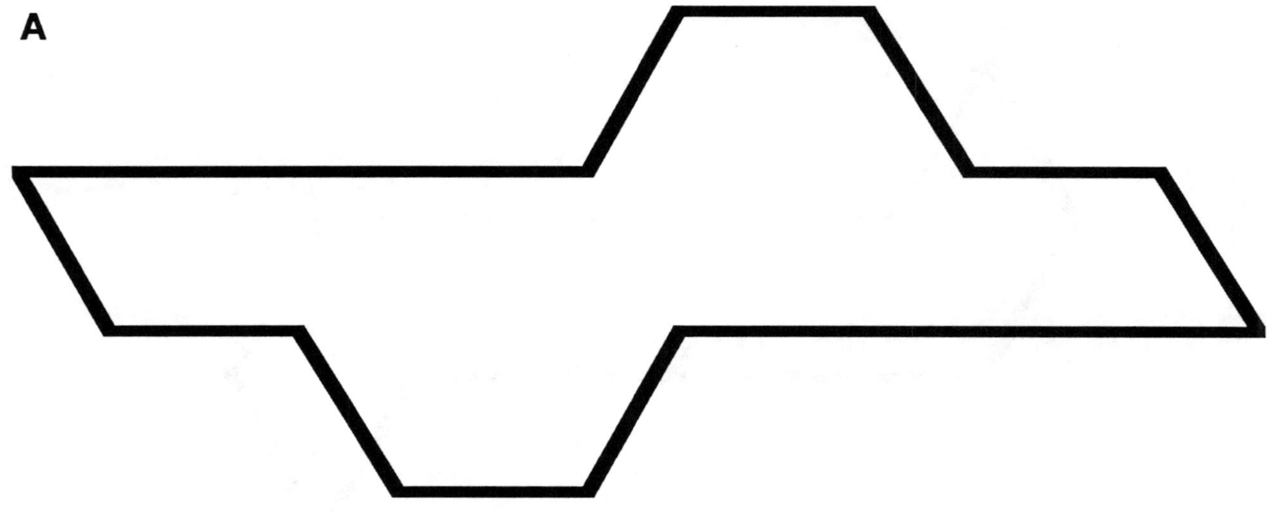

B

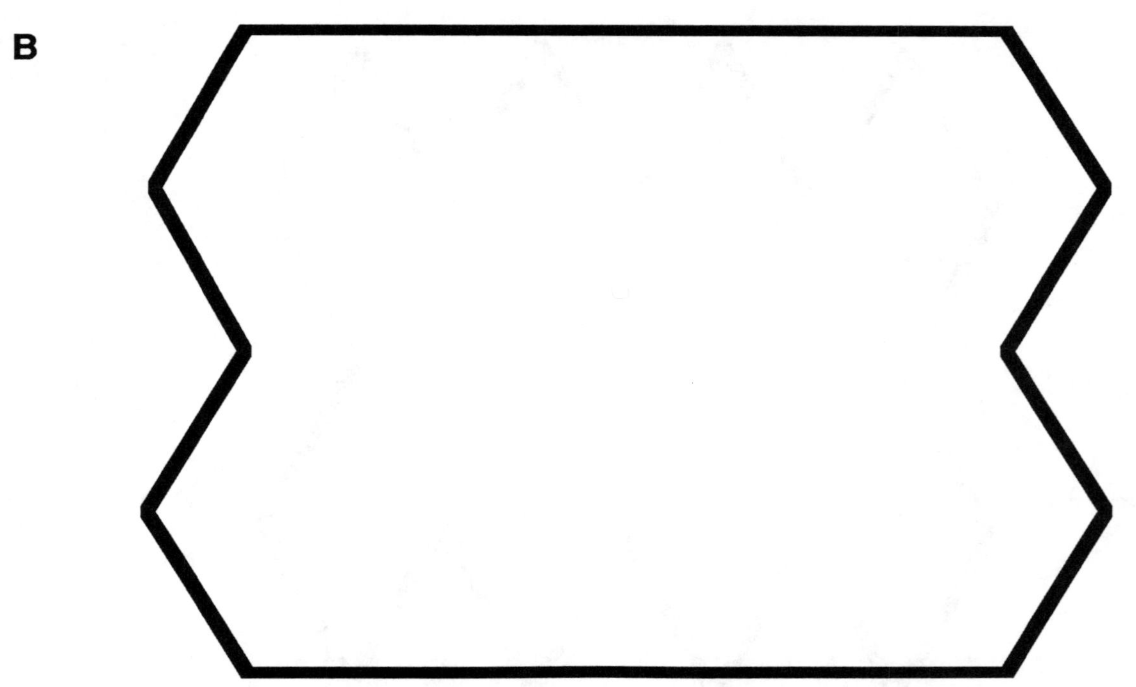

# COVERING A FIGURE

Make each shaded figure using INTERLOCKING CUBES.
Use a different color for each construction.

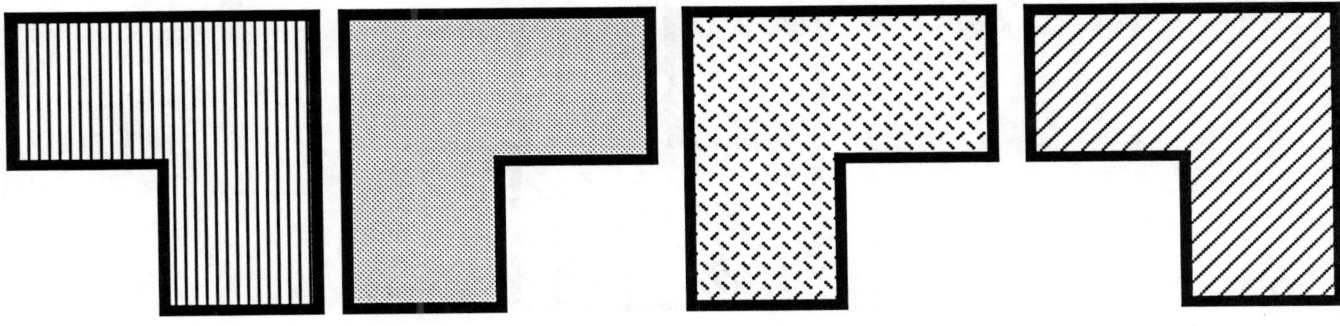

Use the four CUBE constructions to cover the box below.
Trace each figure in the box and color it to match the cubes.

## COVERING A FIGURE

Make six INTERLOCKING CUBE figures like the shaded one below.
Use a different color for each construction.

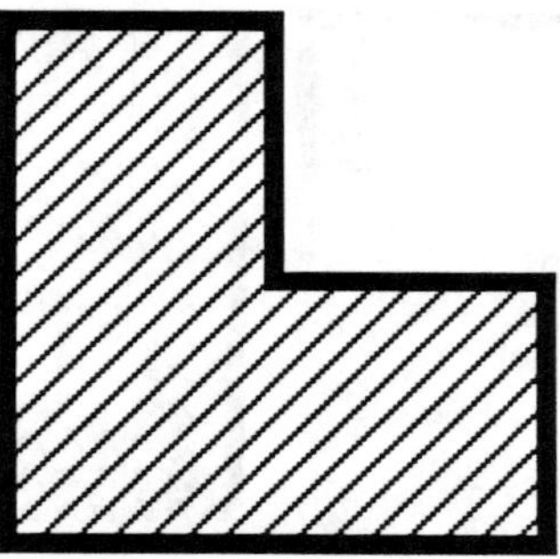

Use the six CUBE constructions to cover the box below.
Trace each figure in the box and color it to match the cubes.

# COPYING A FIGURE

Use ATTRIBUTE BLOCKS to make figures that look like the pictures below.
The pictures are smaller than your blocks.

---

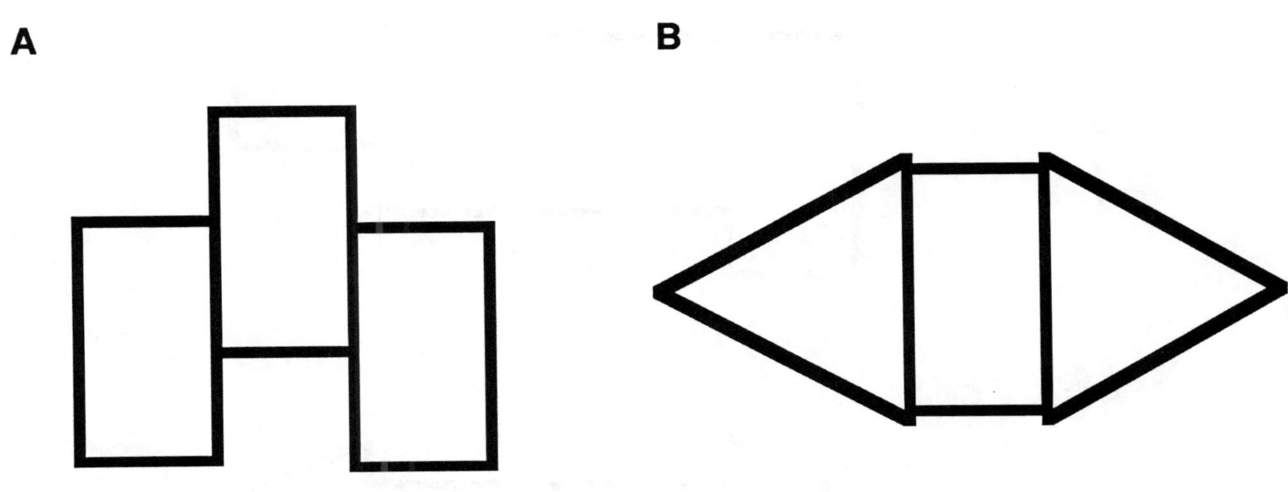


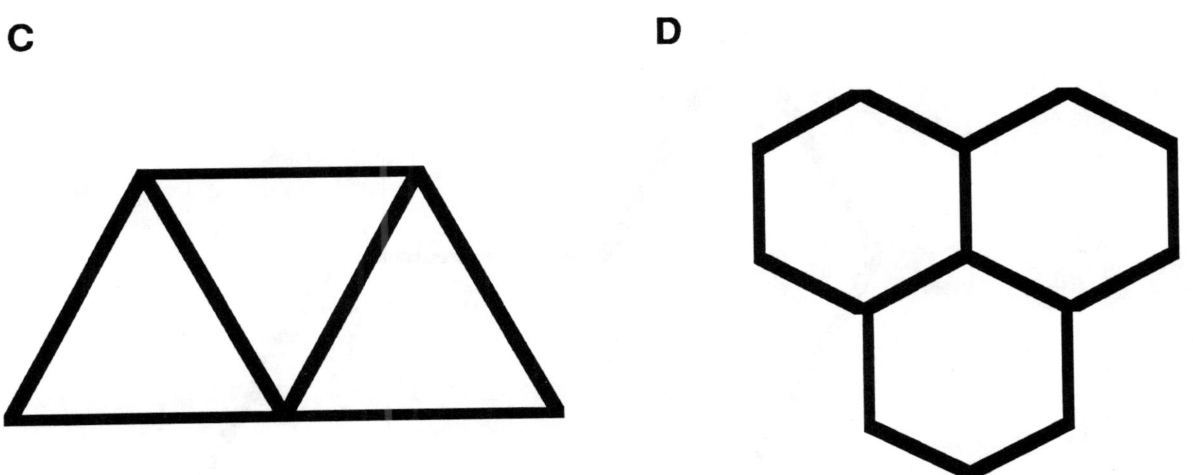

# COPYING A FIGURE

Use ATTRIBUTE BLOCKS to make figures that look like the pictures below.
The pictures are smaller than your blocks.

---

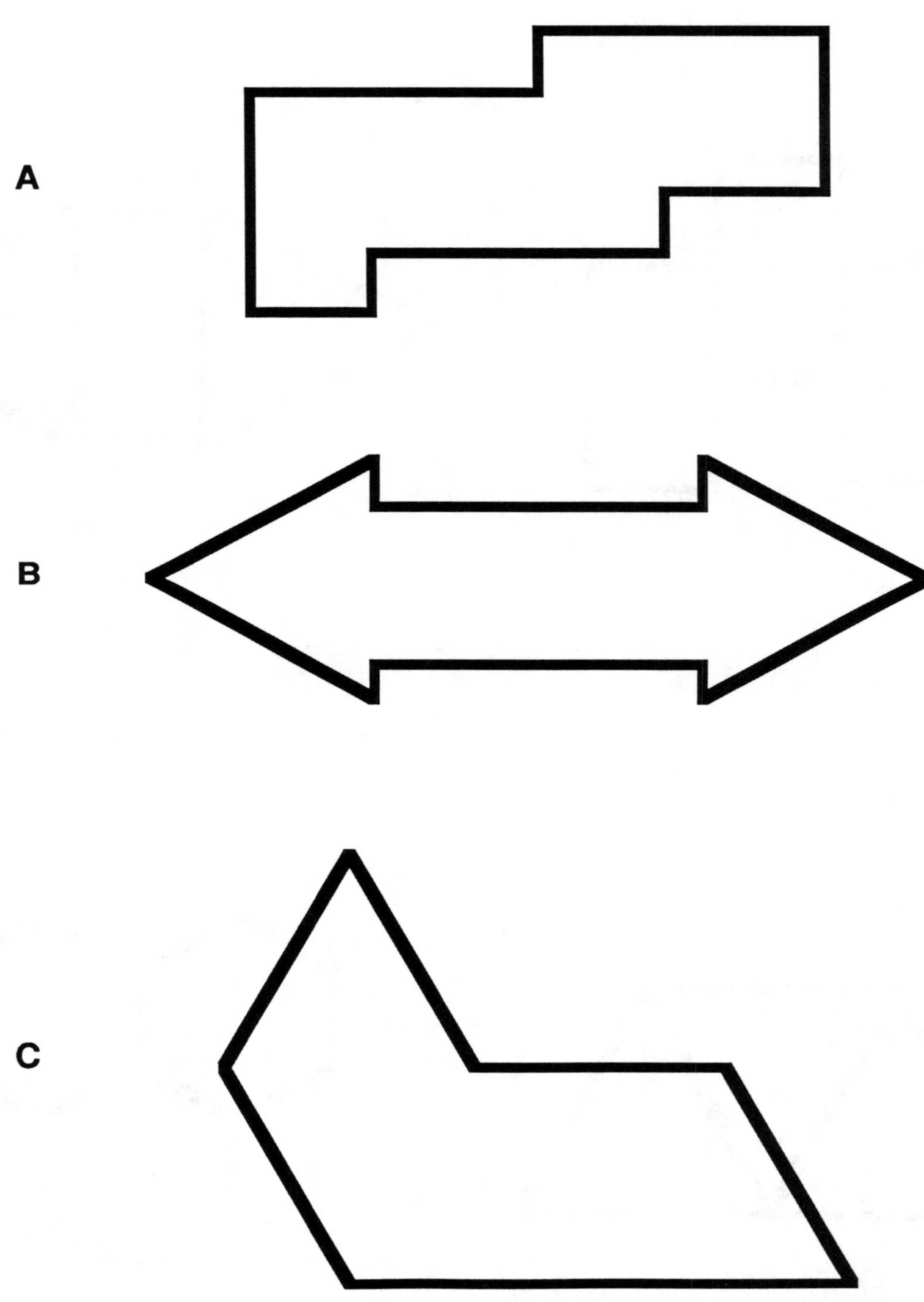

# COPYING A FIGURE

Use PATTERN BLOCKS to make figures that look like the pictures below.
The pictures are smaller than your blocks.

---

A

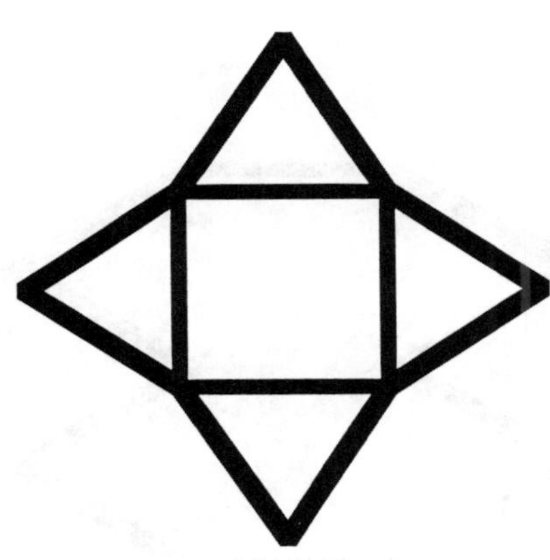

B

C

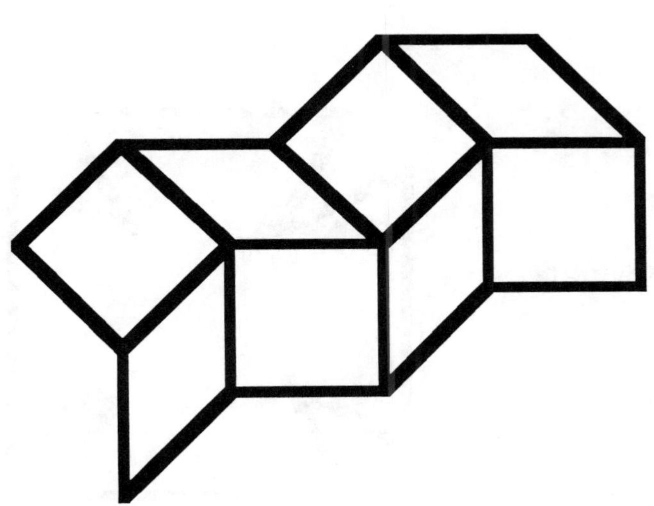

D

# COPYING A FIGURE

Use PATTERN BLOCKS to make figures that look like the pictures below.
The pictures are smaller than your blocks.

---

**A**

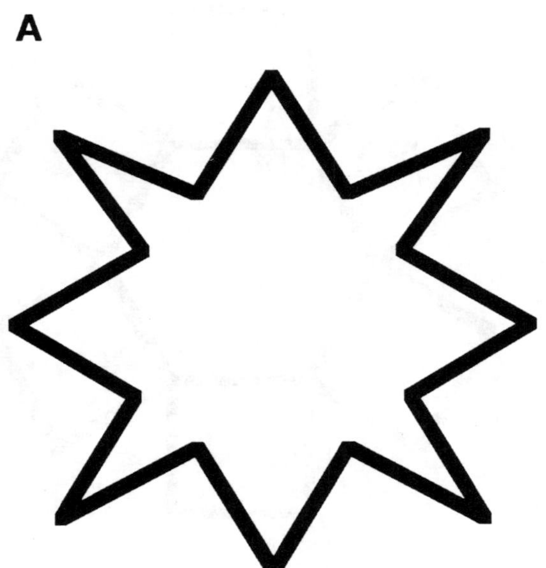

**B**

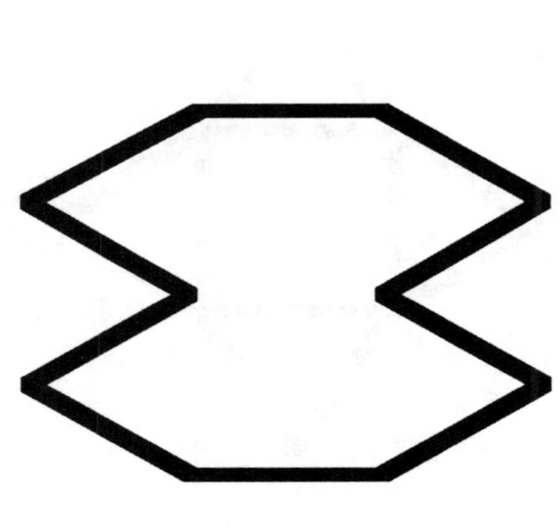

**C**

**D**

## TRACKING

Place a different colored ATTRIBUTE BLOCK on each shape at the top of the sheet.
Choose the same shapes and colors to cover the shapes at the bottom of the sheet.
Color the pictures and connecting paths to match the blocks.

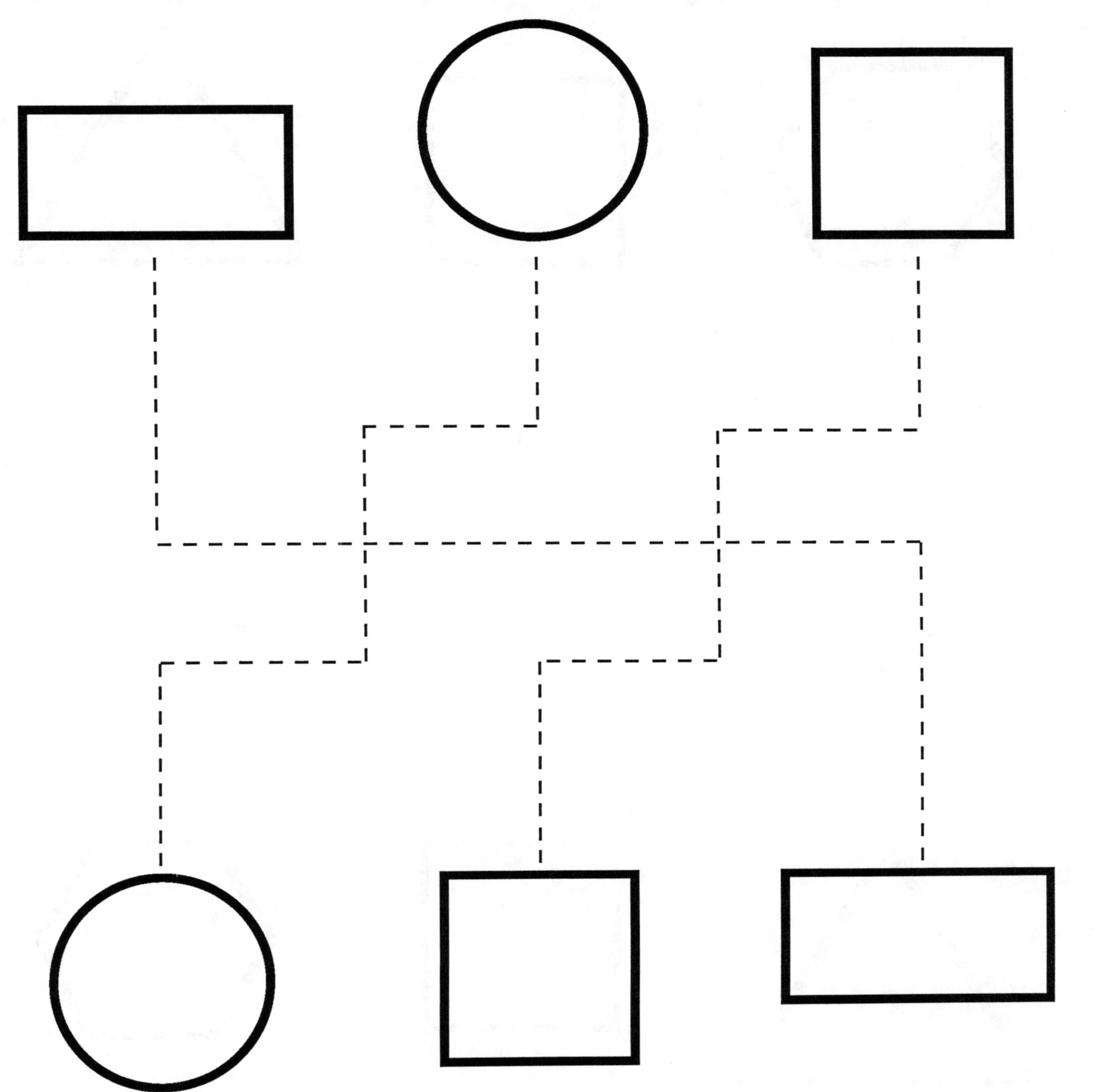

## TRACKING

Place a different colored ATTRIBUTE BLOCK on each shape at the top of the sheet. Choose the same shapes and colors to cover the shapes at the bottom of the sheet. Color the pictures and connecting paths to match the blocks.

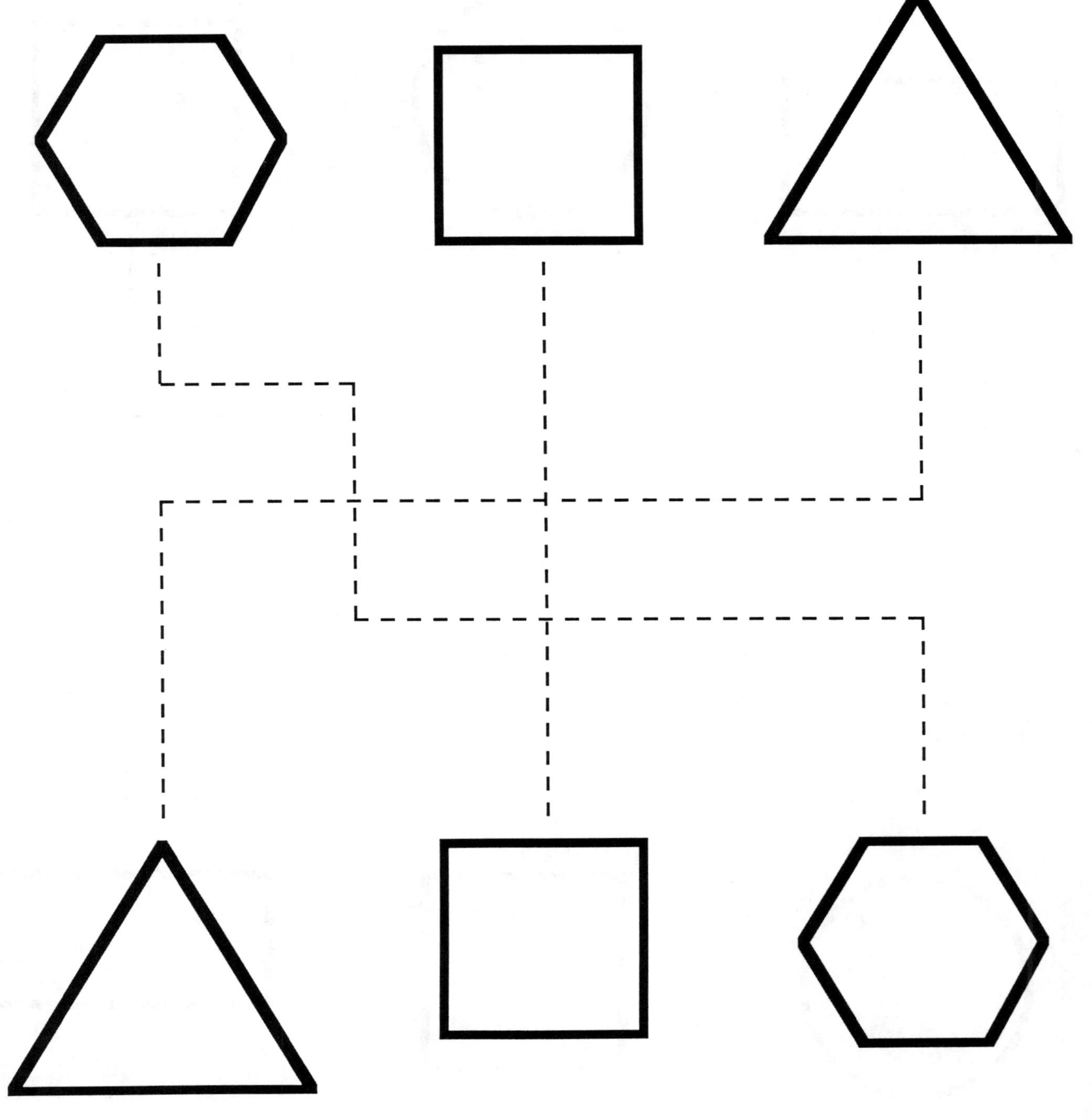

## TRACKING

Cover each shape below with a PATTERN BLOCK.
Color the pictures and connecting paths to match the blocks.

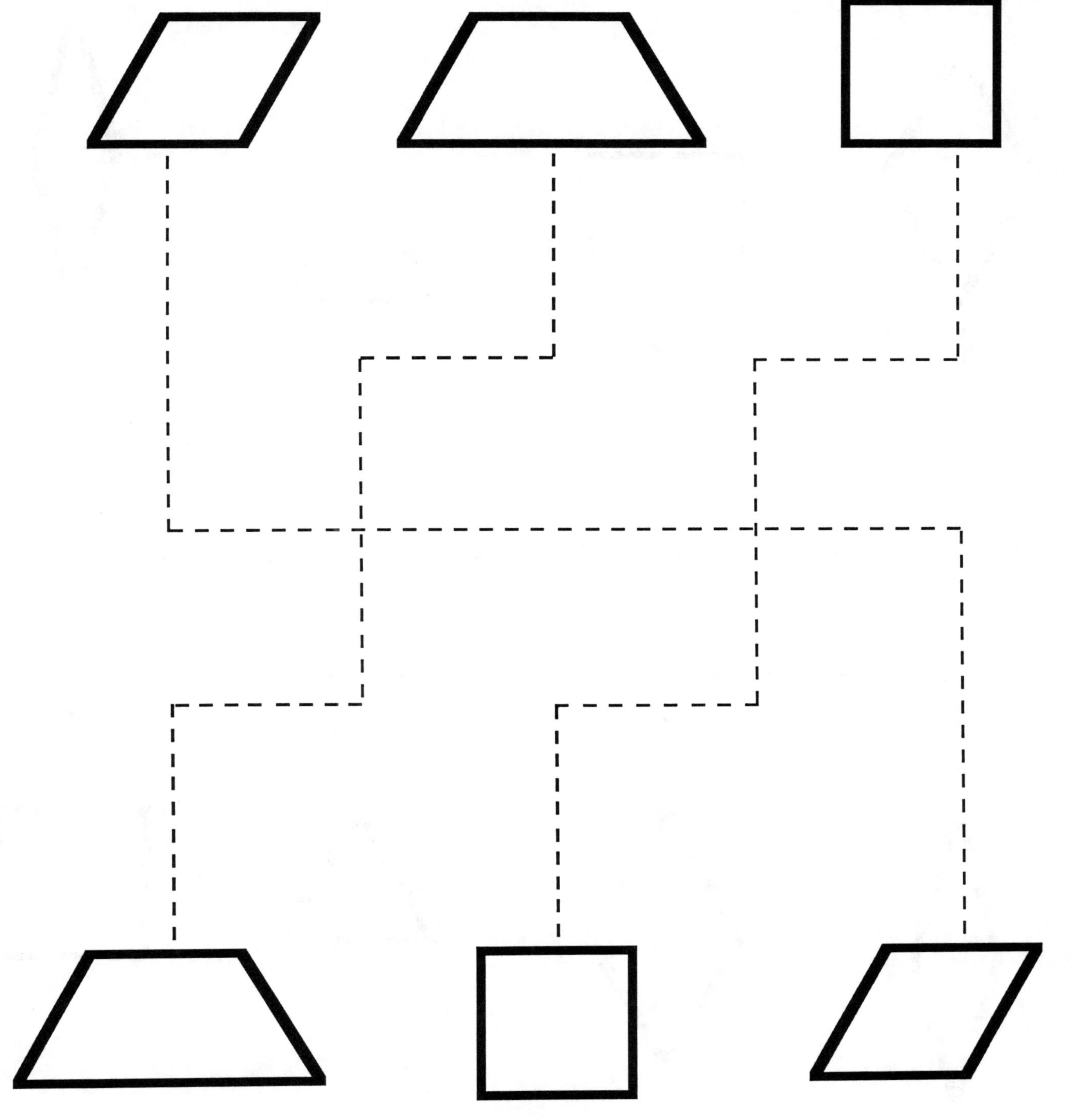

# TRACKING

Cover each shape below with a PATTERN BLOCK.
Color the pictures and connecting paths to match the blocks.

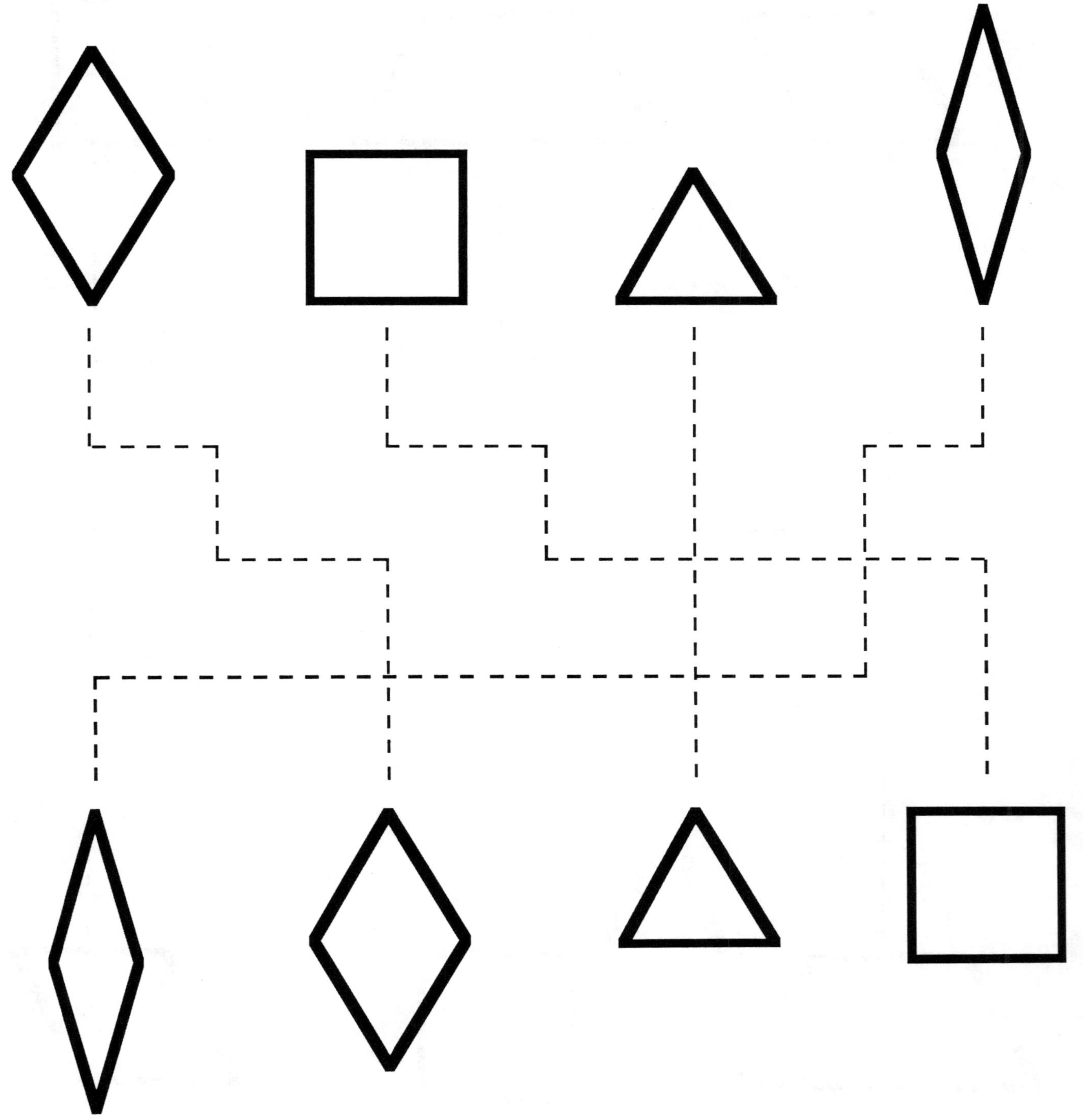

## TRACKING

Place a different colored ATTRIBUTE BLOCK on each shape below.
Move each block along its path and trace the block at the end of its path.
Color the pictures and connecting paths to match the blocks.

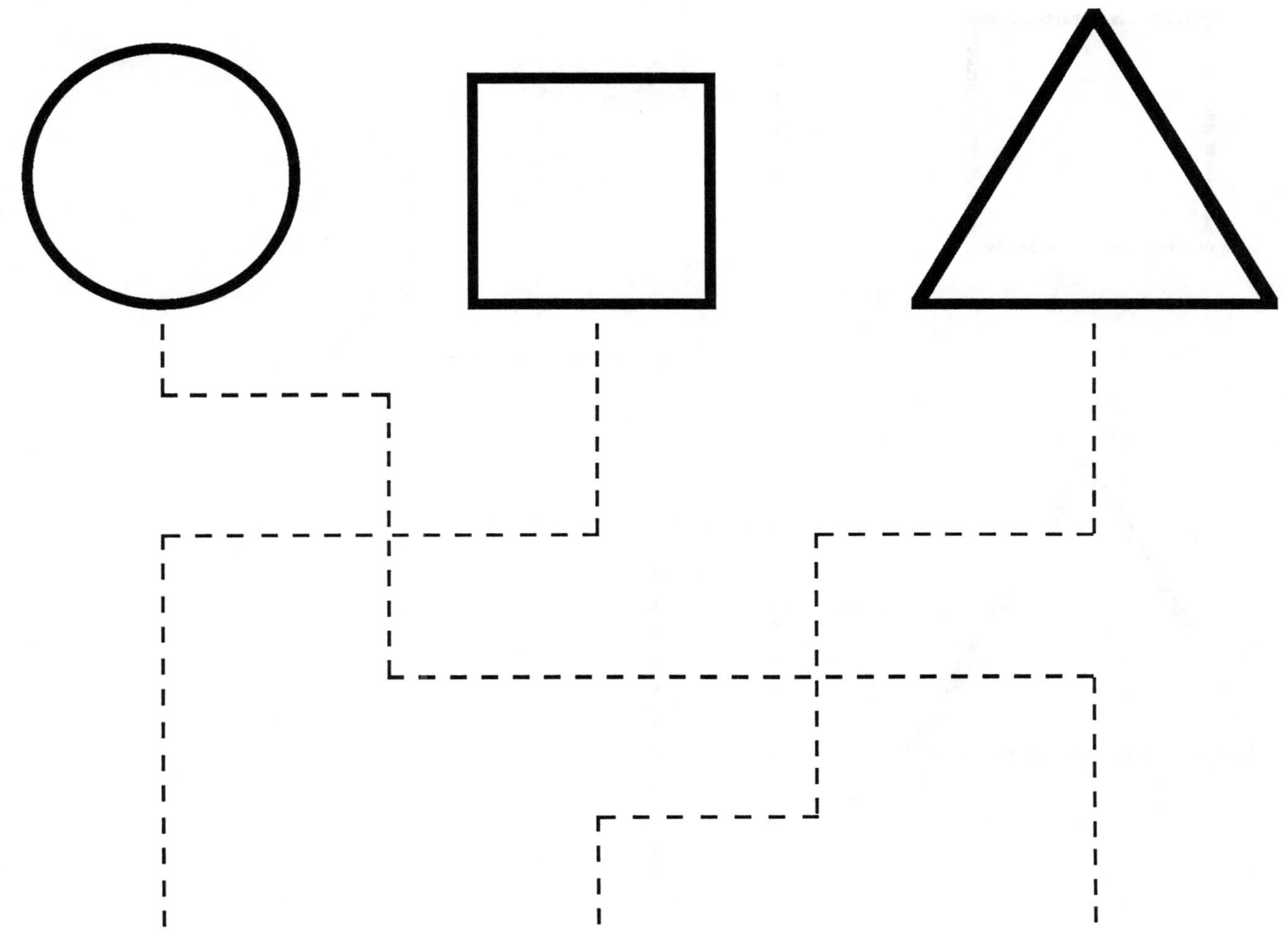

## TRACKING

Place a different colored ATTRIBUTE BLOCK on each shape below.
Move each block along its path and trace the block at the end of its path.
Color the pictures and connecting paths to match the blocks.

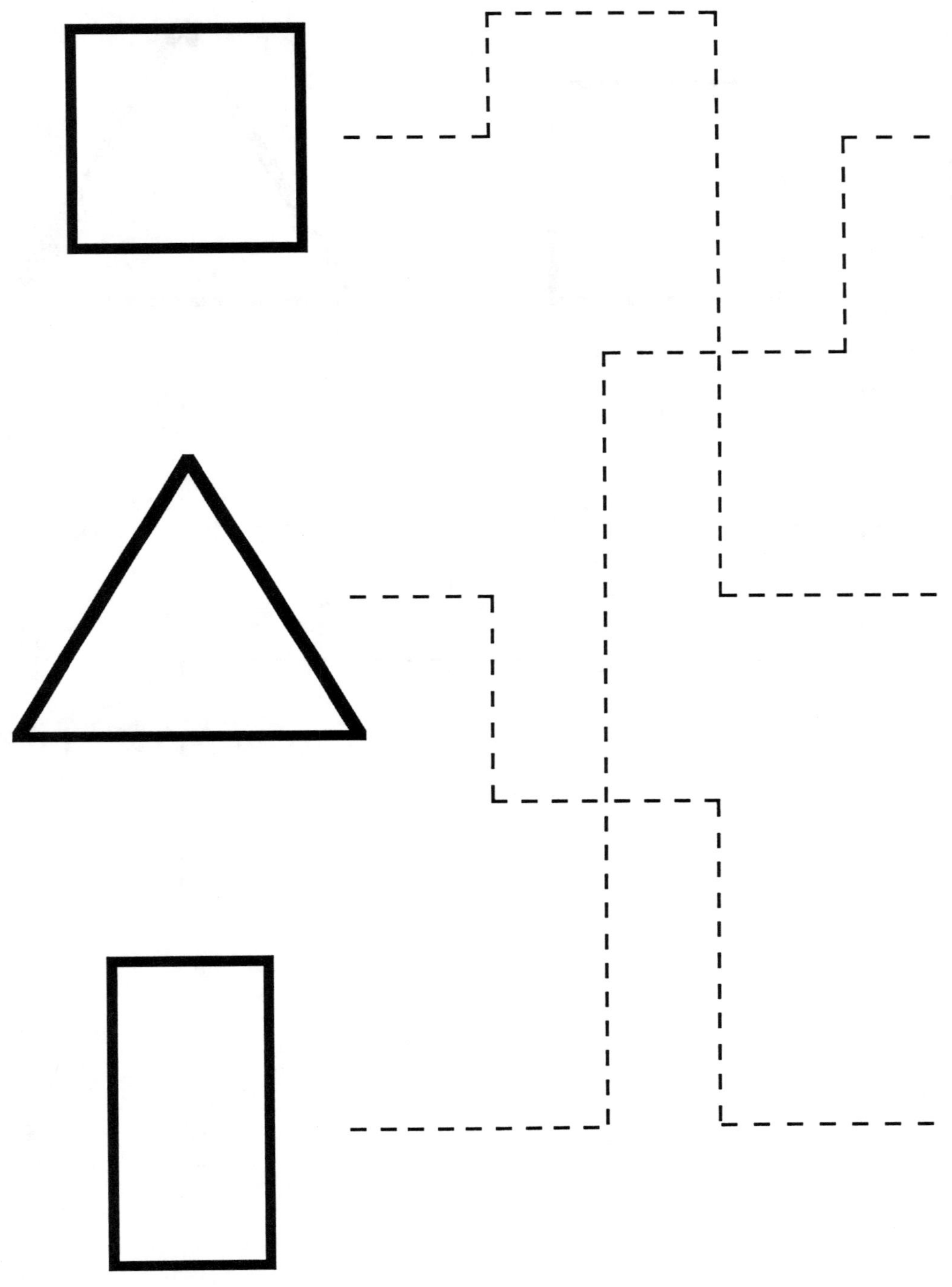

## TRACKING

Cover each shape below with a PATTERN BLOCK.
Move each block along its path and trace it at the end of its path.
Color the pictures and connecting paths to match the blocks.

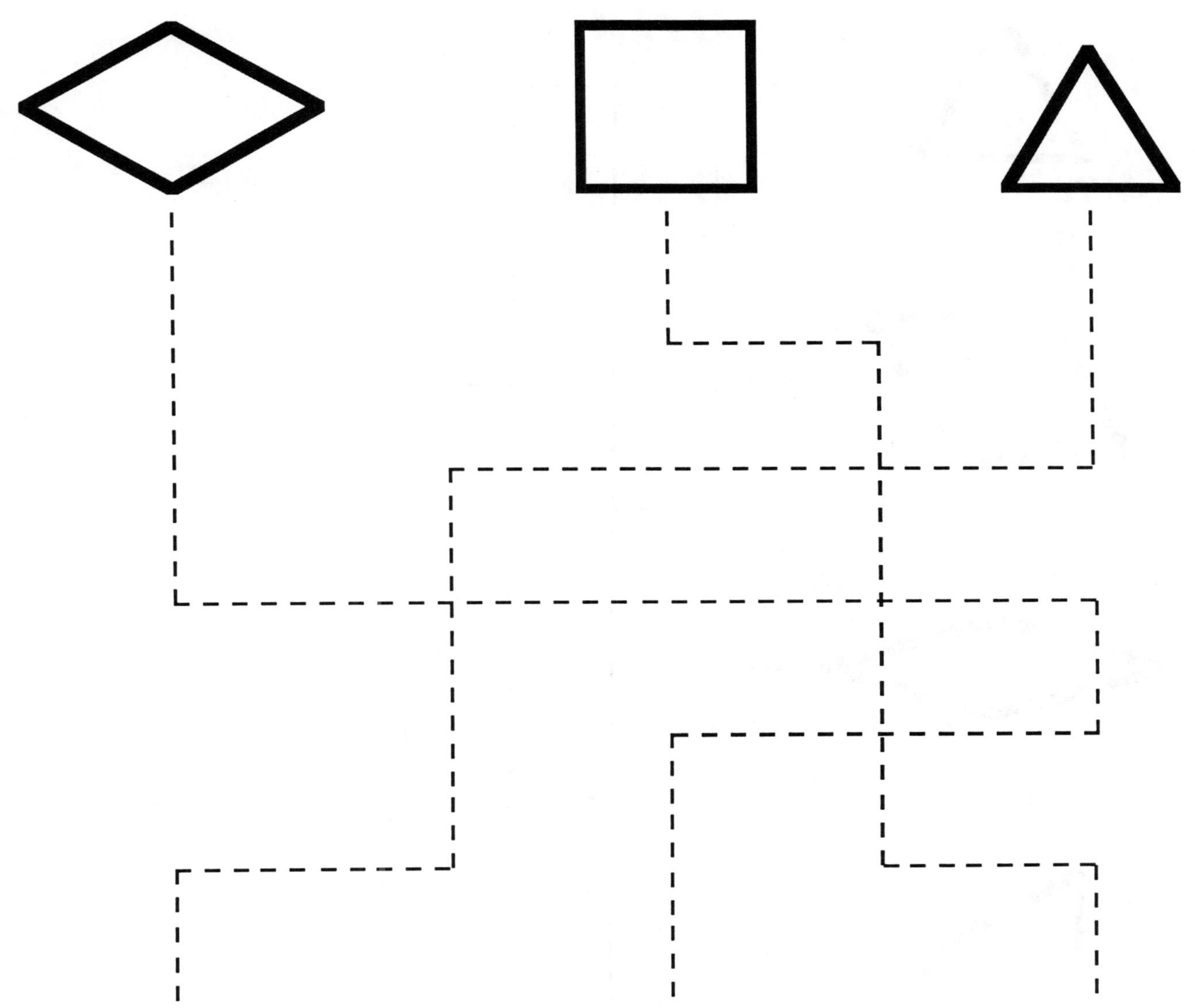

# TRACKING

Cover each shape below with a PATTERN BLOCK.
Move each block along its path and trace it at the end of its path.
Color the pictures and connecting paths to match the blocks.

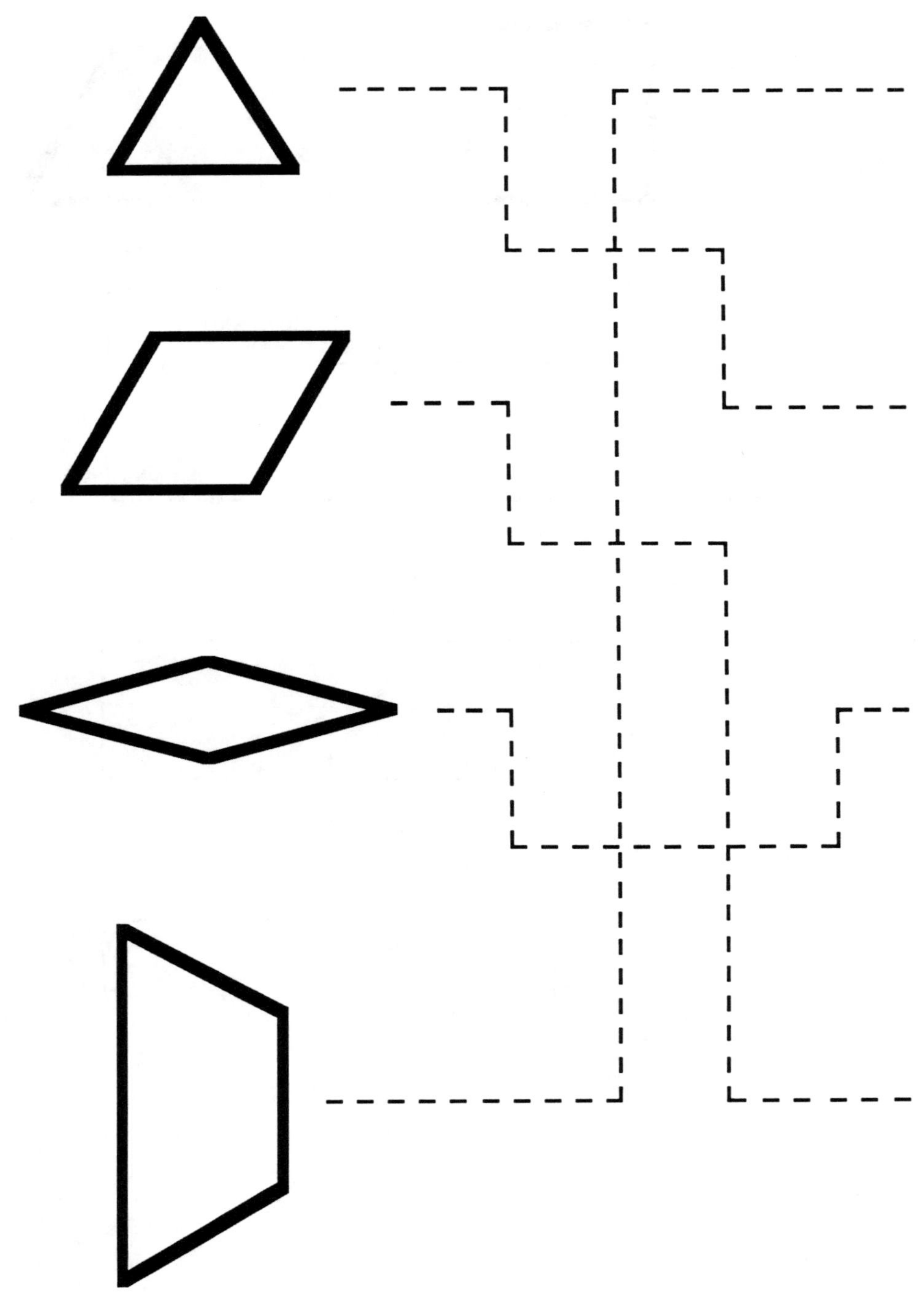

# PATHS

Cover each shape below with a PATTERN BLOCK.
Use the same colors as the blocks to draw paths connecting the matching shapes.
Remove the blocks and color the pictures to match the paths.

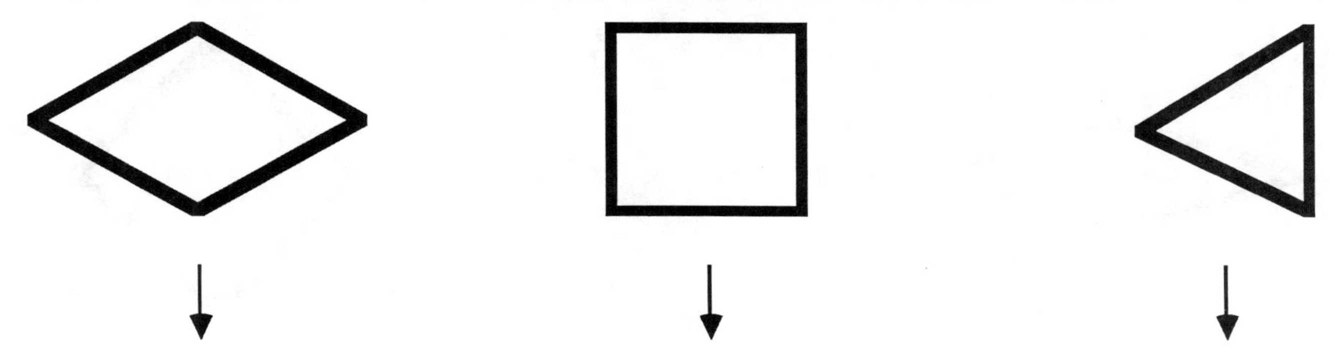

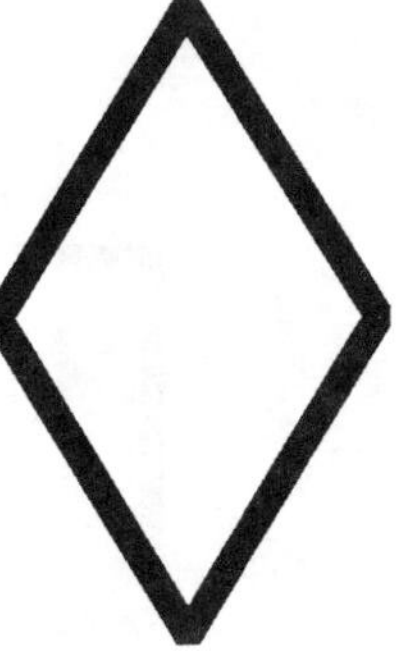

## PATHS

Cover each shape below with a PATTERN BLOCK.
Use the same colors as the blocks to draw paths connecting the matching shapes.
Remove the blocks and color the pictures to match the paths.

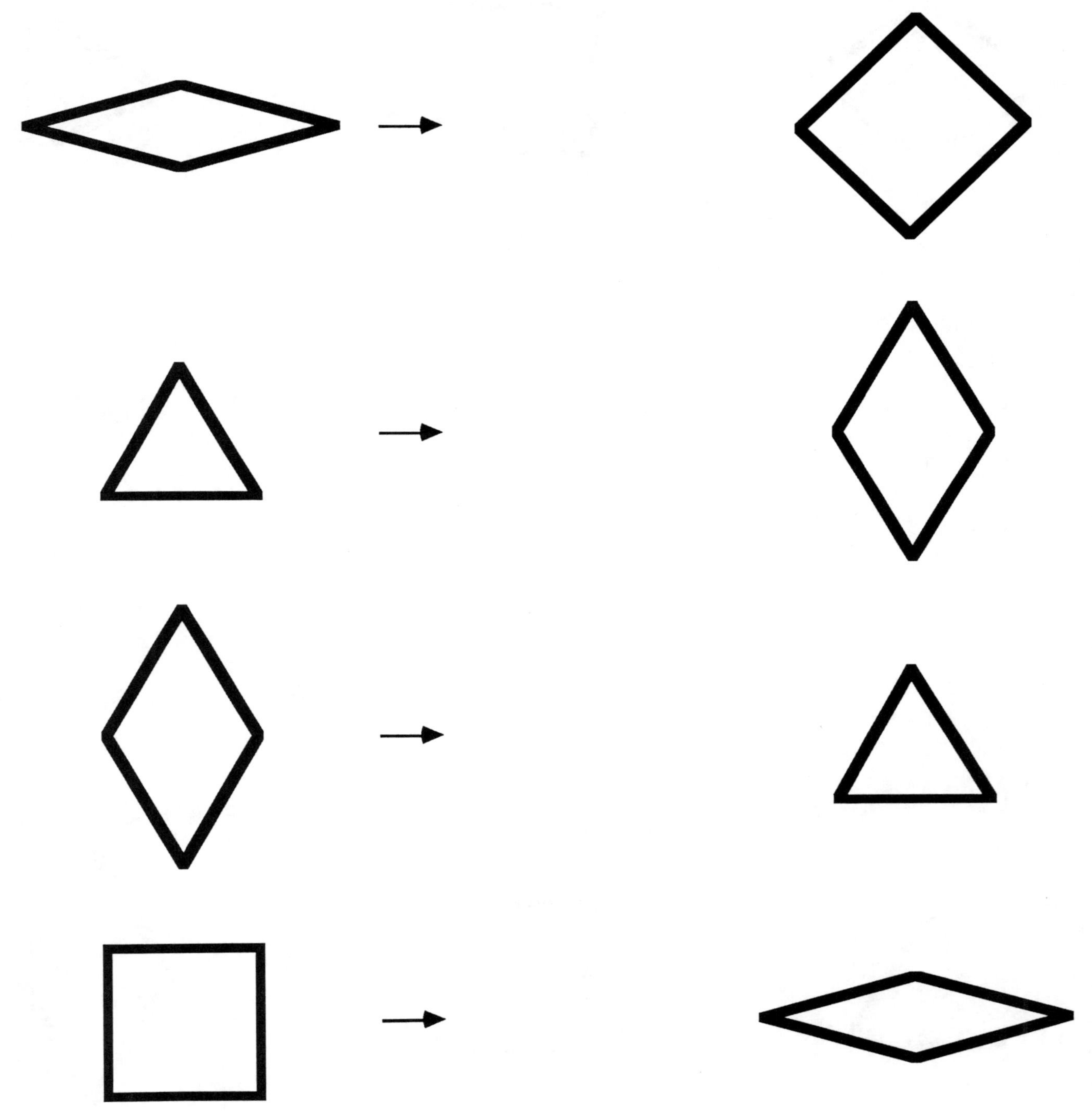

# PATHS

Place a PATTERN BLOCK on the shaded shape at the top of the sheet.
Move the block along the dotted lines to other shapes until you reach the bottom.
Color the pictures and the dotted path you followed.

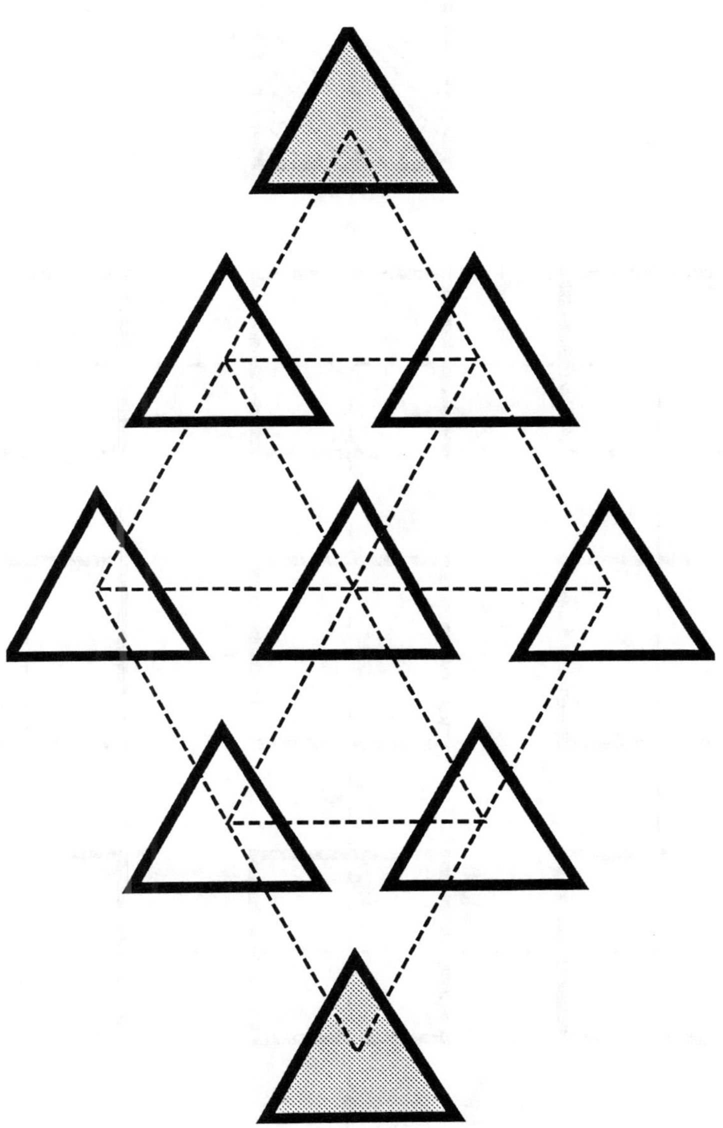

# PATHS

Place a PATTERN BLOCK on the shaded shape at the top of the sheet.
Move the block along the dotted lines to other shapes until you reach the bottom.
Color the pictures and the dotted path you followed.

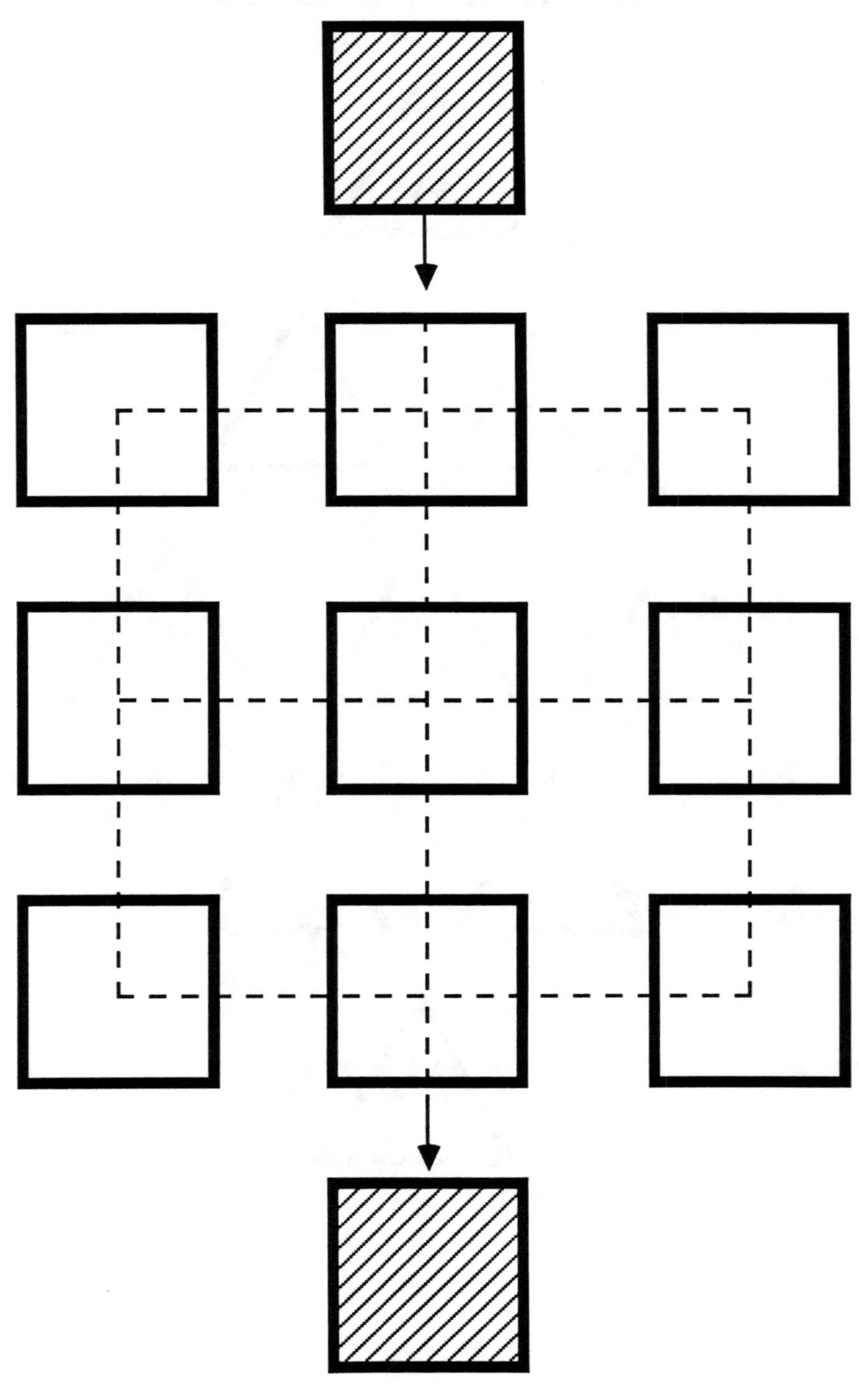

# PATHS

**A** Place a PATTERN BLOCK on the top shape.
Follow the dotted lines to find a path to the bottom shape.
Color the shapes and the path green.

**B** Place a PATTERN BLOCK on the top shape.
Follow the dotted lines to find a different path to the bottom shape.
Color the shapes and the new path green.

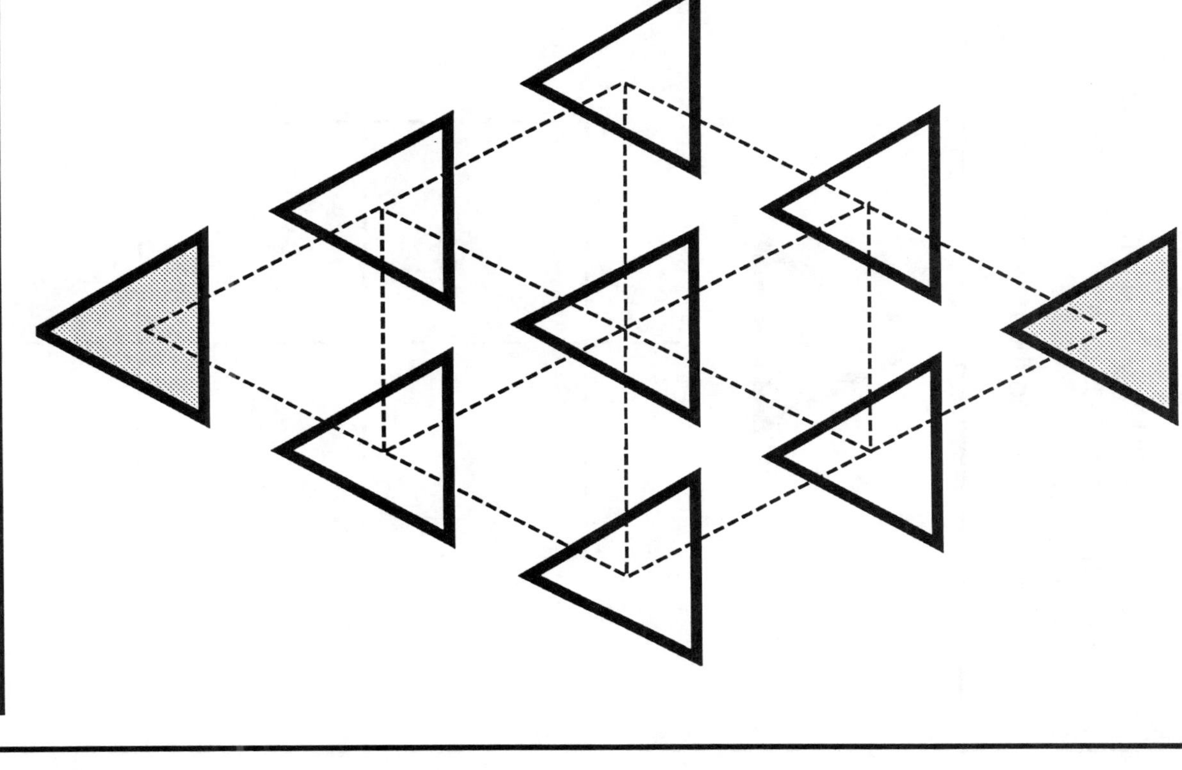

# PATHS

**A** Place a PATTERN BLOCK on the top shape.
Follow the dotted lines to find a path to the bottom shape.
Color the shapes and the path green.

**B** Place a PATTERN BLOCK on the top shape.
Follow the dotted lines to find a different path to the bottom shape.
Color the shapes and the new path green.

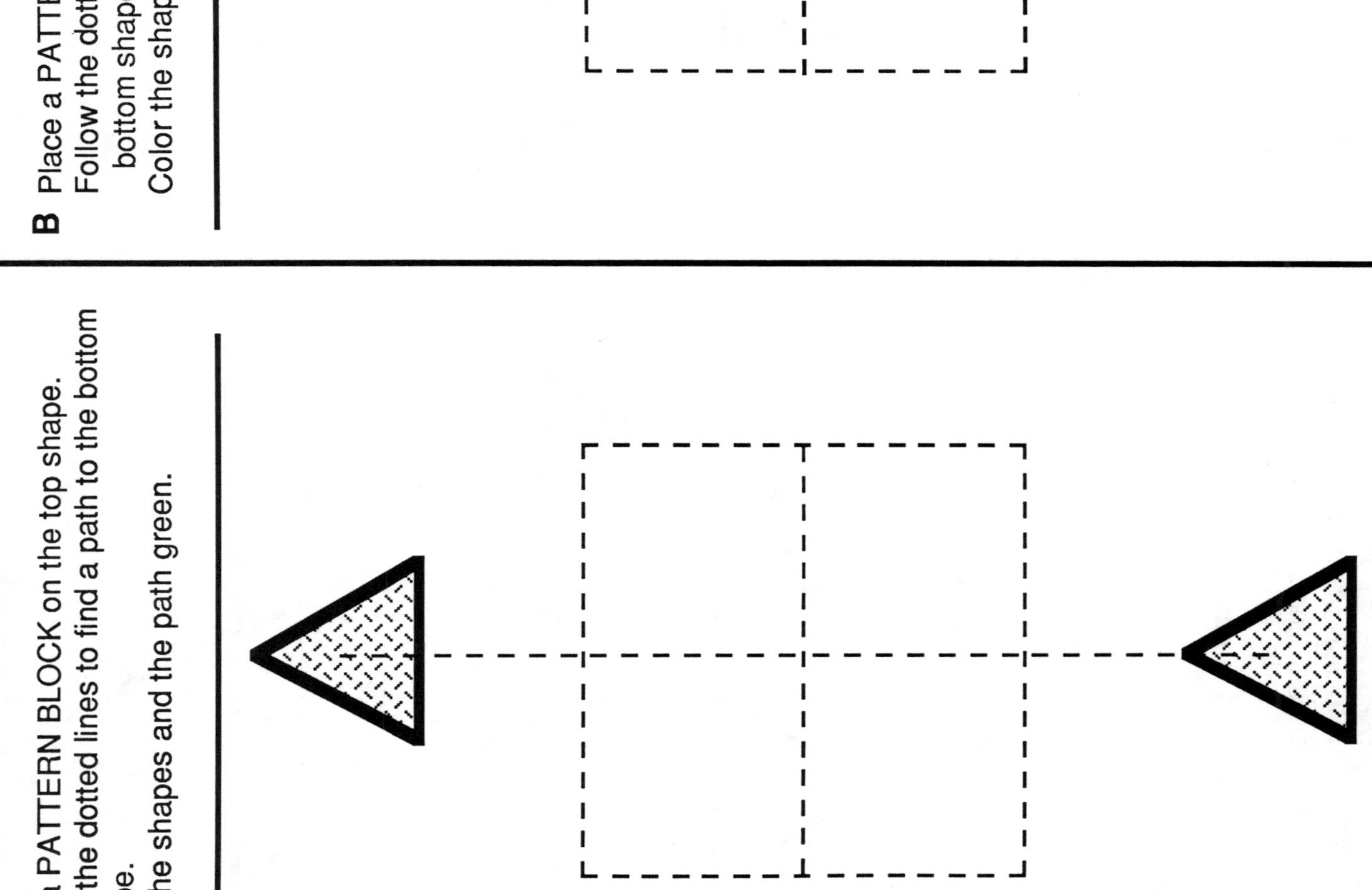

# COPYING A PATTERN

Place a different colored INTERLOCKING CUBE on each shaded shape.

---

Make each pattern below using the two colors you selected.
Color the patterns to match the cubes.

**A** 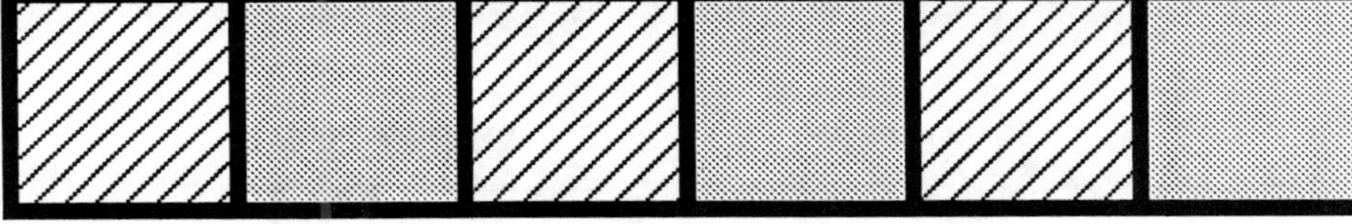

**B** 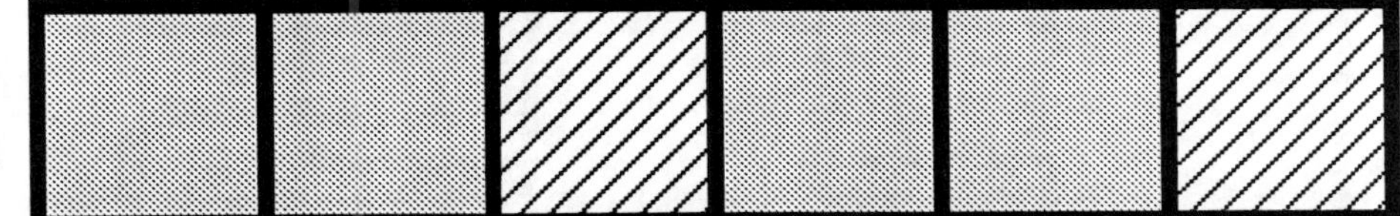

**C** 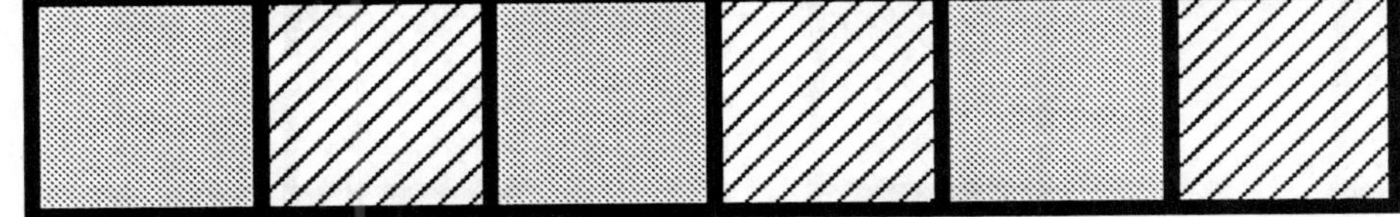

**D** 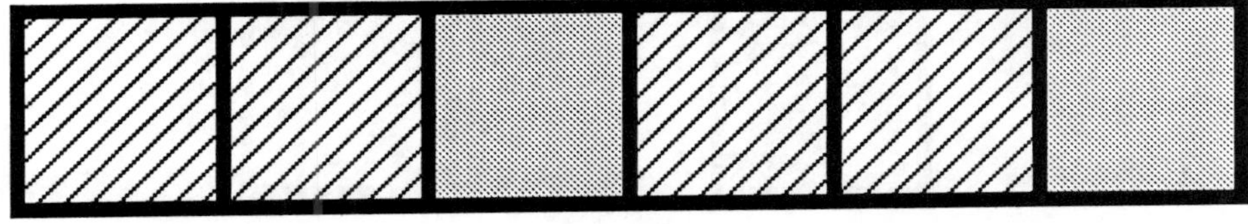

## COPYING A PATTERN

Place a different colored INTERLOCKING CUBE on each shaded shape.

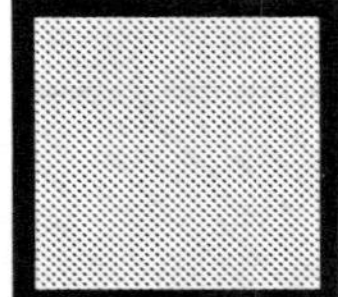

---

Make each pattern below using the two colors you selected.
Color the patterns to match the cubes.

A B C D

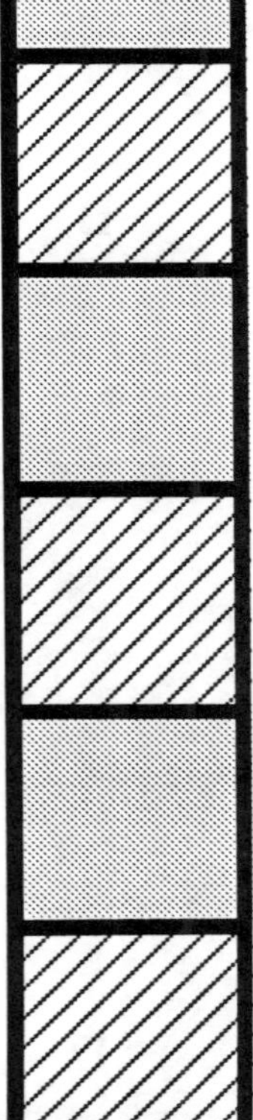

## COPYING A PATTERN

Place a PATTERN BLOCK on each shape below.
In each dotted box, copy the pattern using matching blocks.
Trace the blocks and color the pictures to match them.

A

B

# COPYING A PATTERN

Place a PATTERN BLOCK on each shape below.
In each dotted box, copy the pattern using matching blocks.
Trace the blocks and color the pictures to match them.

A

B

# COPYING A PATTERN

Place the correct red (R), yellow (Y), or blue (B) ATTRIBUTE BLOCK on each shape below.
Color the pictures to match the blocks.

A Y R Y R

B B Y B Y

C B R B R

# COPYING A PATTERN

Place the correct red (R), yellow (Y), or blue (B) ATTRIBUTE BLOCK on each shape below. Color the pictures to match the blocks.

A R B R B

B Y B Y B

C R Y R Y

# COPYING A PATTERN

Rows A and B show patterns of PATTERN BLOCKS. The pictures are smaller than your blocks.
In each dotted box, copy the pattern using PATTERN BLOCKS.
Trace the blocks and color the pictures to match them.

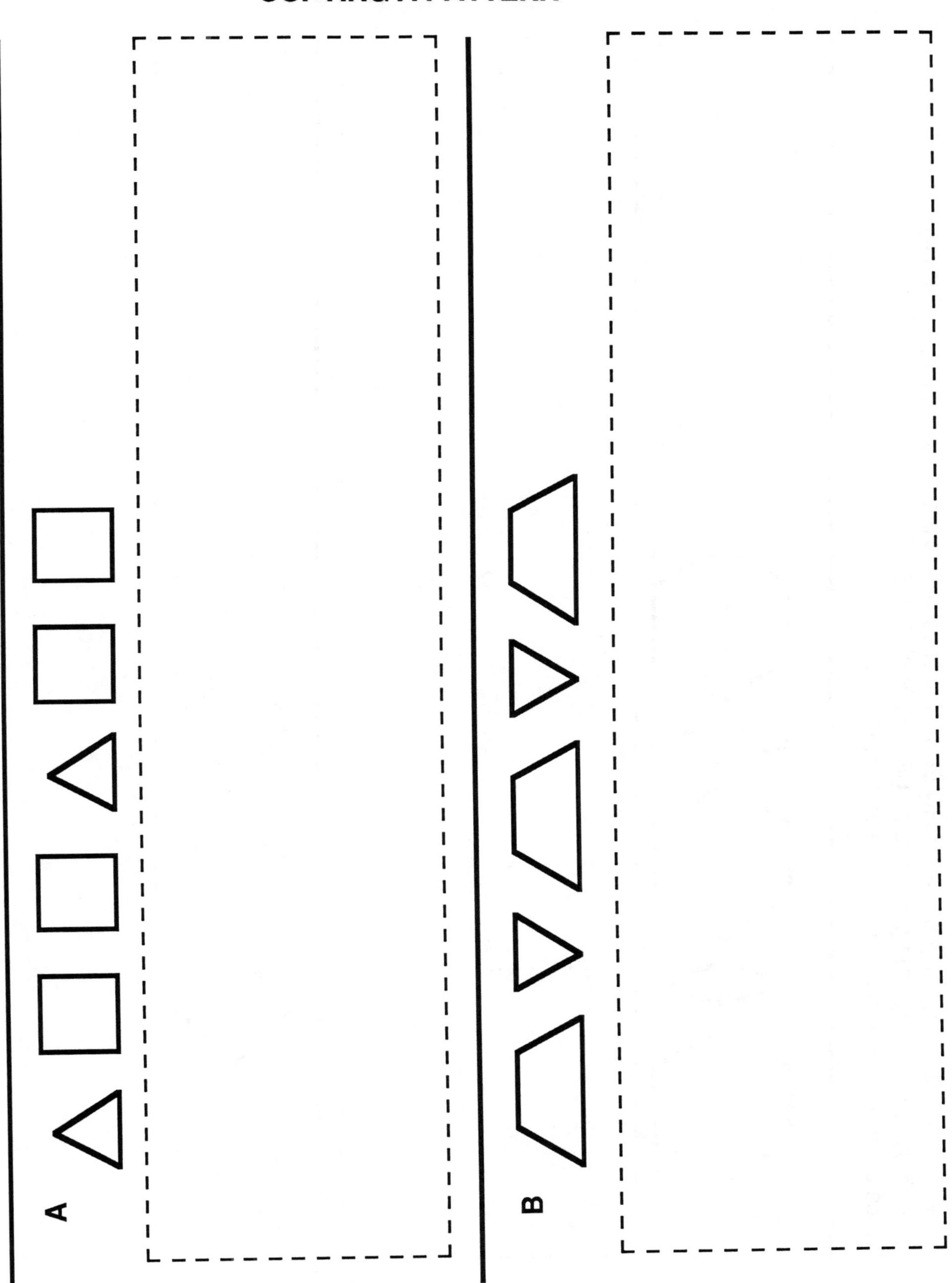

# COPYING A PATTERN

Rows A and B show patterns of PATTERN BLOCKS. The pictures are smaller than your blocks. In each dotted box, copy the pattern using PATTERN BLOCKS. Trace the blocks and color the pictures to match them.

A

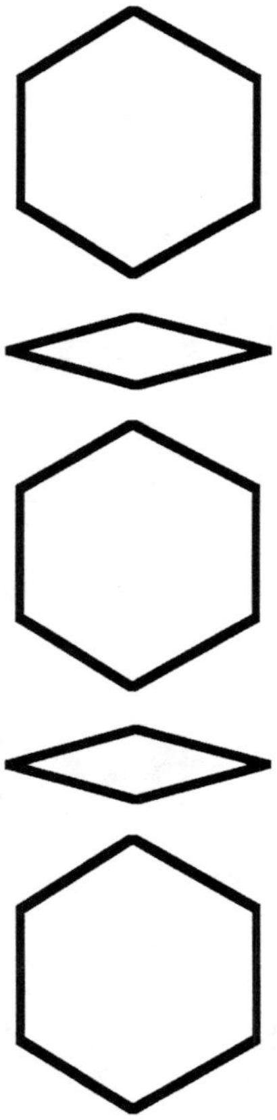

B

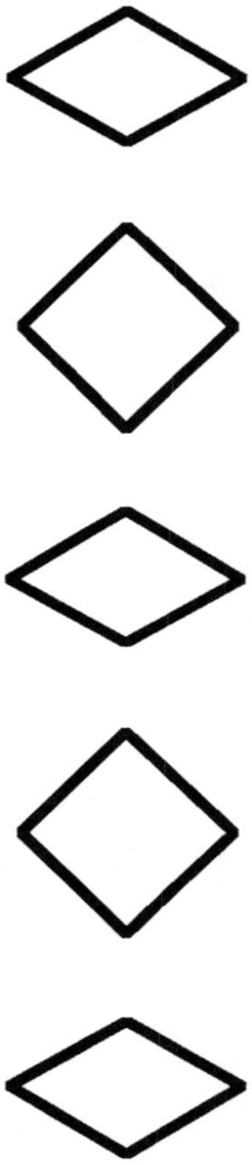

# WHAT COMES NEXT?

Place a different colored INTERLOCKING CUBE on each shaded shape.

Make each pattern below using the two colors you selected.
In each unshaded space, add the cube that comes next in the pattern.
Color the pictures to match the cubes.

A ?

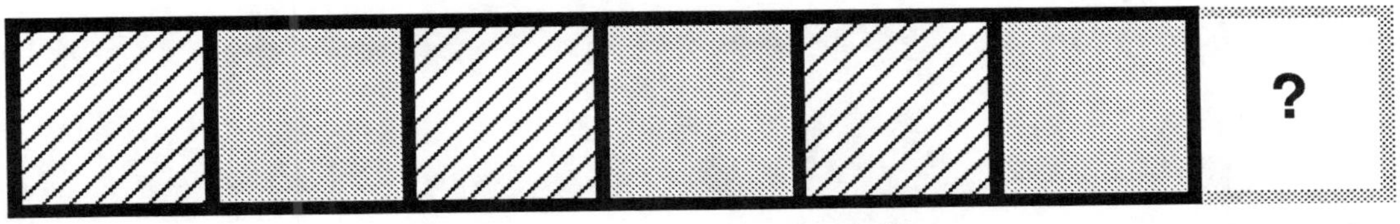

B ?

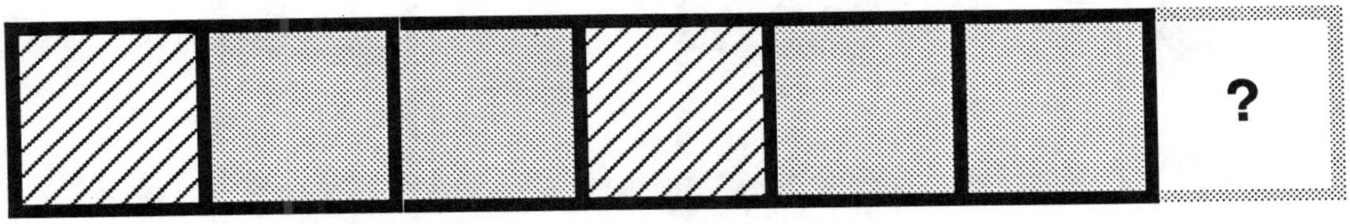

C ?

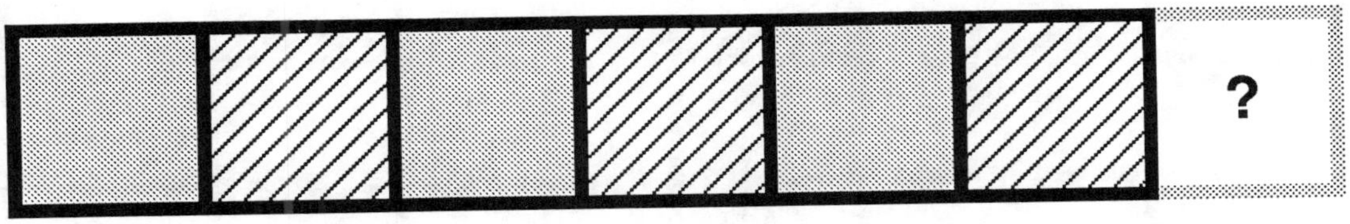

D ?

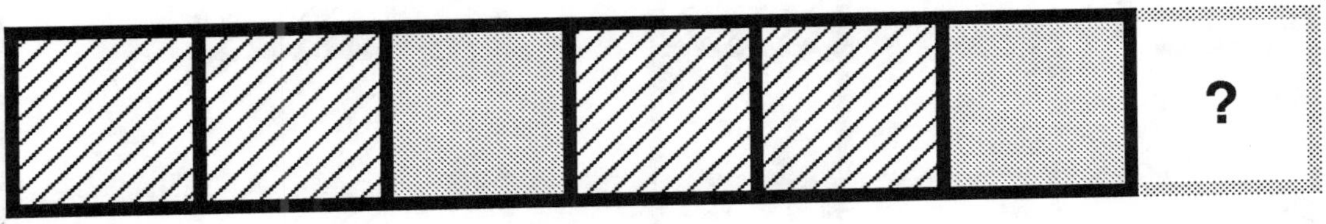

## WHAT COMES NEXT?

Place a different colored INTERLOCKING CUBE on each shaded shape.

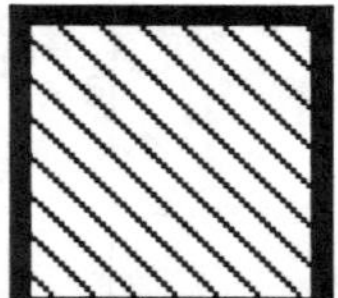

Make each pattern below using the two colors you selected.
In each unshaded space, add the cube that comes next in the pattern.
Color the pictures to match the cubes.

A B C D

? ? ? ?

# WHAT COMES NEXT?

Place an ATTRIBUTE BLOCK on each shape below. Use any colors you wish.
In each dotted box, place the block that comes next in that pattern.
Trace the block that continues the pattern.

**A**

**B**

# WHAT COMES NEXT?

Place an ATTRIBUTE BLOCK on each shape below. Use any colors you wish.
In each dotted box, place the block that comes next in that pattern.
Trace the block that continues the pattern.

A

B

## WHAT COMES NEXT?

Place a PATTERN BLOCK on each shape below.
In each dotted box, place the block that comes next in that pattern.
Trace the blocks and color the pictures to match them.

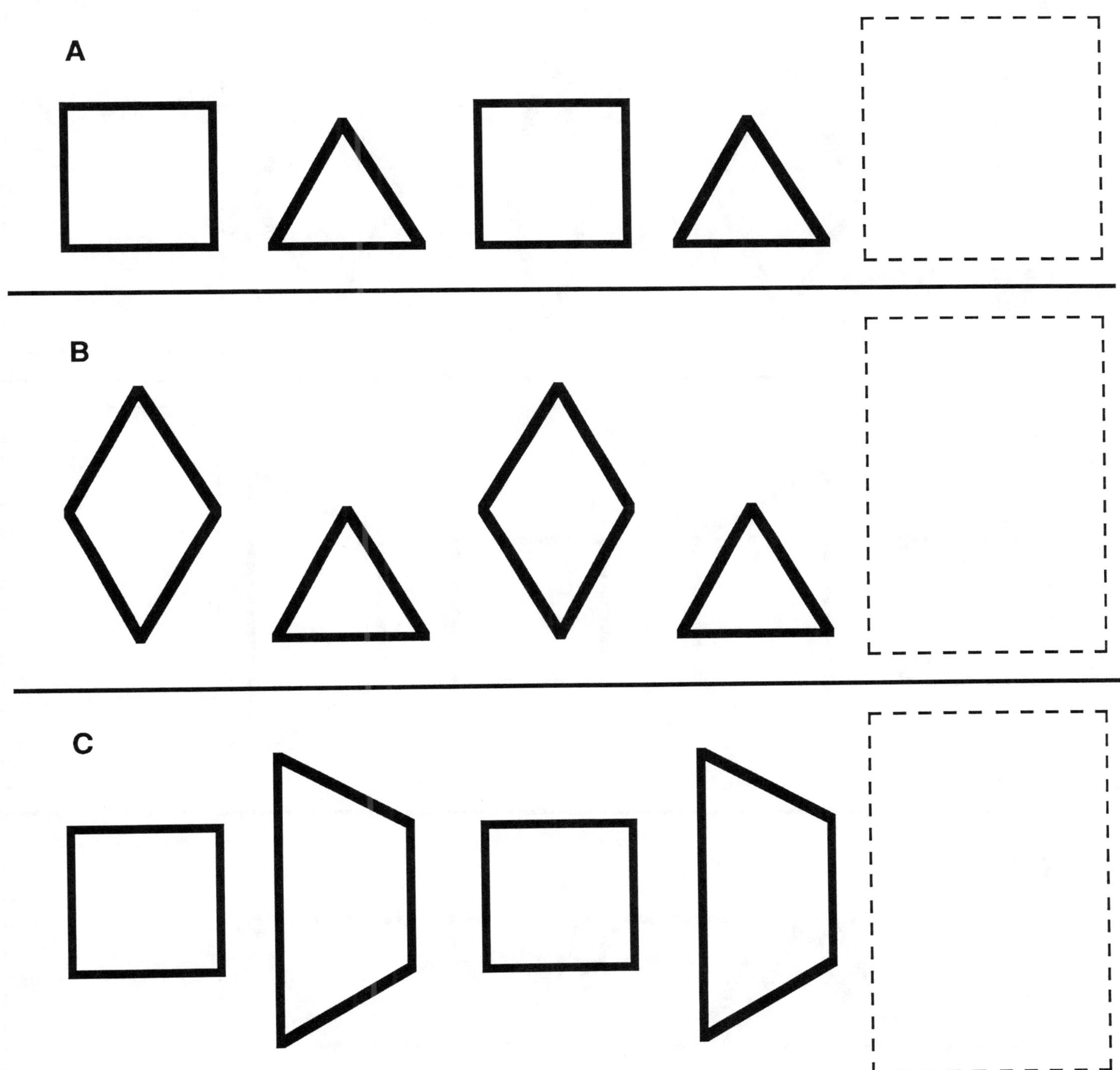

## WHAT COMES NEXT?

Place a PATTERN BLOCK on each shape below.
In each dotted box, place the block that comes next in that pattern.
Trace the blocks and color the pictures to match them.

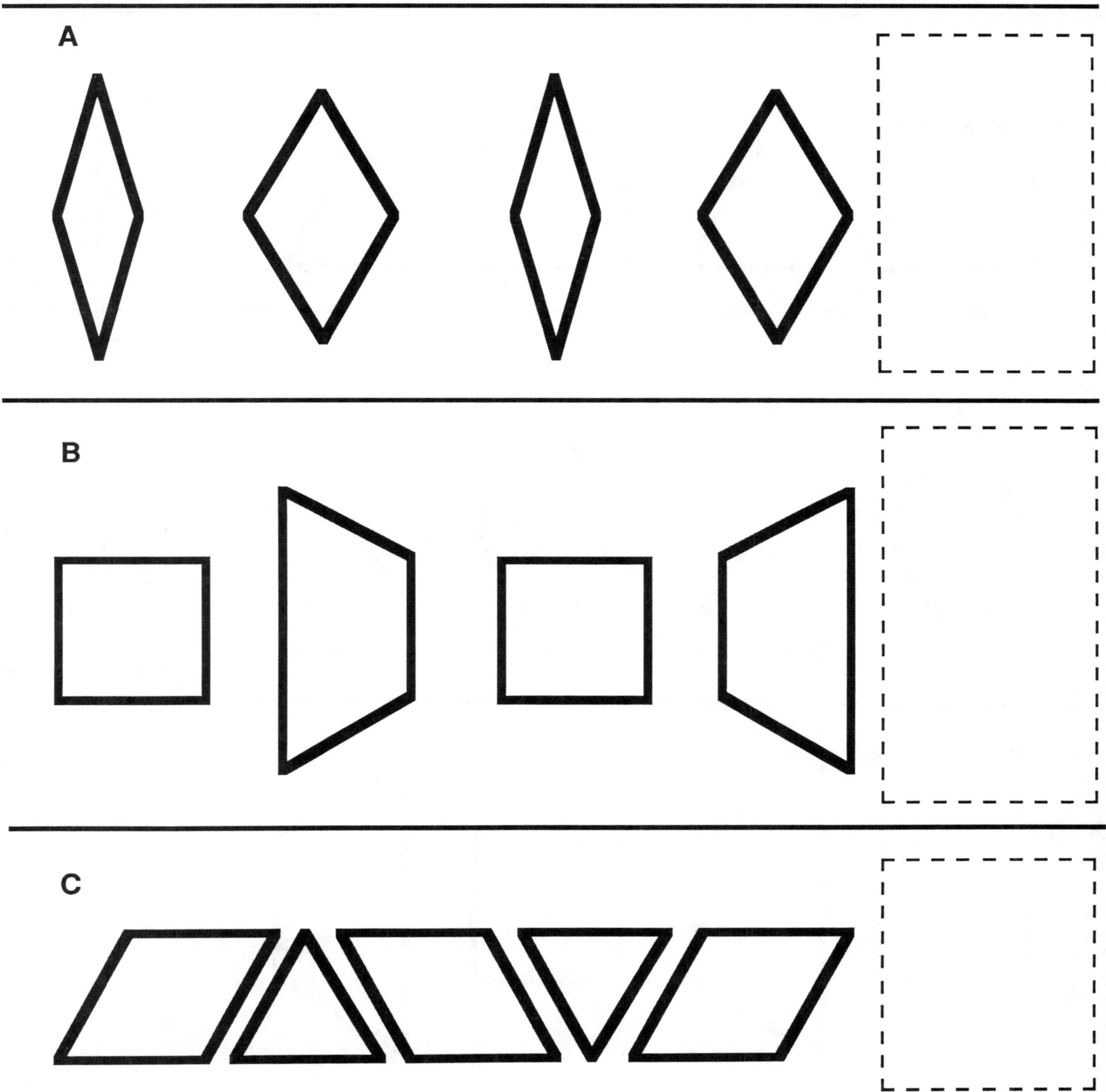

## WHAT COMES NEXT?

The pictures below show patterns using both large and small ATTRIBUTE BLOCKS.
The pictures are smaller than your blocks.
On a piece of paper, build a copy of each pattern using the large and small blocks.
Add the block that comes next in each pattern.

**A**

**B**

**C**

**D**

## WHAT COMES NEXT?

The pictures below show patterns using both large and small ATTRIBUTE BLOCKS.
The pictures are smaller than your blocks.
On a piece of paper, build a copy of each pattern using the large and small blocks.
Add the block that comes next in each pattern.

A

B

C

D

# WHAT COMES NEXT?

Place a different colored INTERLOCKING CUBE on each shaded shape.

Make each pattern below using the two colors you selected.
Make the figure that comes next in the pattern and place it in the dotted box.
Trace the figure and color the pictures to match the cubes.

**A**

**B**

**C**

# WHAT COMES NEXT?

Place a different colored INTERLOCKING CUBE on each shaded shape.

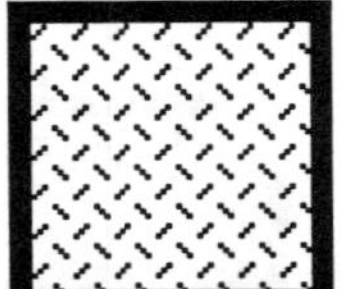

Make each pattern below using the two colors you selected.
Make the figure that comes next in the pattern and place it in the dotted box.
Trace the figure and color the pictures to match the cubes.

**A**

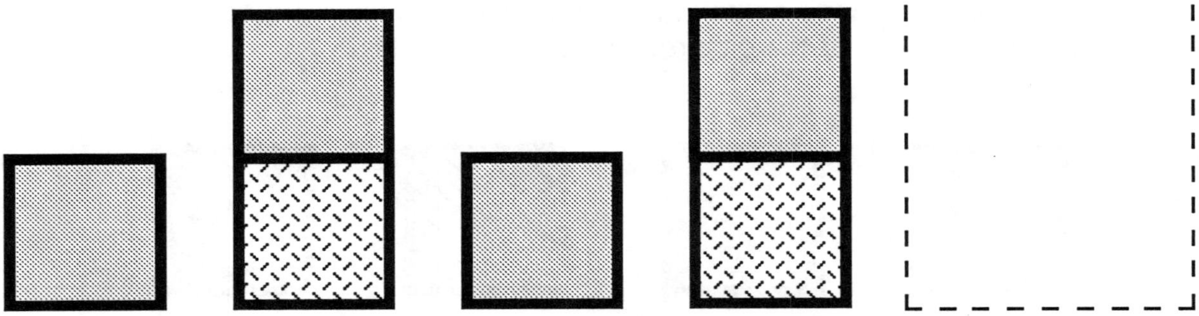

**B**

**C**

## WHAT COMES NEXT?

Place a different colored INTERLOCKING CUBE on each shaded shape.

Make each pattern below using the two colors you selected.
Make the figure that comes next in the pattern and place it in the dotted box .
Trace the figure and color the pictures to match the cubes.

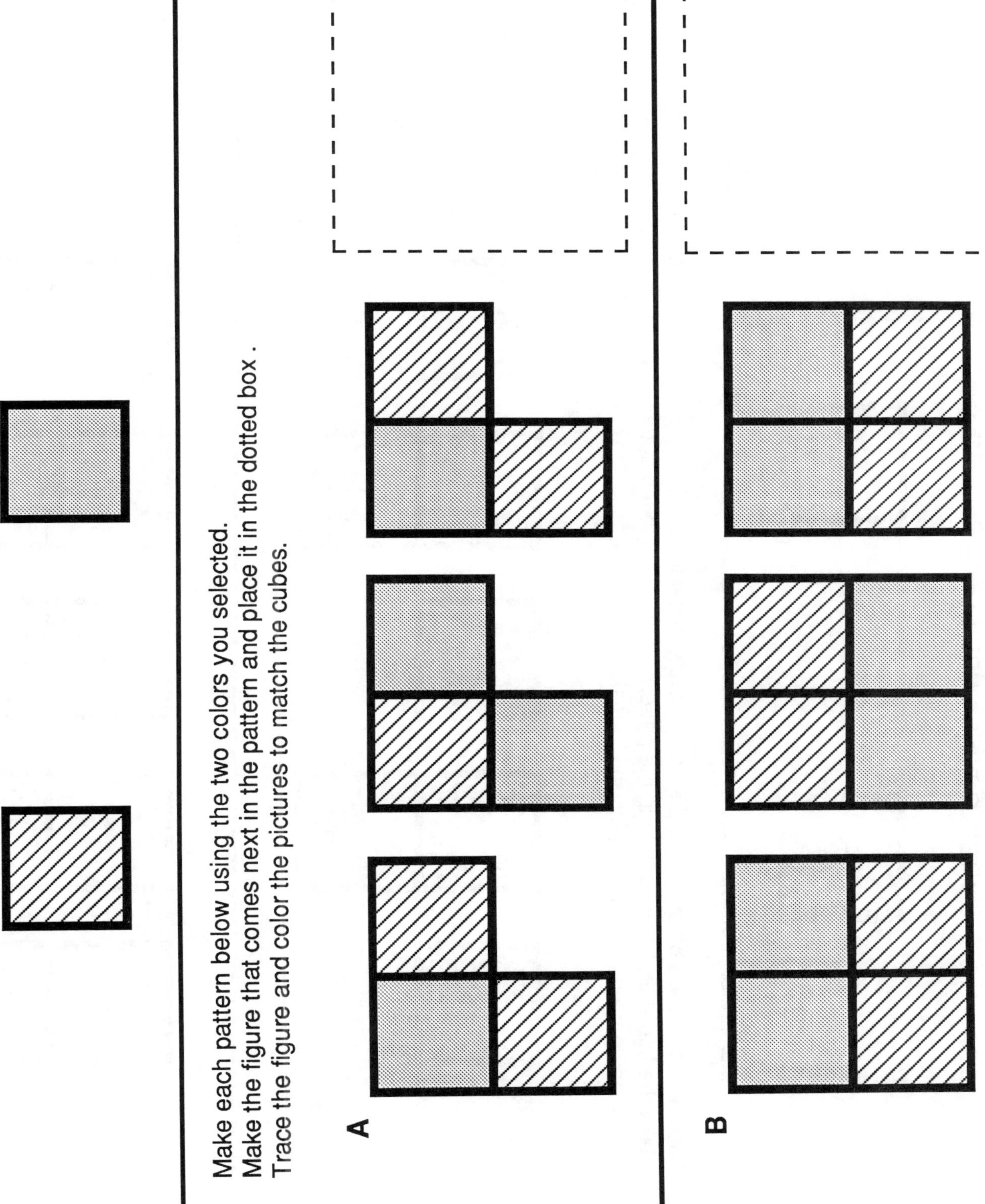

# WHAT COMES NEXT?

Place a different colored INTERLOCKING CUBE on each shaded shape.

Make each pattern below using the two colors you selected.
Make the figure that comes next in the pattern and place it in the dotted box .
Trace the figure and color the pictures to match the cubes.

**A**

**B**

# COMPLETING A PATTERN

Place a different colored INTERLOCKING CUBE on each shaded shape.

---

Make each pattern below using the two colors you selected.
Find the correct cube for the unshaded space and complete each pattern.
Color the pictures to match the cubes.

**A**

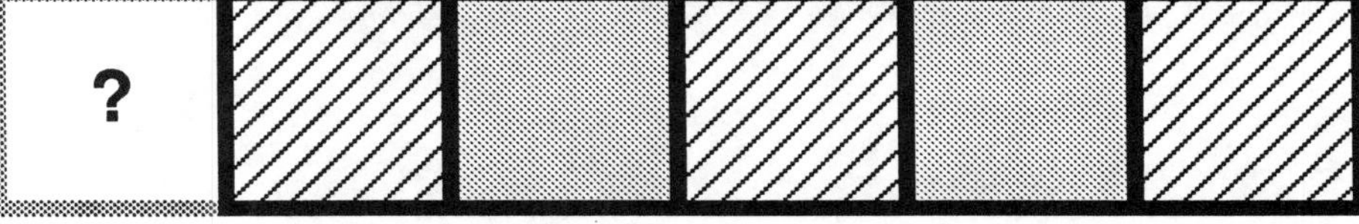


**B**

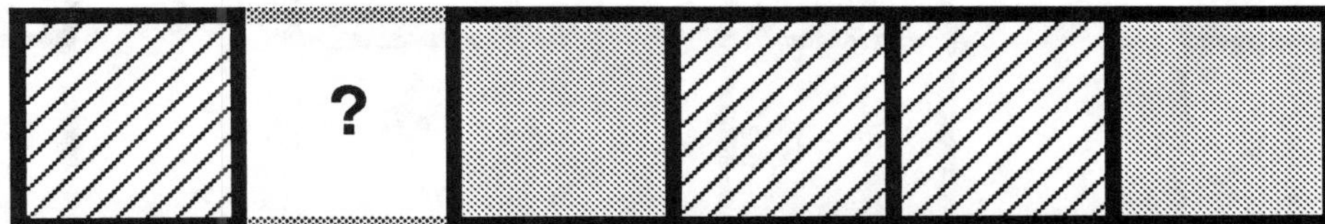


**C**

**D**

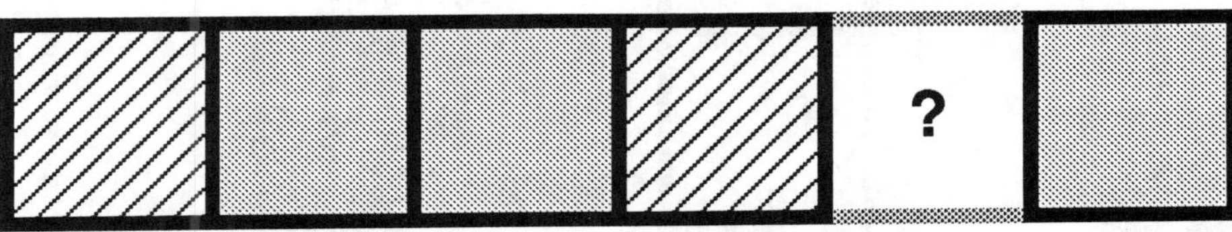

# COMPLETING A PATTERN

Place a different colored INTERLOCKING CUBE on each shaded shape.

---

Make each pattern below using the two colors you selected.
Find the correct cube for the unshaded space and complete each pattern.
Color the pictures to match the cubes.

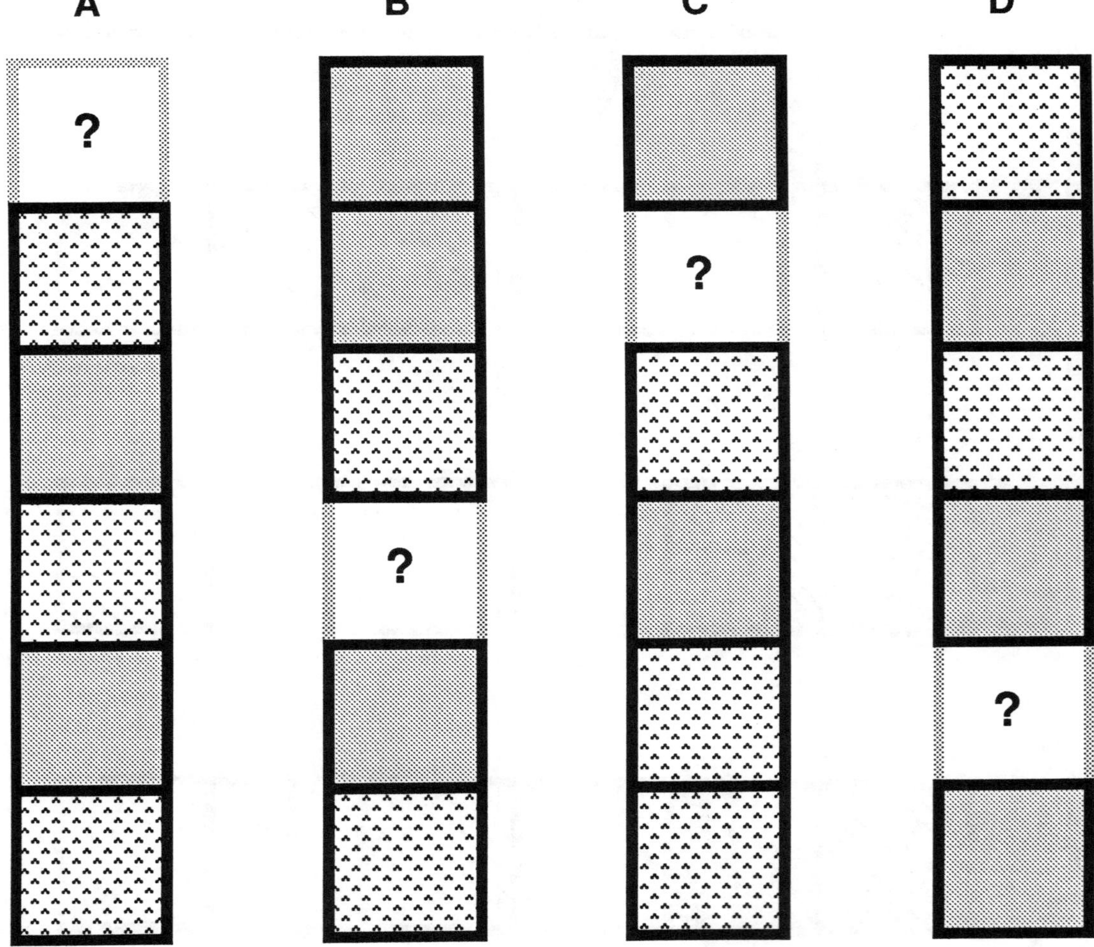

## COMPLETING A PATTERN

Use two different colors of INTERLOCKING CUBES to cover the patterns below.
Find the correct cubes for the unshaded spaces and complete each pattern.
Color the pictures to match the cubes.

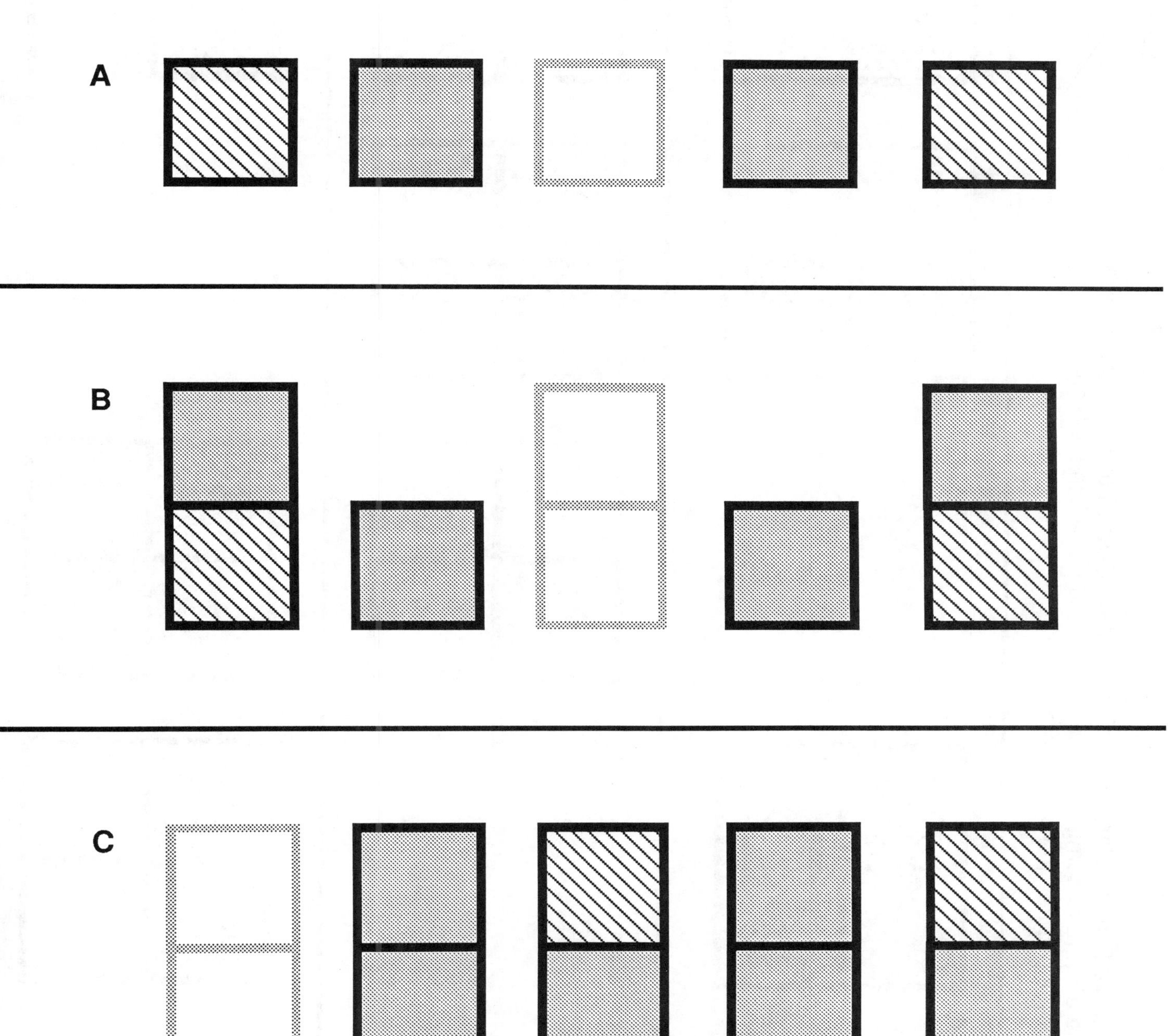

# COMPLETING A PATTERN

Use two different colors of INTERLOCKING CUBES to make and cover each figure below.
Make a figure to complete each pattern and place it in the blank box.
Color the pictures to match the cubes.

A

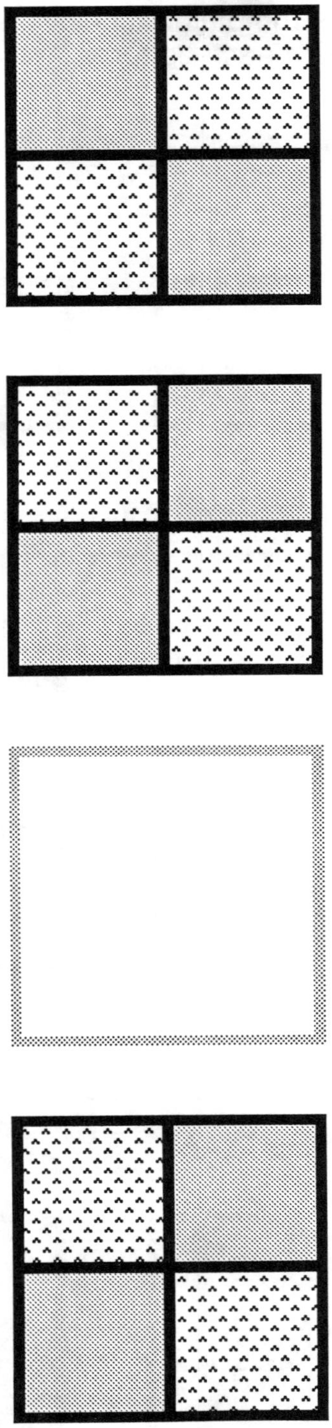

B

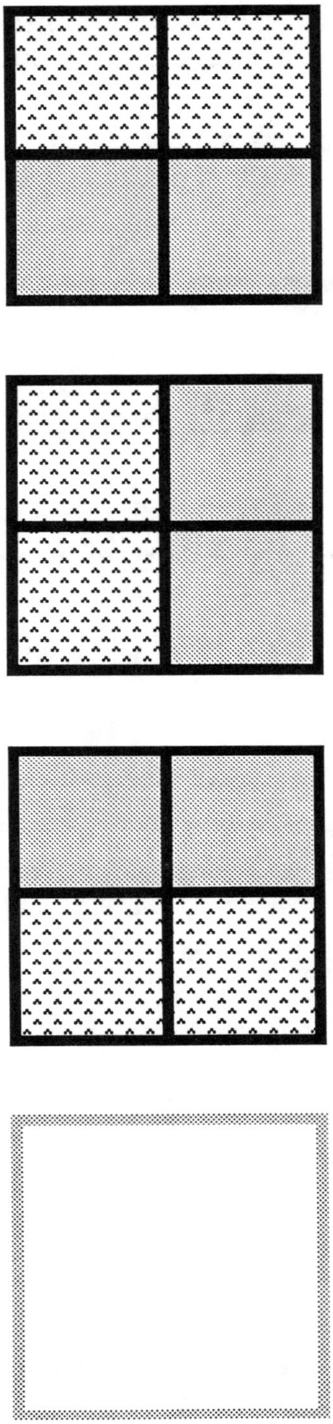

C

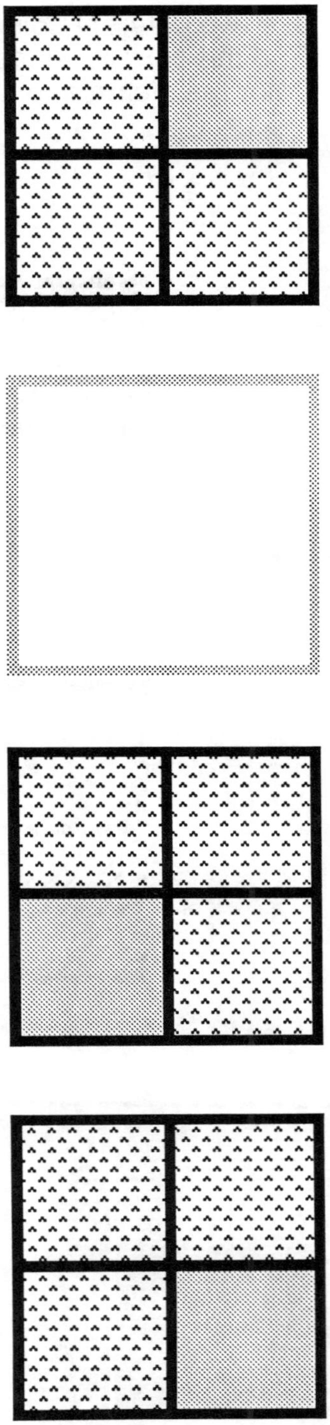

## COMPLETING A PATTERN

Place an ATTRIBUTE BLOCK on each shape below. Use any colors you wish.
Choose the block that completes each pattern and place it in the dotted box.
Trace the block that completes each pattern.

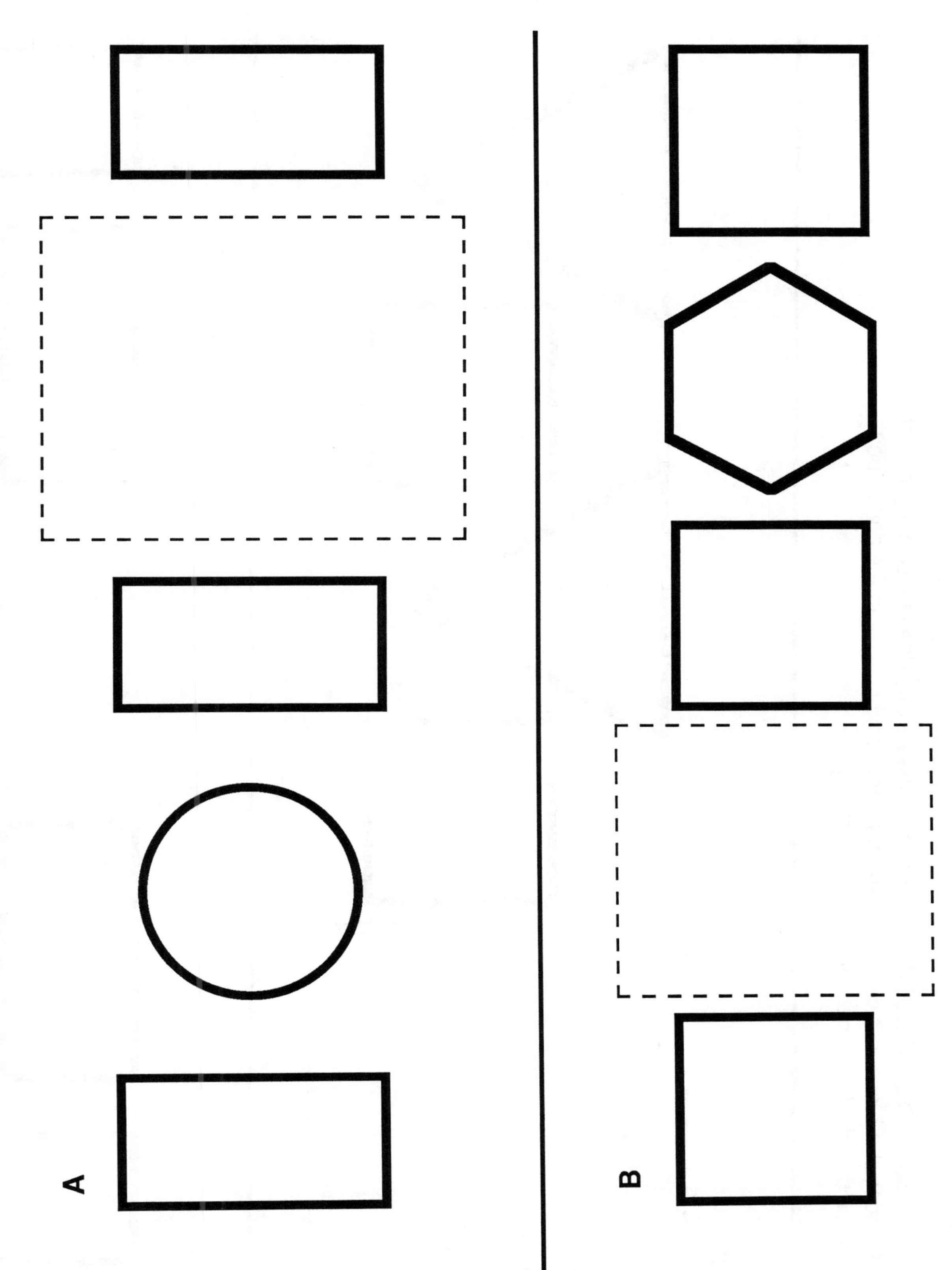

# COMPLETING A PATTERN

Place an ATTRIBUTE BLOCK on each shape below. Use any colors you wish.
Choose the block that completes each pattern and place it in the dotted box.
Trace the block that completes each pattern.

A

B

# COMPLETING A PATTERN

Place a PATTERN BLOCK on each shape below.
Choose the block that completes each pattern and place it in the dotted box.
Trace the blocks and color the pictures to match them.

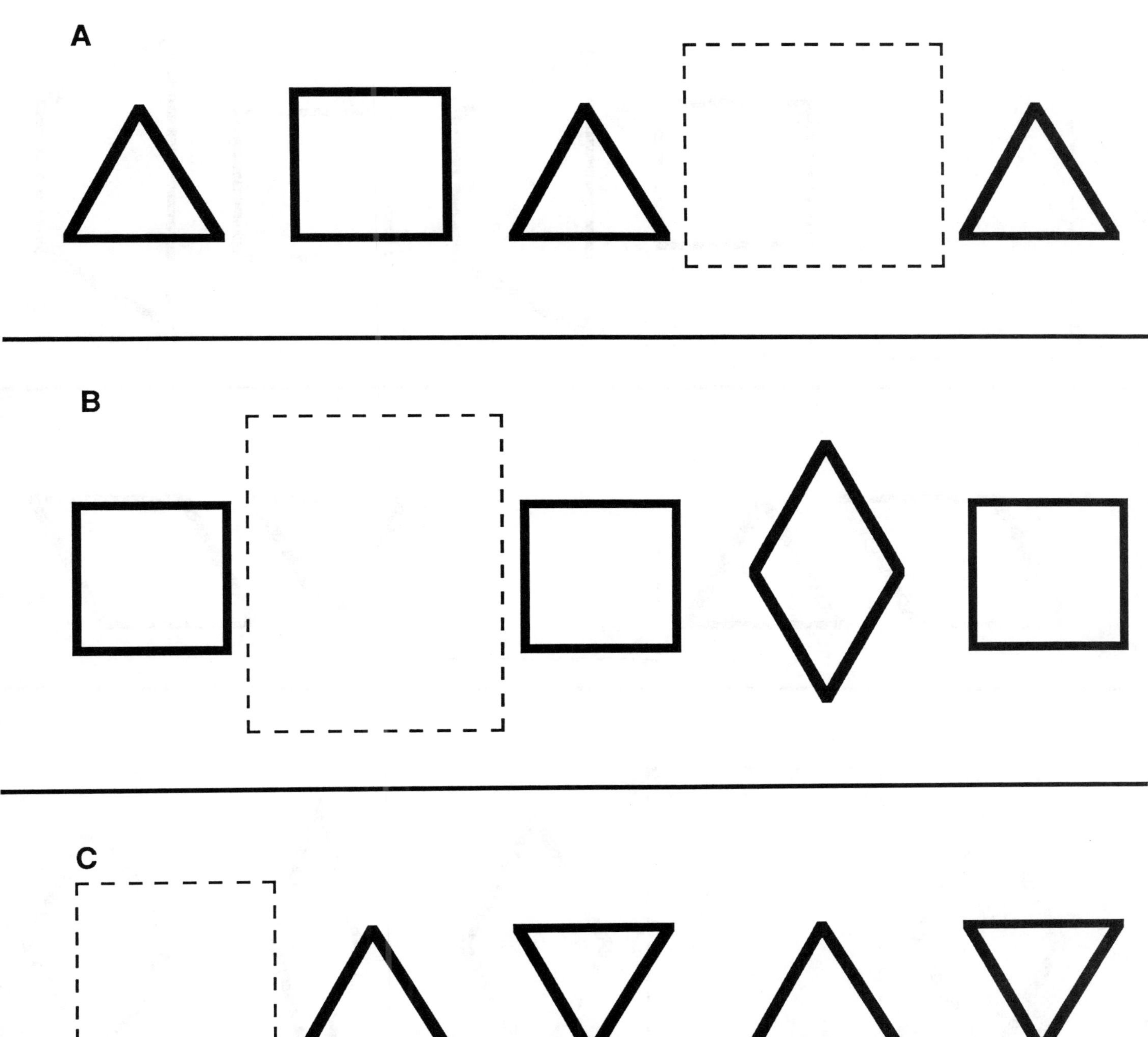

## COMPLETING A PATTERN

Place a PATTERN BLOCK on each shape below.
Choose the block that completes each pattern and place it in the dotted box.
Trace the blocks and color the pictures to match them.

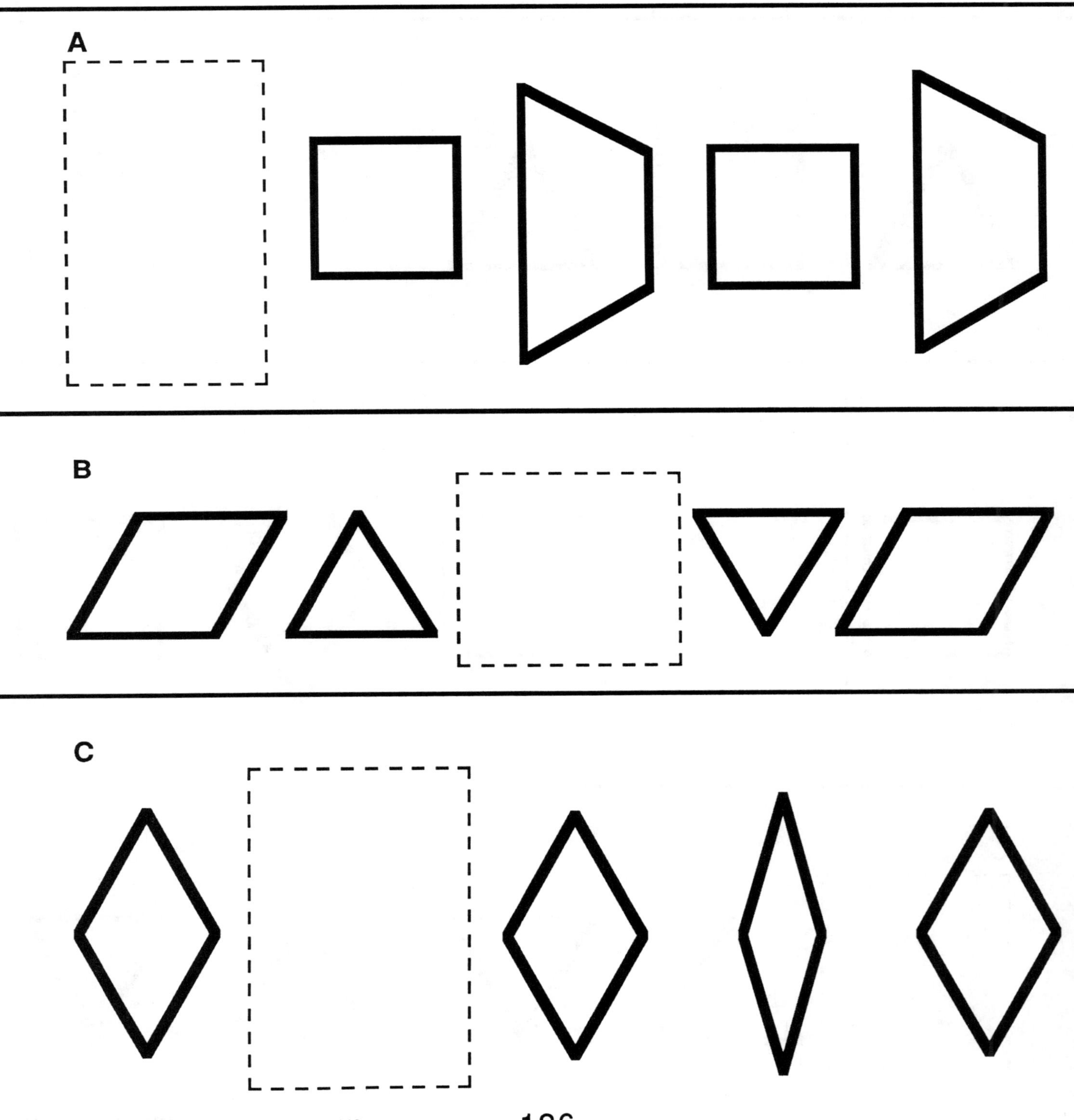

## COMPLETING A PATTERN

Place the correct red (R), yellow (Y), or blue (B) ATTRIBUTE BLOCK on each shape below.
Choose the block that completes each pattern and place it in the dotted box.
Trace the blocks and color the pictures to match them.

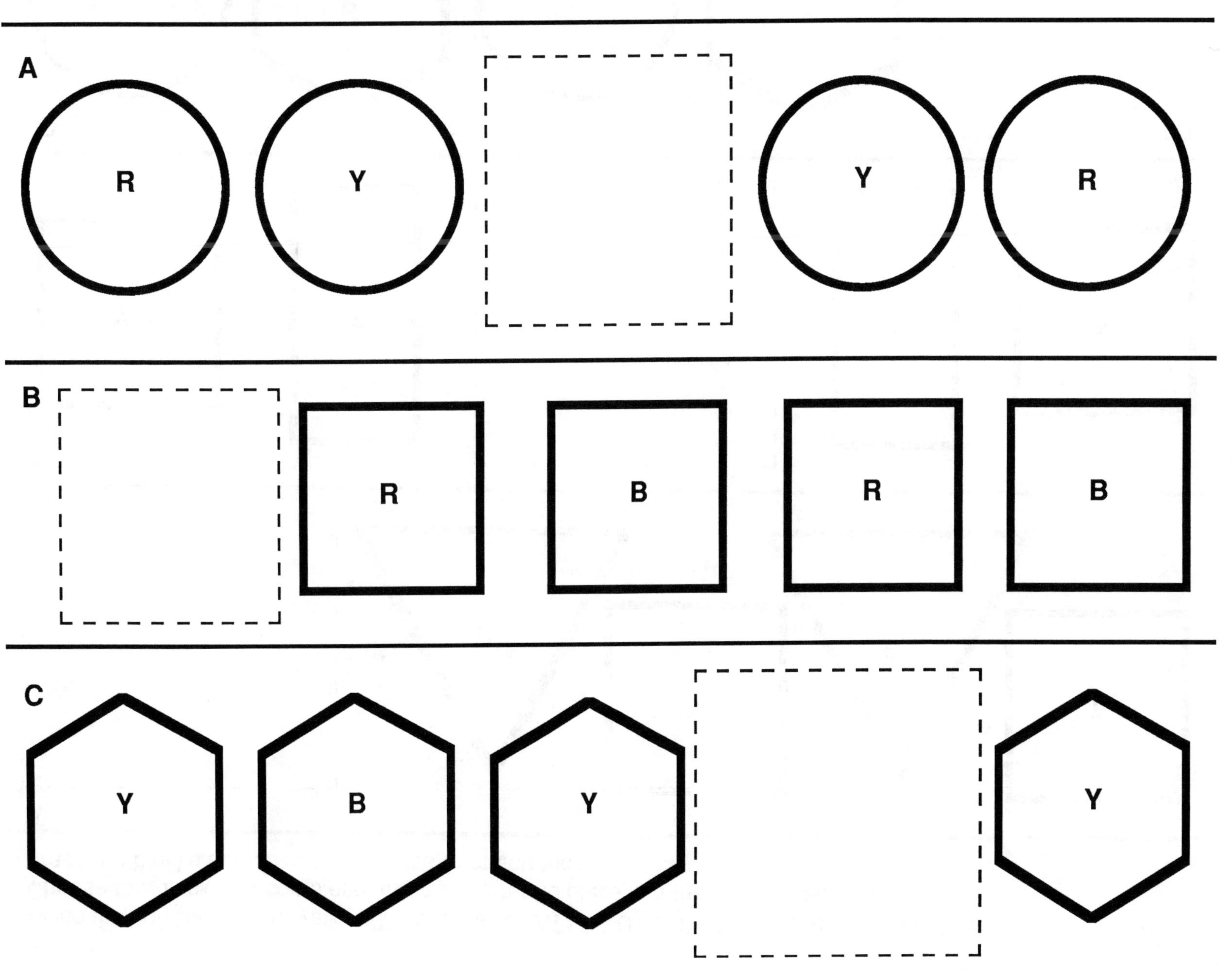

# COMPLETING A PATTERN

Place the correct red (R), yellow (Y), or blue (B) ATTRIBUTE BLOCK on each shape below.
Choose the block that completes each pattern and place it in the dotted box.
Trace the blocks and color the pictures to match them.

A

R Y R Y

B

Y B B Y

C

R B R B

## SEQUENCES OF SHAPES

Place a PATTERN BLOCK on each shape below.
Make a sequence of blocks to continue the pattern and place it in the dotted box.
Trace the blocks and color the pictures.

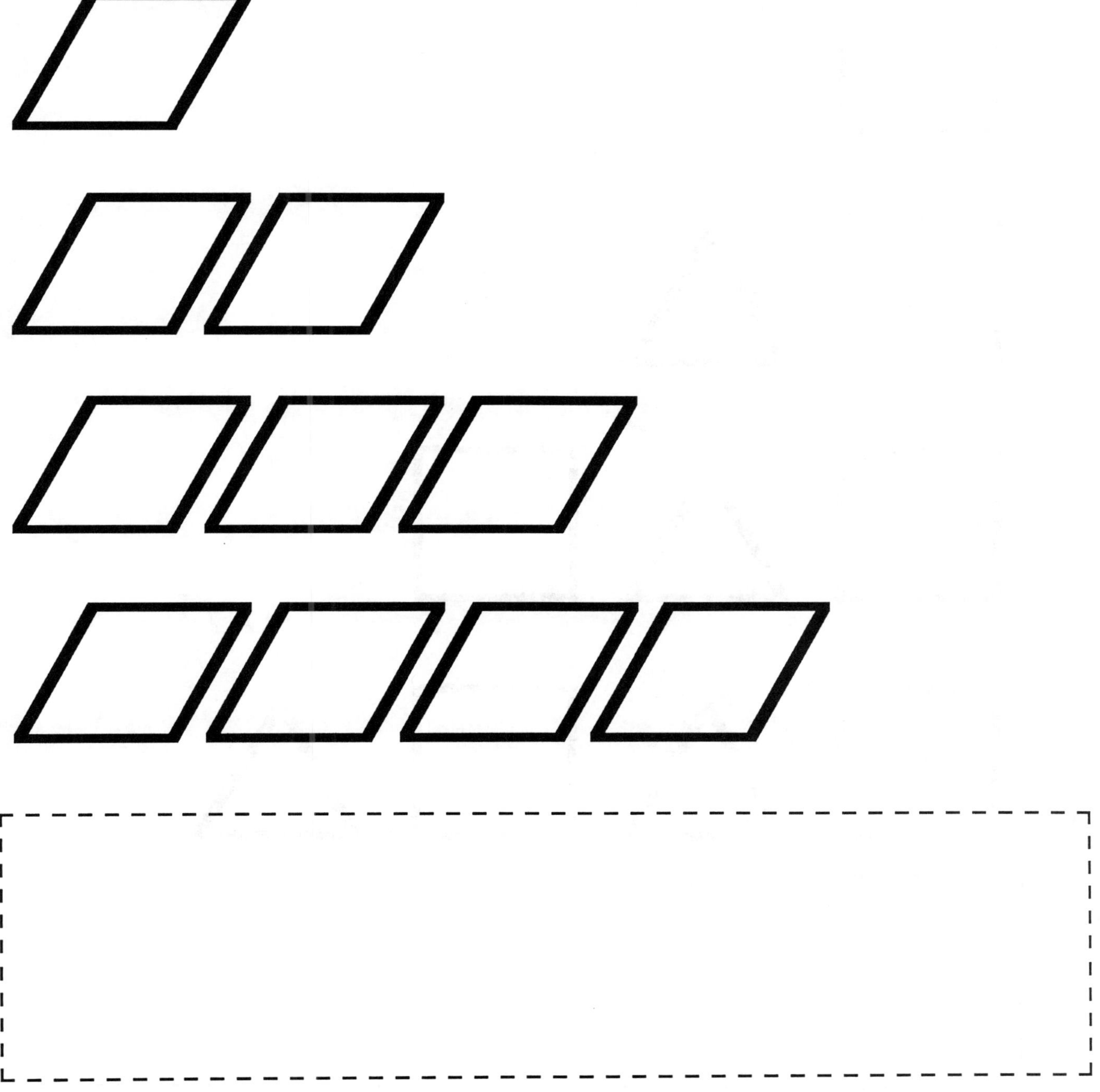

## SEQUENCES OF SHAPES

Place a PATTERN BLOCK on each shape below.
Make a sequence of blocks to continue the pattern and place it in the dotted box.
Trace the blocks and color the pictures.

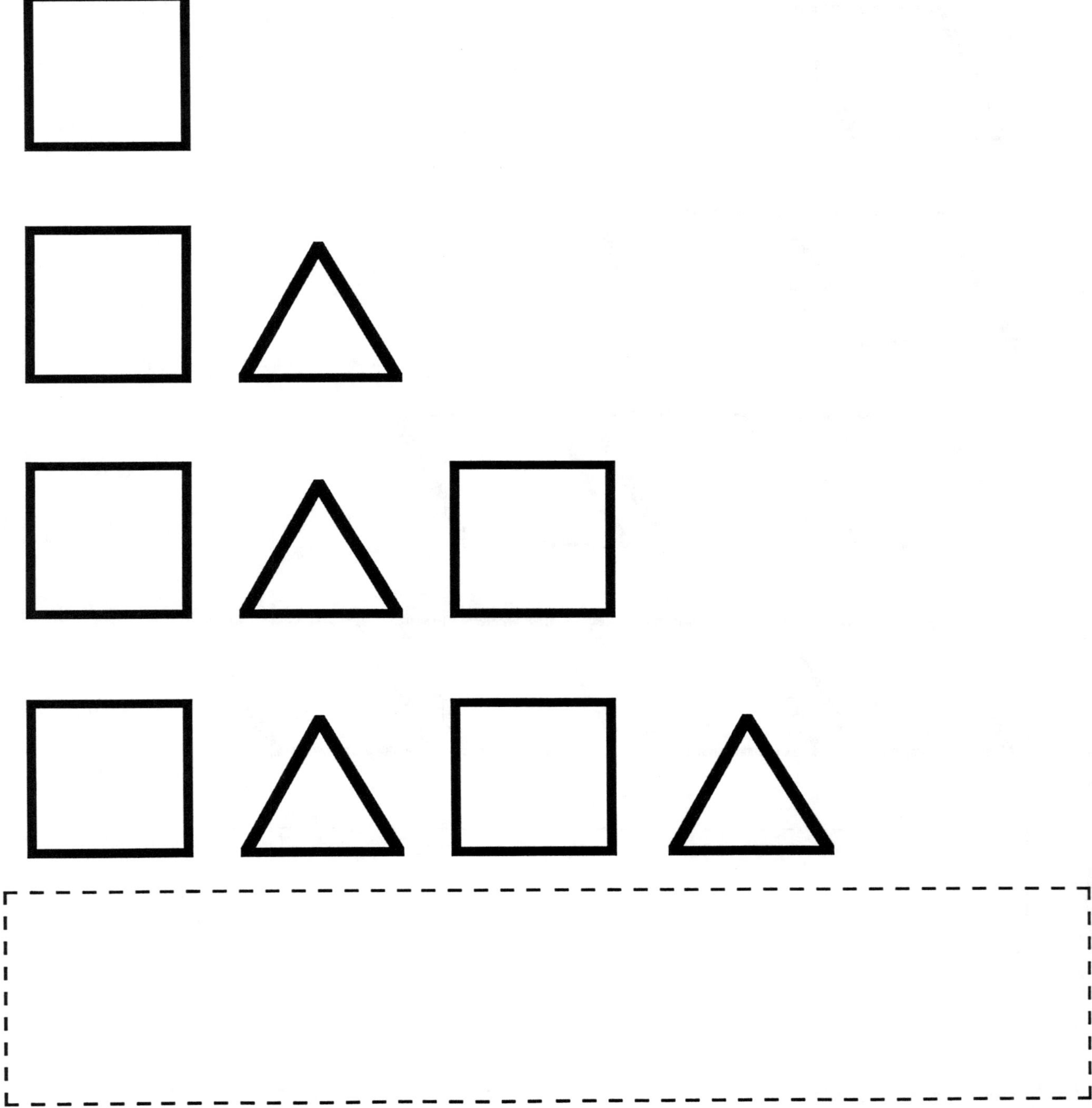

## SEQUENCES OF SHAPES

Use two different colors of INTERLOCKING CUBES to cover the sequences below.
Make a sequence of cubes to continue the pattern and place it in the dotted box.
Trace the cubes and color the pictures.

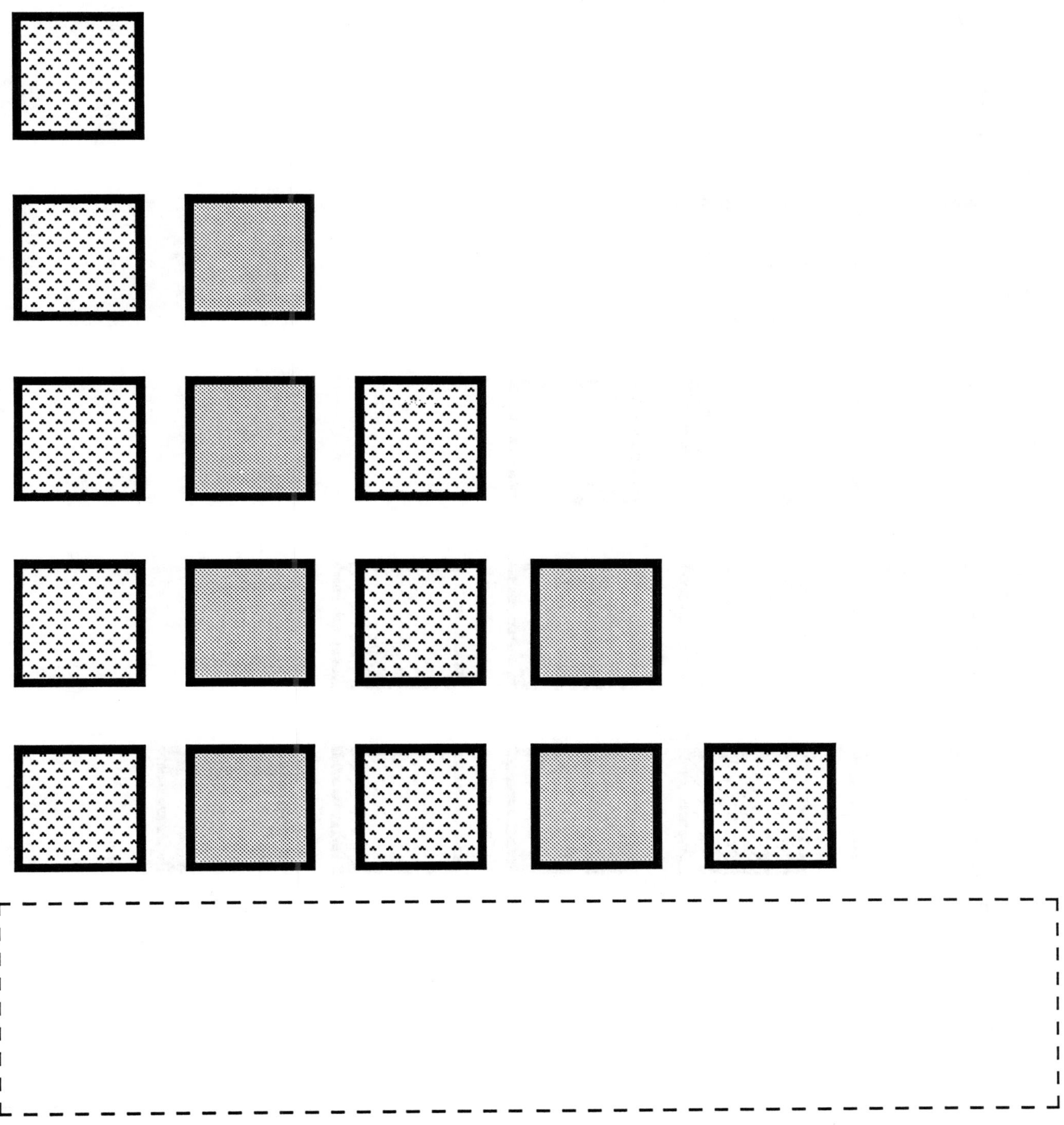

## SEQUENCES OF SHAPES

Use two different colors of INTERLOCKING CUBES to cover the sequences below. Make a sequence of cubes to continue the pattern and place it in the dotted box. Trace the cubes and color the pictures.

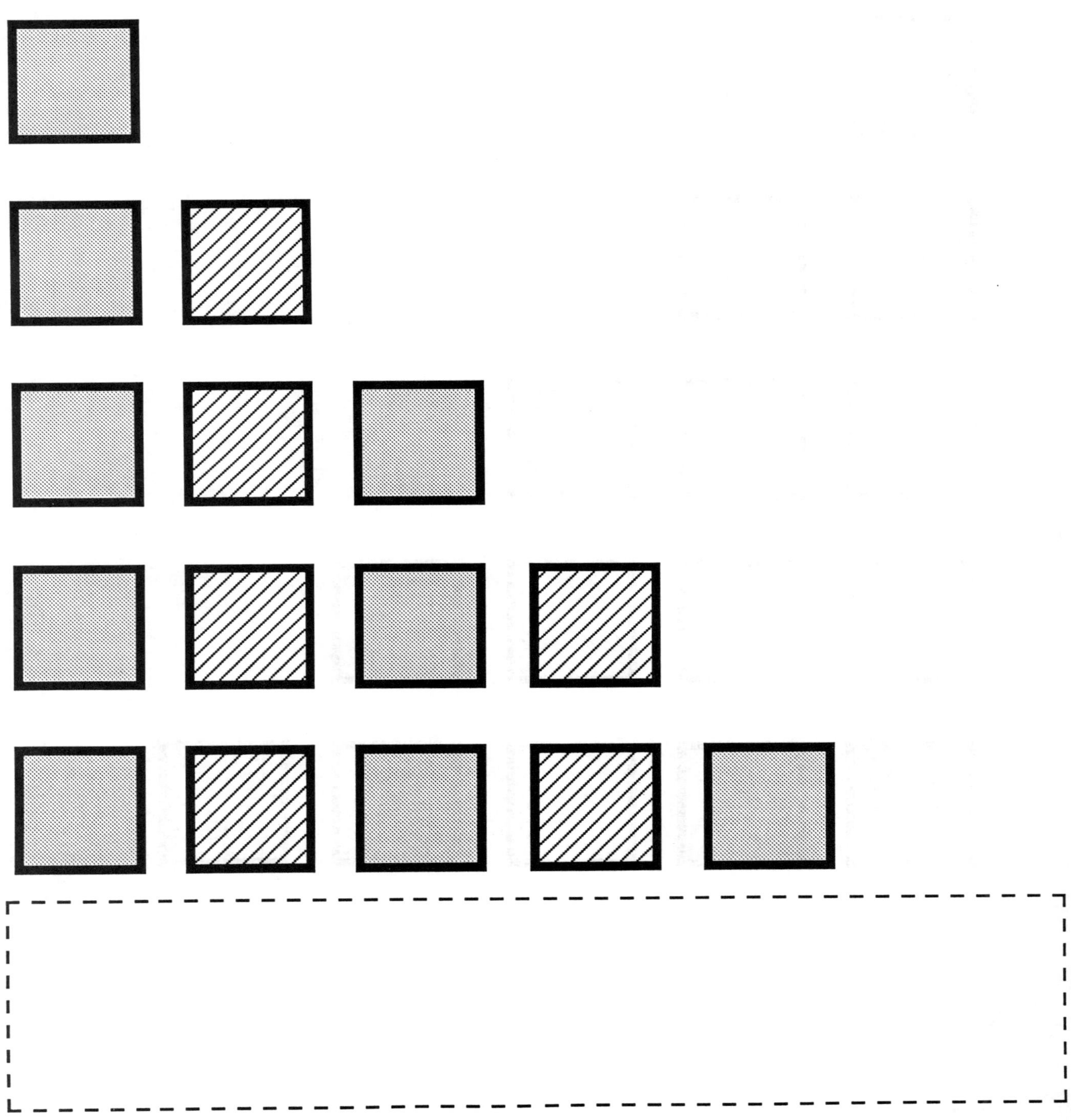

# SEQUENCES OF FIGURES

Use PATTERN BLOCK triangles to make and cover the figures below.
Use triangles to make a figure that continues the pattern and place it in the dotted box.
Trace the blocks in the figure and color the pictures to match the blocks.

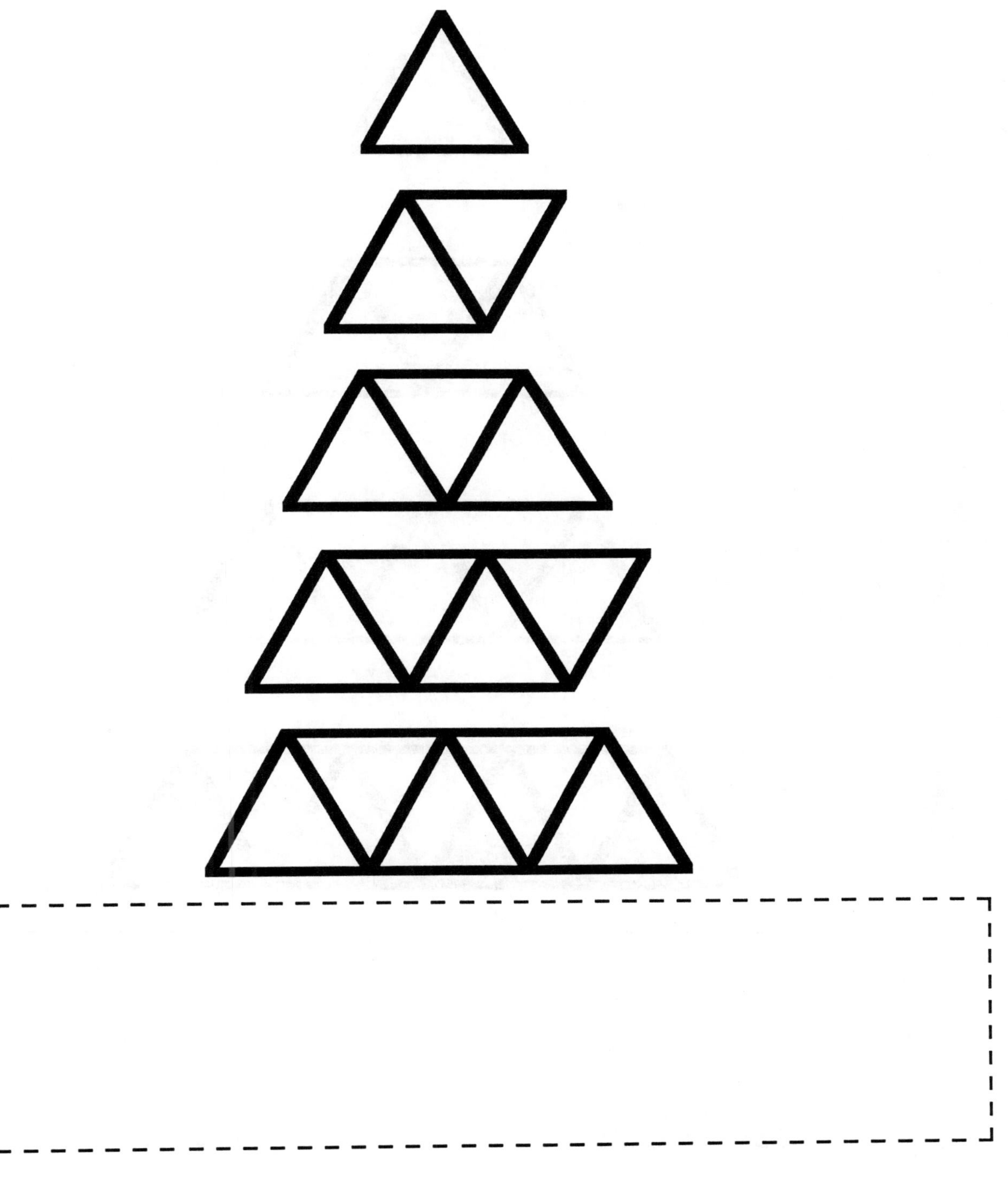

## SEQUENCES OF FIGURES

Use PATTERN BLOCK triangles to make and cover the figures below.
Use triangles to make a figure that continues the pattern and place it in the dotted box.
Trace the blocks in the figure and color the pictures to match the blocks.

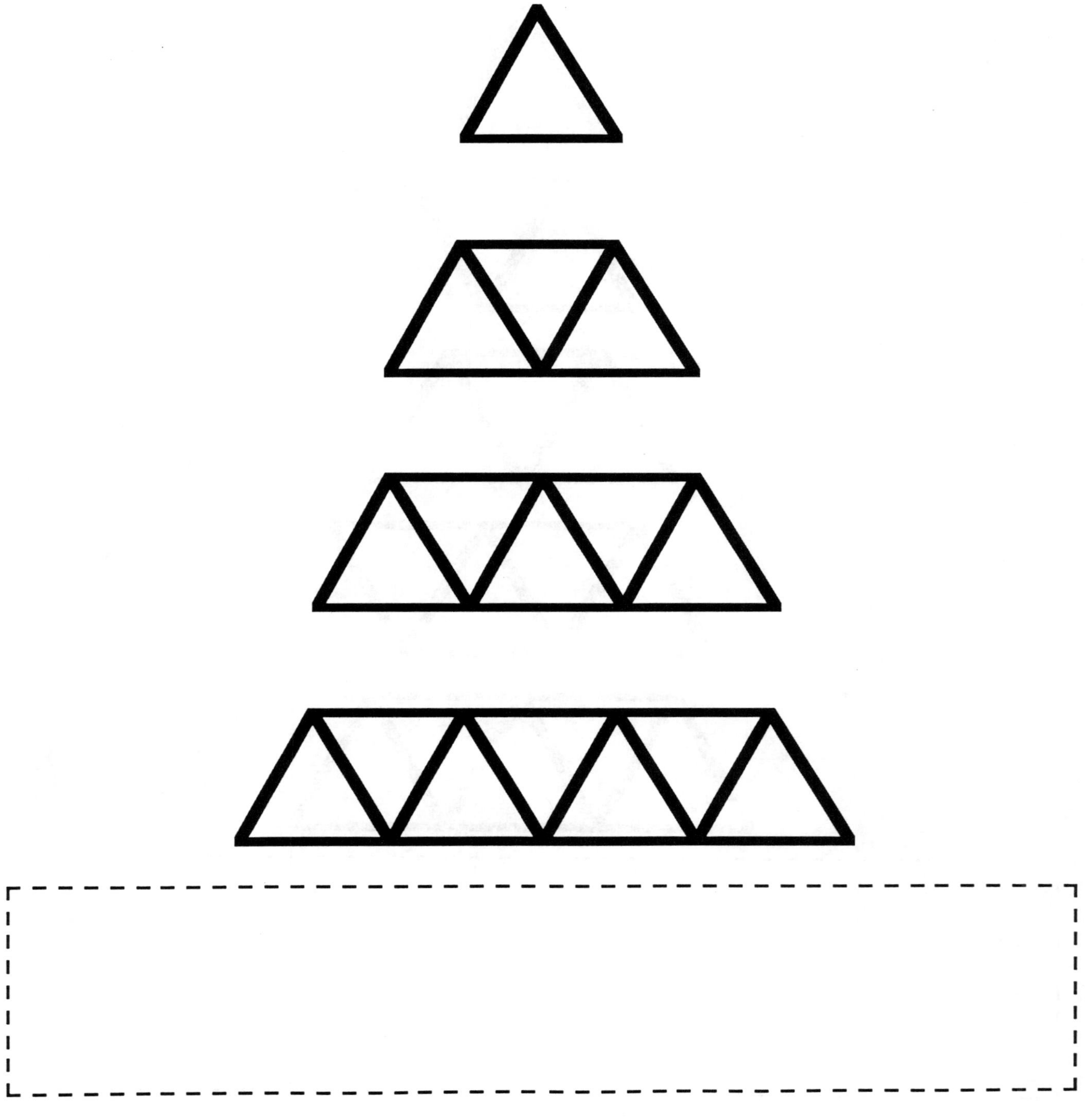

## SEQUENCES OF FIGURES

Use two different colors of INTERLOCKING CUBES to make and cover the figures below.
Make the figure that completes the pattern and place it in the dotted box.
Trace the figure and color the pictures to match the cubes.

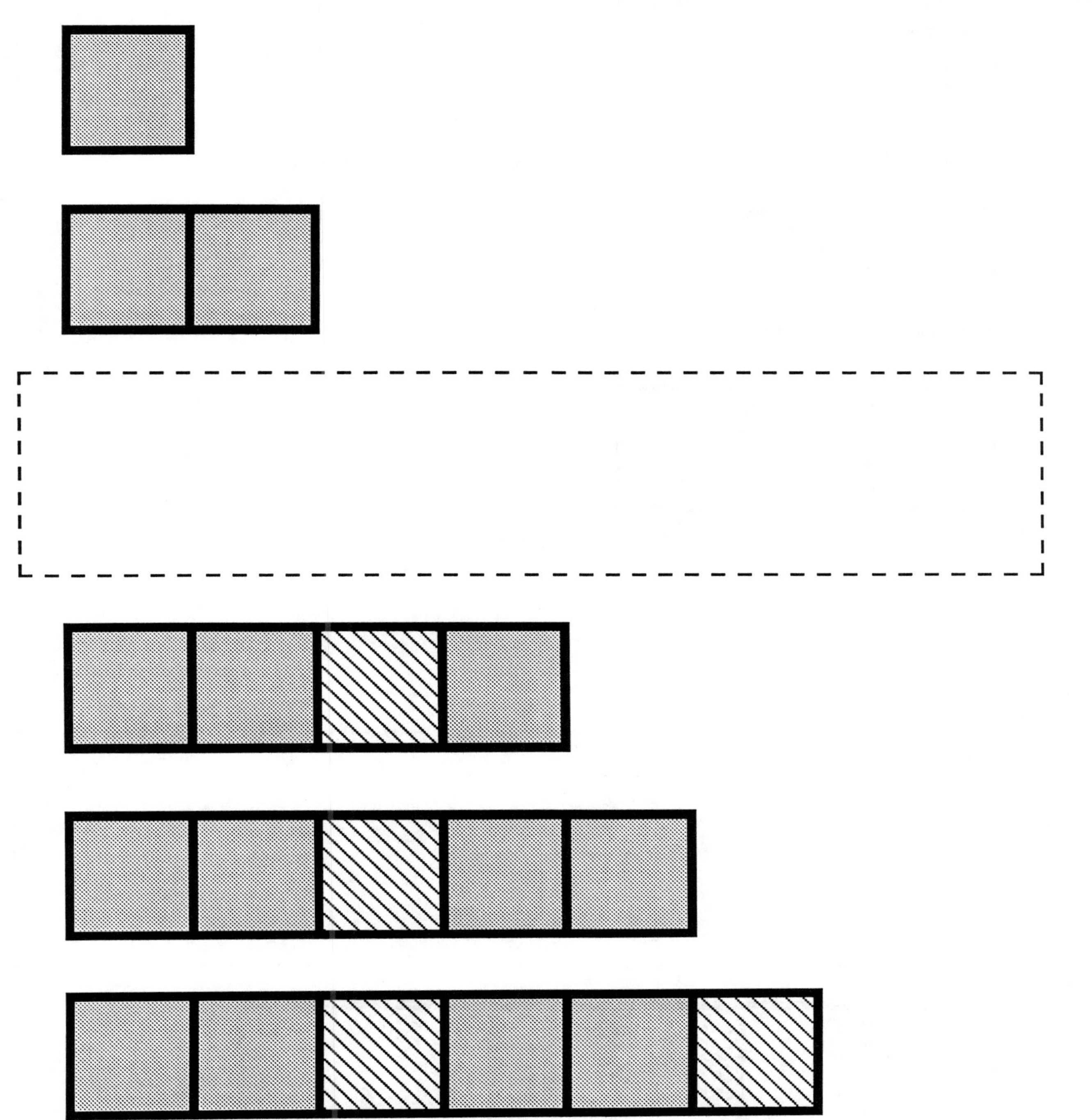

# SEQUENCES OF FIGURES

Use two different colors of INTERLOCKING CUBES to make and cover the figures below. Make the TWO figures that complete the pattern and place them in the dotted boxes. Trace the figures and color the pictures to match the cubes.

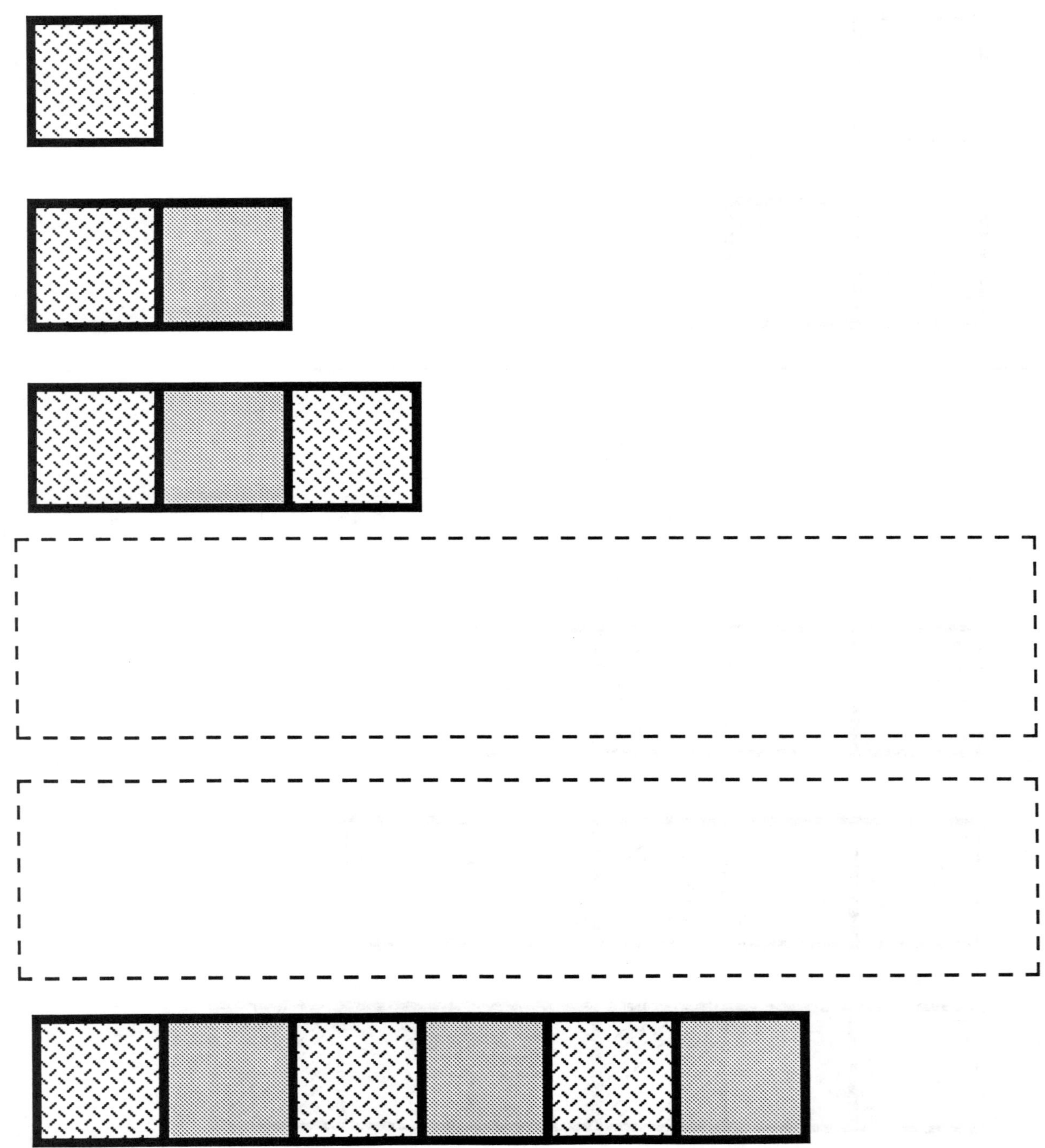

# SEQUENCES OF SHAPES

Place a PATTERN BLOCK on each shape below.
Make a sequence of blocks to complete the pattern and place it in the dotted box.
Trace the blocks and color the pictures.

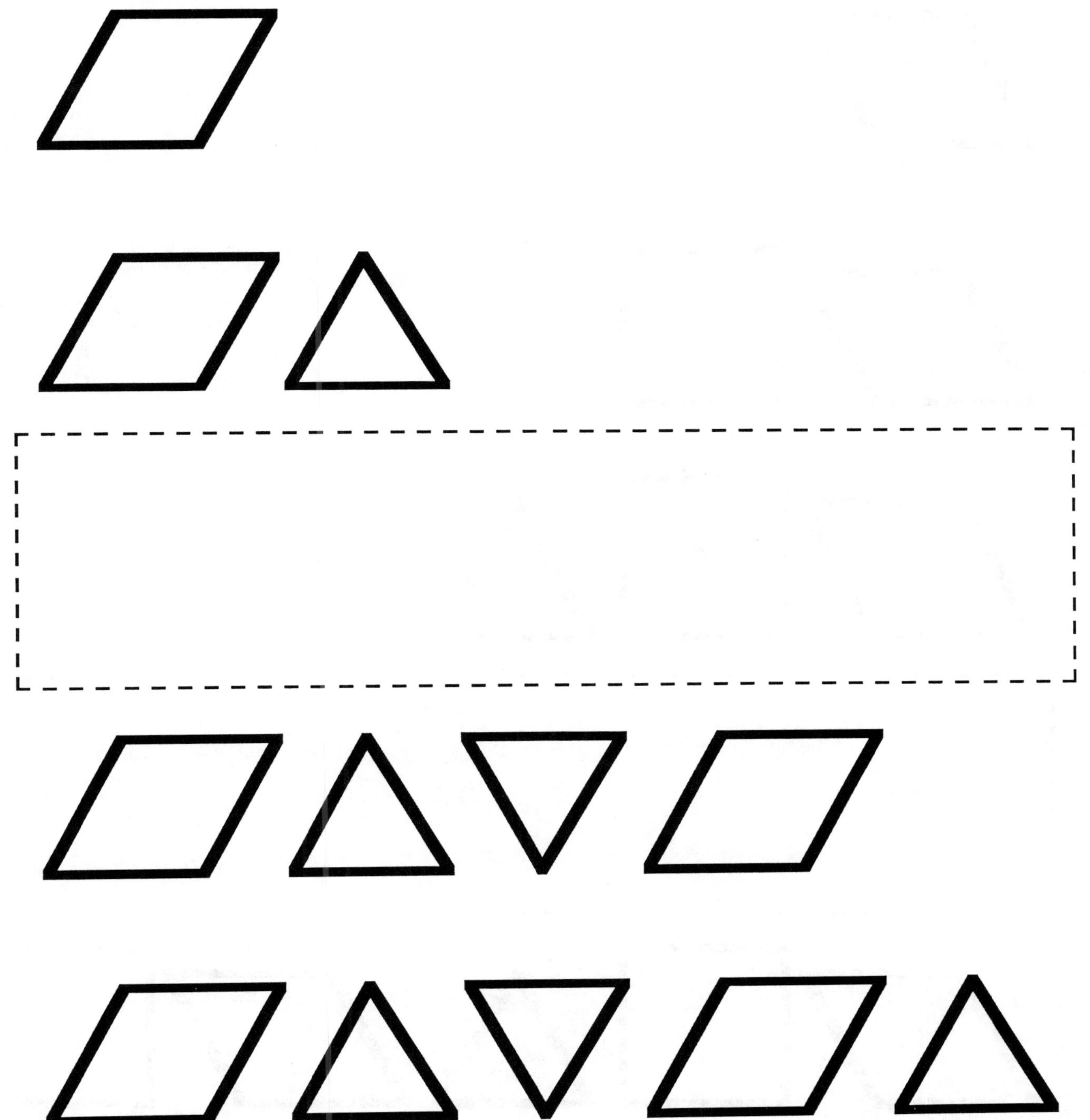

## SEQUENCES OF SHAPES

Place a PATTERN BLOCK on each shape below.
Make a sequence of blocks to complete the pattern and place it in the dotted box.
Trace the blocks and color the pictures.

---

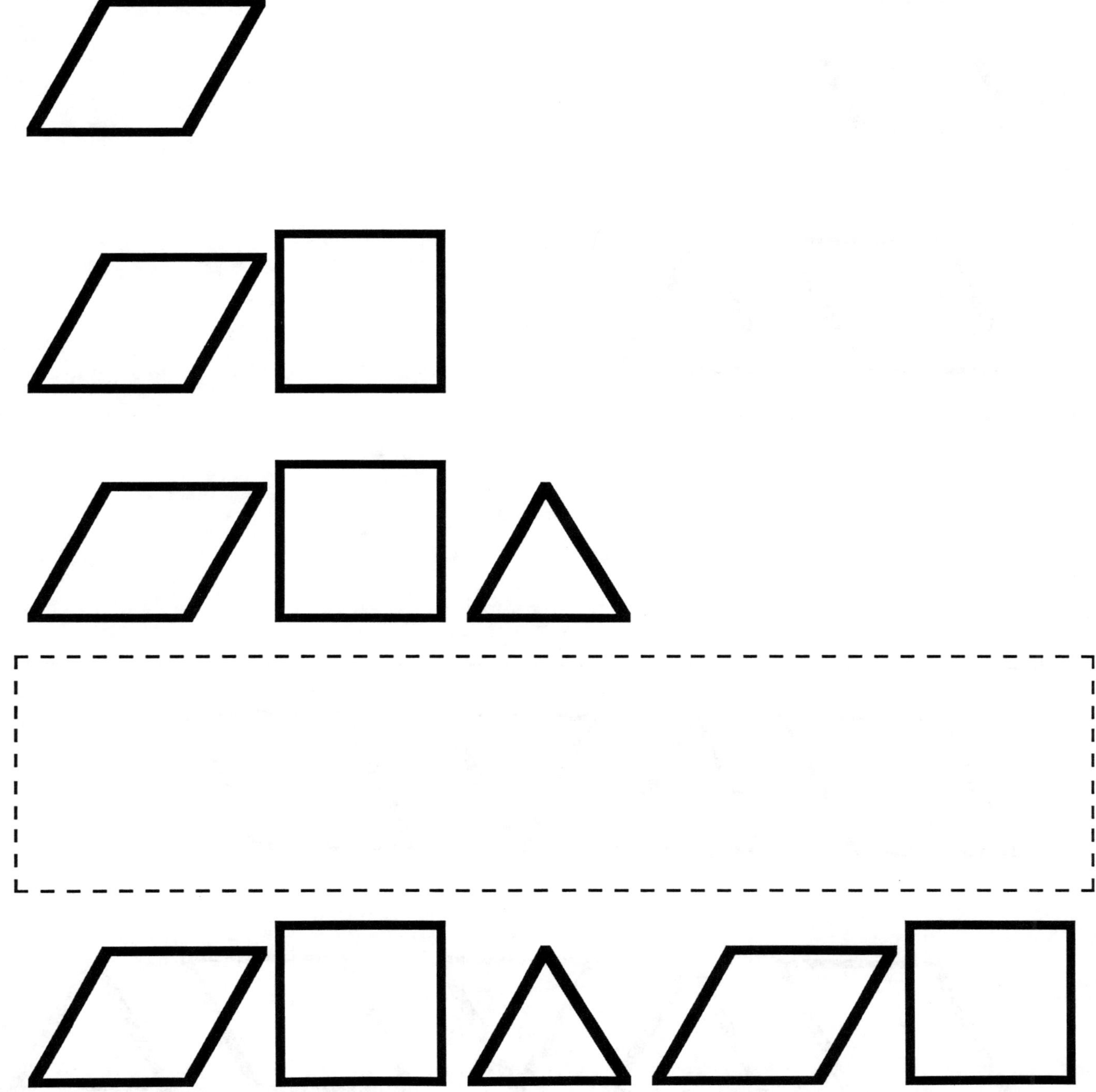

# PAPER FOLDING

On a folded piece of paper, a red PATTERN BLOCK shape is traced and cut out.

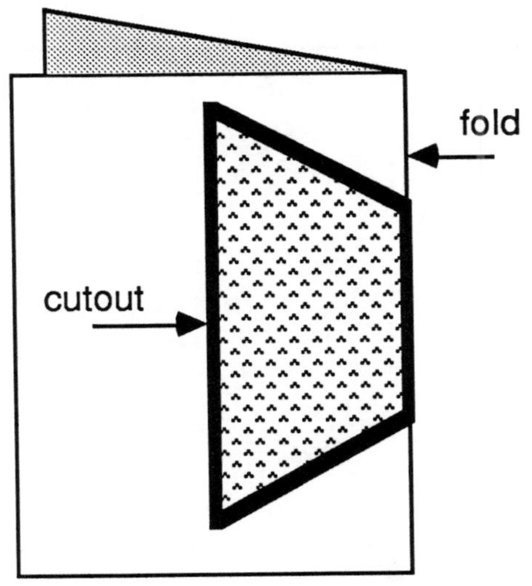


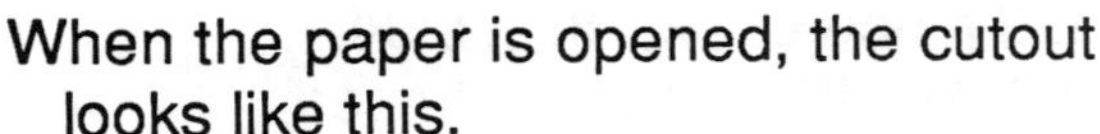
When the paper is opened, the cutout looks like this.

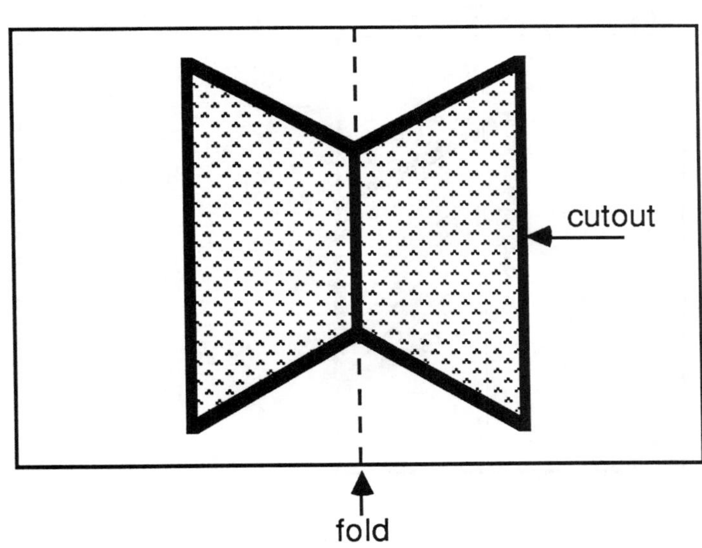


---

On a folded piece of paper, a blue PATTERN BLOCK shape is traced and cut out.

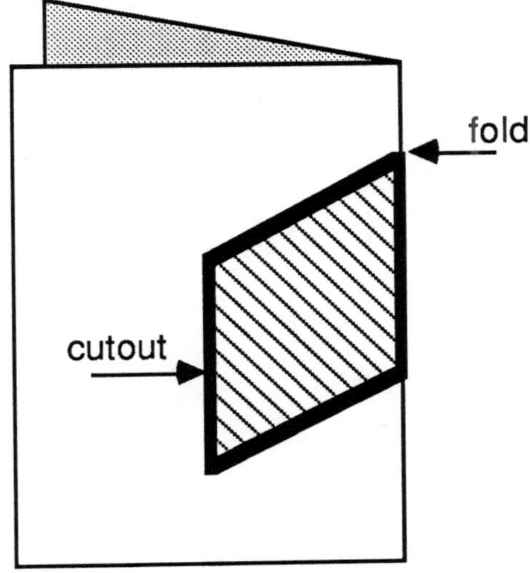


On the opened paper below, place PATTERN BLOCKS to show what the cutout looks like. Trace the blocks and color the picture.

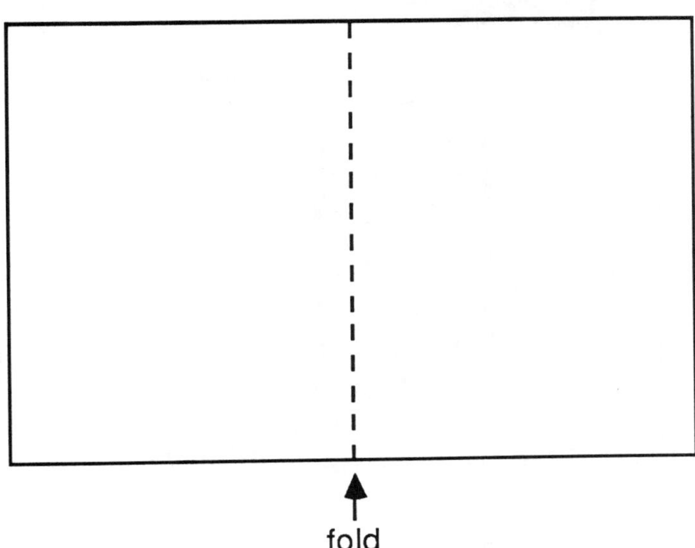

# PAPER FOLDING

On a folded piece of paper, a blue PATTERN BLOCK shape is traced and cut out.

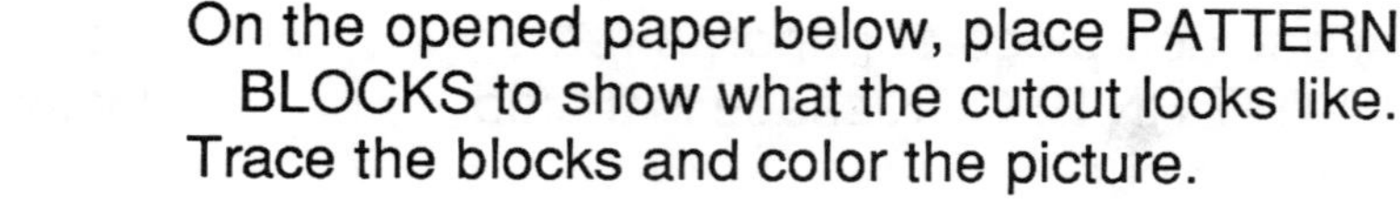

On the opened paper below, place PATTERN BLOCKS to show what the cutout looks like. Trace the blocks and color the picture.

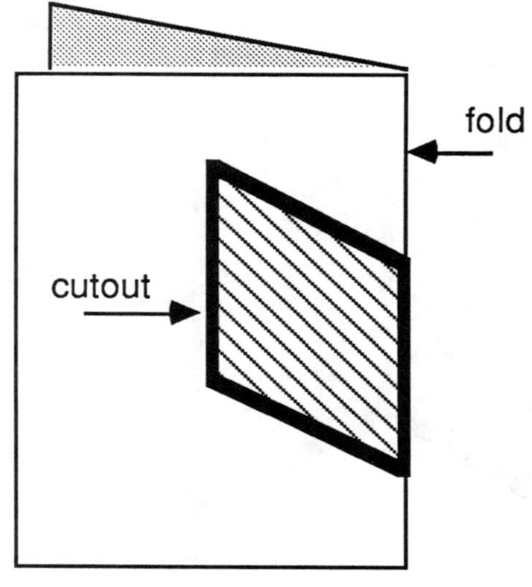


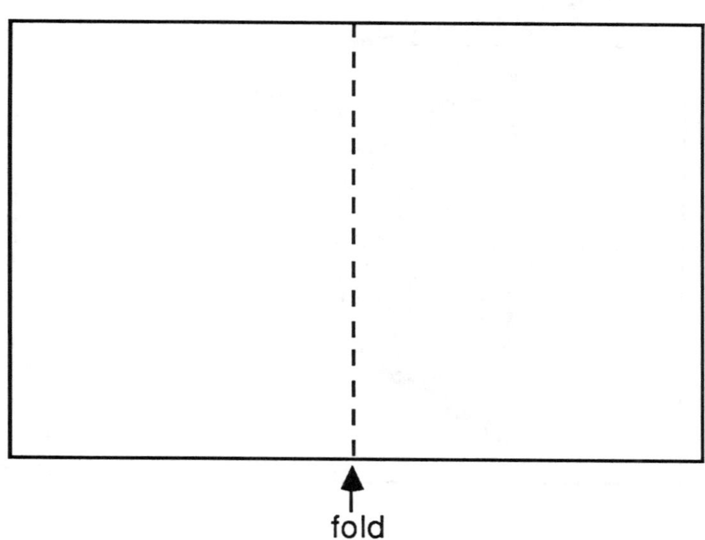


---

On a folded piece of paper, a red PATTERN BLOCK shape is traced and cut out.

On the opened paper below, place PATTERN BLOCKS to show what the cutout looks like. Trace the blocks and color the picture.

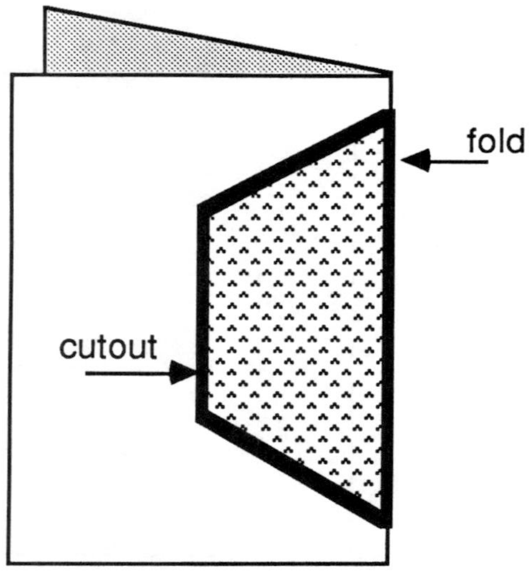


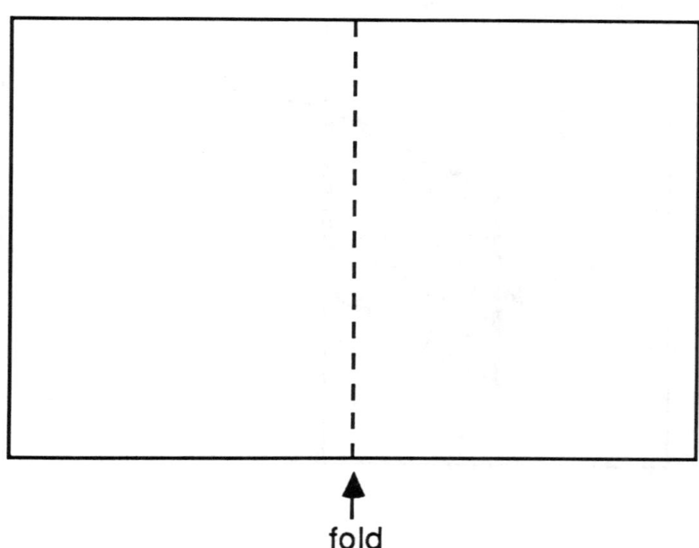

# PAPER FOLDING

On a folded piece of paper, a tan PATTERN BLOCK shape is traced and cut out.

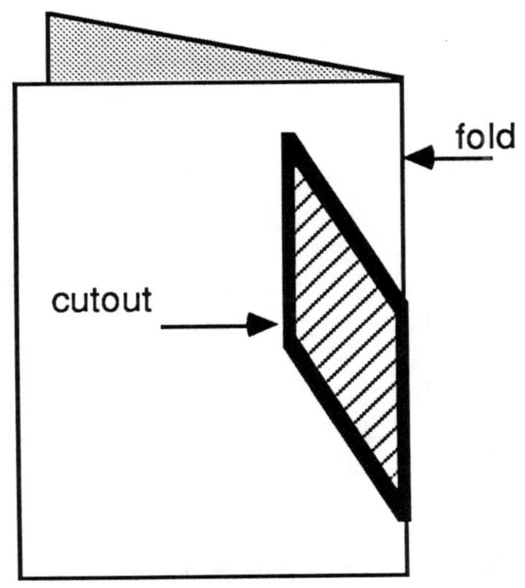


On the opened paper below, place PATTERN BLOCKS to show what the cutout looks like. Trace the blocks and color the picture.

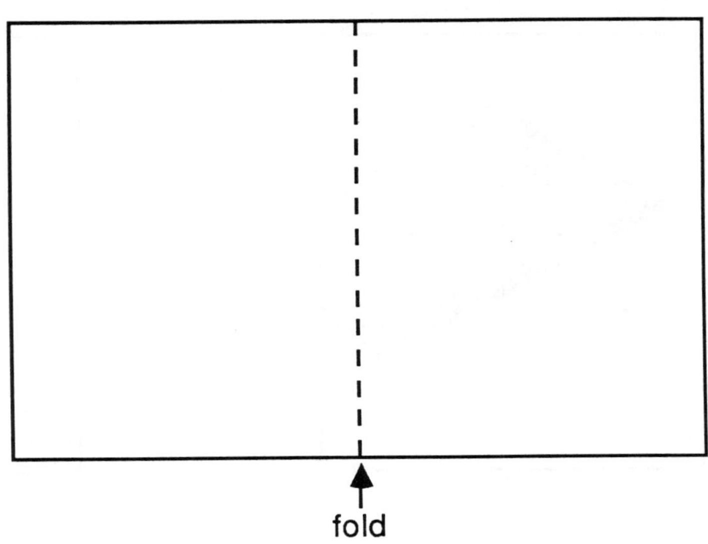


---

On a folded piece of paper, an orange PATTERN BLOCK shape is traced and cut out.

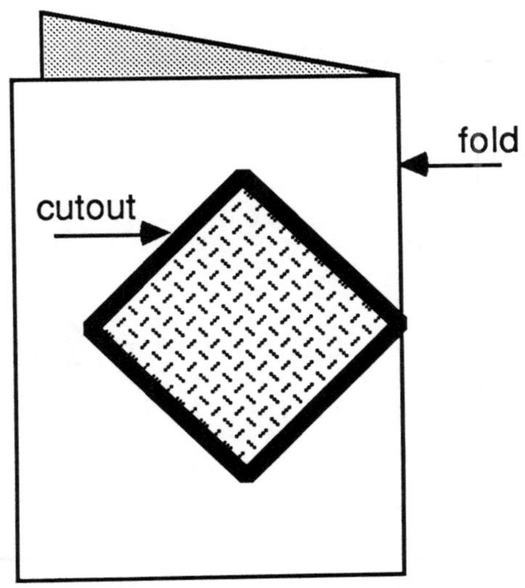


On the opened paper below, place PATTERN BLOCKS to show what the cutout looks like. Trace the blocks and color the picture.

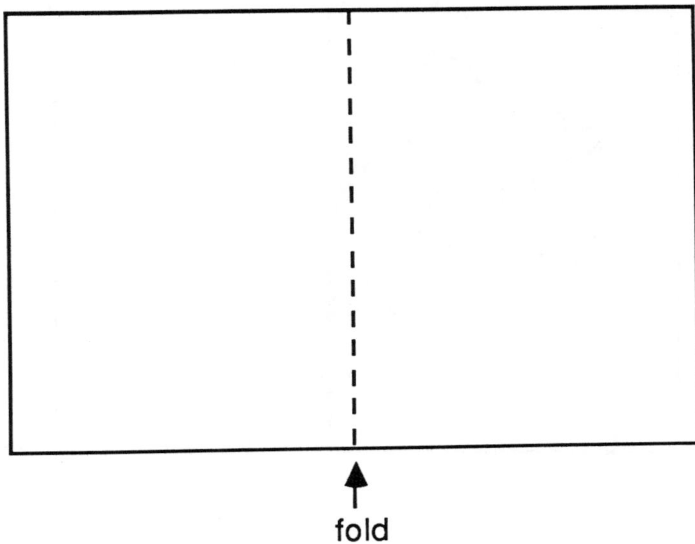

# PAPER FOLDING

On a folded piece of paper, a red PATTERN BLOCK shape is traced and cut out.

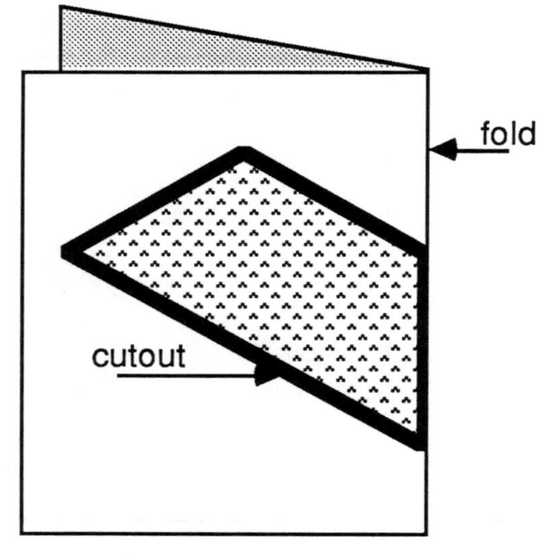


On the opened paper below, place PATTERN BLOCKS to show what the cutout looks like. Trace the blocks and color the picture.

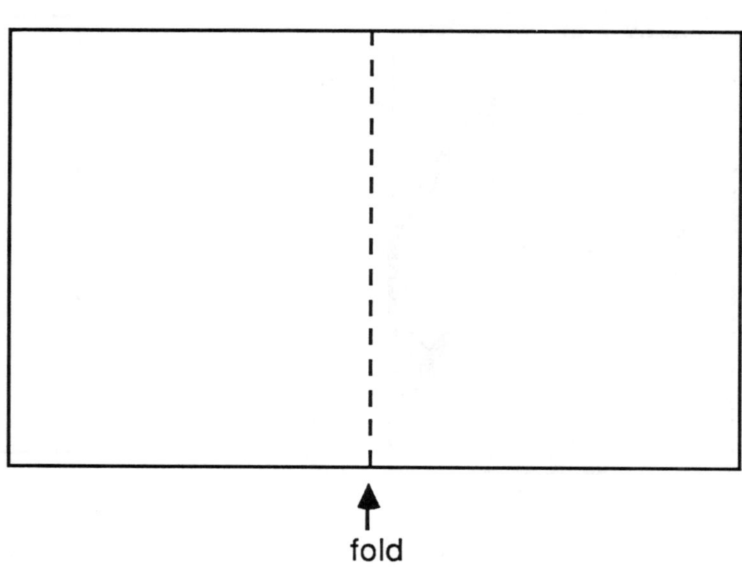


---

On a folded piece of paper, tan and green PATTERN BLOCK shapes are traced and cut out.

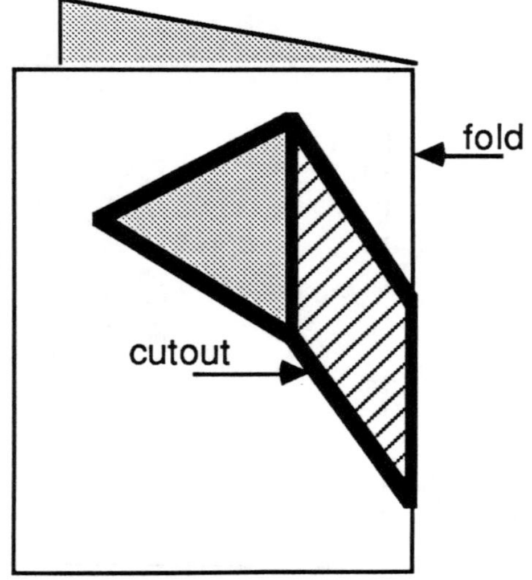


On the opened paper below, place PATTERN BLOCKS to show what the cutout looks like. Trace the blocks and color the picture.

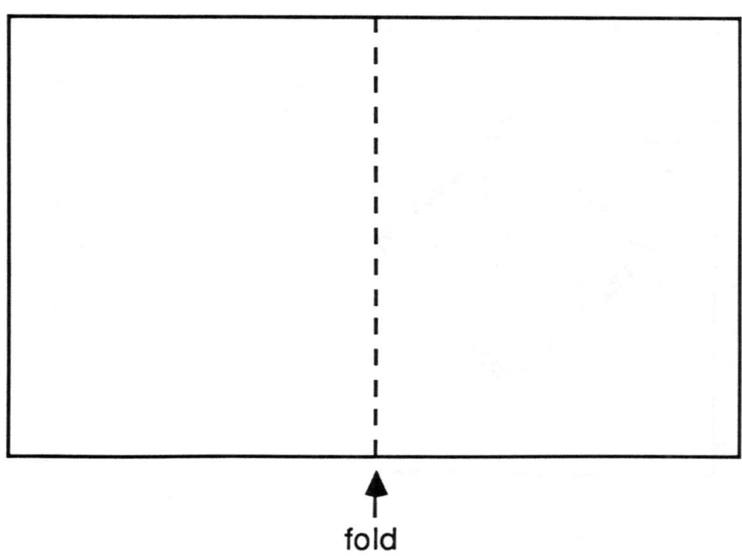

# PAPER FOLDING

On the folded piece of paper below, place a PATTERN BLOCK to show which shape to cut out to make the shaded design. Trace the block and color the picture.

This is what the paper looks like when it is opened.

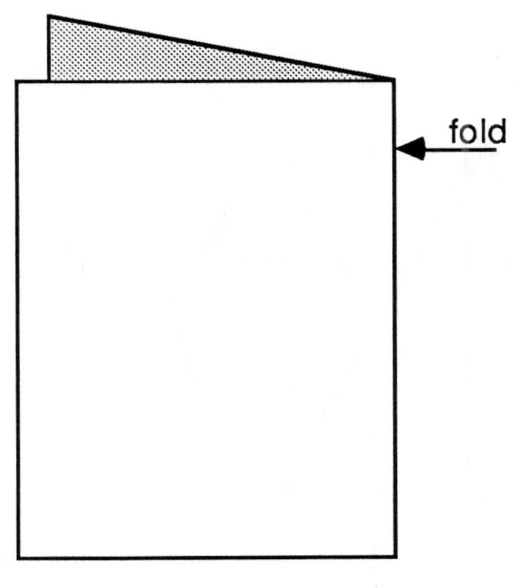


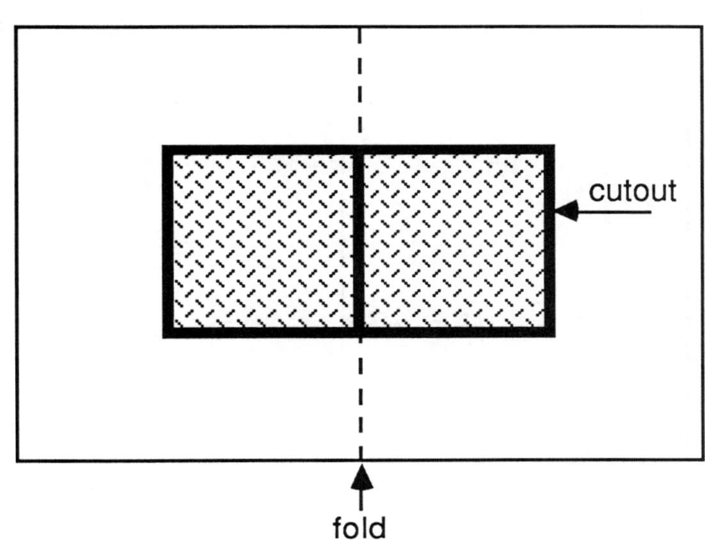


On the folded piece of paper below, place a PATTERN BLOCK to show which shape to cut out to make the shaded design. Trace the block and color the picture.

This is what the paper looks like when it is opened.

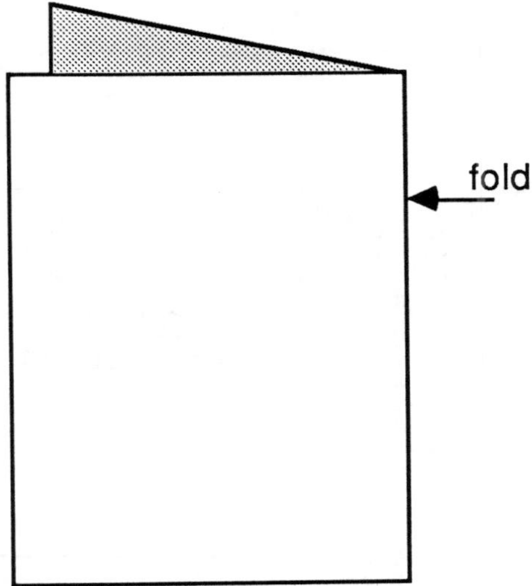


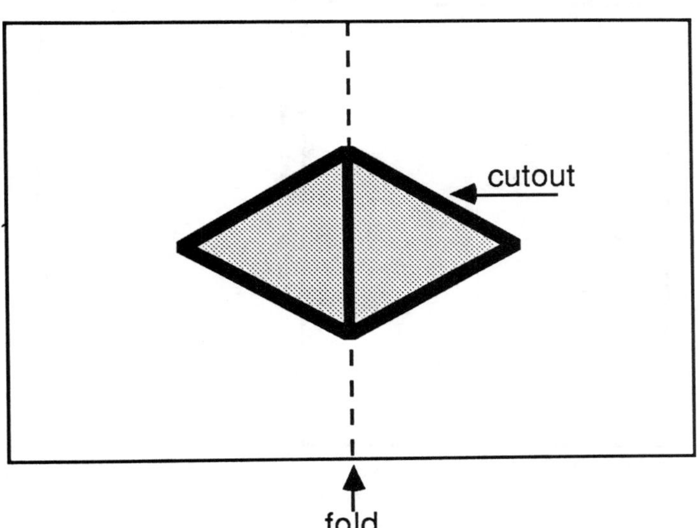

# PAPER FOLDING

On the folded piece of paper below, place a PATTERN BLOCK to show which shape to cut out to make the shaded design. Trace the block and color the picture.

This is what the paper looks like when it is opened.

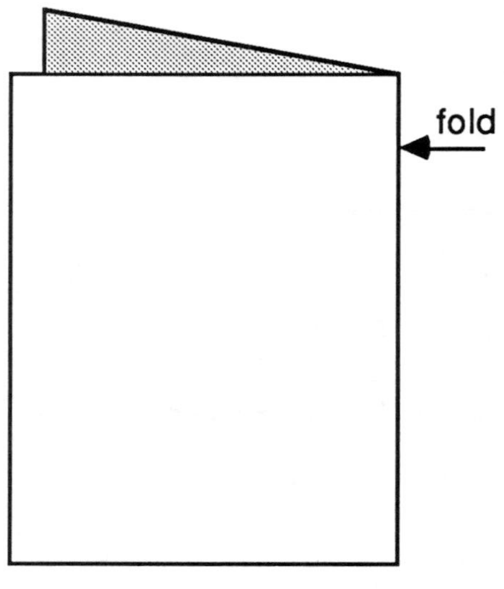


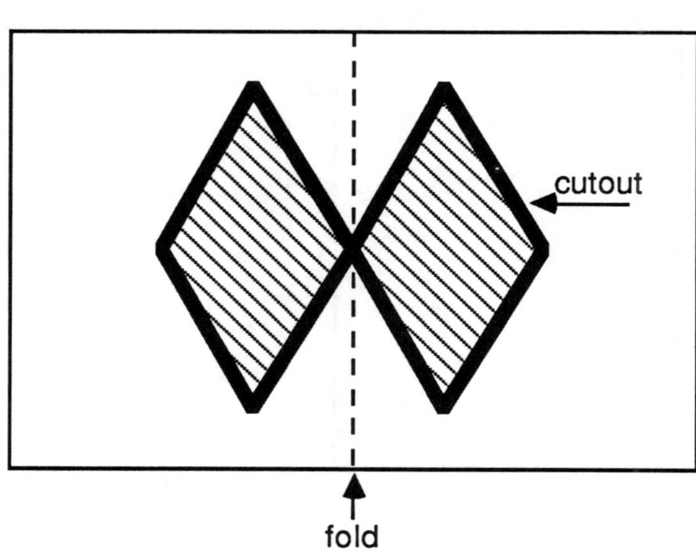


---

On the folded piece of paper below, place a PATTERN BLOCK to show which shape to cut out to make the shaded design. Trace the block and color the picture.

This is what the paper looks like when it is opened.

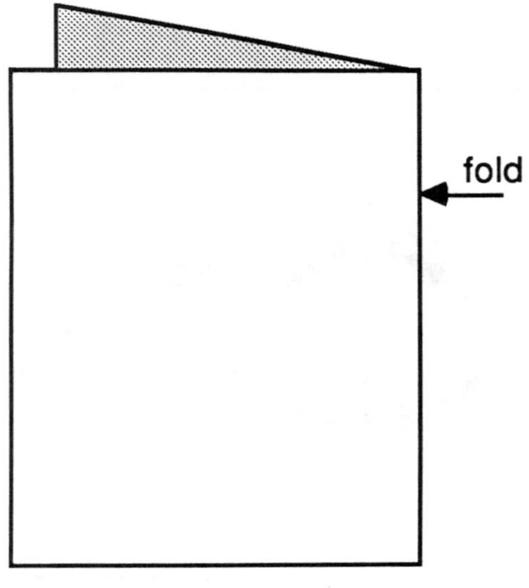


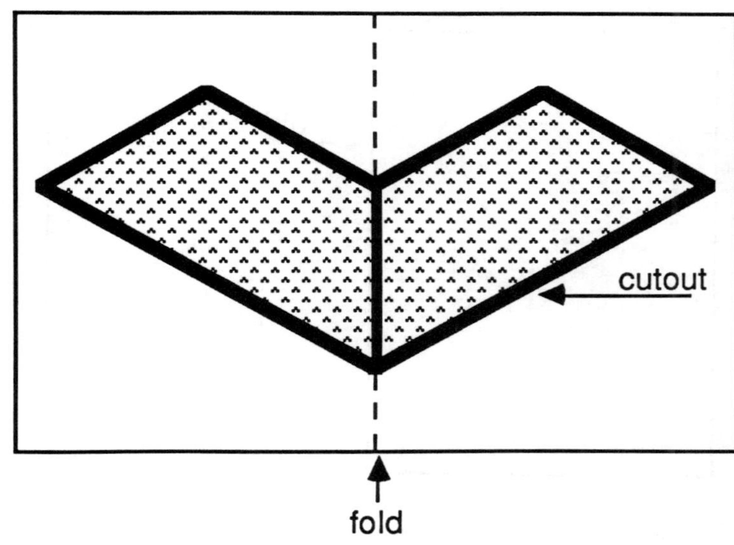

# CLASSIFYING—COLOR AND SHAPE

Place a red (R), yellow (Y), or blue (B) ATTRIBUTE BLOCK on each shape below.
In each dotted box, place a block with the same color and same shape.
Trace the blocks and color the pictures to match.

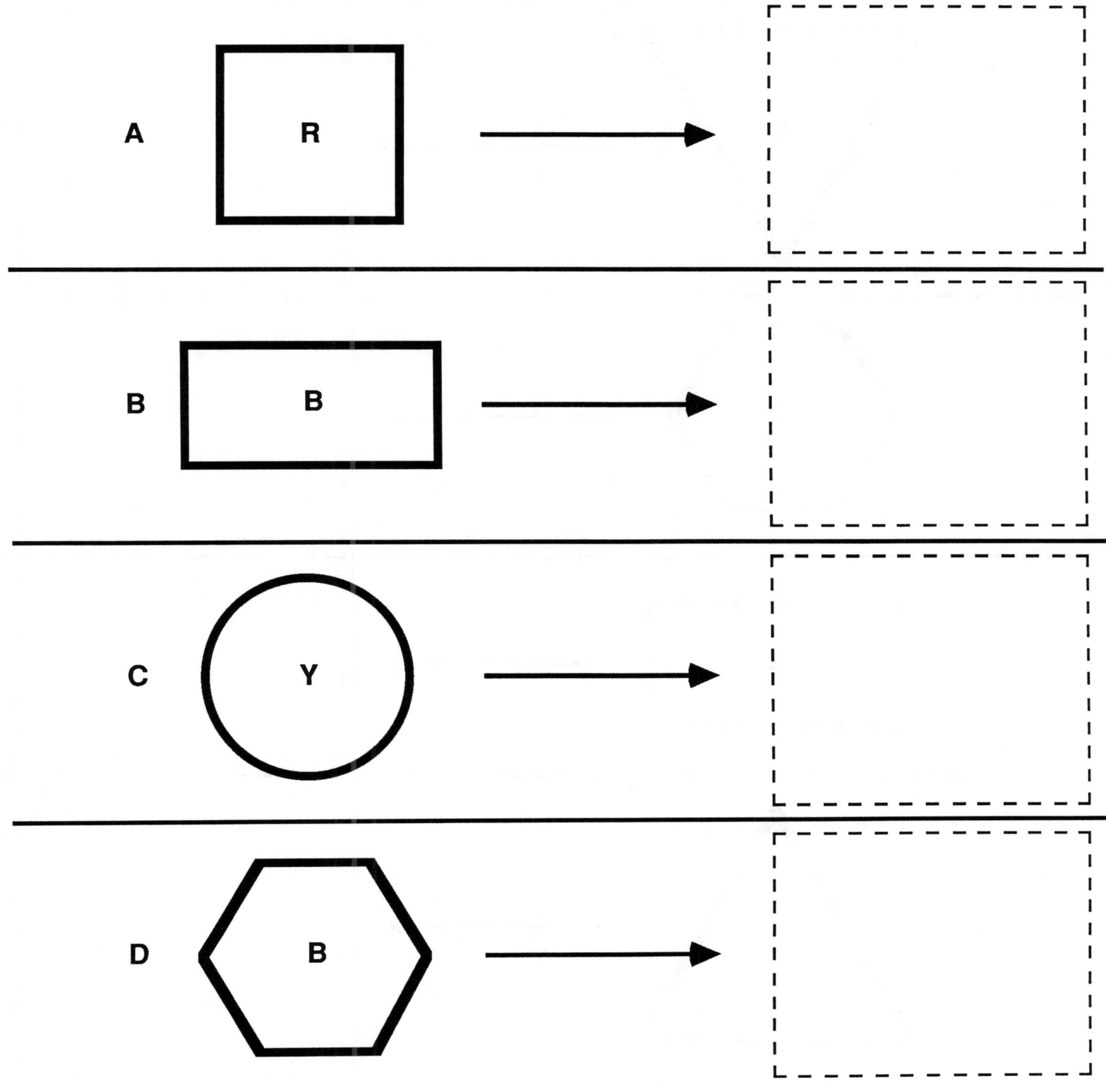

## CLASSIFYING—COLOR AND SHAPE

Place a red (R), yellow (Y), or blue (B) ATTRIBUTE BLOCK on each shape below.
In each dotted box, place a block with the same color and same shape.
Trace the block and color the pictures to match.

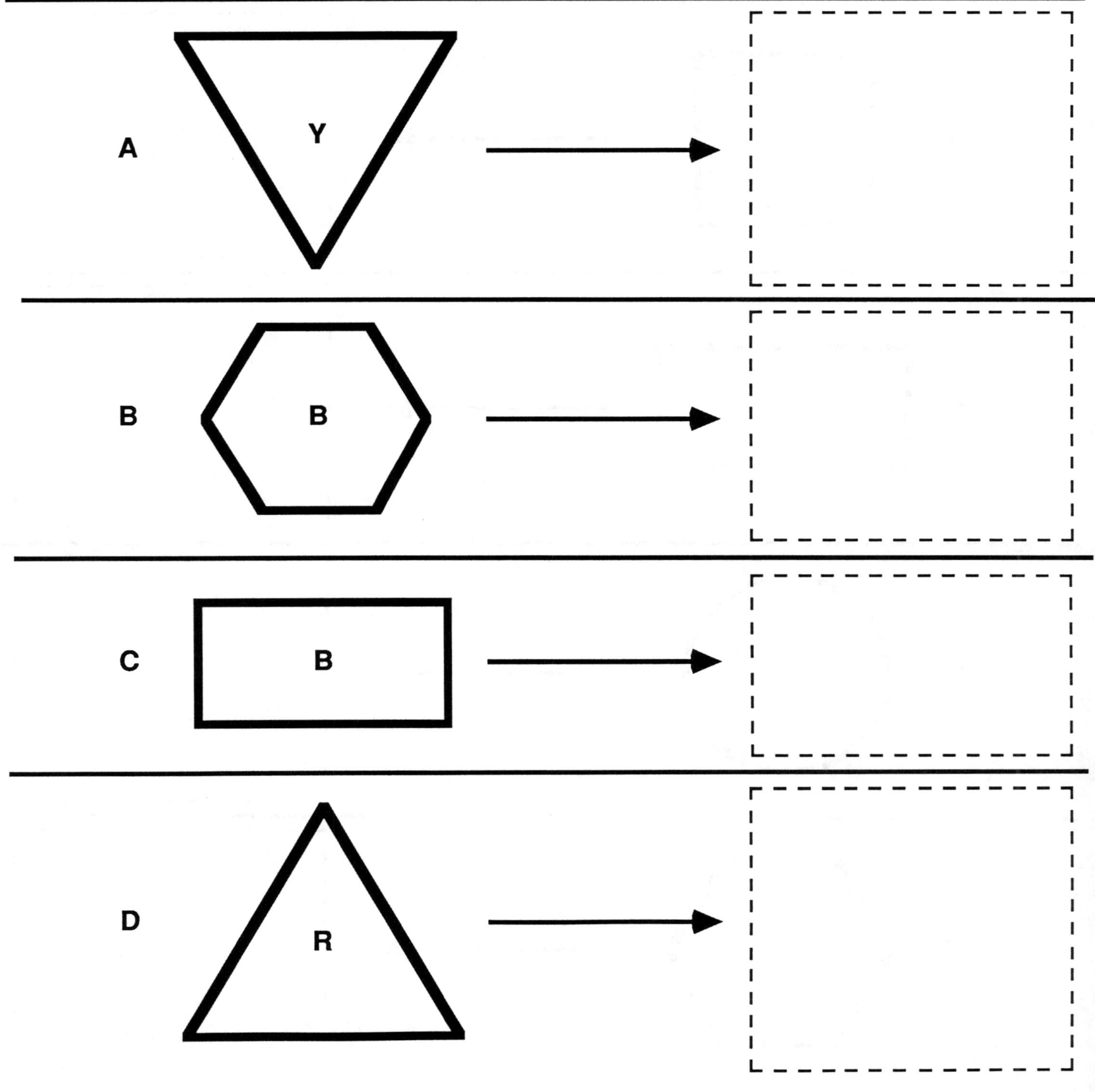

## CLASSIFYING—COLOR AND SHAPE

Place a yellow (Y) or blue (B) ATTRIBUTE BLOCK on each shape below.
In each dotted box, place a block with the same shape but a different color.
Trace the blocks and color the pictures to match.

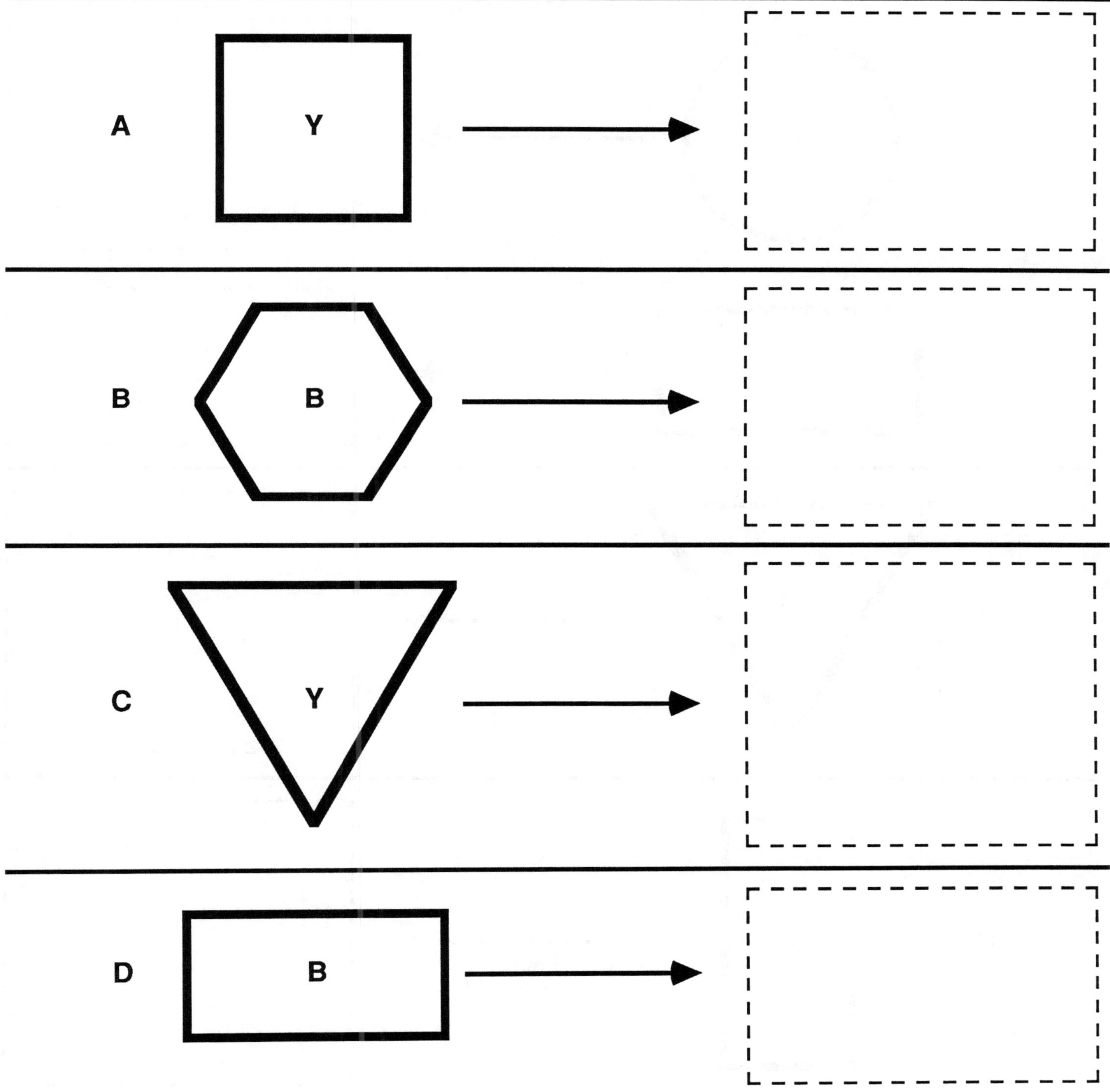

# CLASSIFYING—COLOR AND SHAPE

Place a red (R), yellow (Y), or blue (B) ATTRIBUTE BLOCK on each shape below.
In each dotted box, place a block with the same shape but a different color.
Trace the blocks and color the pictures to match.

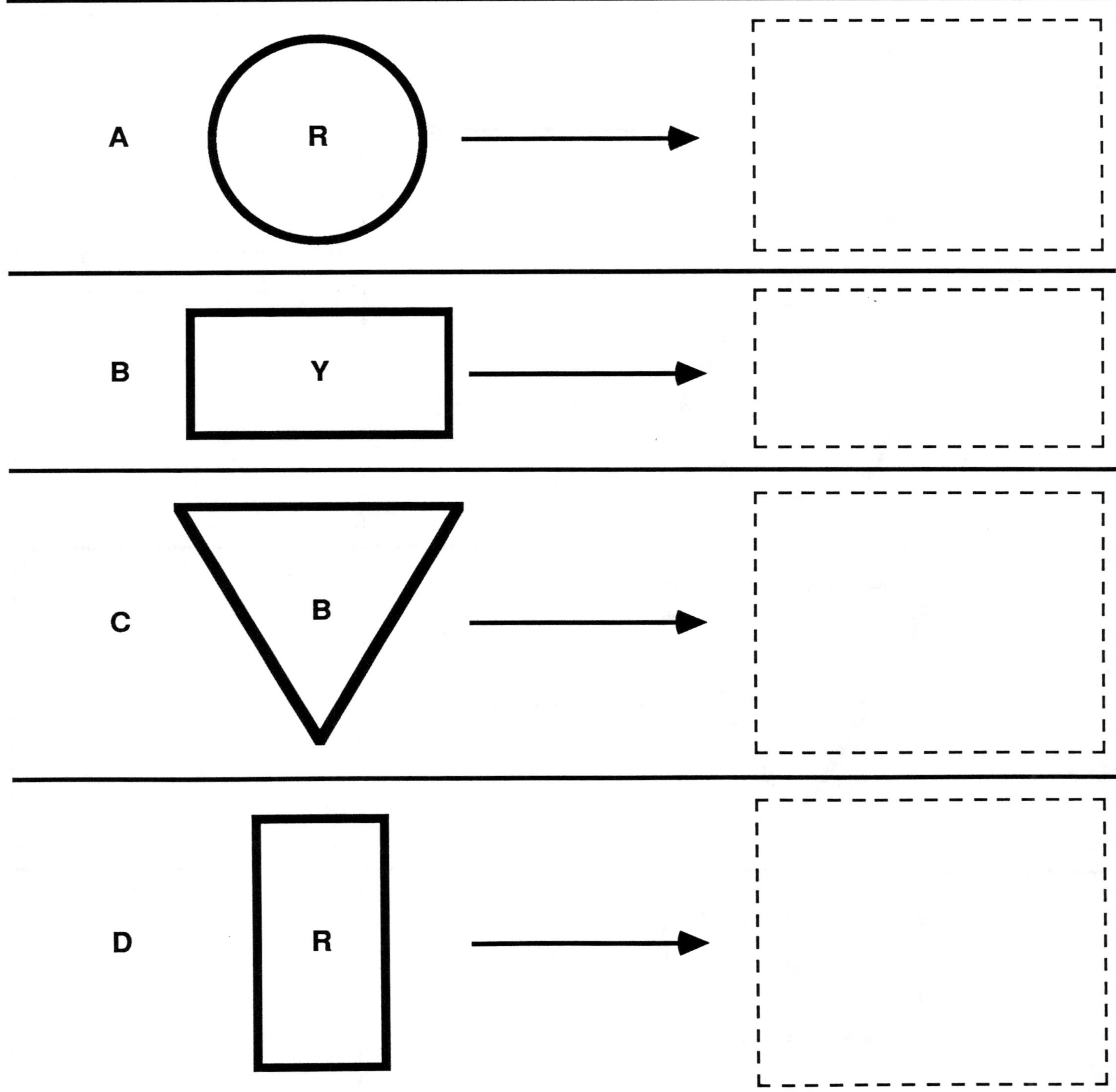

## CLASSIFYING—COLOR AND SHAPE

Place a red (R), yellow (Y), or blue (B) ATTRIBUTE BLOCK on each shape below.
In each dotted box, place a block with the same color but a different shape.
Trace the blocks and color the pictures to match.

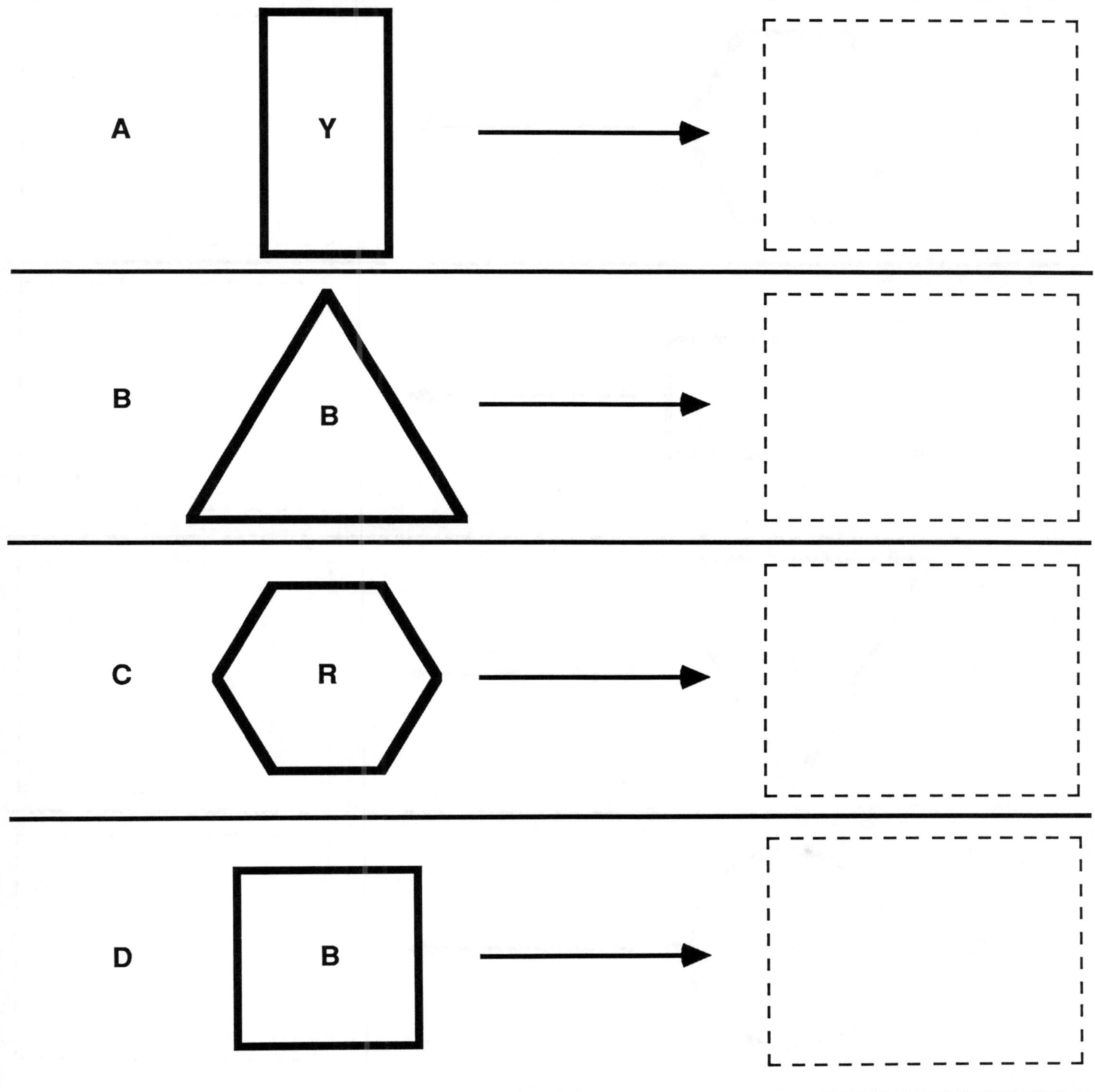

## CLASSIFYING—COLOR AND SHAPE

Place a red (R), yellow (Y), or blue (B) ATTRIBUTE BLOCK on each shape below.
In each dotted box, place a block with the same color but a different shape.
Trace the blocks and color the pictures to match.

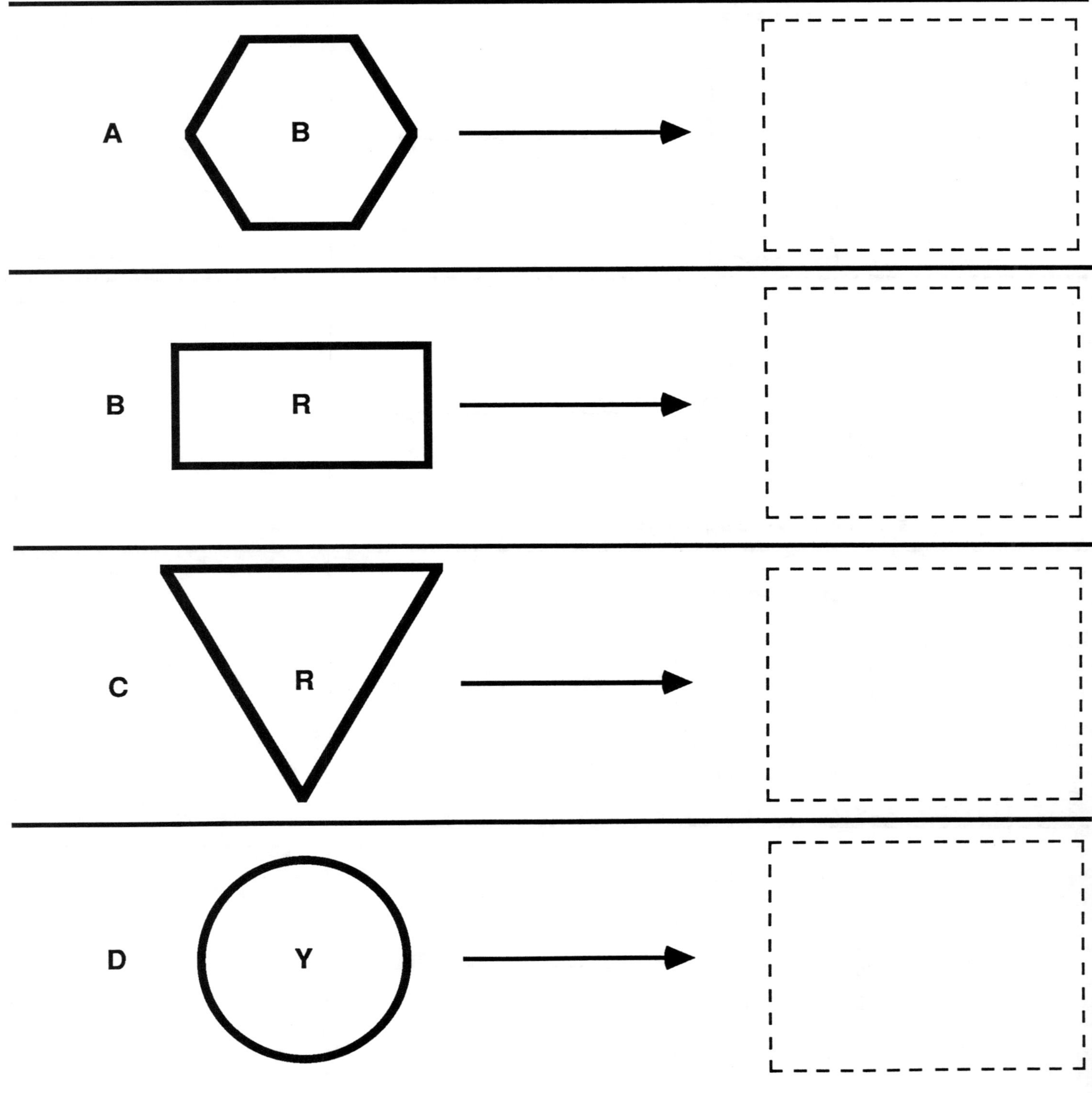

# CLASSIFYING—COLOR AND SHAPE

Place a red (R), yellow (Y), or blue (B) ATTRIBUTE BLOCK on each shape below.
In each dotted box, place a block with a different color and different shape.
Trace the blocks and color the pictures to match.

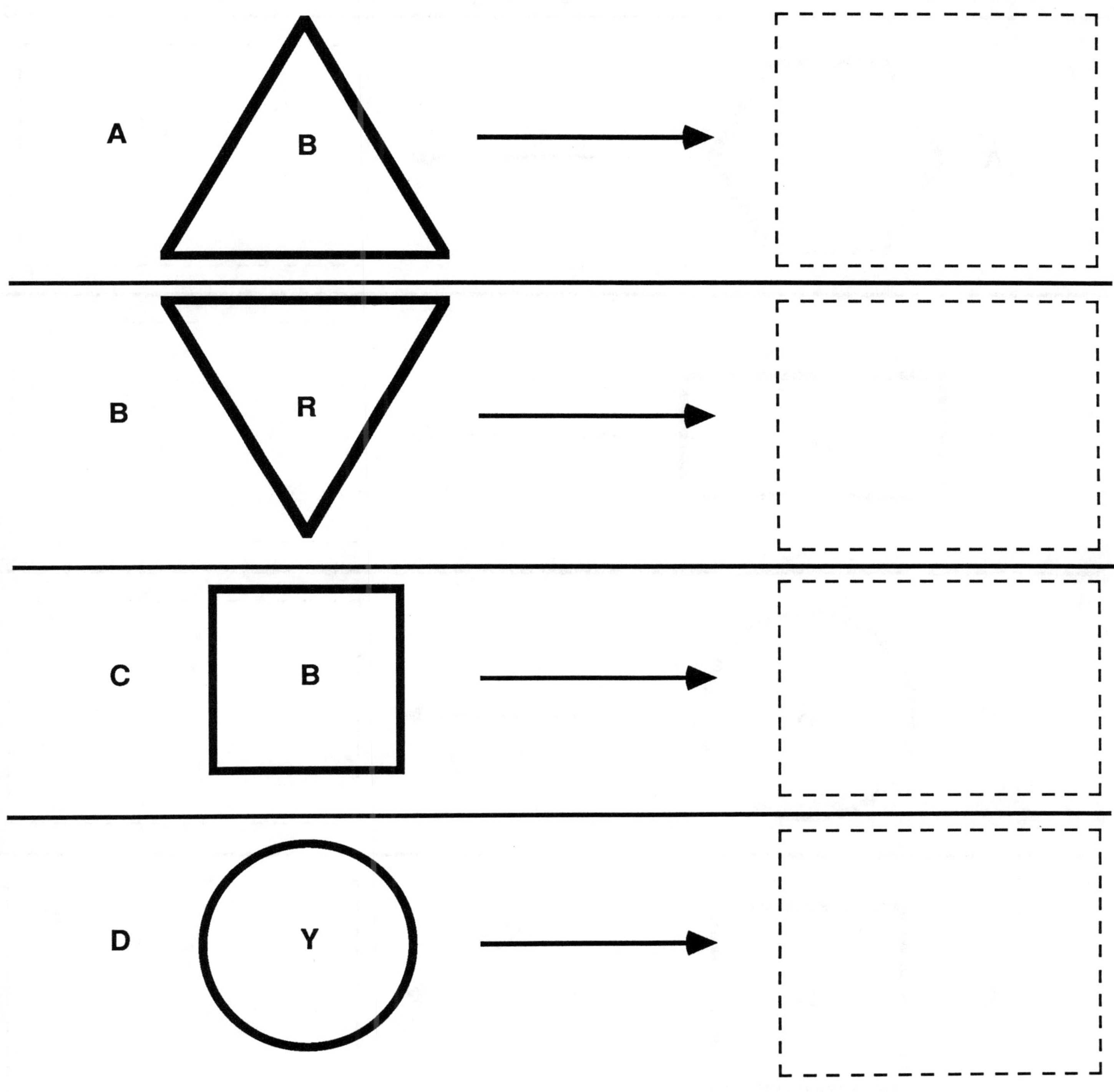

## CLASSIFYING—COLOR AND SHAPE

Place a red (R), yellow (Y), or blue (B) ATTRIBUTE BLOCK on each shape below.
In each dotted box, place a block with a different color and different shape.
Trace the blocks and color the pictures to match.

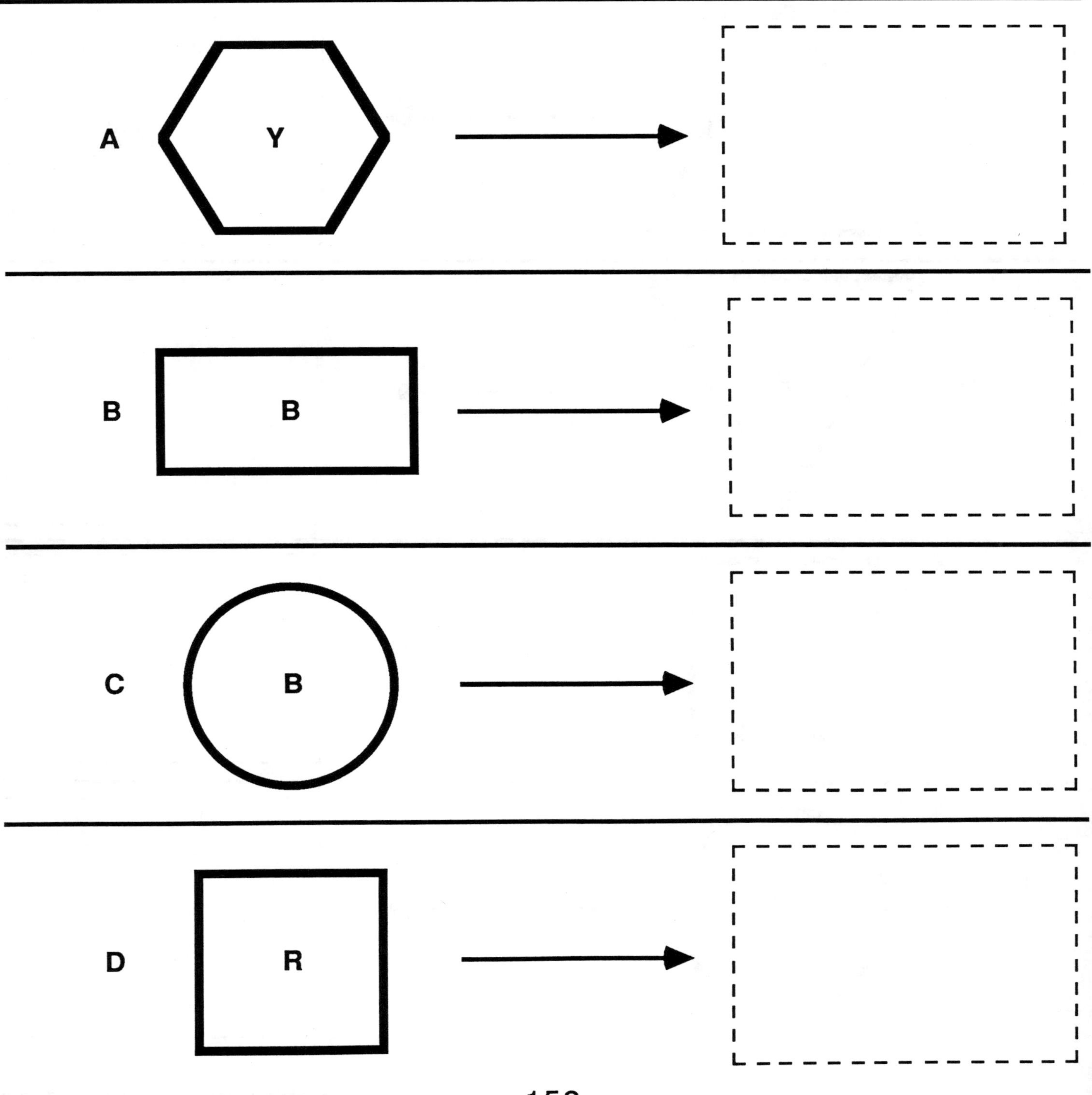

# CLASSIFYING—COLOR AND SHAPE

Using two different colors of INTERLOCKING CUBES, make two copies of each figure below.

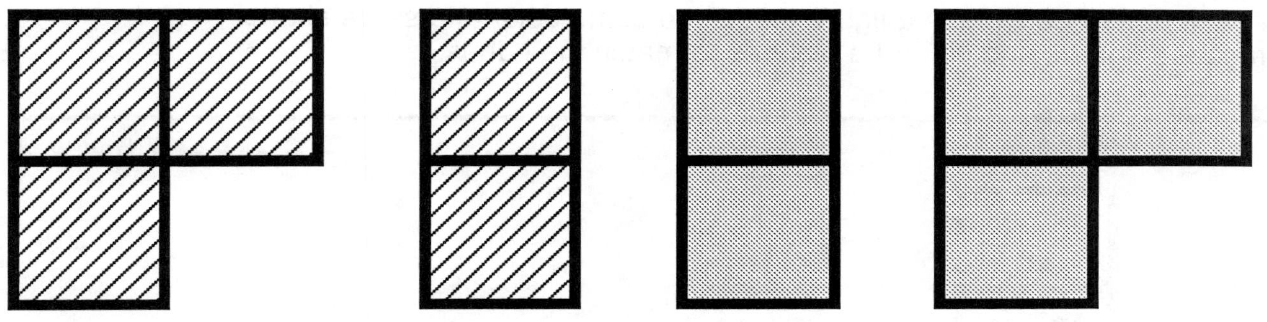

Place a correct INTERLOCKING CUBE figure on each picture below.
In each dotted box, place a figure that is the same color and same shape.
Trace the figures and color the pictures to match the cubes.

A B C

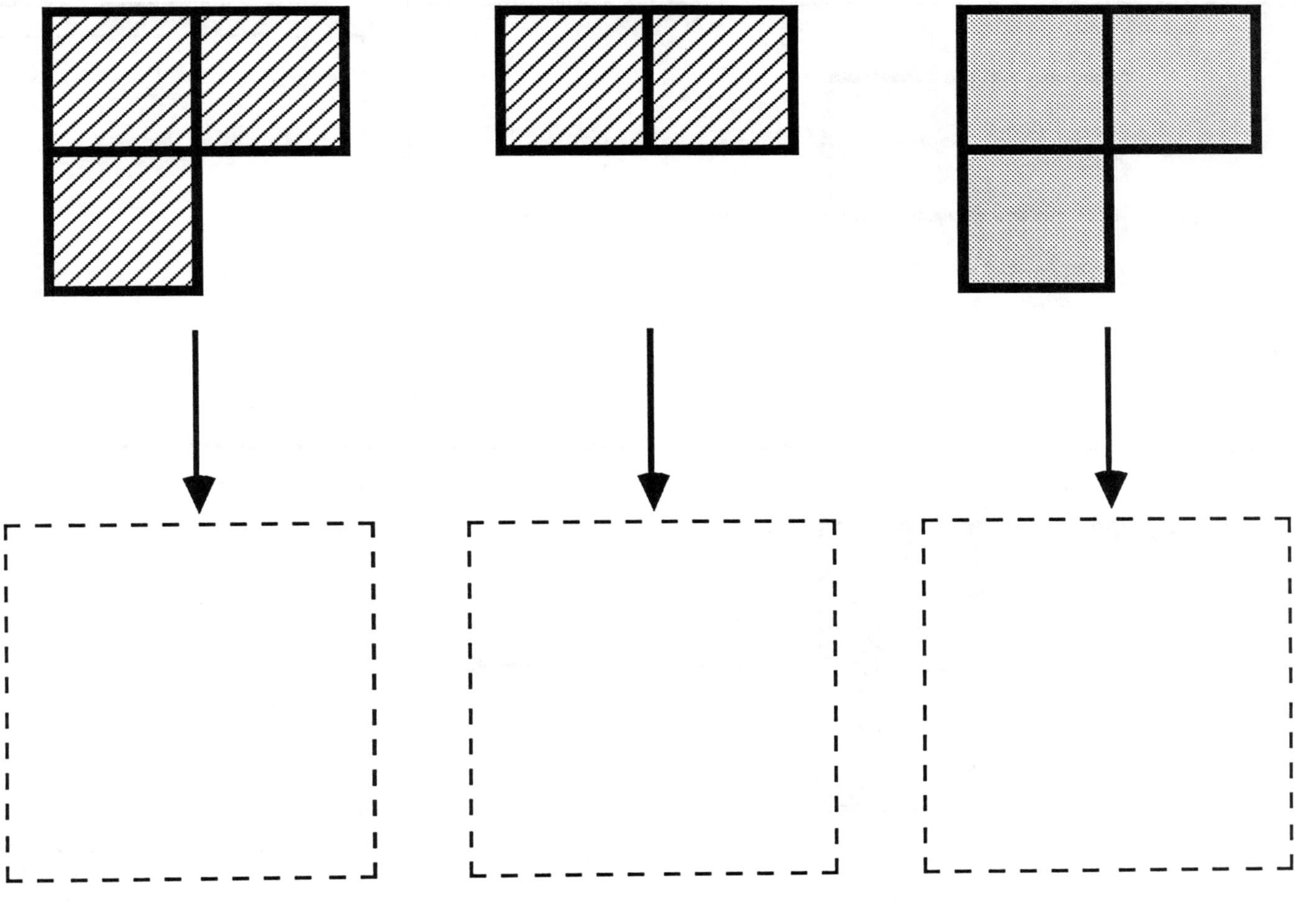

## CLASSIFYING—COLOR AND SHAPE

Use the eight INTERLOCKING CUBE figures constructed for Activity Sheet 153.
Place a correct INTERLOCKING CUBE figure on each picture below.
In each dotted box, place a figure that is the same color and same shape.
Trace the figures and color the pictures to match the cubes.

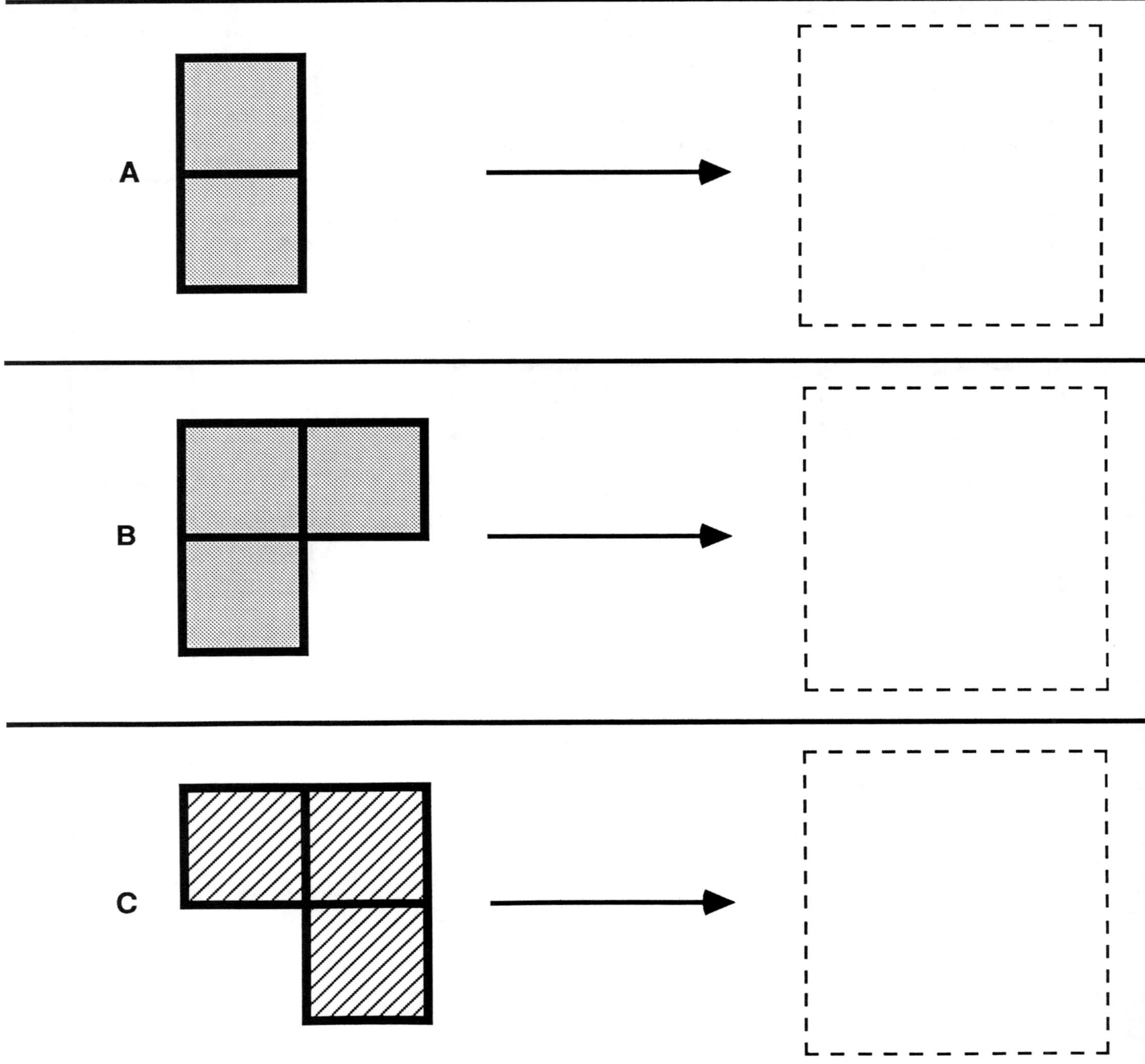

# CLASSIFYING—COLOR AND SHAPE

Using two different colors of INTERLOCKING CUBES, make two copies of each figure below.

Place a correct INTERLOCKING CUBE figure on each picture below.
In each dotted box, place a figure that is the same shape but a different color.
Trace the figures and color the pictures to match the cubes.

A

B

C

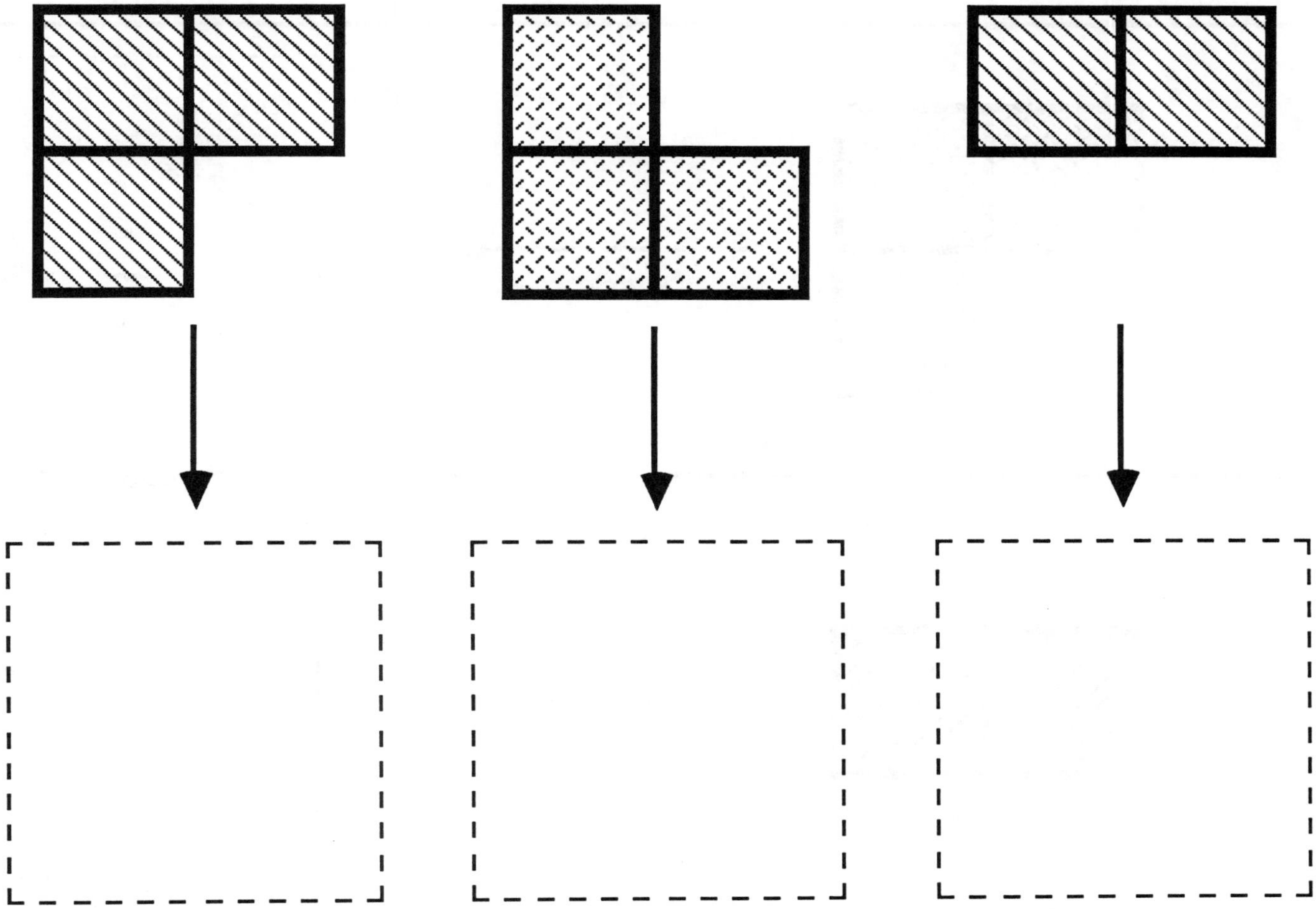

# CLASSIFYING—COLOR AND SHAPE

Use the eight INTERLOCKING CUBE figures constructed for Activity Sheet 155.
Place a correct INTERLOCKING CUBE figure on each picture below.
In each dotted box, place a figure that is the same shape but a different color.
Trace the figures and color the pictures to match the cubes.

A

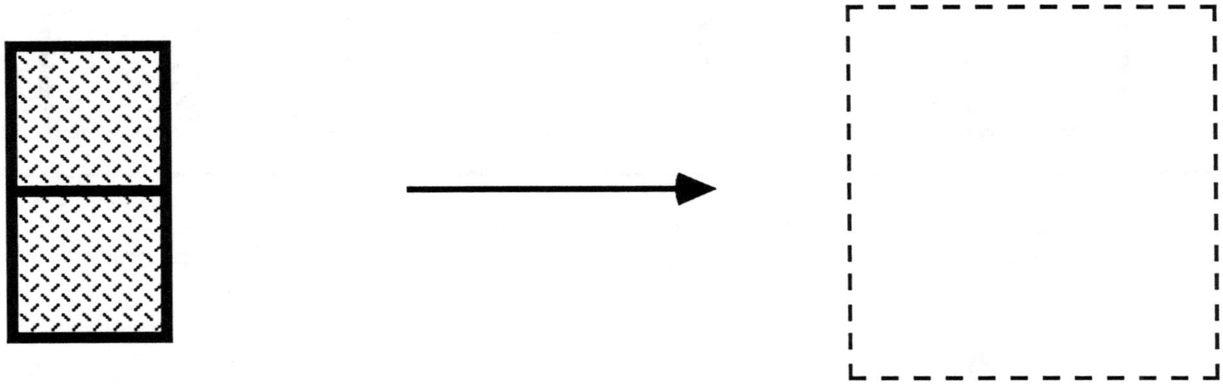

B

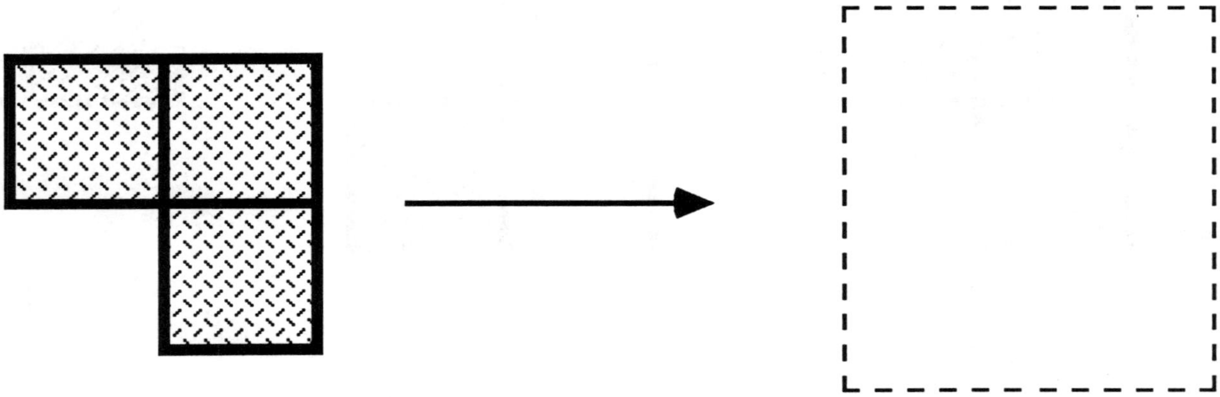

C

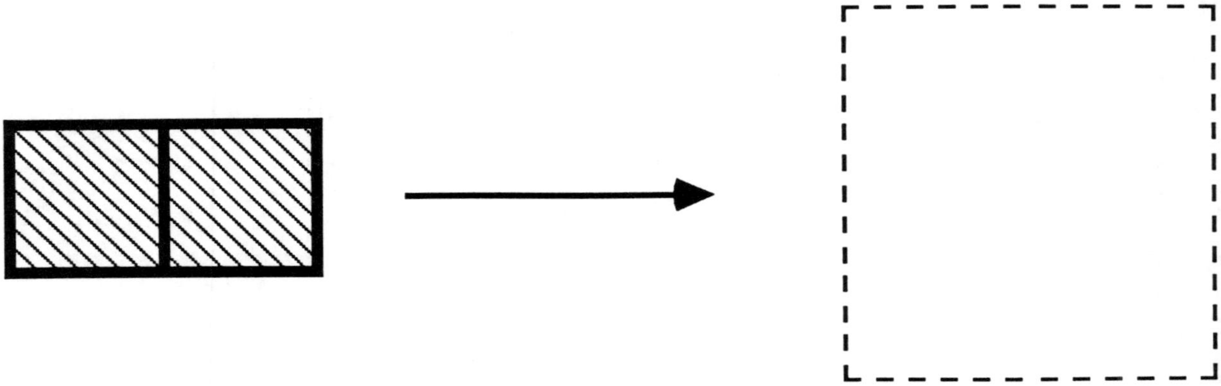

# CLASSIFYING—COLOR AND SHAPE

Using two different colors of INTERLOCKING CUBES, make two copies of each figure below.

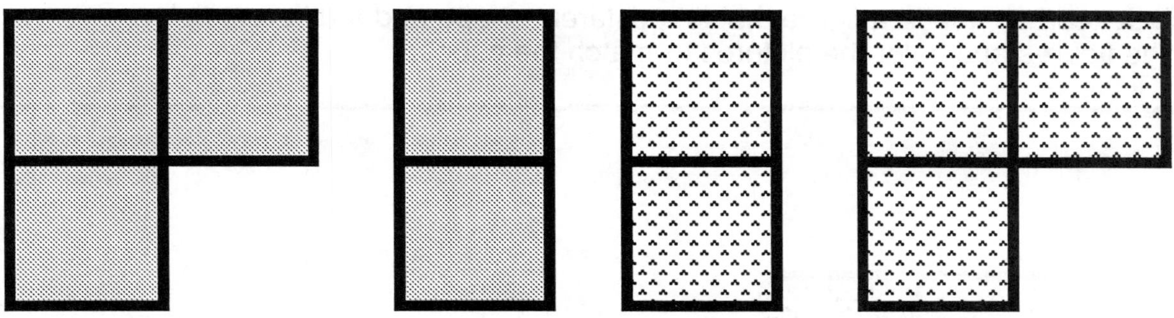

Place a correct INTERLOCKING CUBE figure on each picture below.
In each dotted box, place a figure that is a different shape and a different color.
Trace the figures and color the pictures to match the cubes.

A

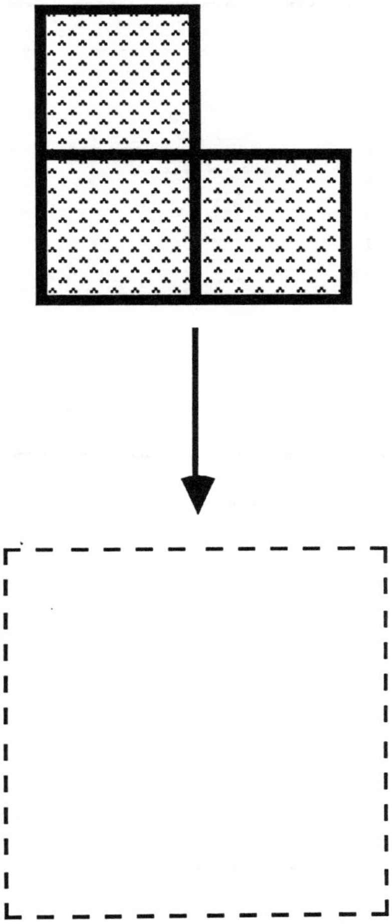

B

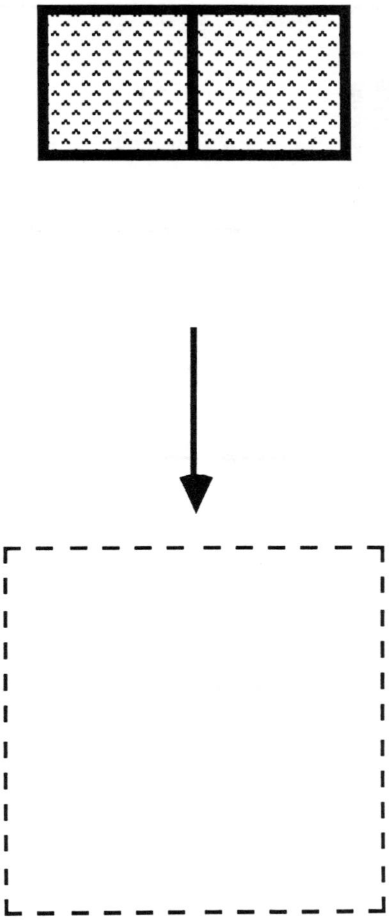

C

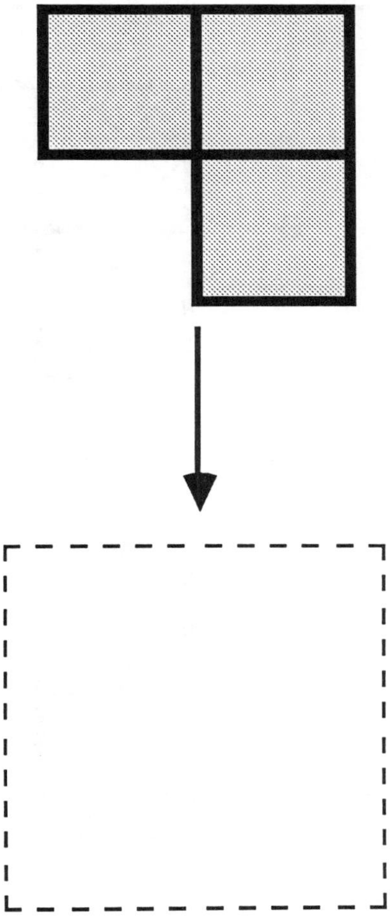

# CLASSIFYING—COLOR AND SHAPE

Use the eight INTERLOCKING CUBE figures constructed for Activity Sheet 157.
Place a correct INTERLOCKING CUBE figure on each picture below.
In each dotted box, place a figure that is a different shape and a different color.
Trace the figures and color the pictures to match the cubes.

A

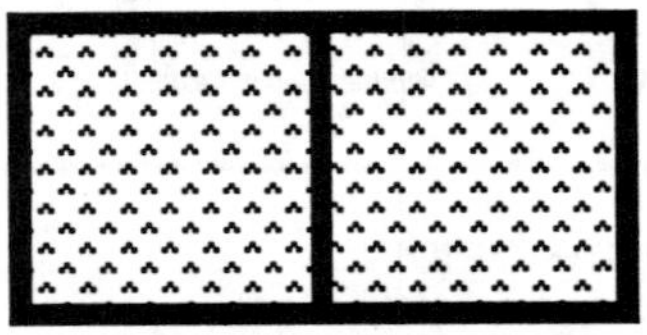

B

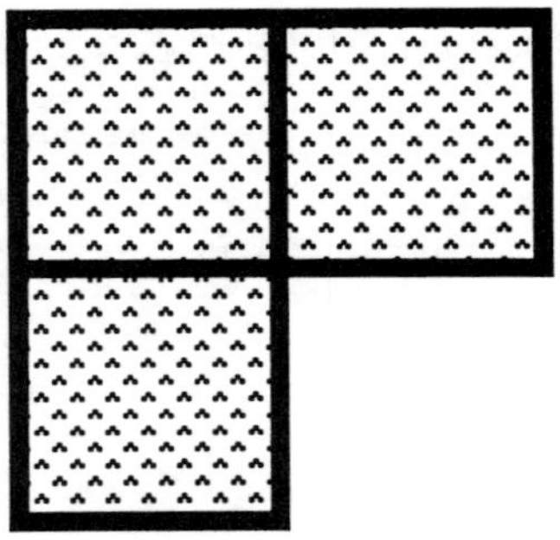

C

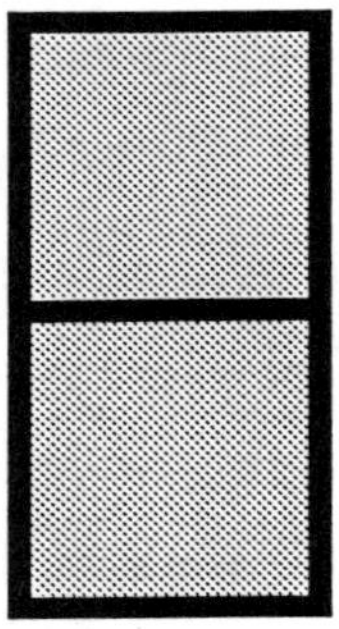

## CLASSIFYING—COLOR, SHAPE, AND SIZE

Place a red (R) or yellow (Y) ATTRIBUTE BLOCK on each shape below.
In each dotted box, place a block that is the same color and same shape but a different size.
Trace the blocks and color the pictures to match.

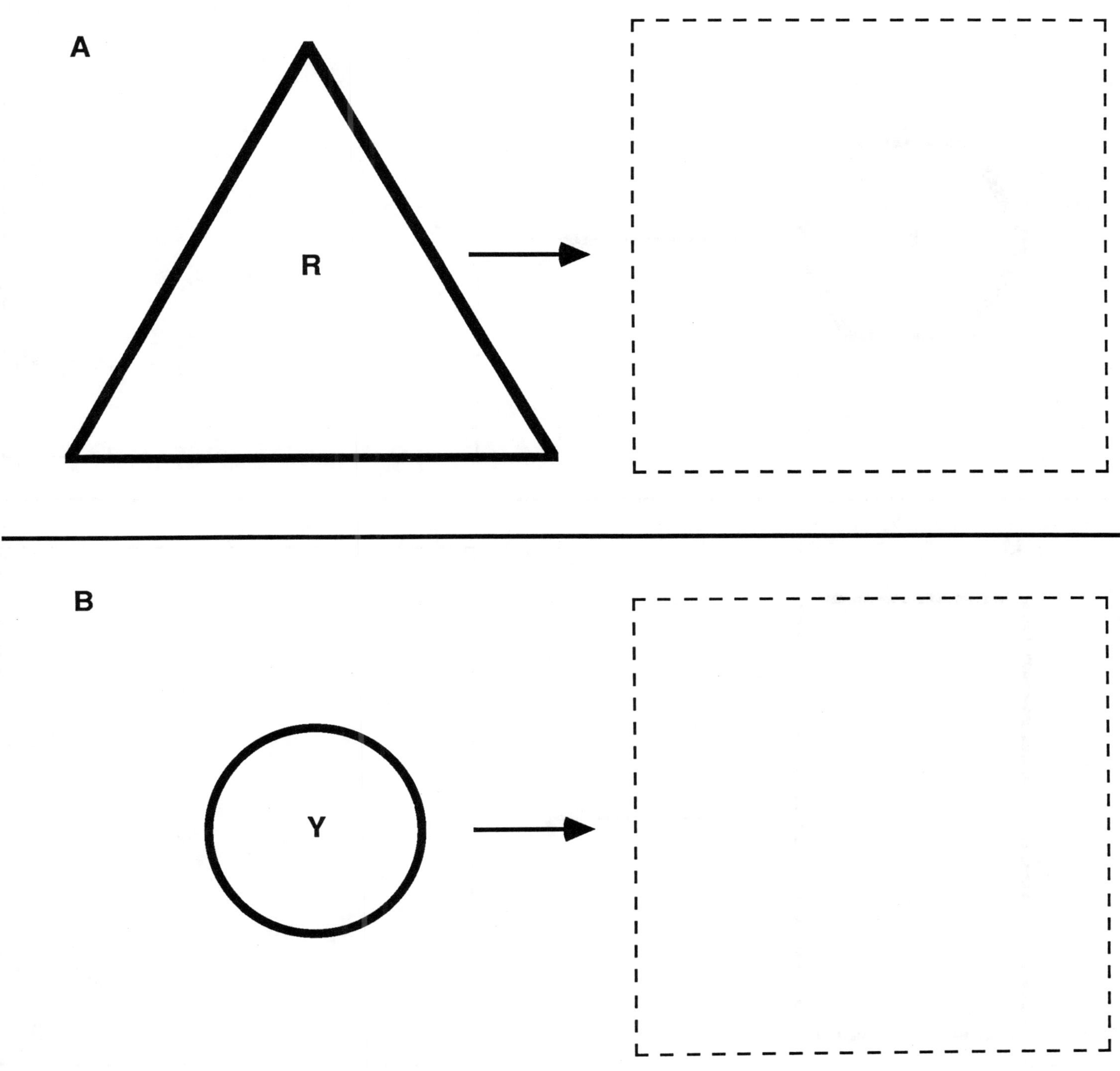

# CLASSIFYING—COLOR, SHAPE, AND SIZE

Place a red (R) or blue (B) ATTRIBUTE BLOCK on each shape below.
In each dotted box, place a block that is the same color and same shape but a different size.
Trace the blocks and color the pictures to match.

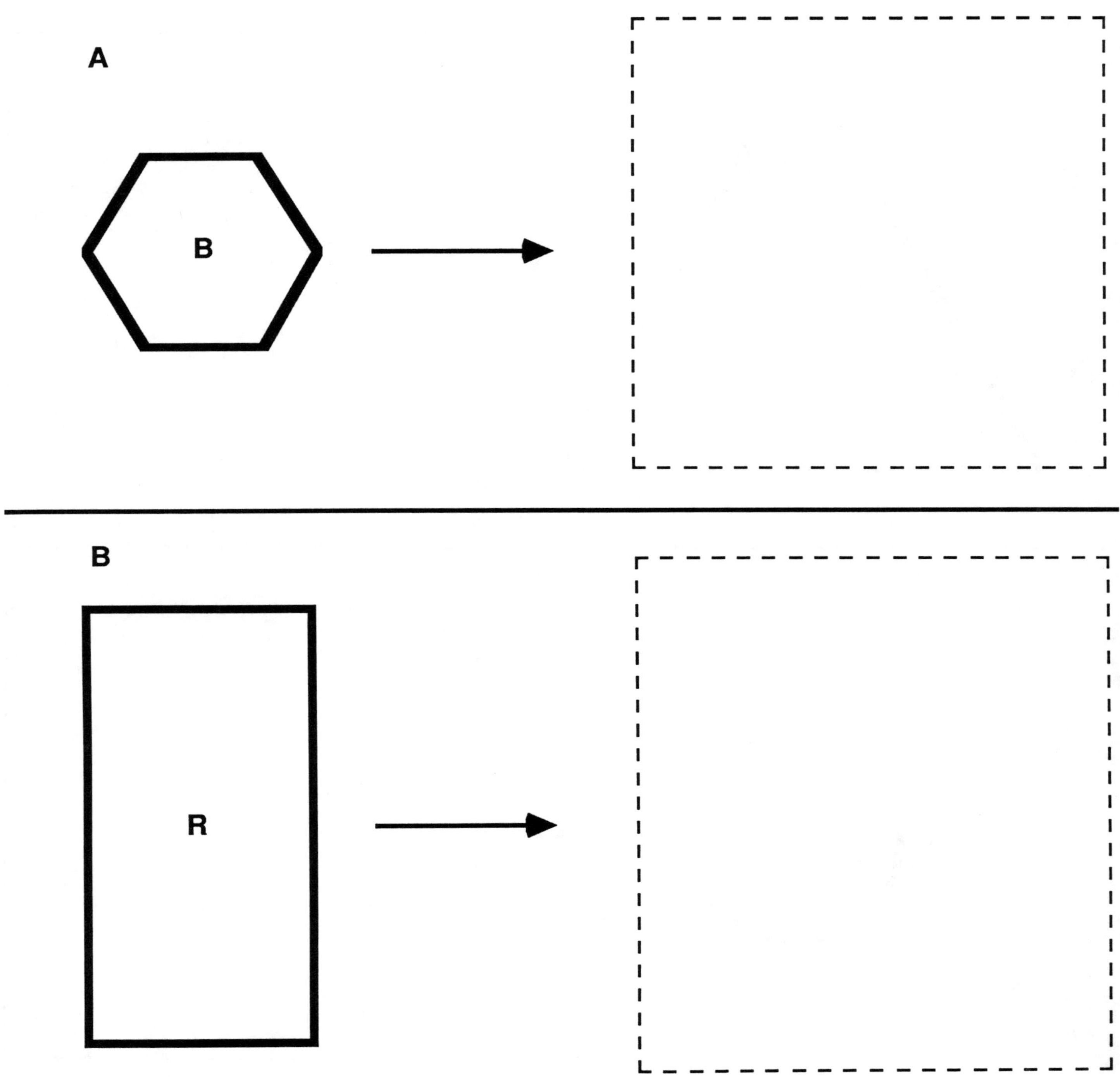

## CLASSIFYING—COLOR, SHAPE, AND SIZE

Place a red (R) or blue (B) ATTRIBUTE BLOCK on each shape below.
In each dotted box, place a block with the same shape but a different color and different size.
Trace the blocks and color the pictures to match.

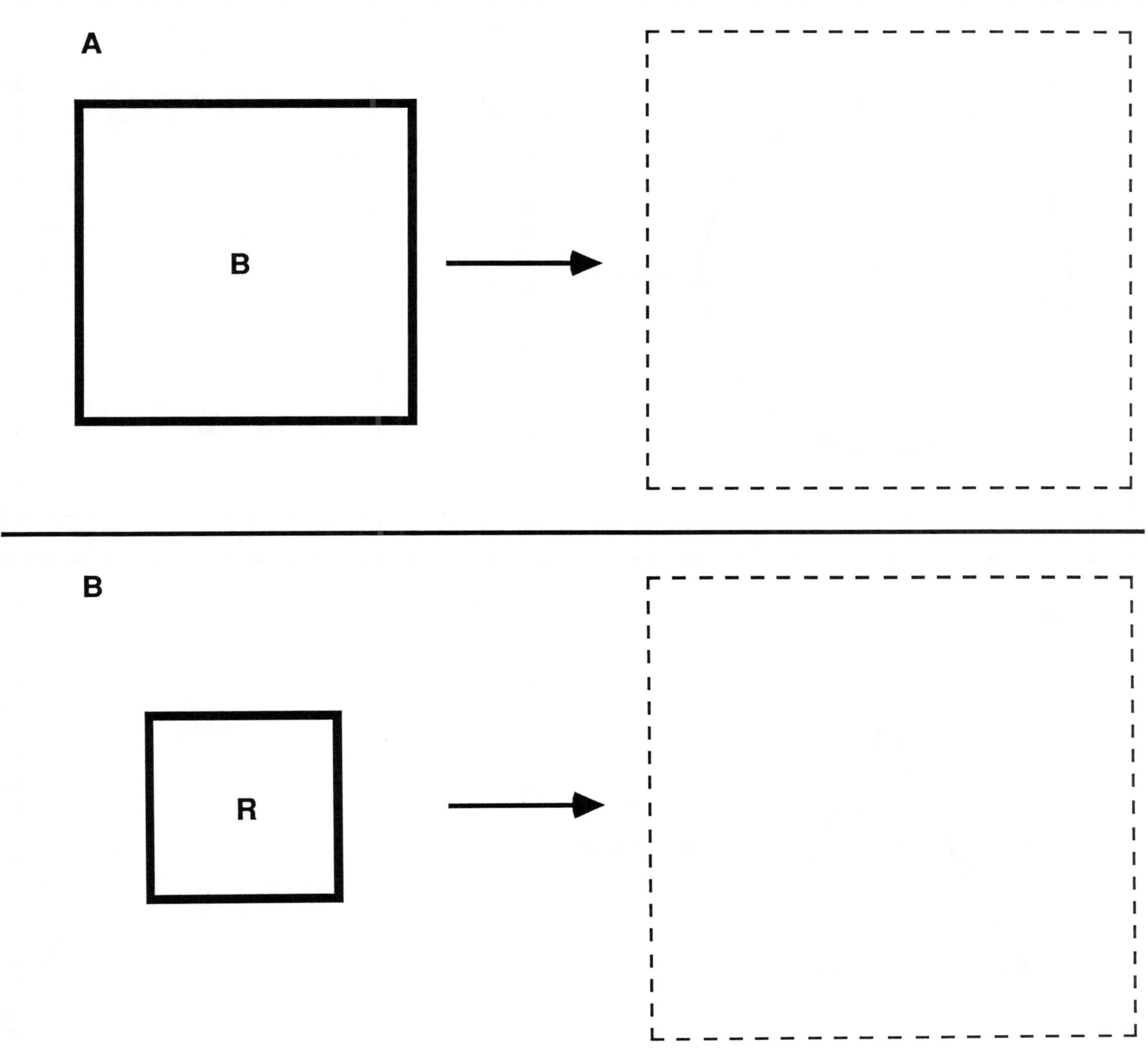

## CLASSIFYING—COLOR, SHAPE, AND SIZE

Place a yellow (Y) or blue (B) ATTRIBUTE BLOCK on each shape below.
In each dotted box, place a block with the same shape but a different color and different size.
Trace the blocks and color the pictures to match.

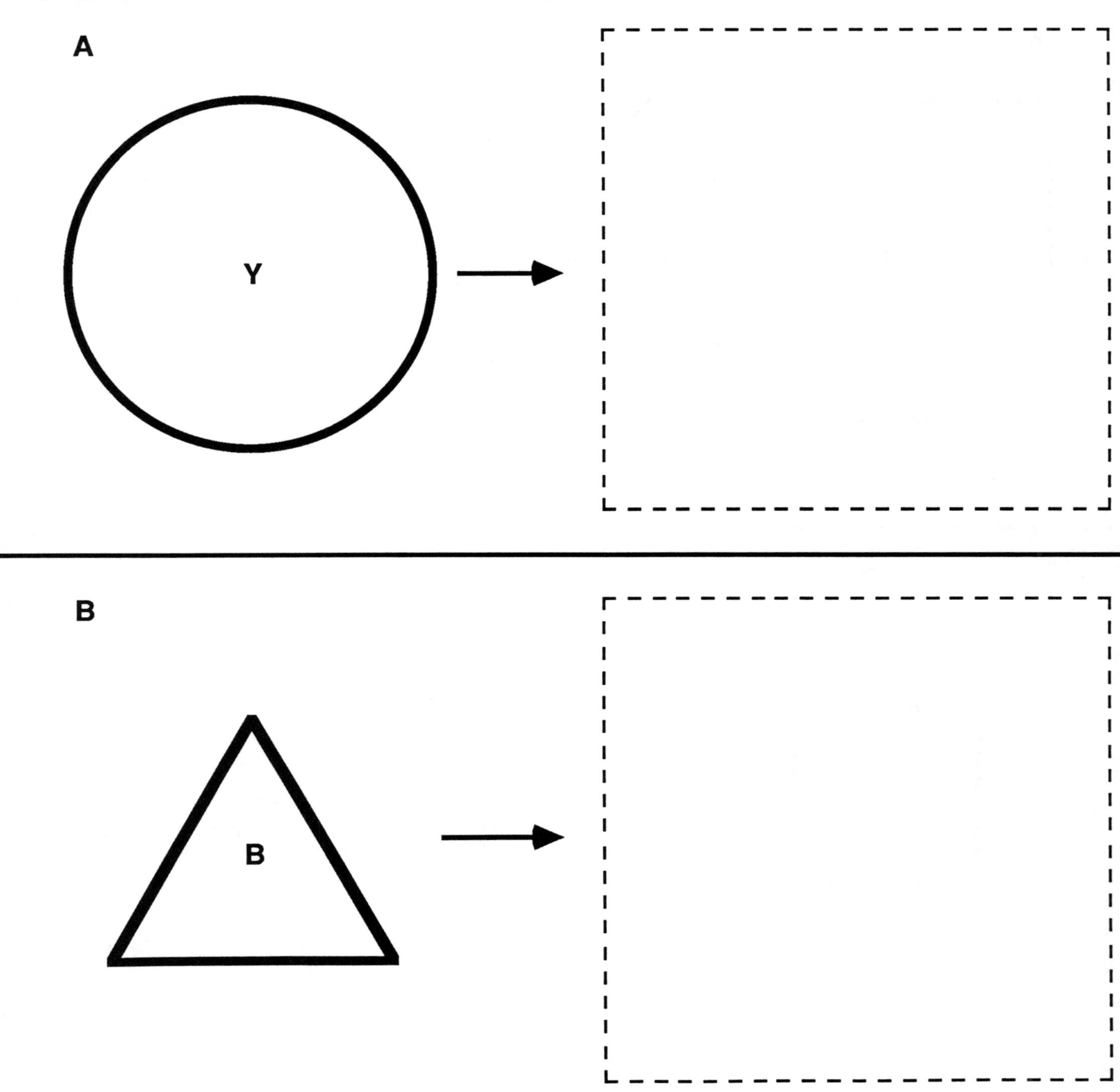

# CLASSIFYING—COLOR, SHAPE, AND SIZE

Place a yellow (Y) or blue (B) ATTRIBUTE BLOCK on each shape below.
In each dotted box, place a block with the same color but a different shape and different size.
Trace the blocks and color the pictures to match.

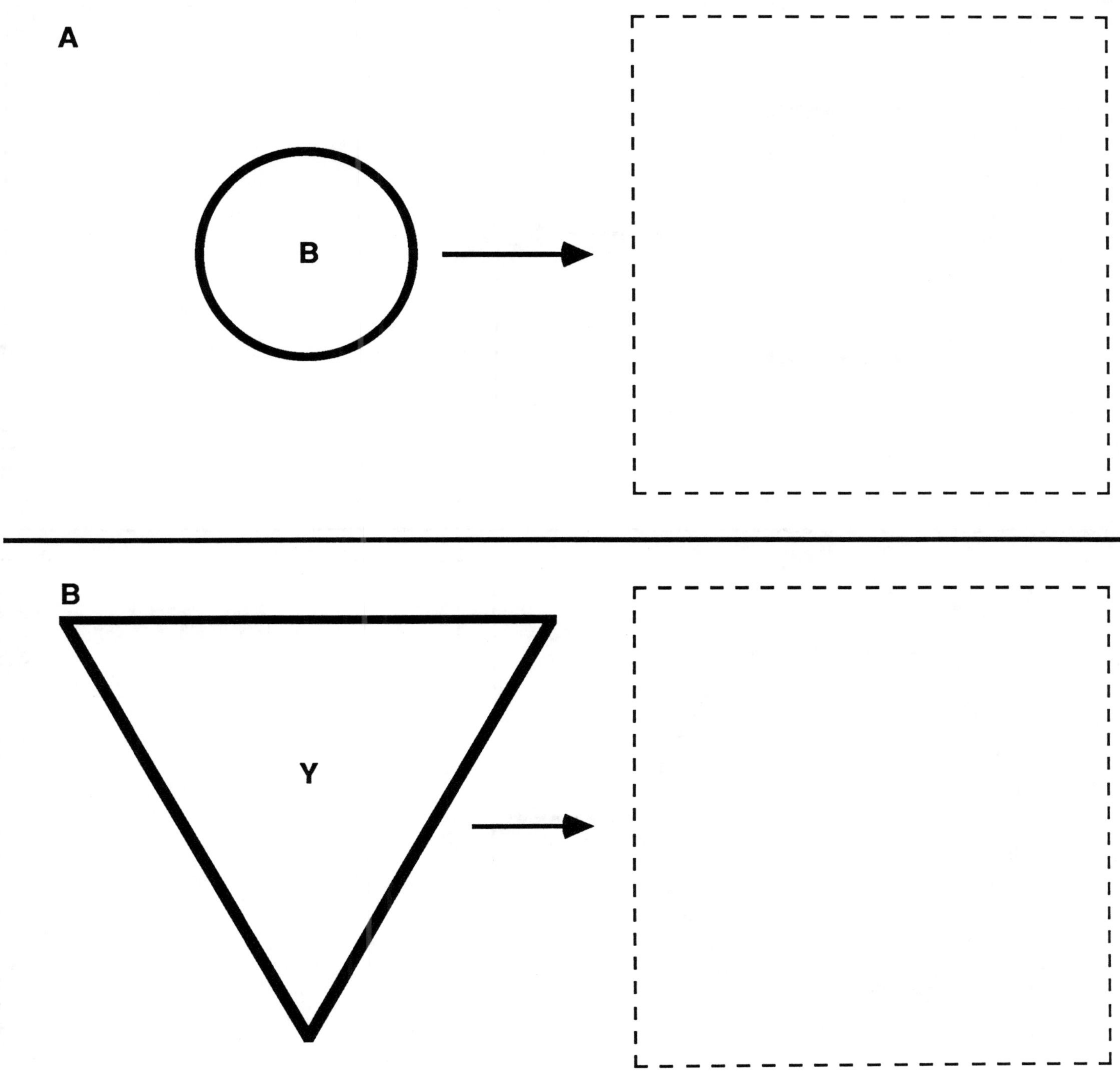

# CLASSIFYING—COLOR, SHAPE, AND SIZE

Place a red (R) ATTRIBUTE BLOCK on each shape below.
In each dotted box, place a block with the same color but a different shape and different size.
Trace the blocks and color the pictures to match.

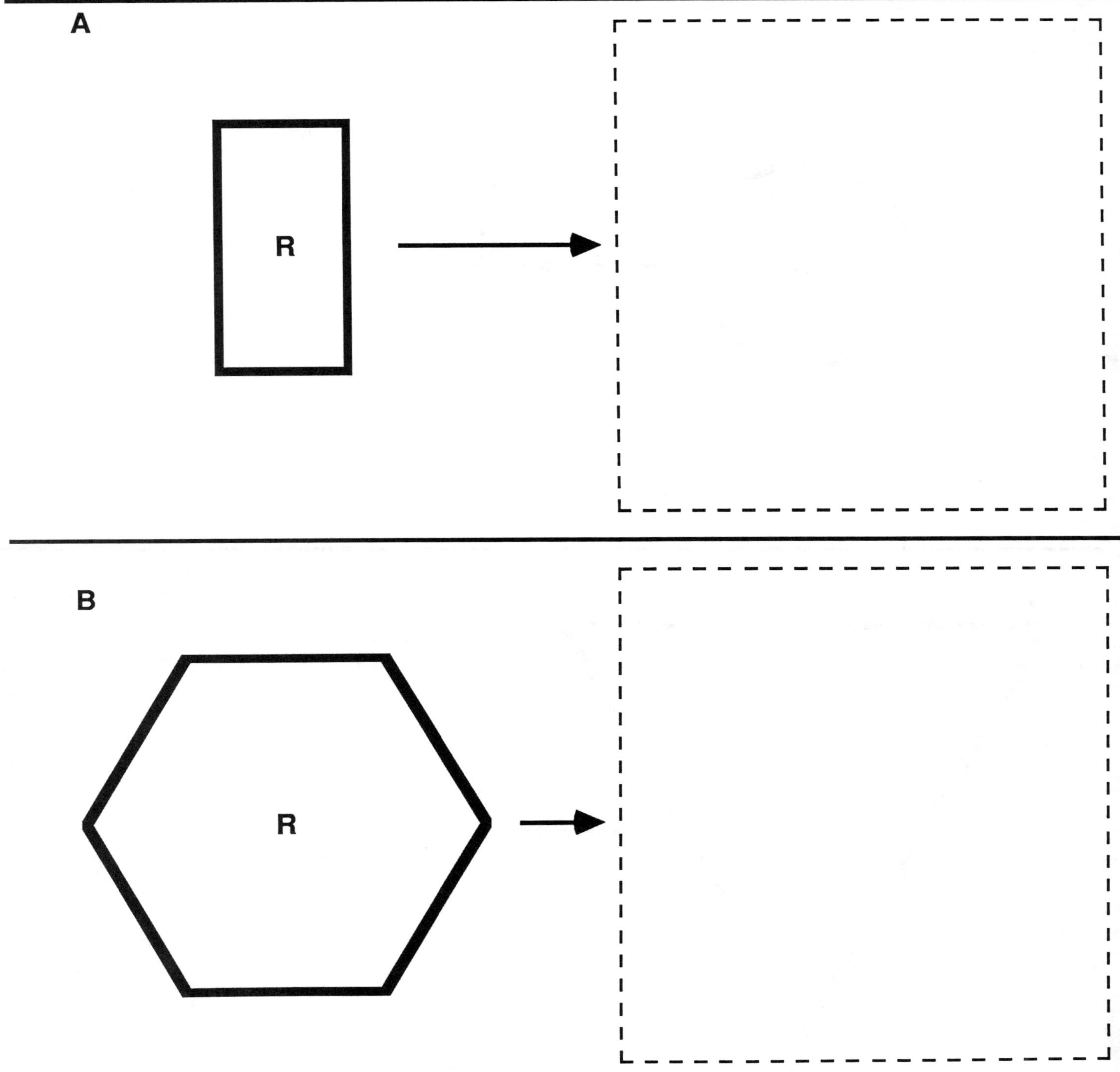

## CLASSIFYING—COLOR, SHAPE, AND SIZE

Place a red (R) or blue (B) ATTRIBUTE BLOCK on each shape below.
In each dotted box, place a block with a different shape, different color, and different size.
Trace the blocks and color the pictures to match.

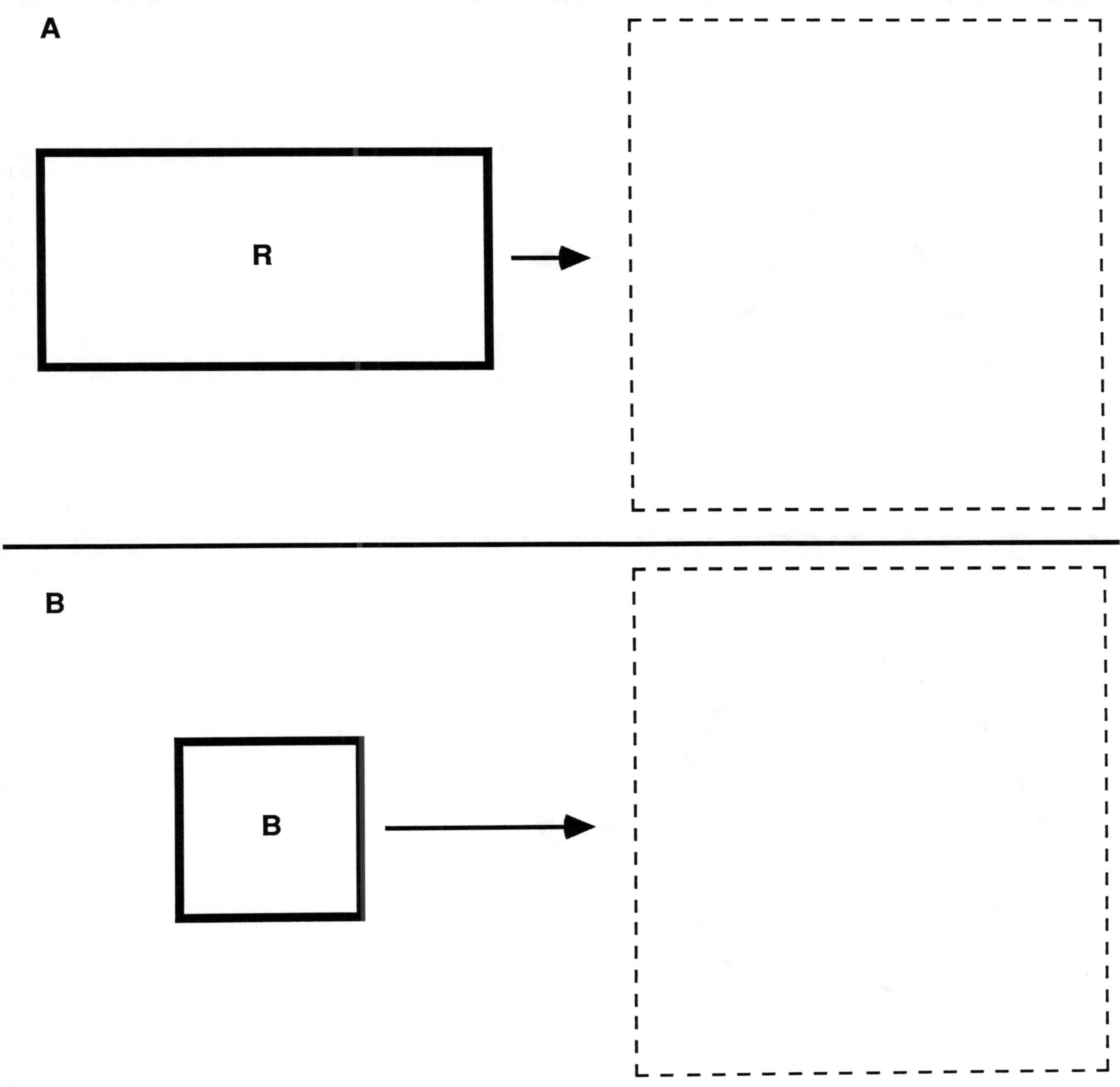

# CLASSIFYING—COLOR, SHAPE, AND SIZE

Place a red (R) or yellow (Y) ATTRIBUTE BLOCK on each shape below.
In each dotted box, place a block with a different shape, different color, and different size.
Trace the blocks and color the pictures to match.

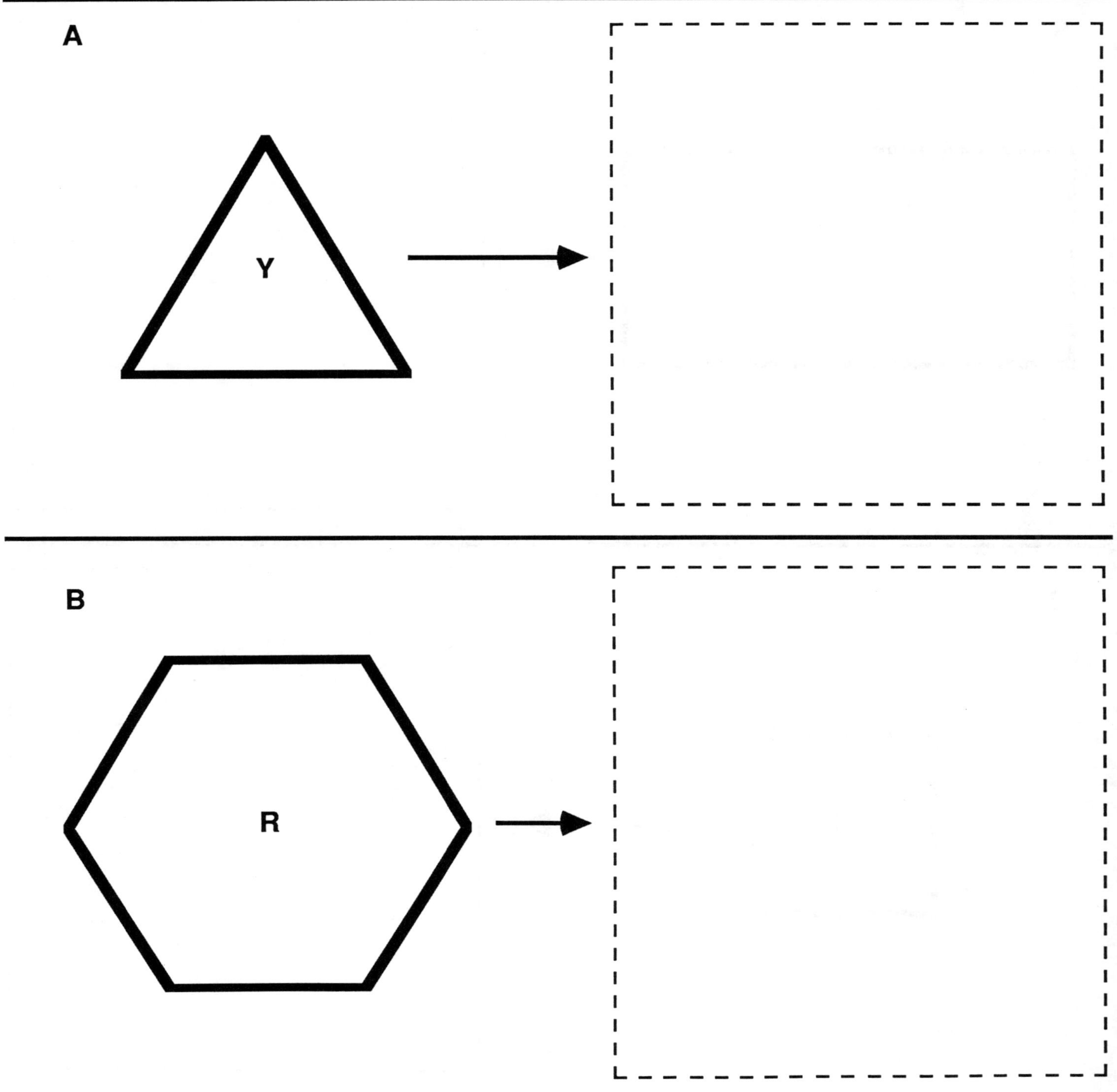

# GROUPING BY SHAPE

Place an ATTRIBUTE BLOCK on each shaded shape below. Use any colors you wish.
In each box, place all the small blocks that are the same shape.
Trace the blocks and color the pictures to match.

**A**

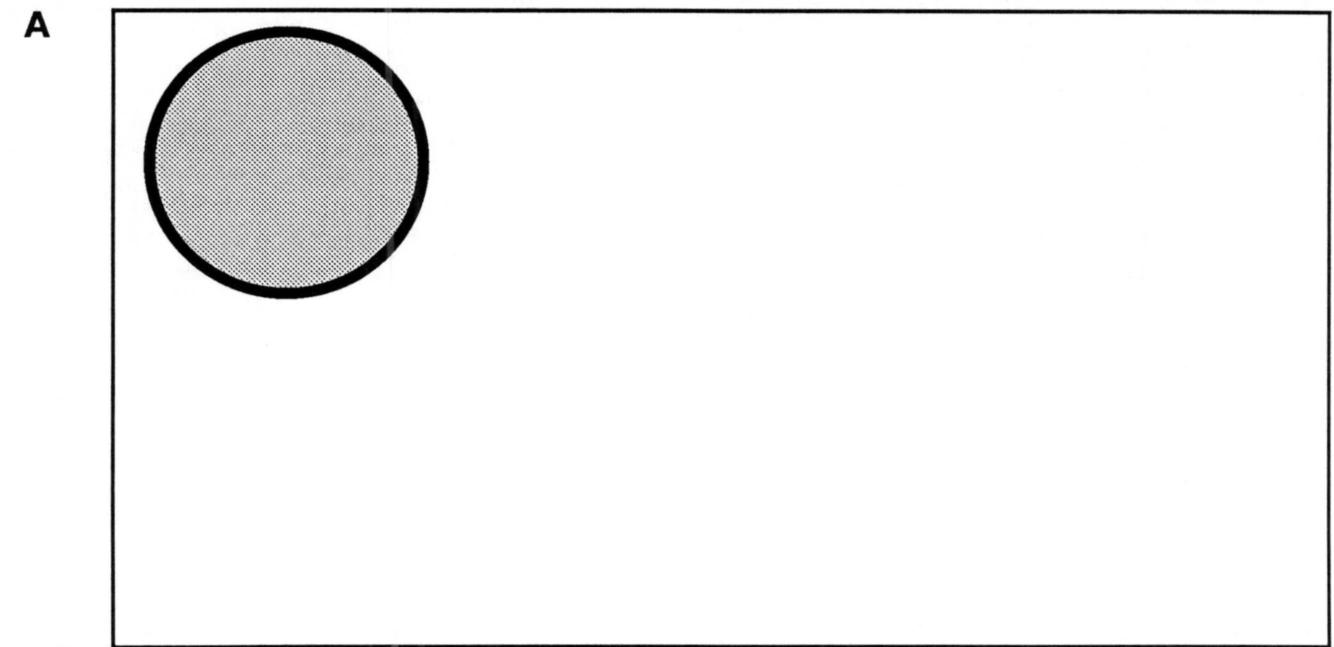

**B**

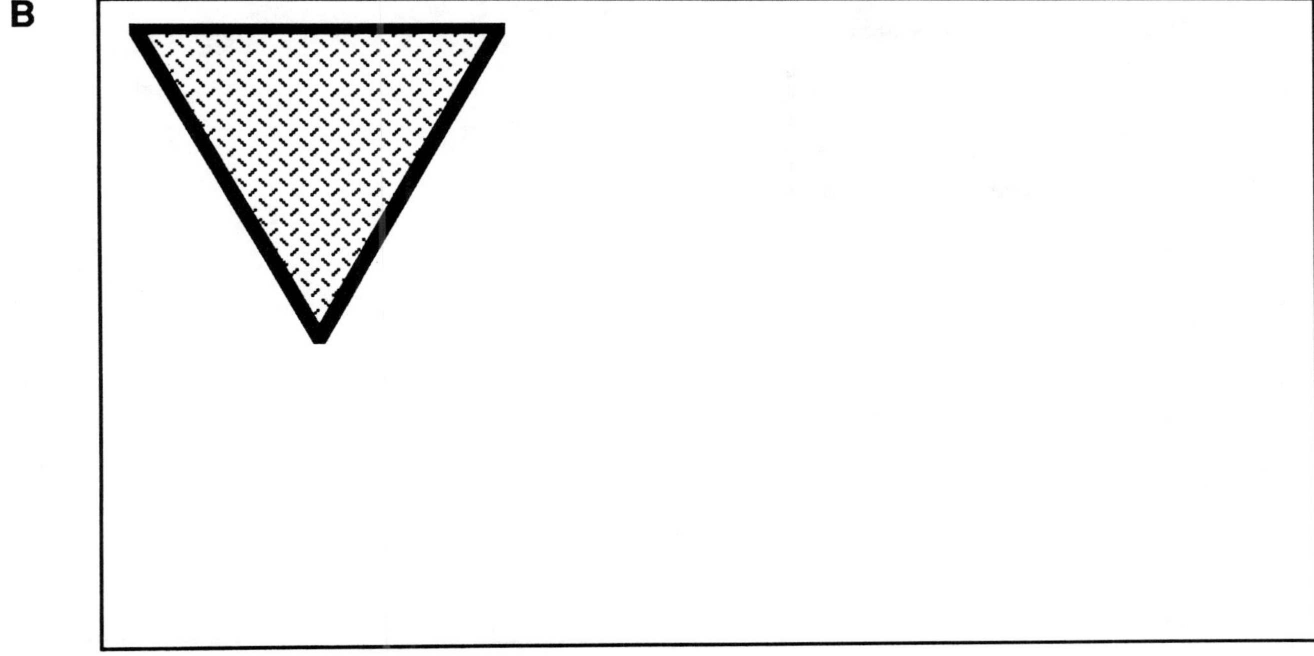

## GROUPING BY SHAPE

Place an ATTRIBUTE BLOCK on each shaded shape below. Use any colors you wish.
In each box, place all the small blocks that are the same shape.
Trace the blocks and color the pictures to match.

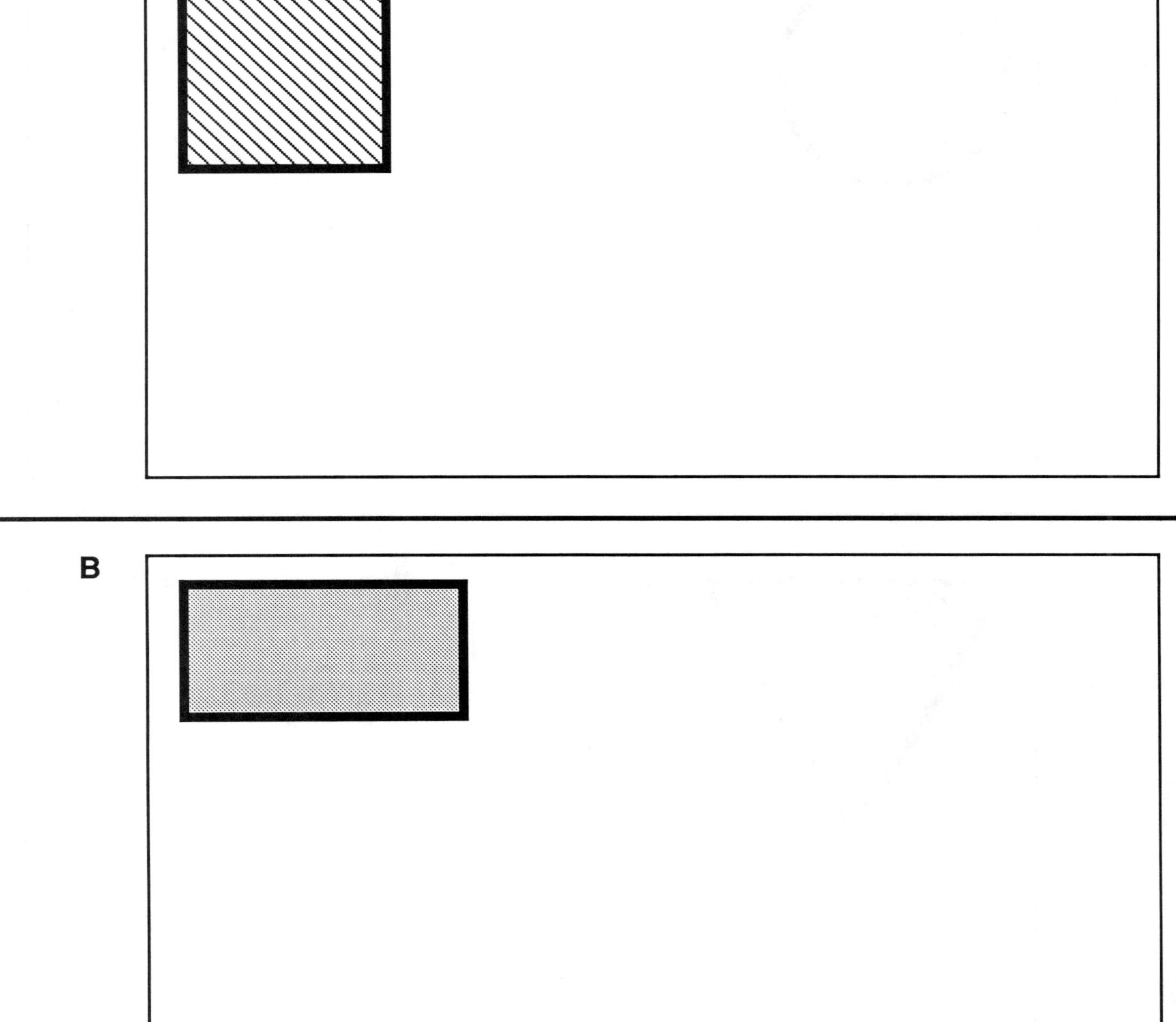

## GROUPING BY SHAPE

Place a PATTERN BLOCK on each shaded shape below.
In each box, place blocks with the same shape in the dotted circles.
Trace the blocks and color the pictures to match.

**A**

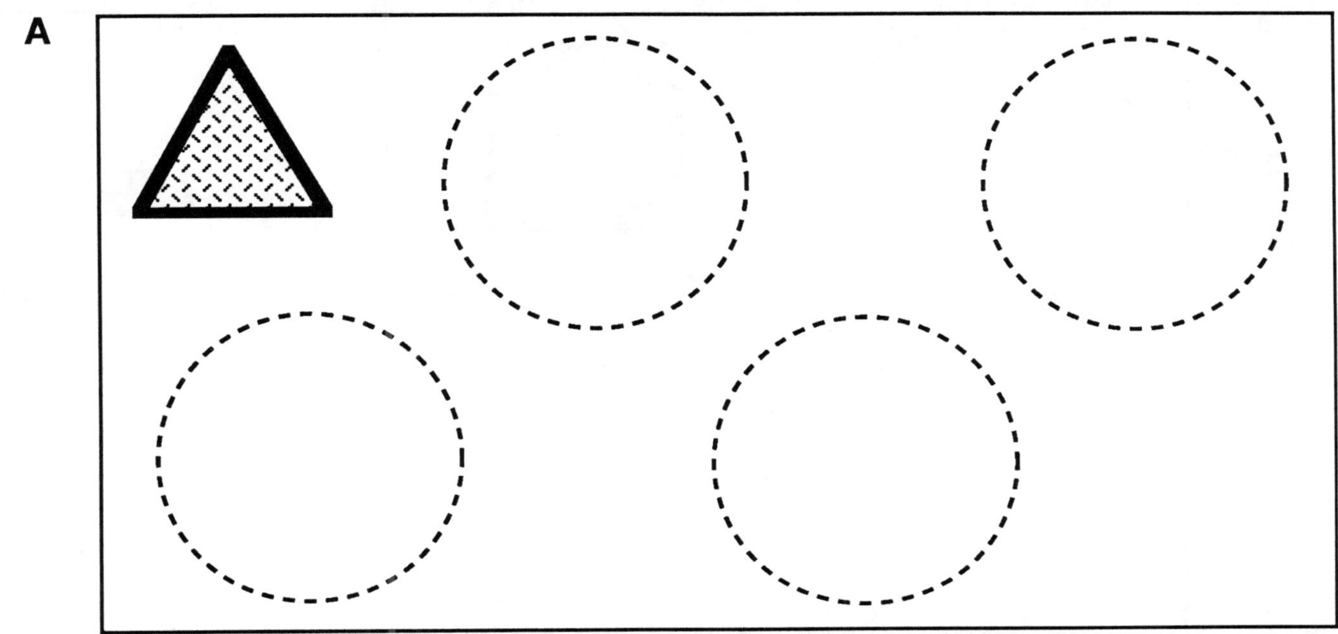

**B**

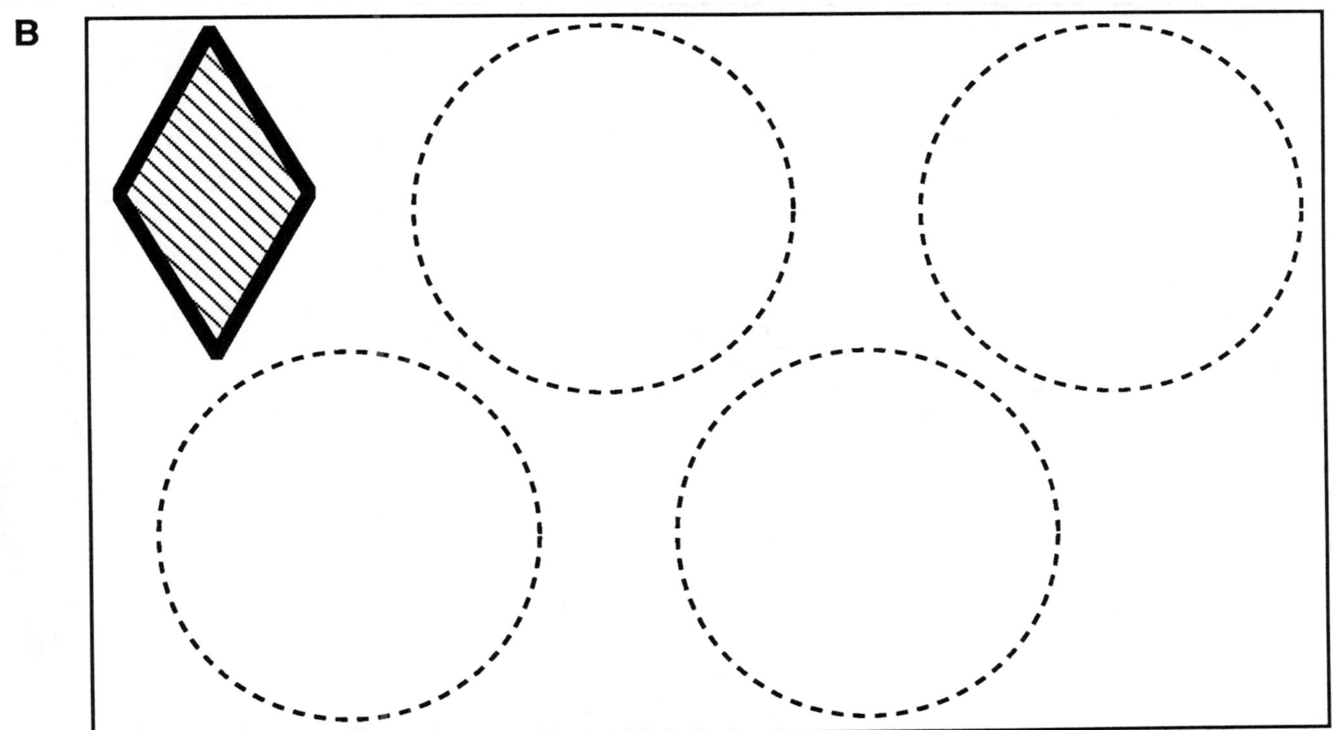

## GROUPING BY SHAPE

Place a PATTERN BLOCK on each shaded shape below.
In each box, place blocks with the same shape in the dotted circles.
Trace the blocks and color the pictures to match.

**A**

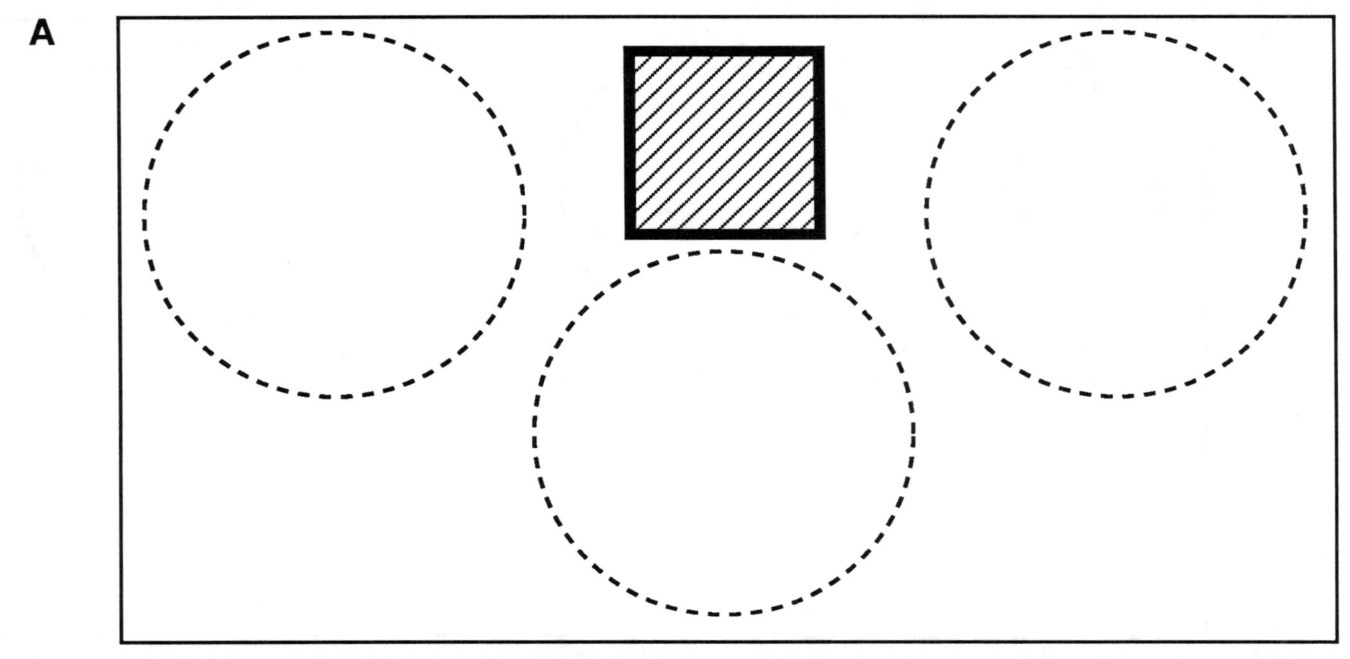

**B**

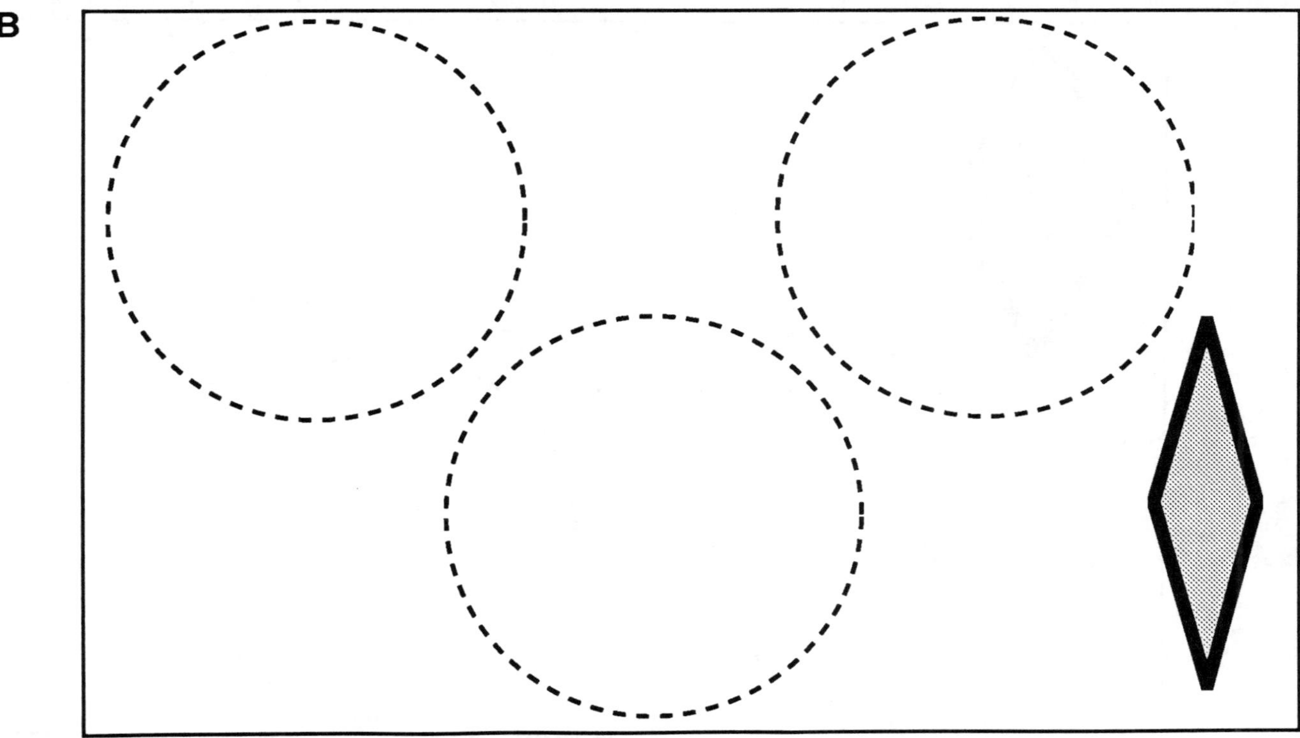

## GROUPING BY SHAPE

Using two different colors of INTERLOCKING CUBES, make two copies of each figure below.

Place a correct INTERLOCKING CUBE figure on each picture below.
In each box, place all the figures that are the same shape.
Trace the figures and color the pictures to match the cubes.

**A**

**B**

## GROUPING BY COLOR

Use the eight INTERLOCKING CUBE figures constructed for Activity Sheet 171.
Place a correct INTERLOCKING CUBE figure on each picture below.
In each box, place all the figures that are the same color.
Trace the figures and color the pictures to match the cubes.

A

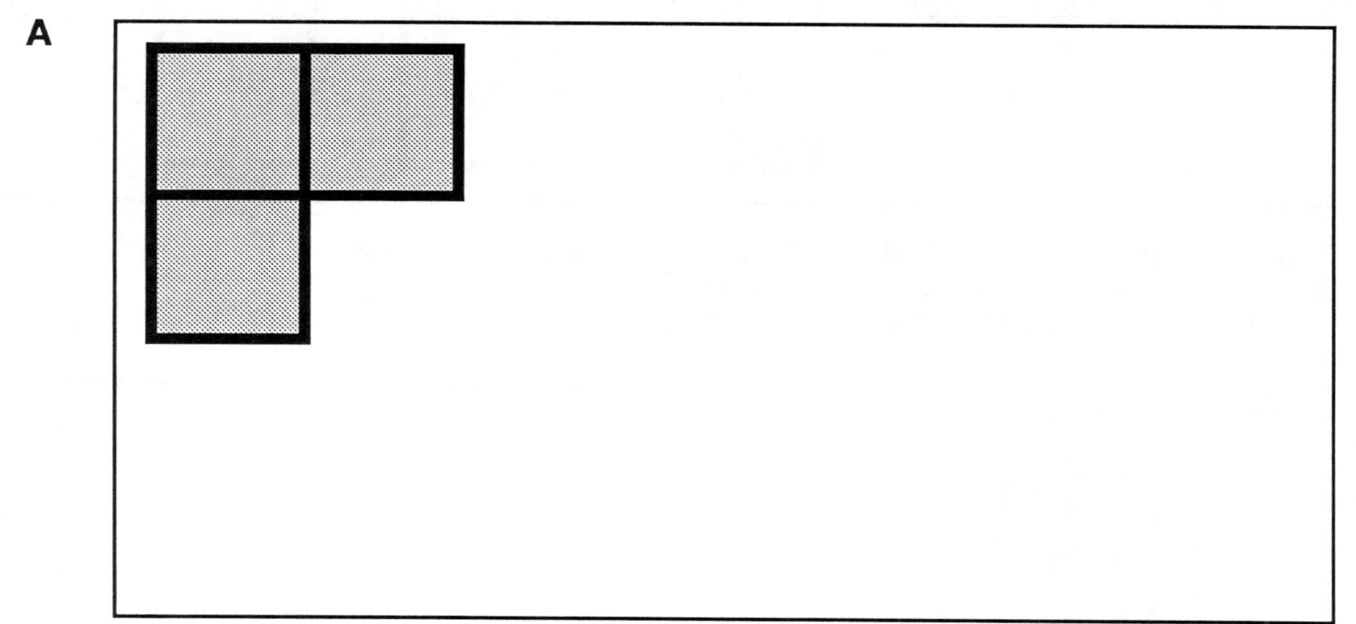

B

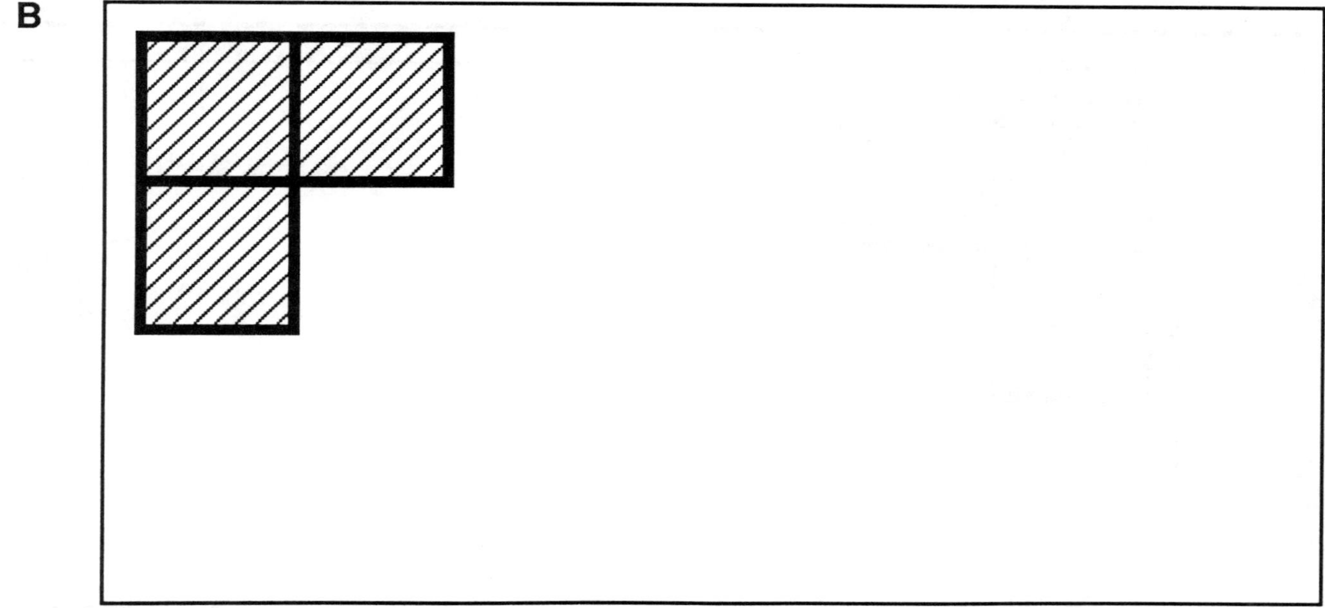

## GROUPING BY COLOR

Place a red (R) or yellow (Y) ATTRIBUTE BLOCK on the top shape in each box.
Cover the other shapes in each box with blocks that are the same color.
Color the pictures to match the blocks.

A

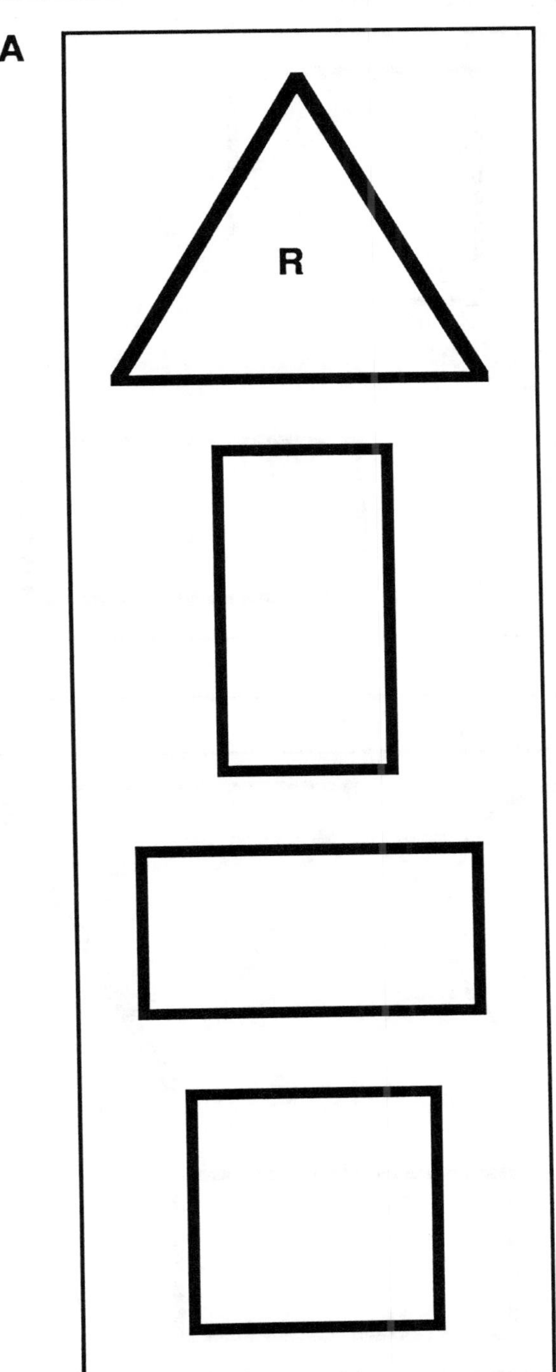


B

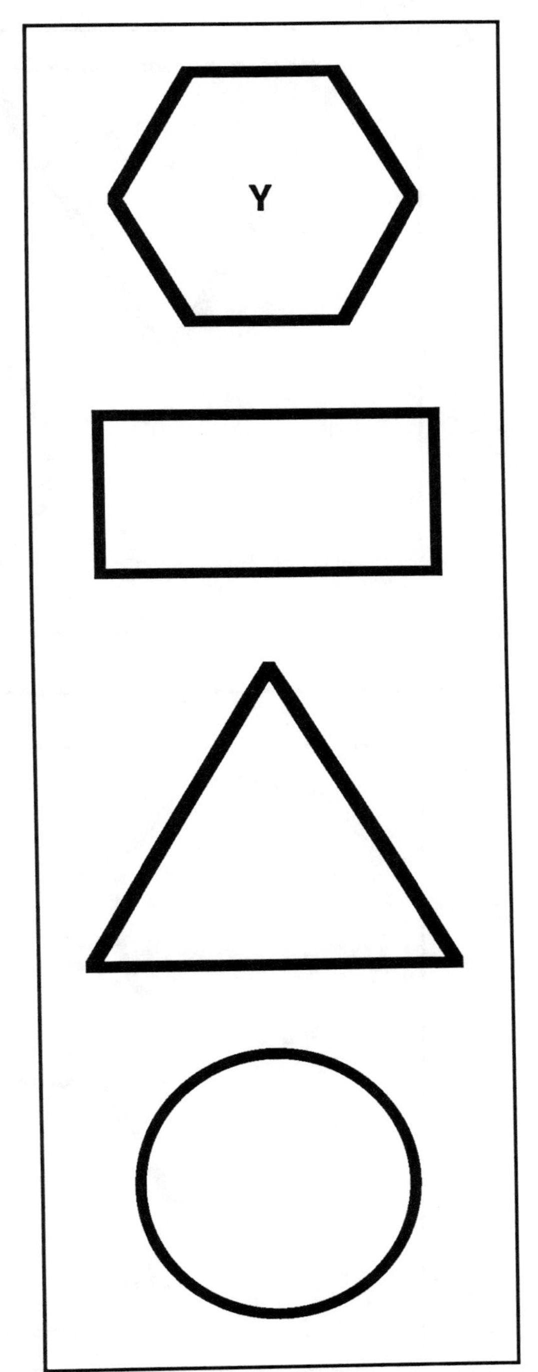

## GROUPING BY COLOR

Place a red (R) or blue (B) ATTRIBUTE BLOCK on the first shape in each box.
Cover the other shapes in each box with blocks that are the same color.
Color the pictures to match the blocks.

**A**

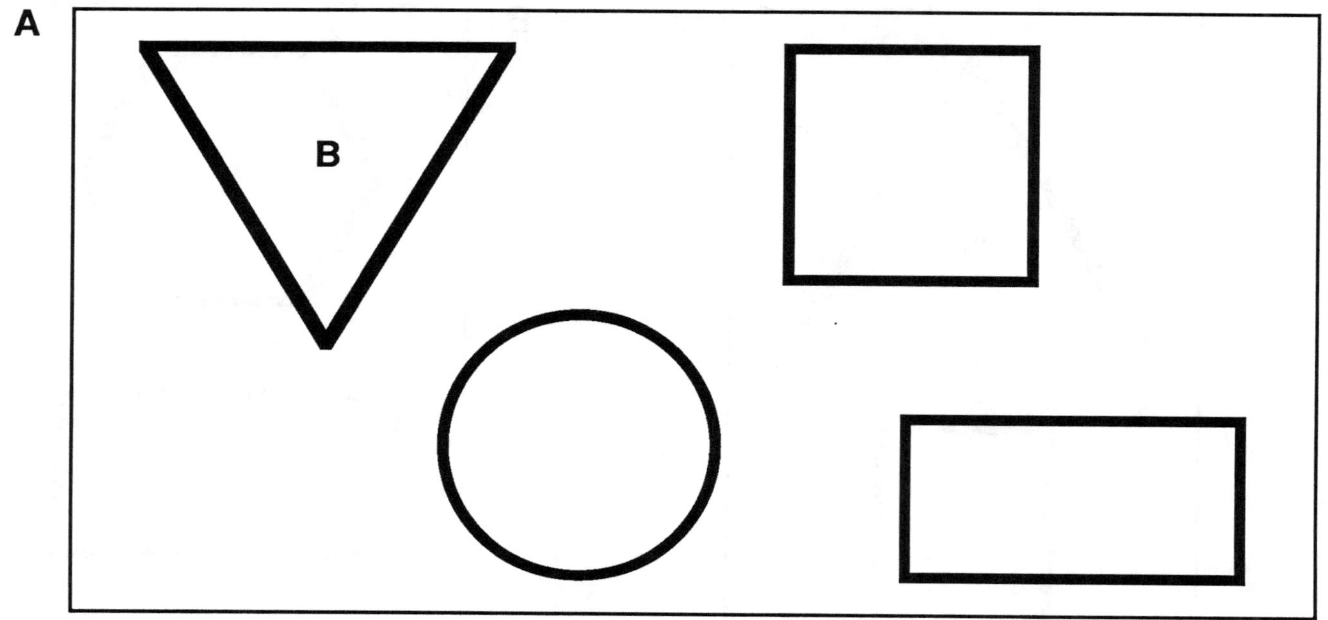


**B**

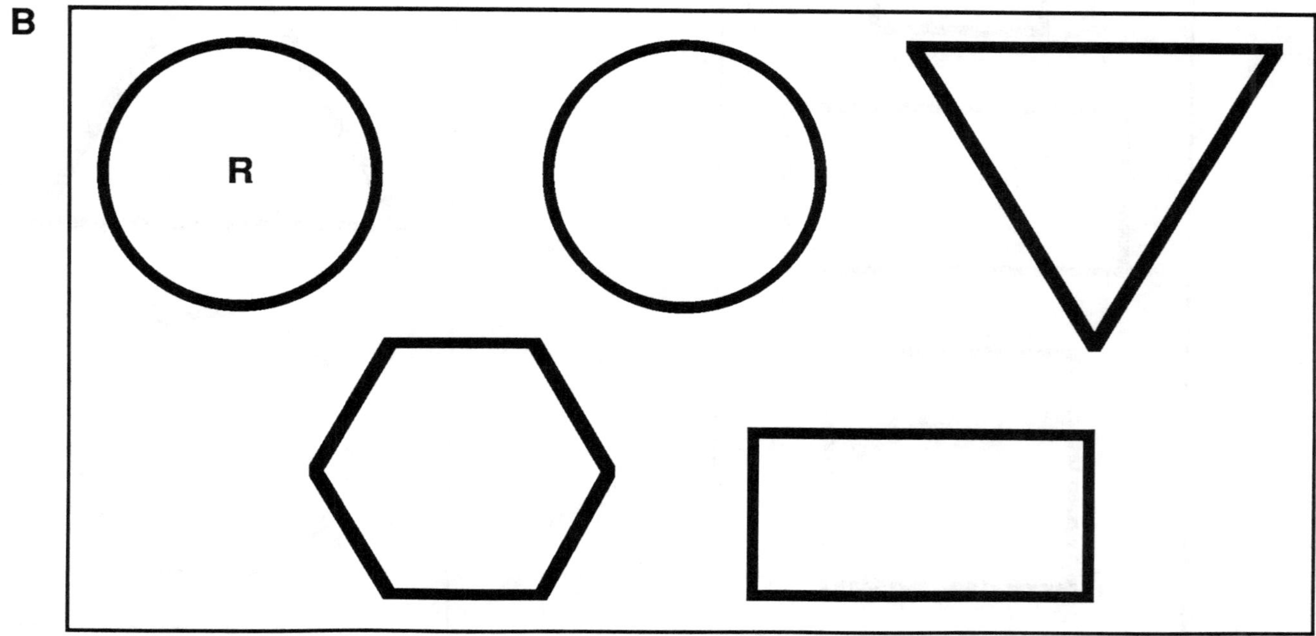

## GROUPING—COLOR AND SHAPE

Place a yellow (Y) or blue (B) ATTRIBUTE BLOCK on each shape below.
In each box, place all the blocks that are the same color and same shape.
Trace the blocks and color the pictures to match.

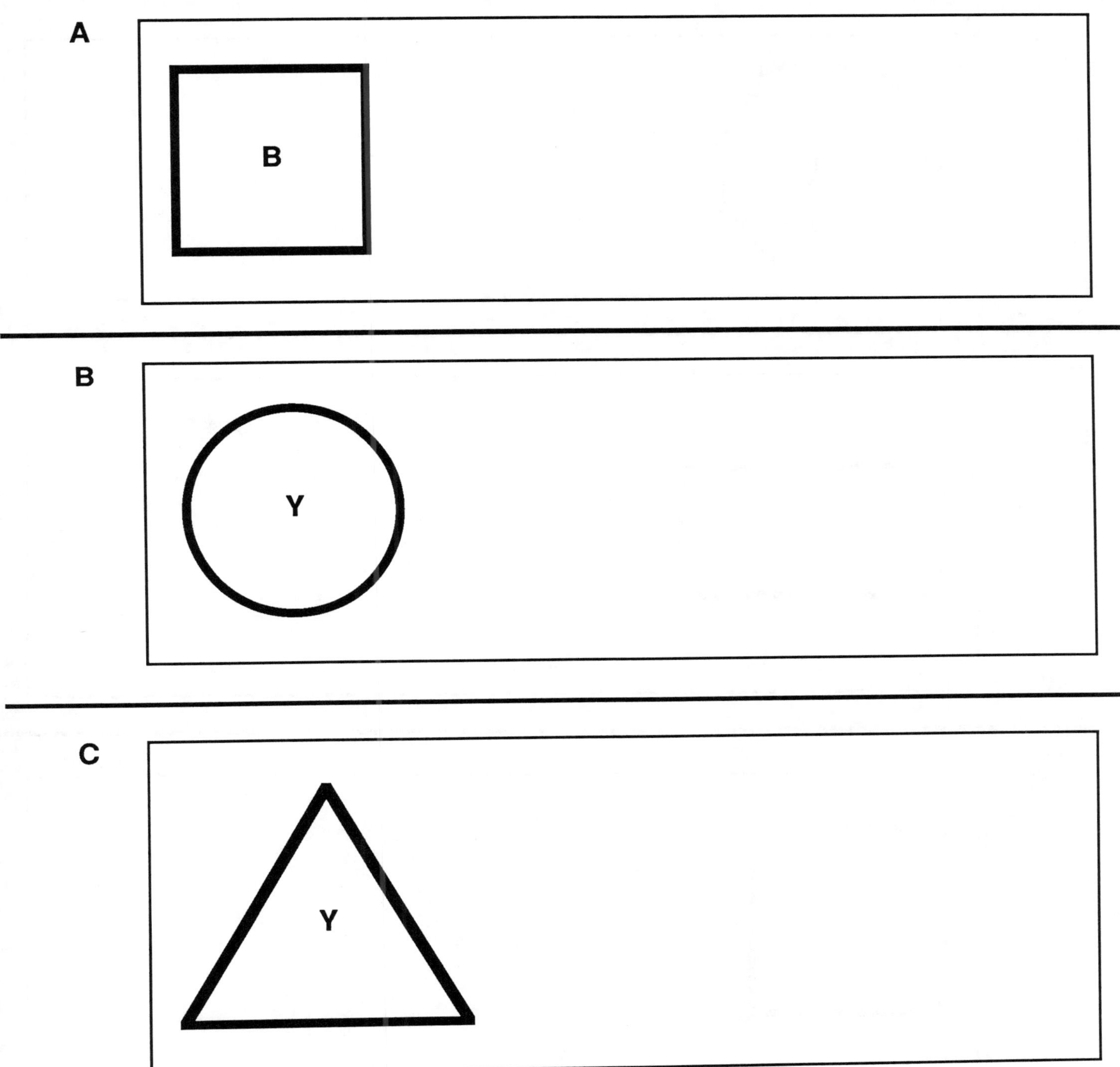

## GROUPING—COLOR AND SHAPE

Place a red (R), yellow (Y), or blue (B) ATTRIBUTE BLOCK on each shape below.
In each box, place all the blocks that are the same color and same shape.
Trace the blocks and color the pictures to match.

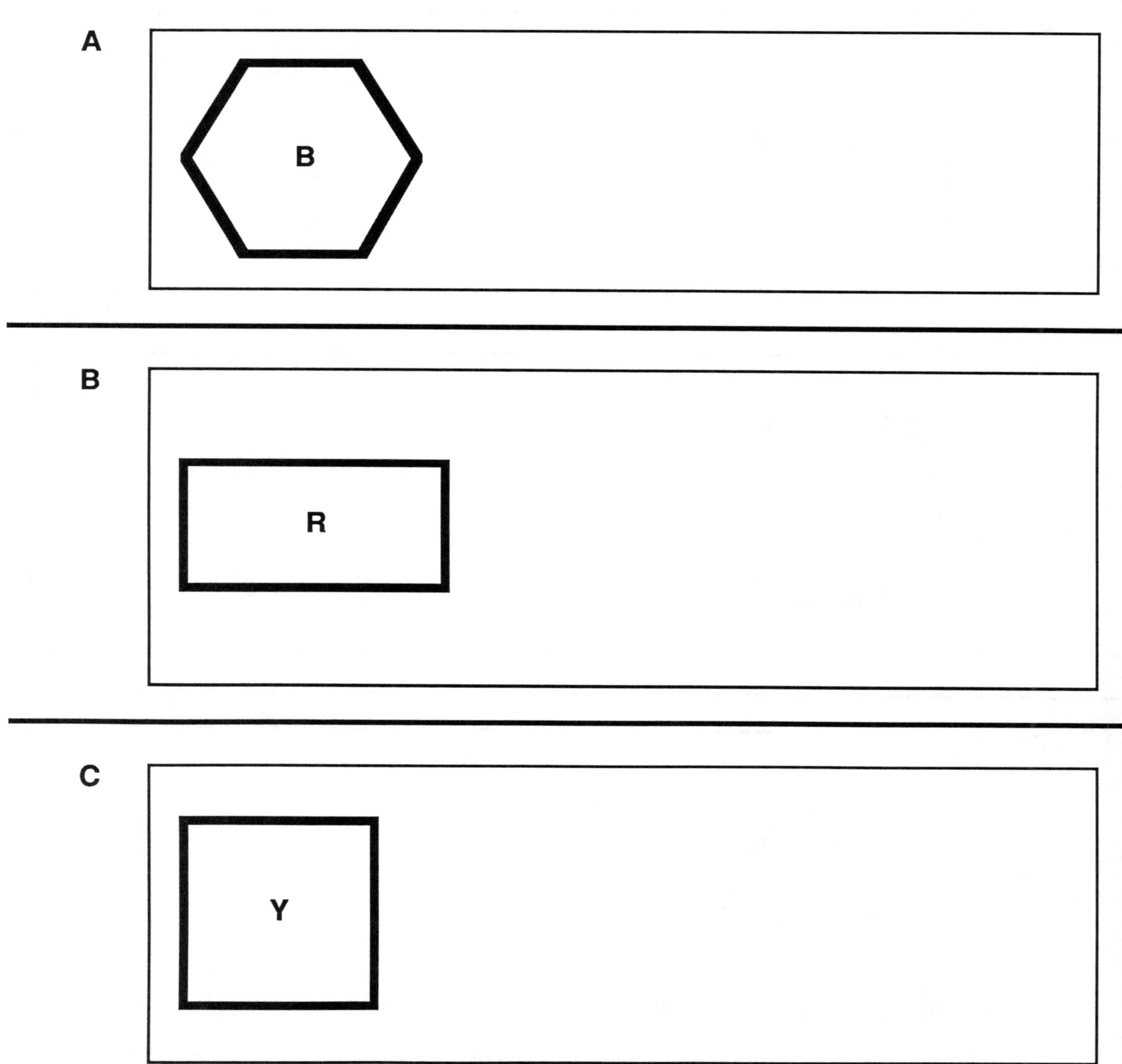

# GROUPING—COLOR AND SHAPE

Place a red (R) or blue (B) ATTRIBUTE BLOCK on each shape below.
In each box, place all the blocks that are the same shape but a different color.
Trace the blocks and color the pictures to match.

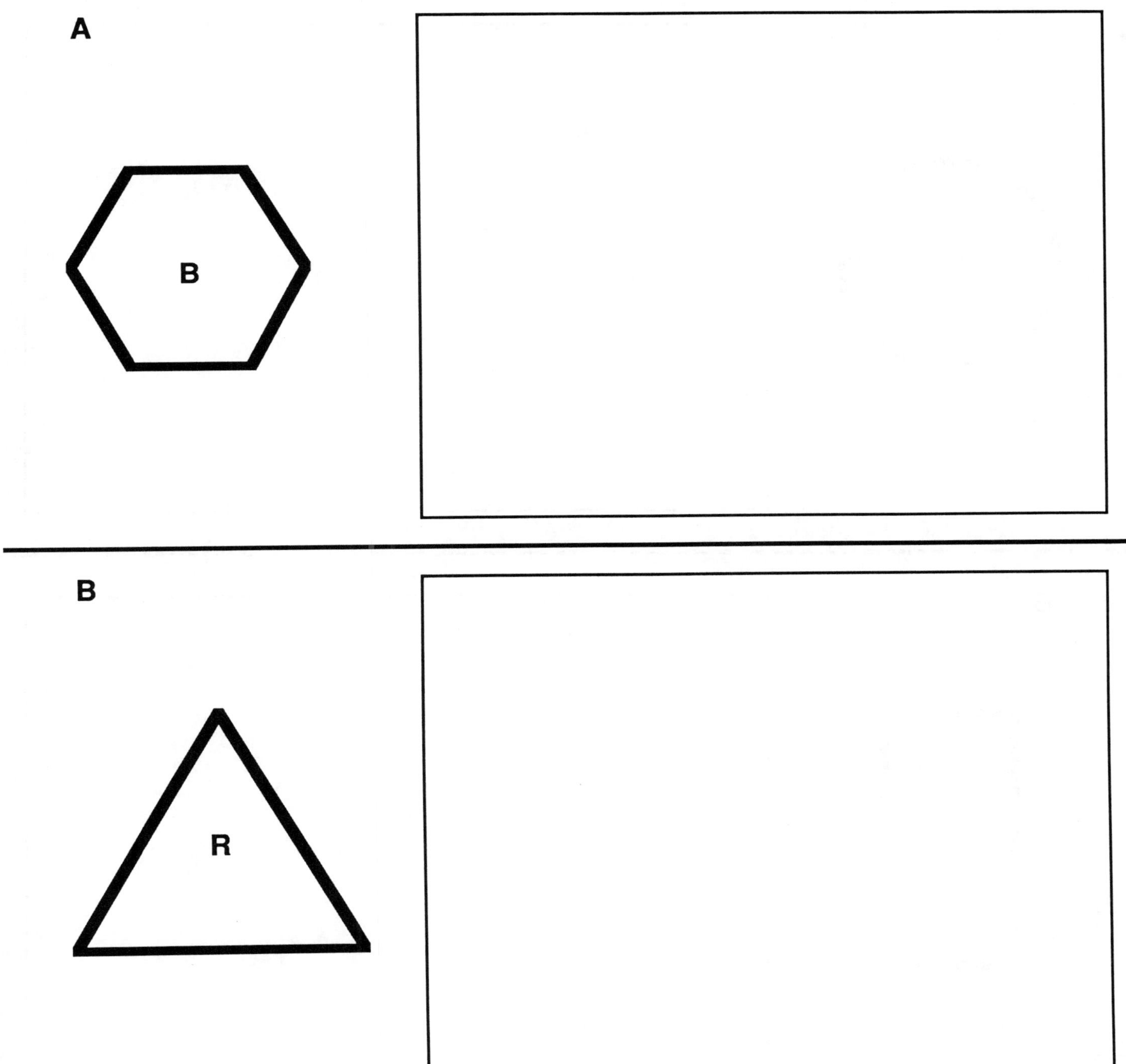

## GROUPING—COLOR AND SHAPE

Place a red (R) or yellow (Y) ATTRIBUTE BLOCK on each shape below.
In each box, place all the blocks that are the same shape but a different color.
Trace the blocks and color the pictures to match.

**A**

Y

**B**

R

## GROUPING—COLOR AND SHAPE

Place a red (R) or yellow (Y) ATTRIBUTE BLOCK on each shape below.
Fill each box with blocks that are the same color but a different shape.
Trace the blocks and color the pictures to match.

**A**

R

**B**

Y

## GROUPING—COLOR AND SHAPE

Place a red (R) or blue (B) ATTRIBUTE BLOCK on each shape below.
Fill each box with blocks that are the same color but a different shape.
Trace the blocks and color the pictures to match.

A

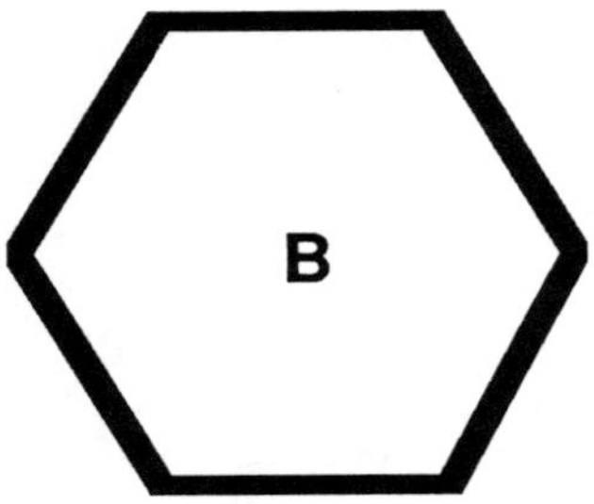

B

B

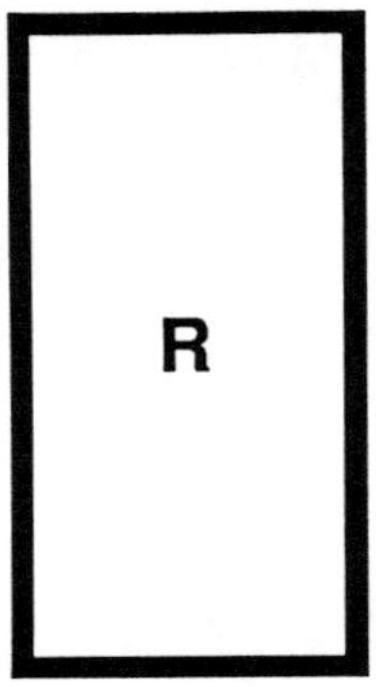

R

## GROUPING—COLOR AND SHAPE

Place a yellow (Y) or blue (B) ATTRIBUTE BLOCK on each shape below.
Fill each box with blocks that are a different shape and different color.
Trace the blocks and color the pictures to match.

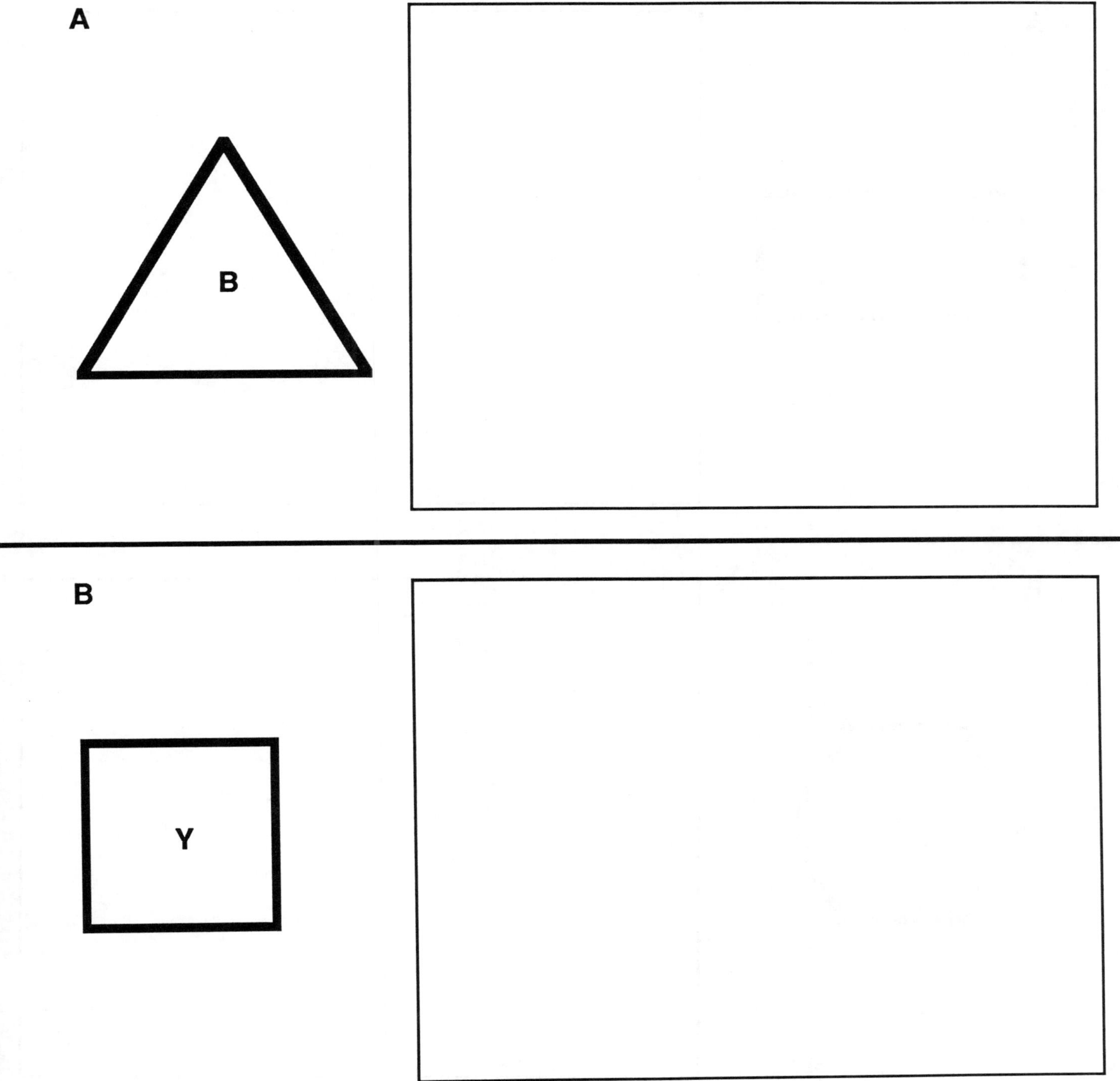

## GROUPING—COLOR AND SHAPE

Place a red (R) or yellow (Y) ATTRIBUTE BLOCK on each shape below.
Fill each box with blocks that are a different shape and different color.
Trace the blocks and color the pictures to match.

**A**

Y

**B**

R

## DESCRIBING A GROUP—WHAT DOES NOT BELONG?

Place a red (R), yellow (Y), or blue (B) ATTRIBUTE BLOCK on each shape below.
In each box, remove the block that does not belong to the group.
Color the pictures of the shapes that do belong to the group.

A

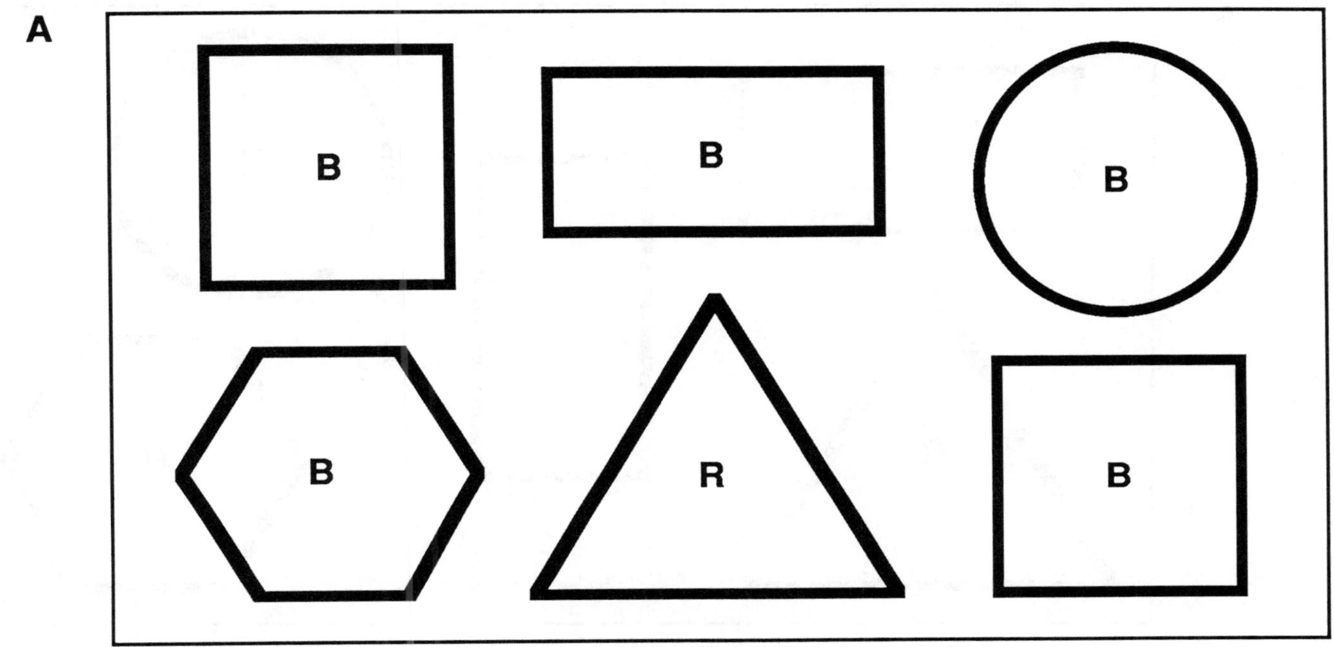


B

## DESCRIBING A GROUP—WHAT DOES NOT BELONG?

Place a red (R), yellow (Y), or blue (B) ATTRIBUTE BLOCK on each shape below.
In each box, remove the block that does not belong to the group.
Color the pictures of the shapes that do belong to the group.

**A**

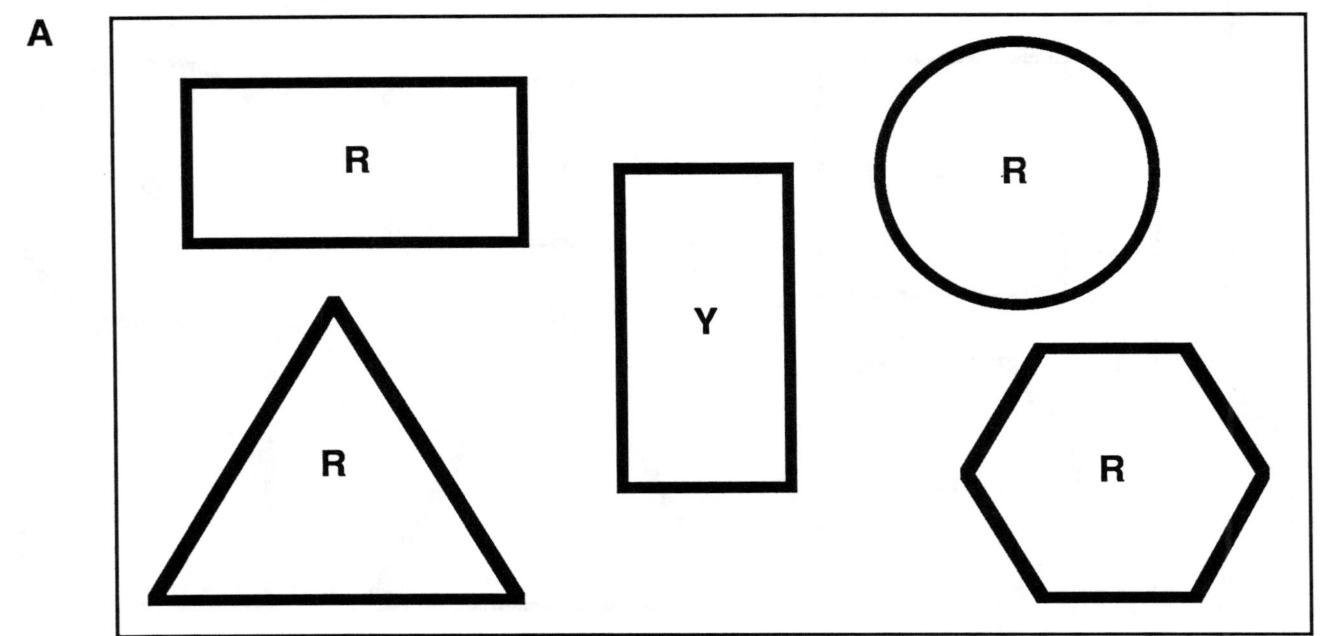


**B**

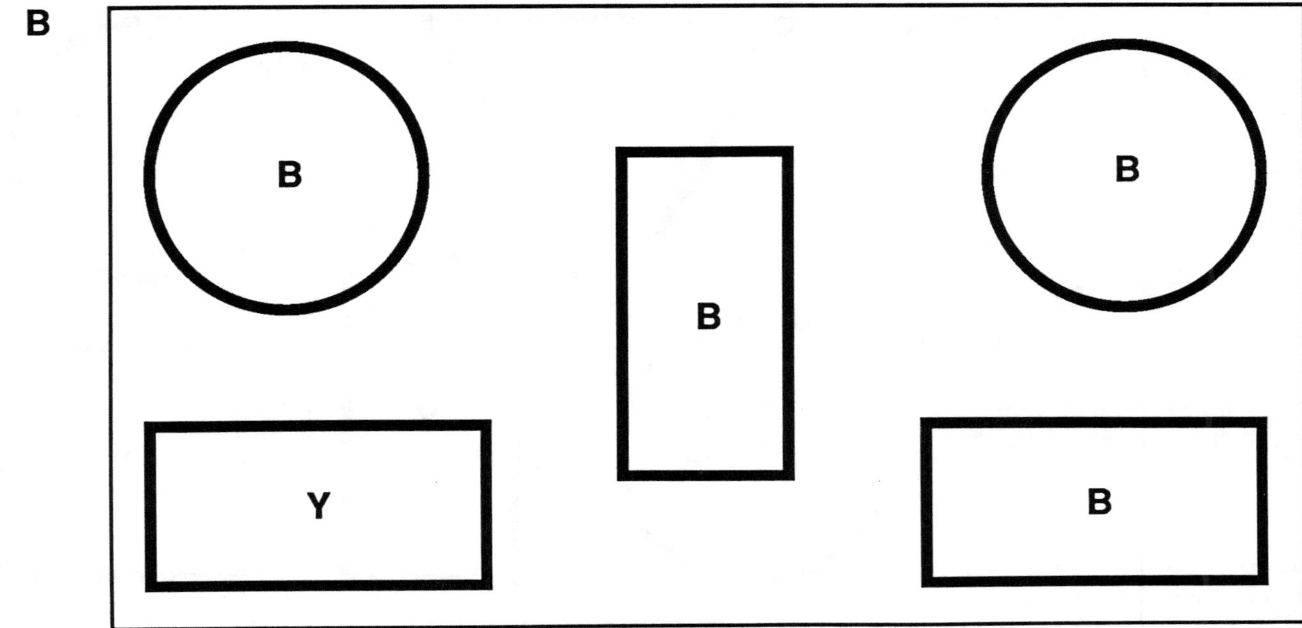

## DESCRIBING A GROUP—WHAT DOES NOT BELONG?

Place a red (R), yellow (Y), or blue (B) ATTRIBUTE BLOCK on each shape below.
In each box, remove the block that does not belong to the group.
Color the pictures of the shapes that do belong to the group.

A

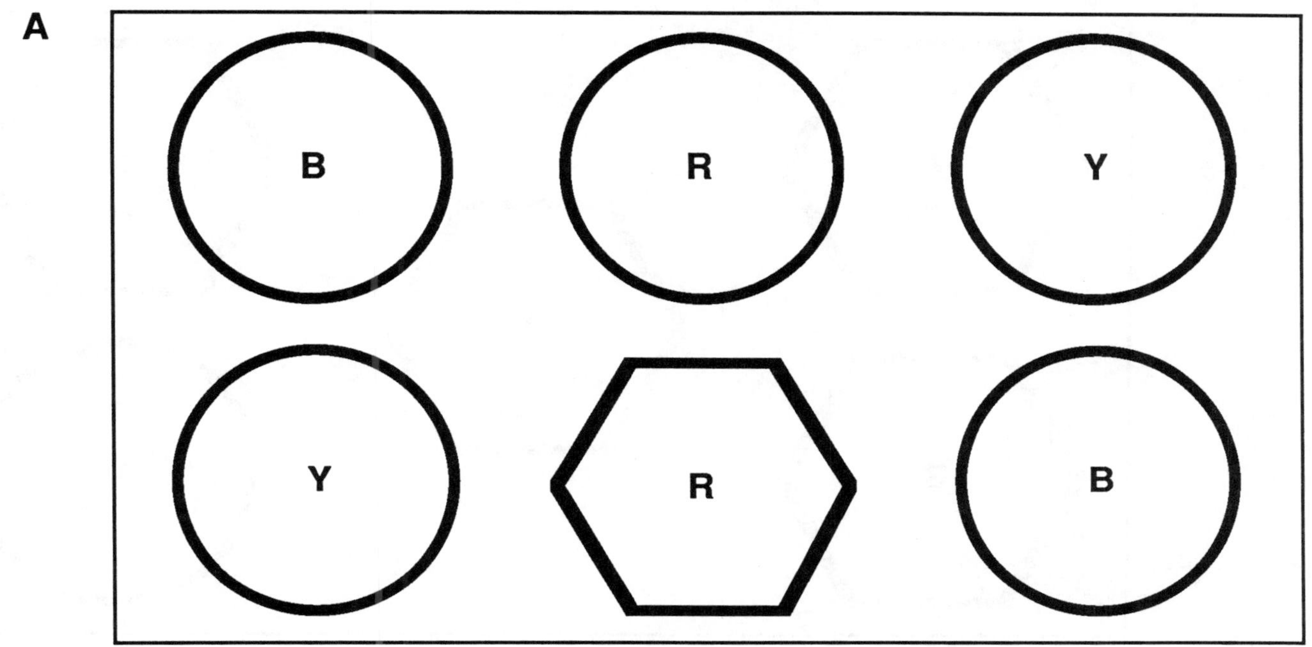


B

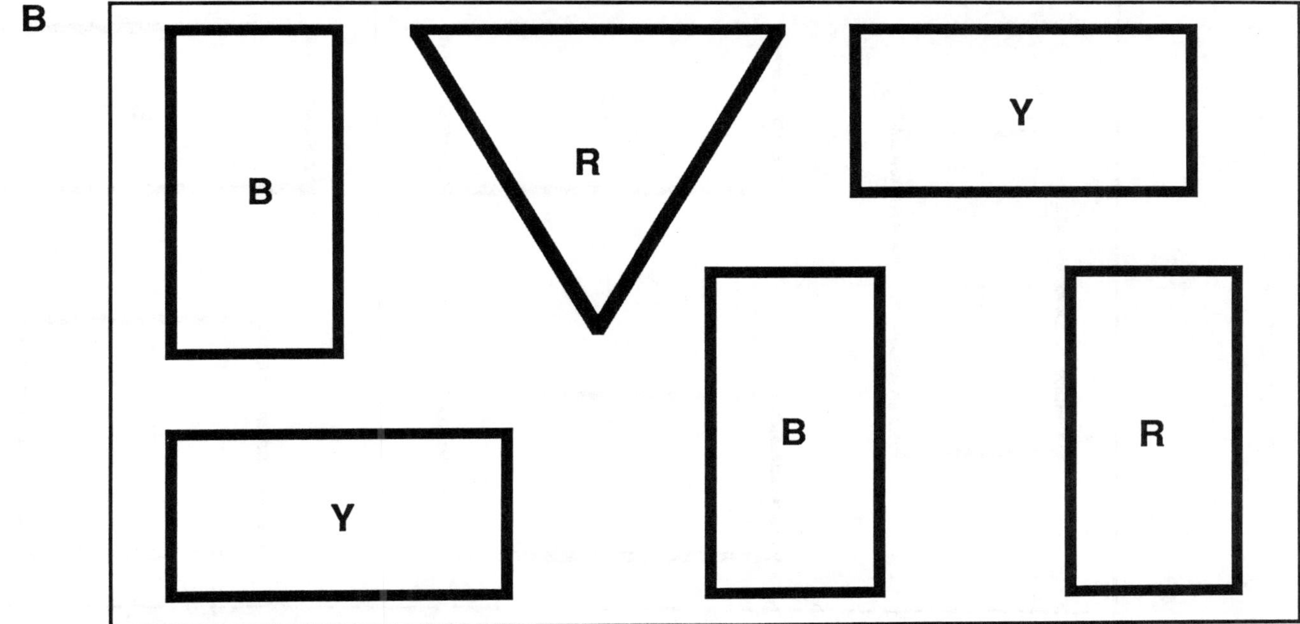

# DESCRIBING A GROUP—WHAT DOES NOT BELONG?

Place a red (R), yellow (Y), or blue (B) ATTRIBUTE BLOCK on each shape below.
In each box, remove the block that does not belong to the group.
Color the pictures of the shapes that do belong to the group.

A

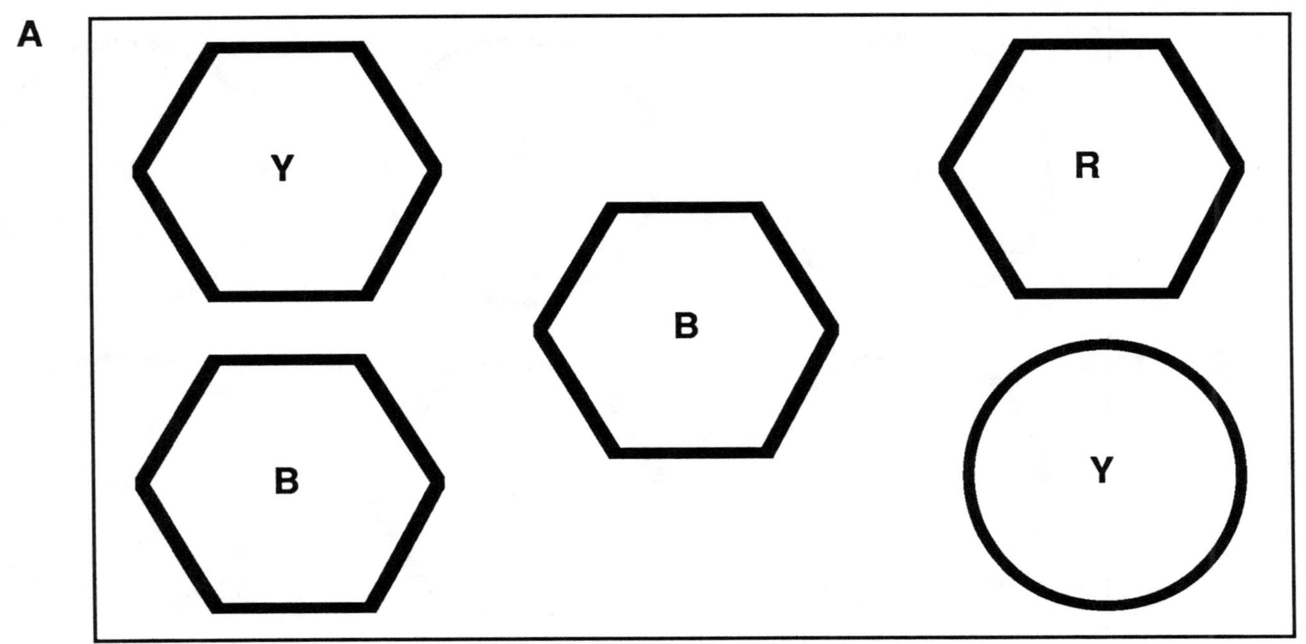


B

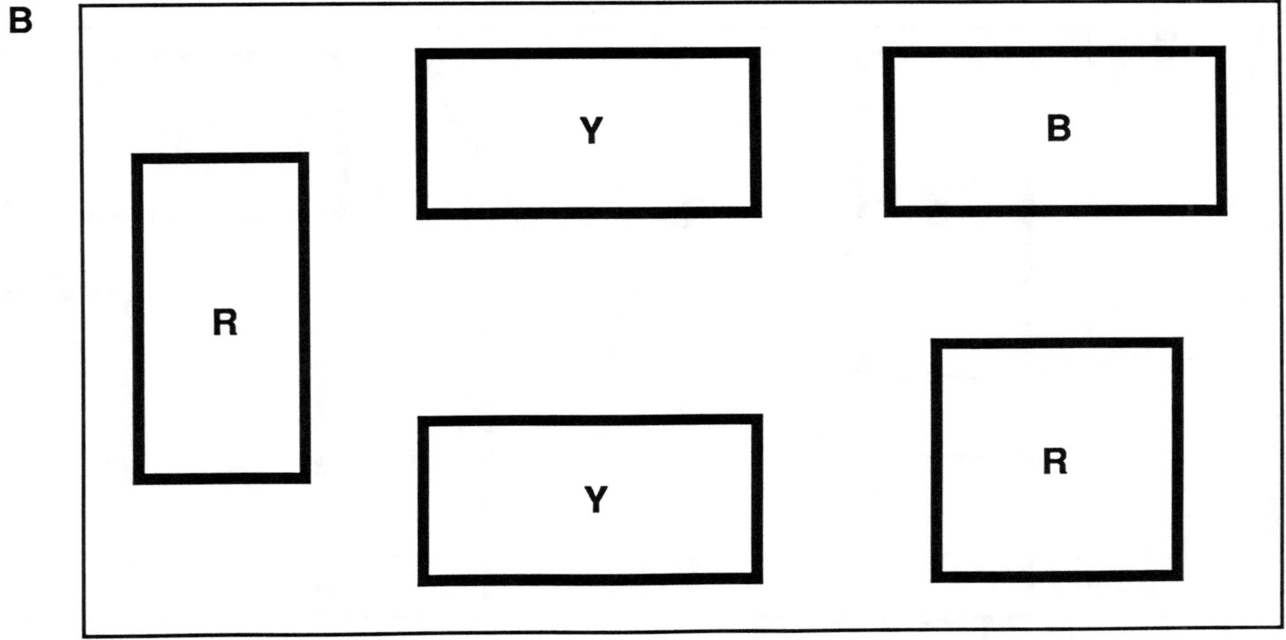

## DESCRIBING A GROUP—WHAT DOES NOT BELONG?

Place a PATTERN BLOCK on each shape below.
In each box, remove the block that does not belong to the group.
Color the pictures of the shapes that do belong to the group.

**A**

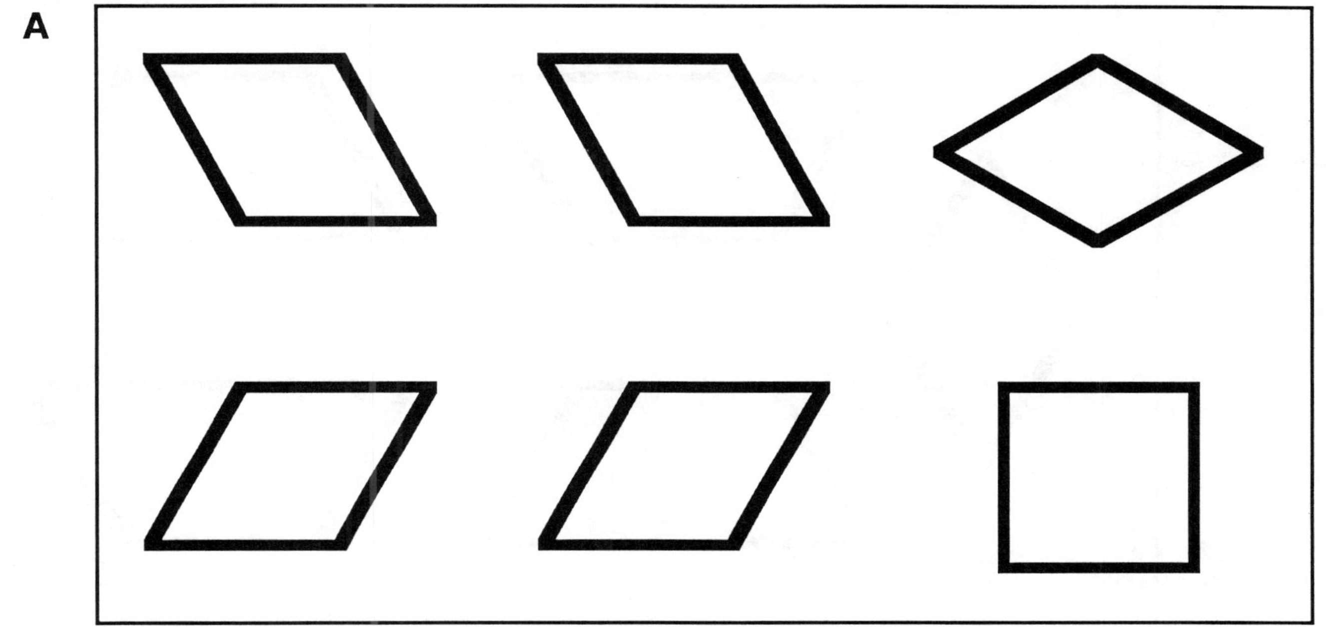

**B**

## DESCRIBING A GROUP—WHAT DOES NOT BELONG?

Place a PATTERN BLOCK on each shape below.
In each box, remove the block that does not belong to the group.
Color the pictures of the shapes that do belong to the group.

**A**

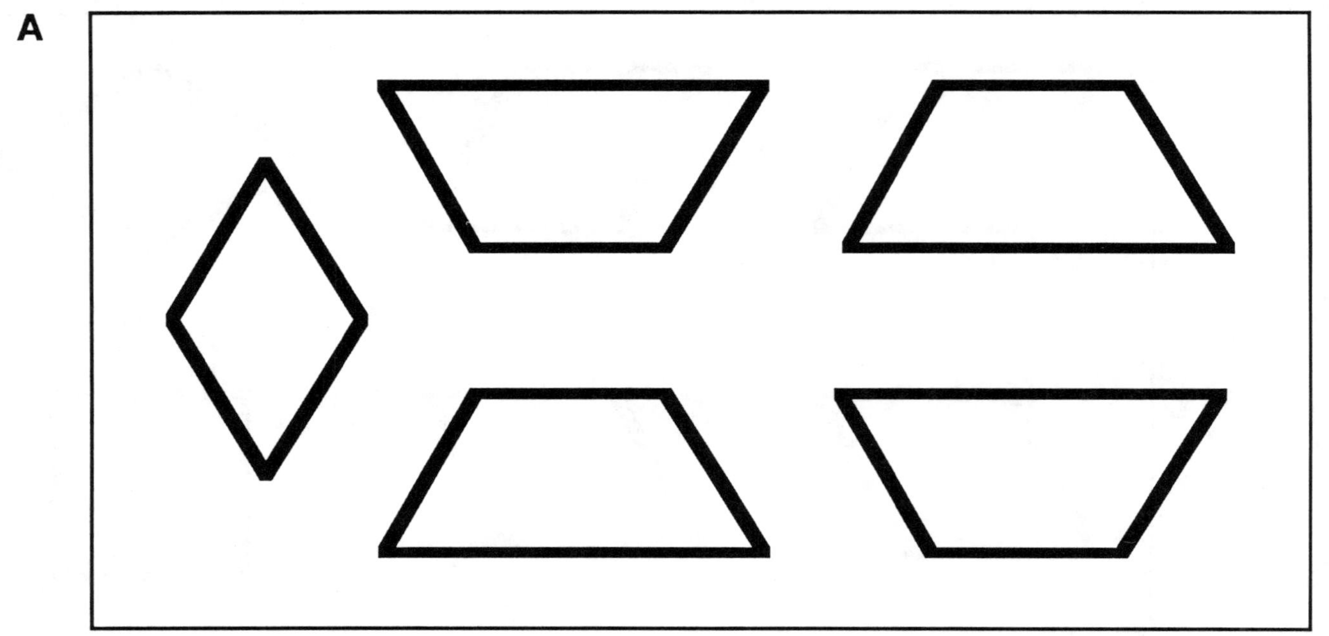

**B**

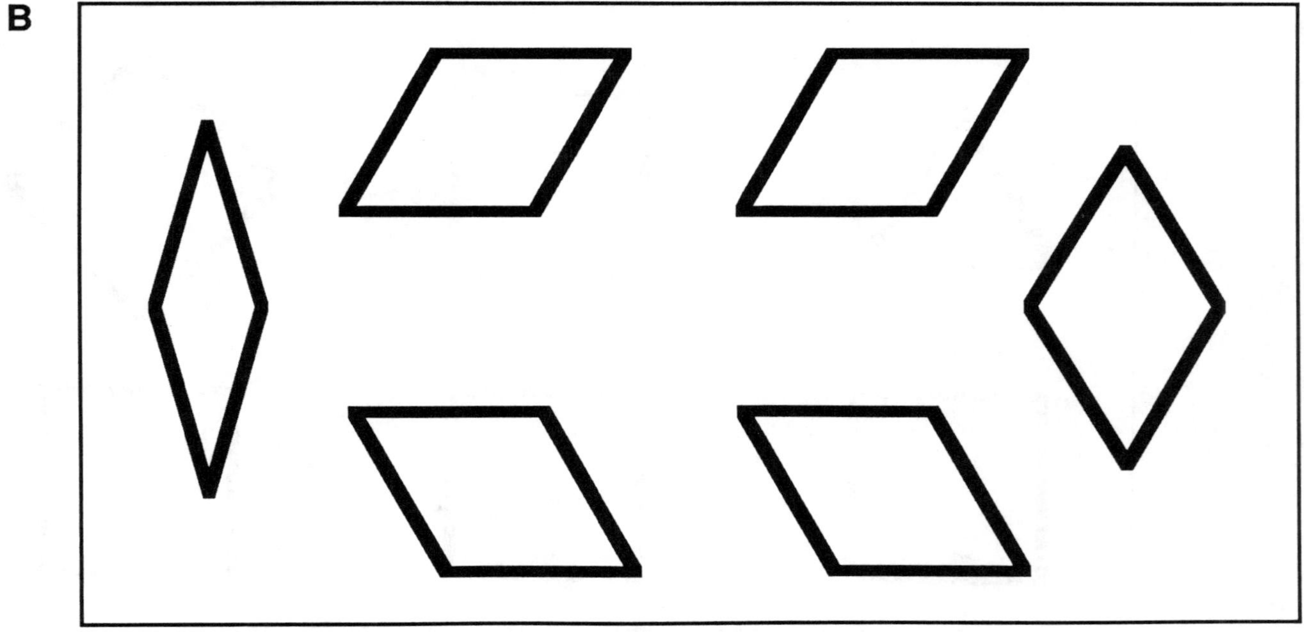

## DESCRIBING A GROUP—ADDING SHAPES

Place a PATTERN BLOCK on each shape below.
In each box, add one more block that belongs to the group.
Trace the blocks and color the pictures to match.

**A**

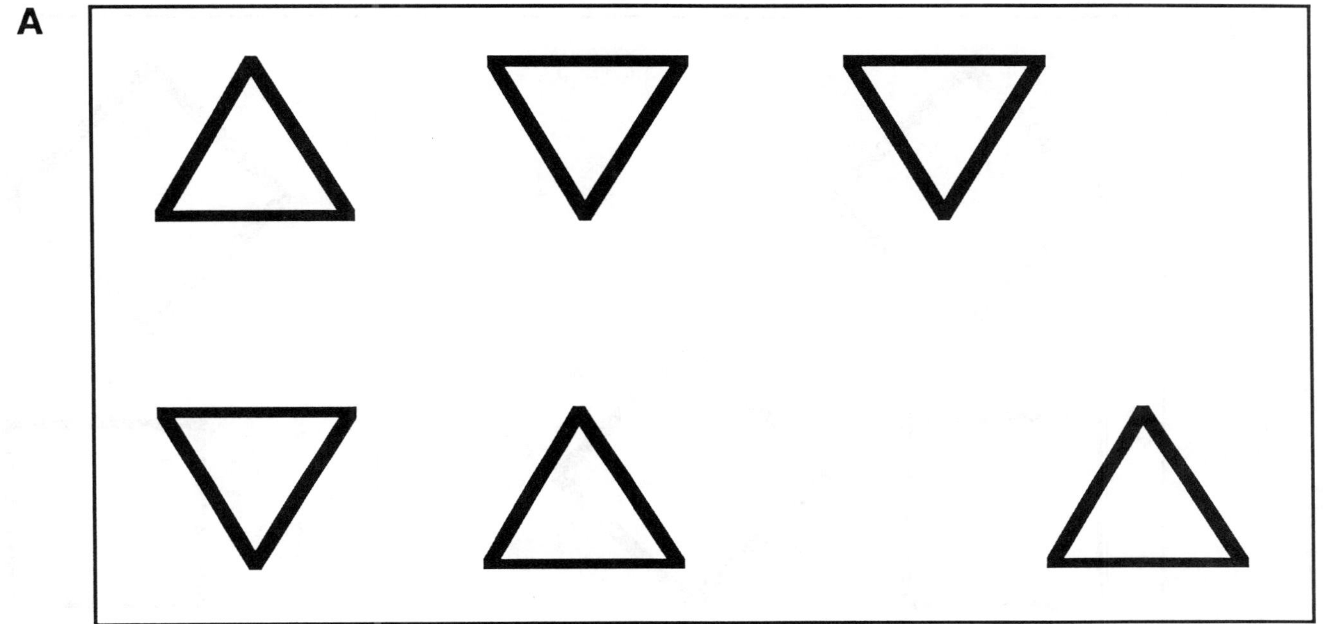

**B**

## DESCRIBING A GROUP—ADDING SHAPES

Place a PATTERN BLOCK on each shape below.
In each box, add TWO more blocks that belong to the group.
Trace the blocks and color the pictures to match.

A

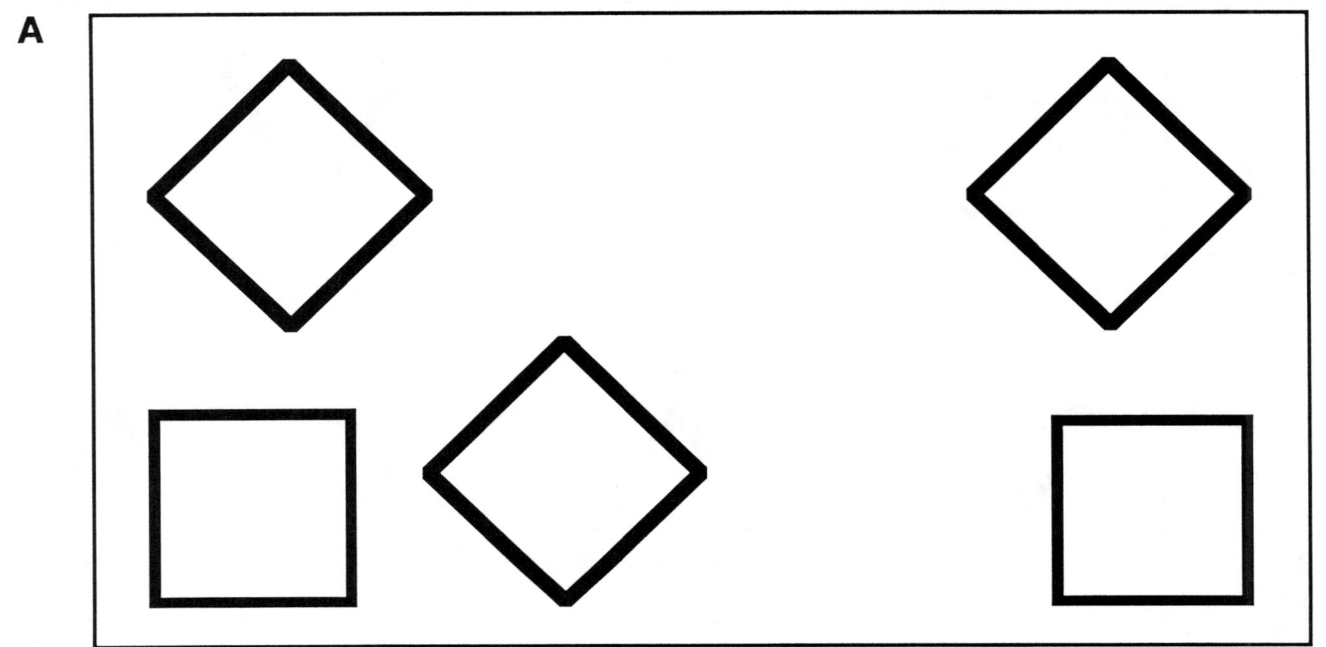

B

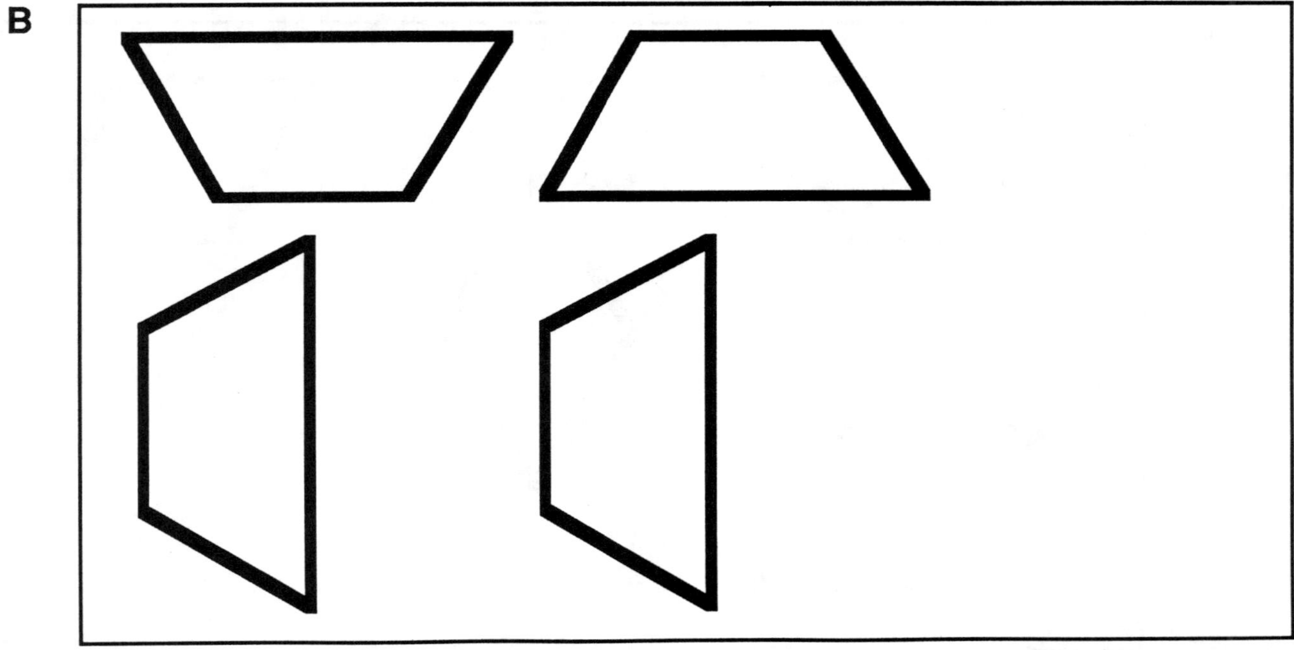

## DESCRIBING A GROUP—ADDING SHAPES

Place a red (R) or blue (B) ATTRIBUTE BLOCK on each shape below.
In each box, add one more block that belongs to the group.
Trace the blocks and color the pictures to match.

A

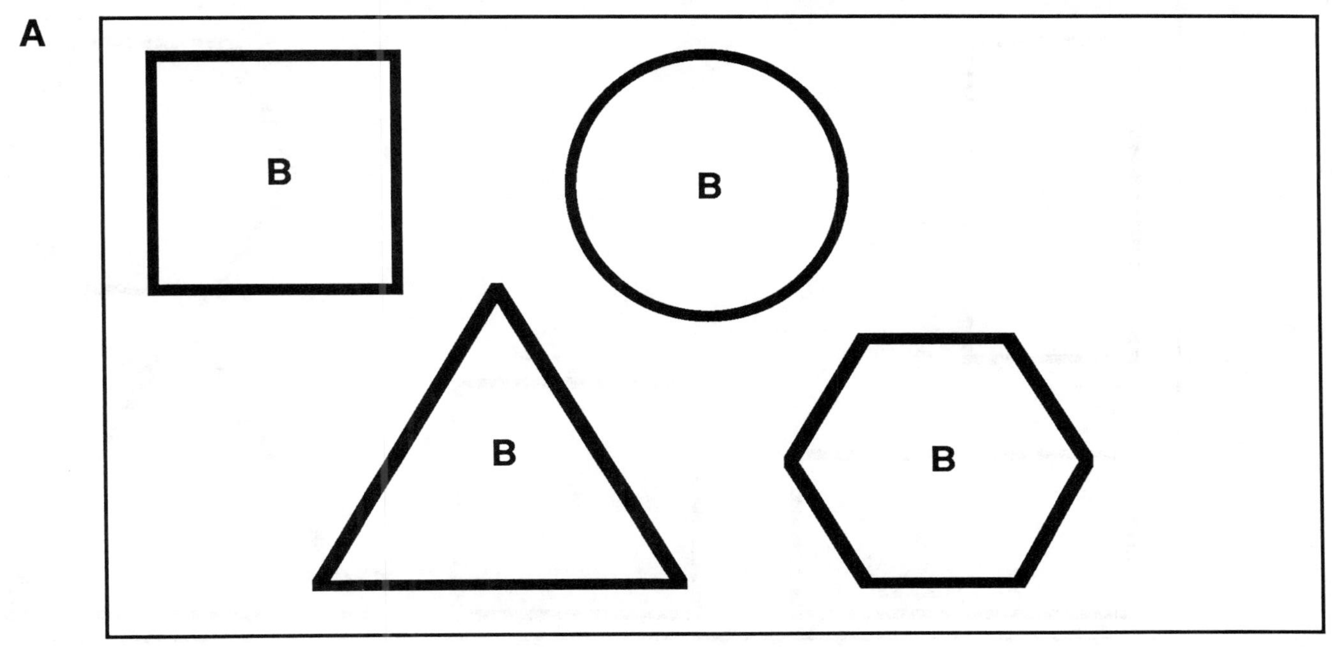


B

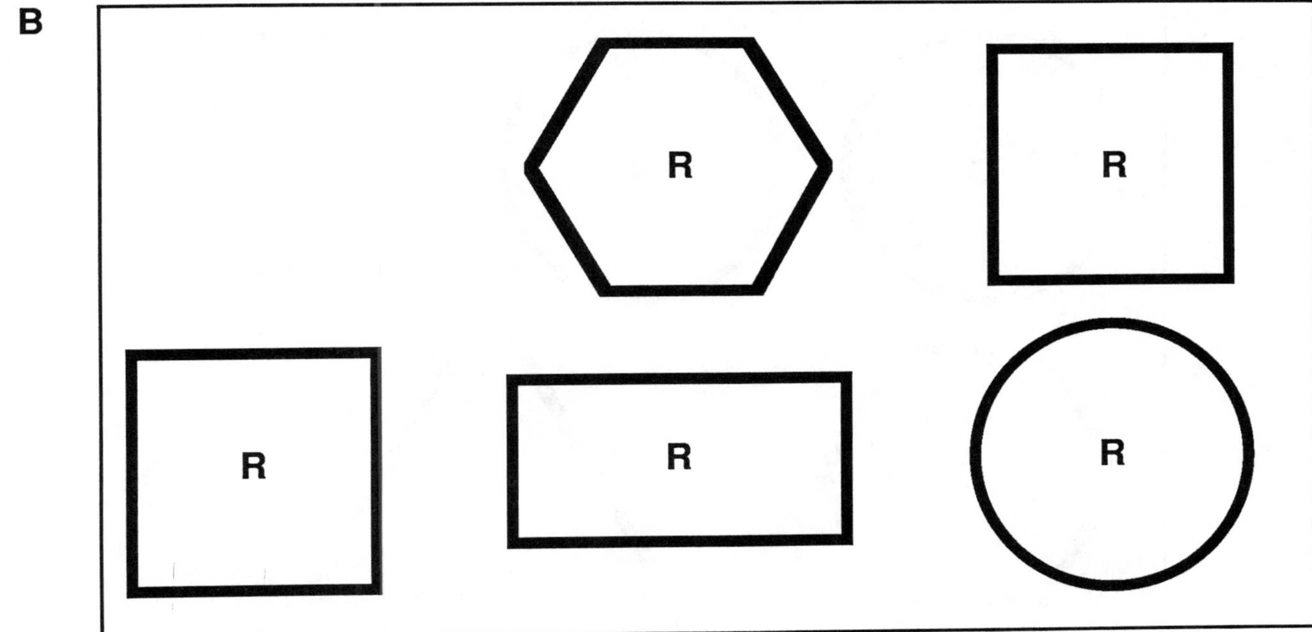

## DESCRIBING A GROUP—ADDING SHAPES

Place a yellow (Y) or blue (B) ATTRIBUTE BLOCK on each shape below.
In each box, add one more block that belongs to the group.
Trace the blocks and color the pictures to match.

**A**

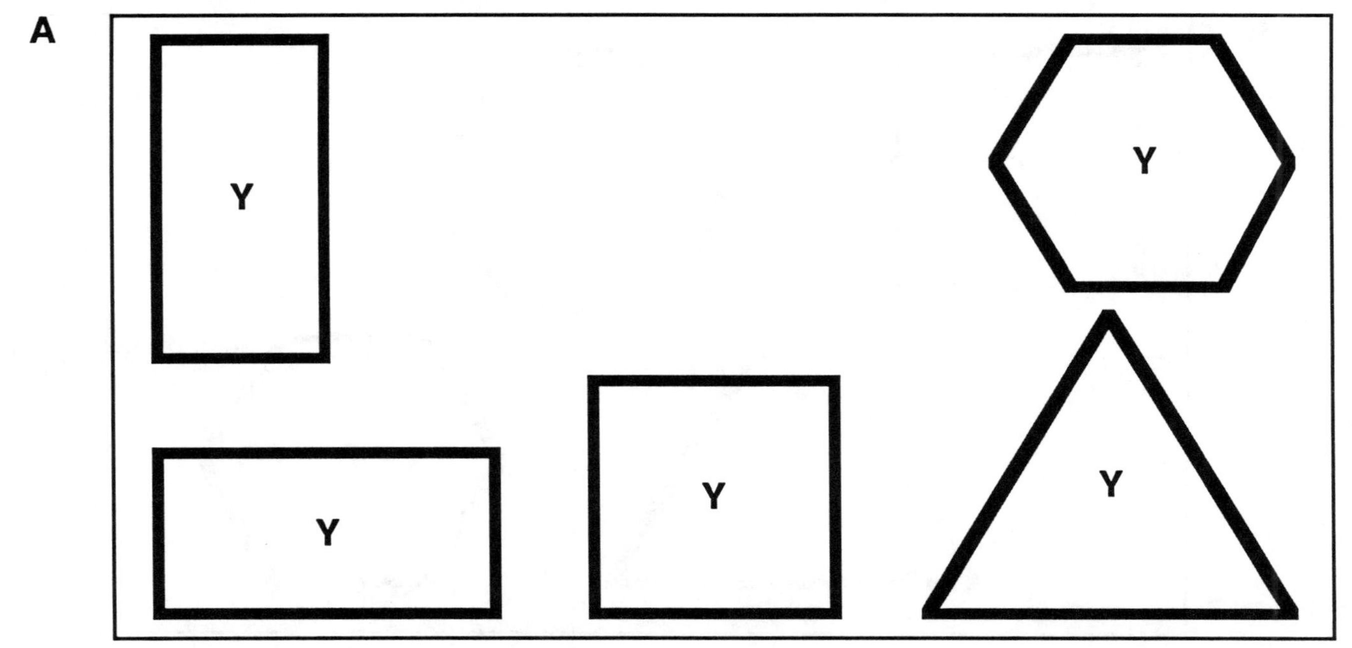


**B**

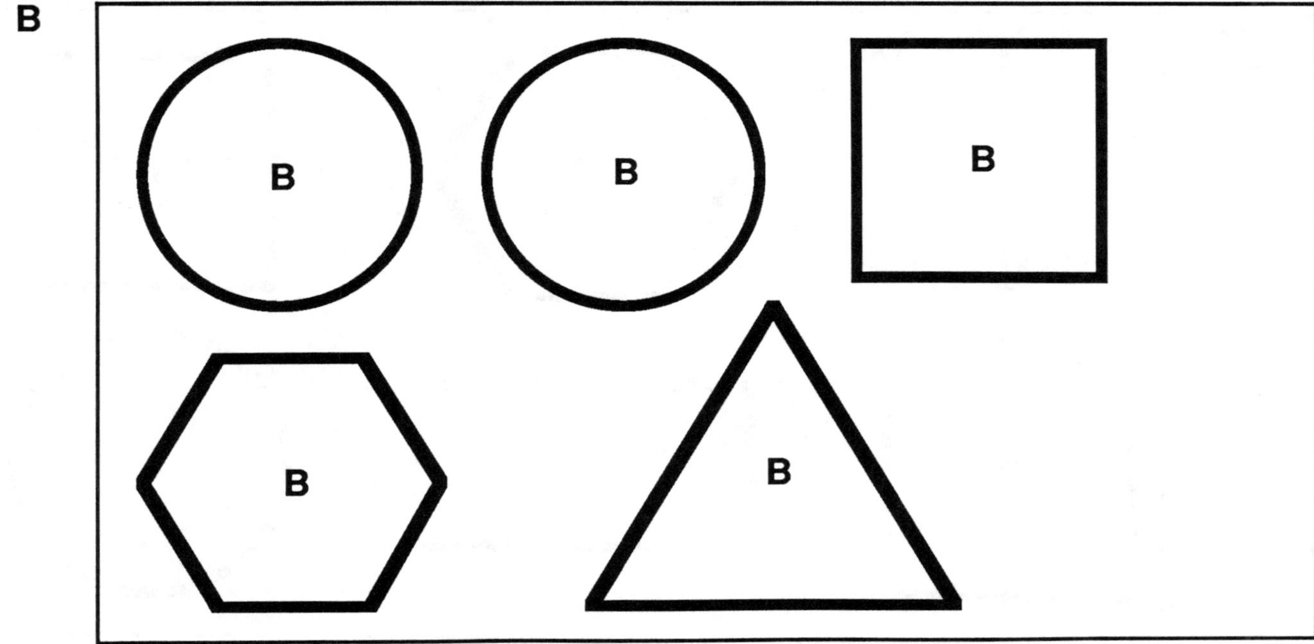

## DESCRIBING A GROUP—ADDING SHAPES

Place a red (R), yellow (Y), or blue (B) ATTRIBUTE BLOCK on each shape below.
In each box, add one more block that belongs to the group.
Trace the blocks and color the pictures to match.

A

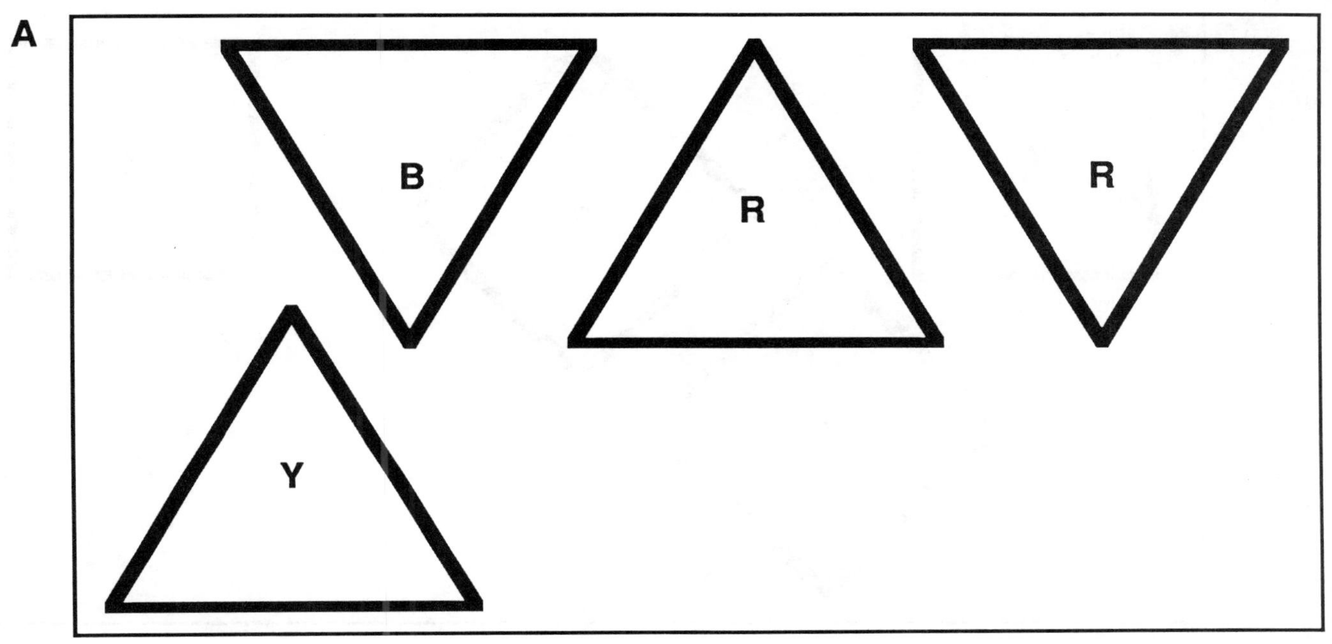


B

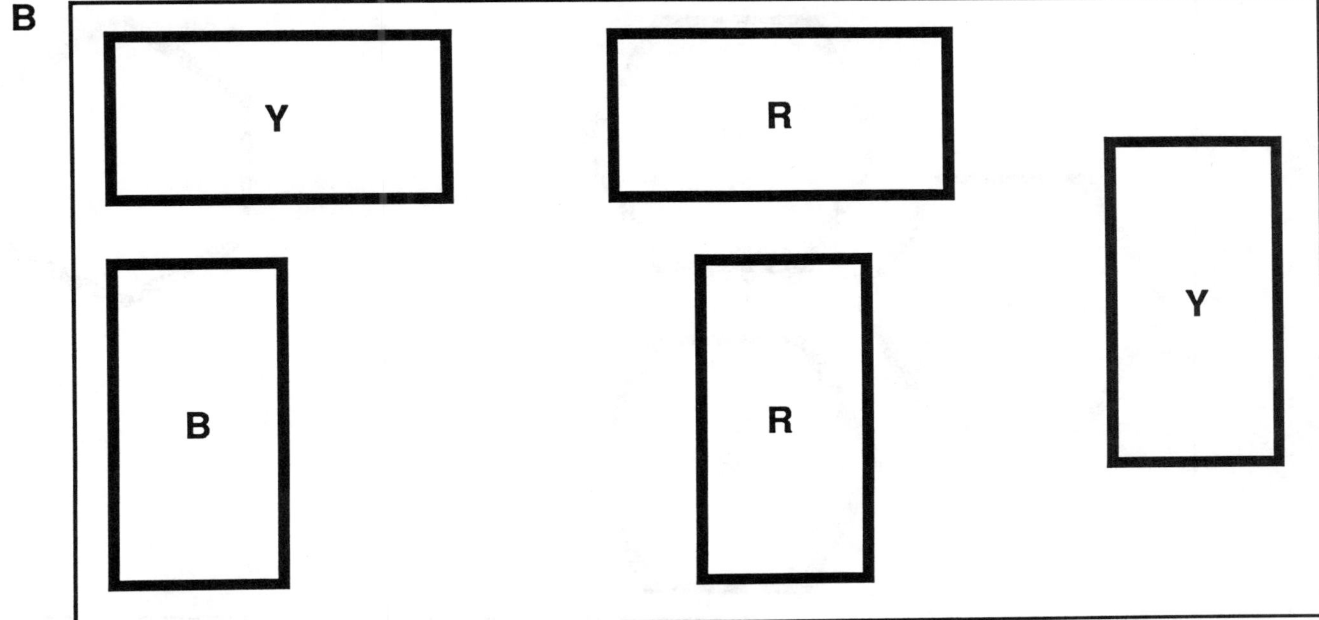

## DESCRIBING A GROUP—ADDING SHAPES

Place a red (R), yellow (Y), or blue (B) ATTRIBUTE BLOCK on each shape below.
In each box, add TWO more blocks that belong to the group.
Trace the blocks and color the pictures to match.

**A**

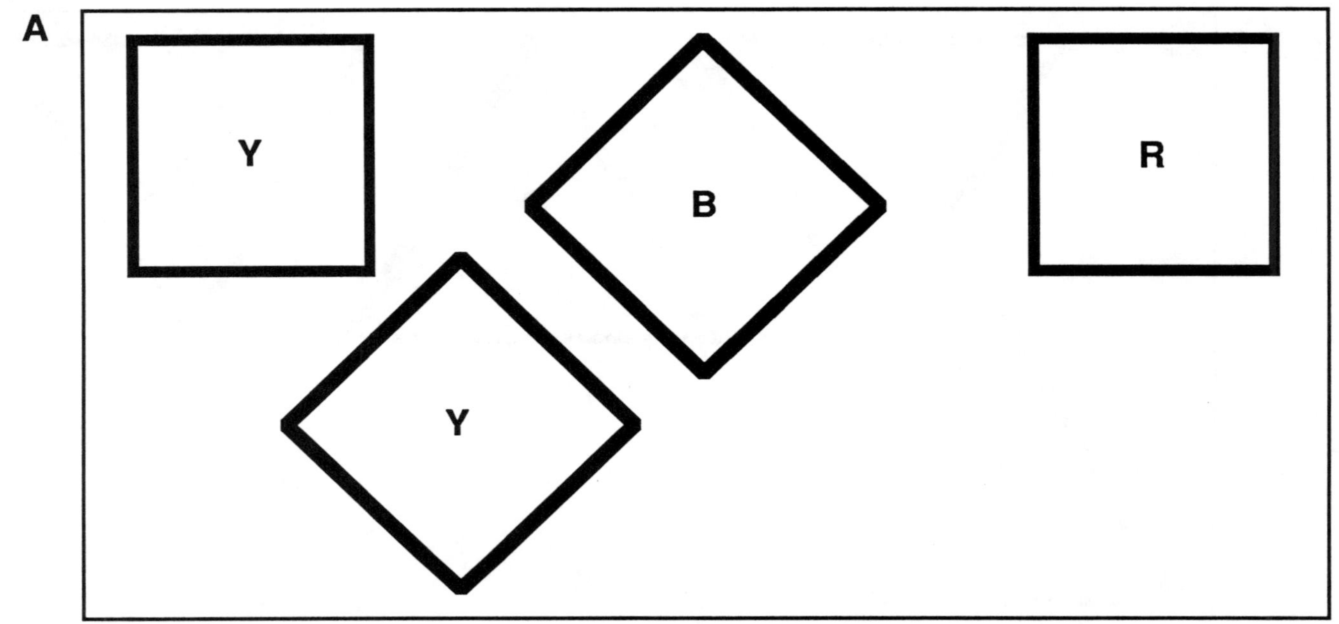


**B**

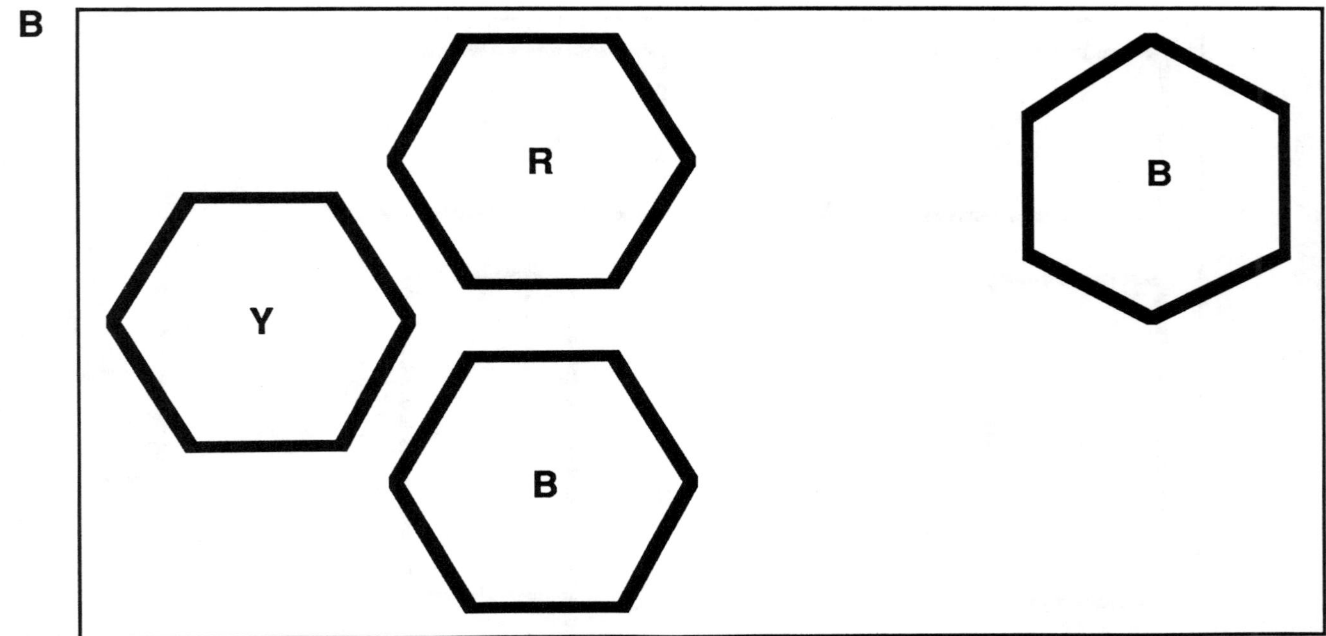

## DESCRIBING A GROUP—WHAT BELONGS?

Place a red (R), yellow (Y), or blue (B) ATTRIBUTE BLOCK on each shape in the first column.
Draw a line from each block to the group in which it belongs.
The pictures of the shapes in each group are smaller than your blocks.

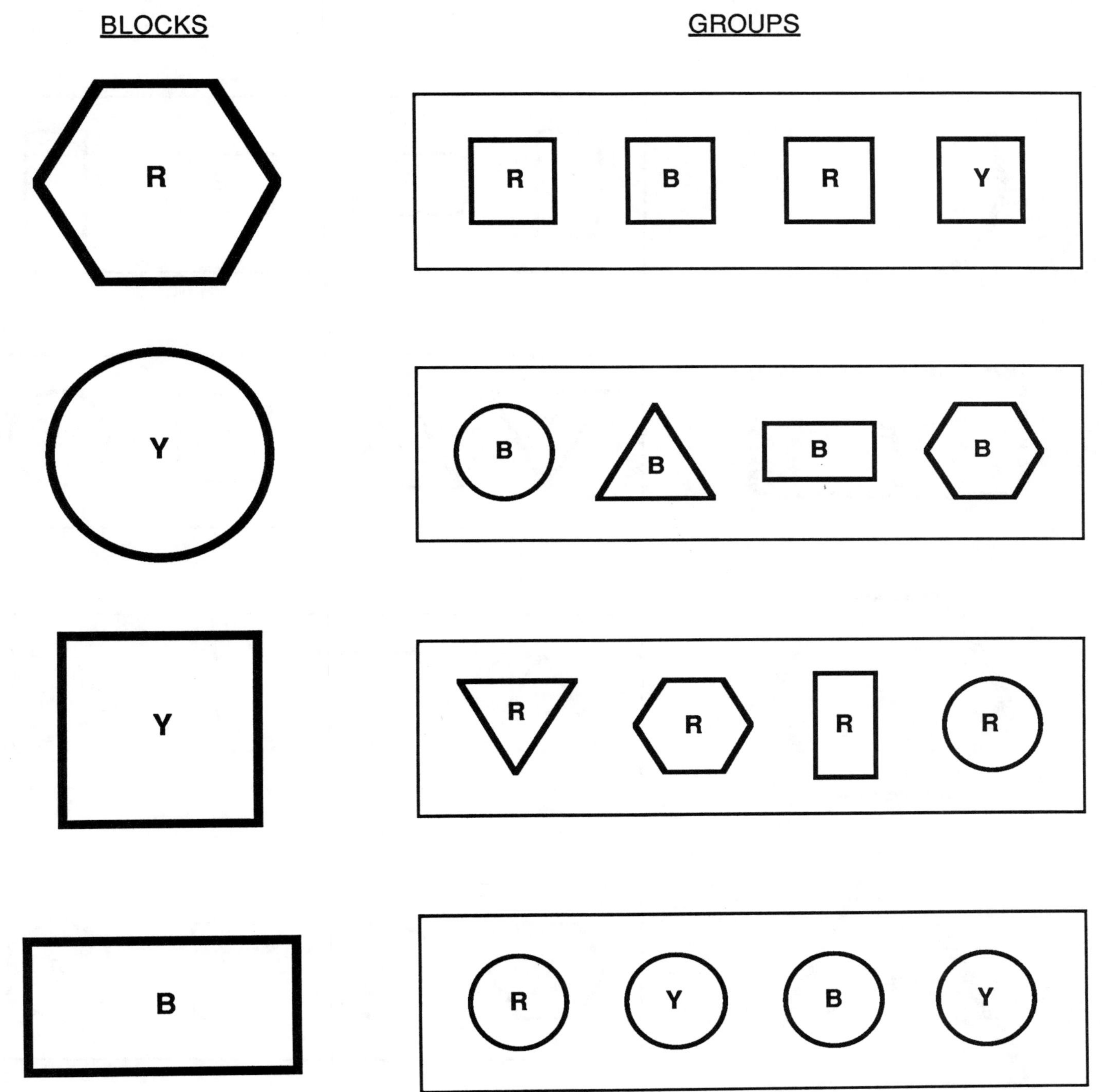

## DESCRIBING A GROUP—WHAT BELONGS?

Place a red (R), yellow (Y), or blue (B) ATTRIBUTE BLOCK on each shape in the first column.
Draw a line from each block to the group in which it belongs.
The pictures of the shapes in each group are smaller than your blocks.

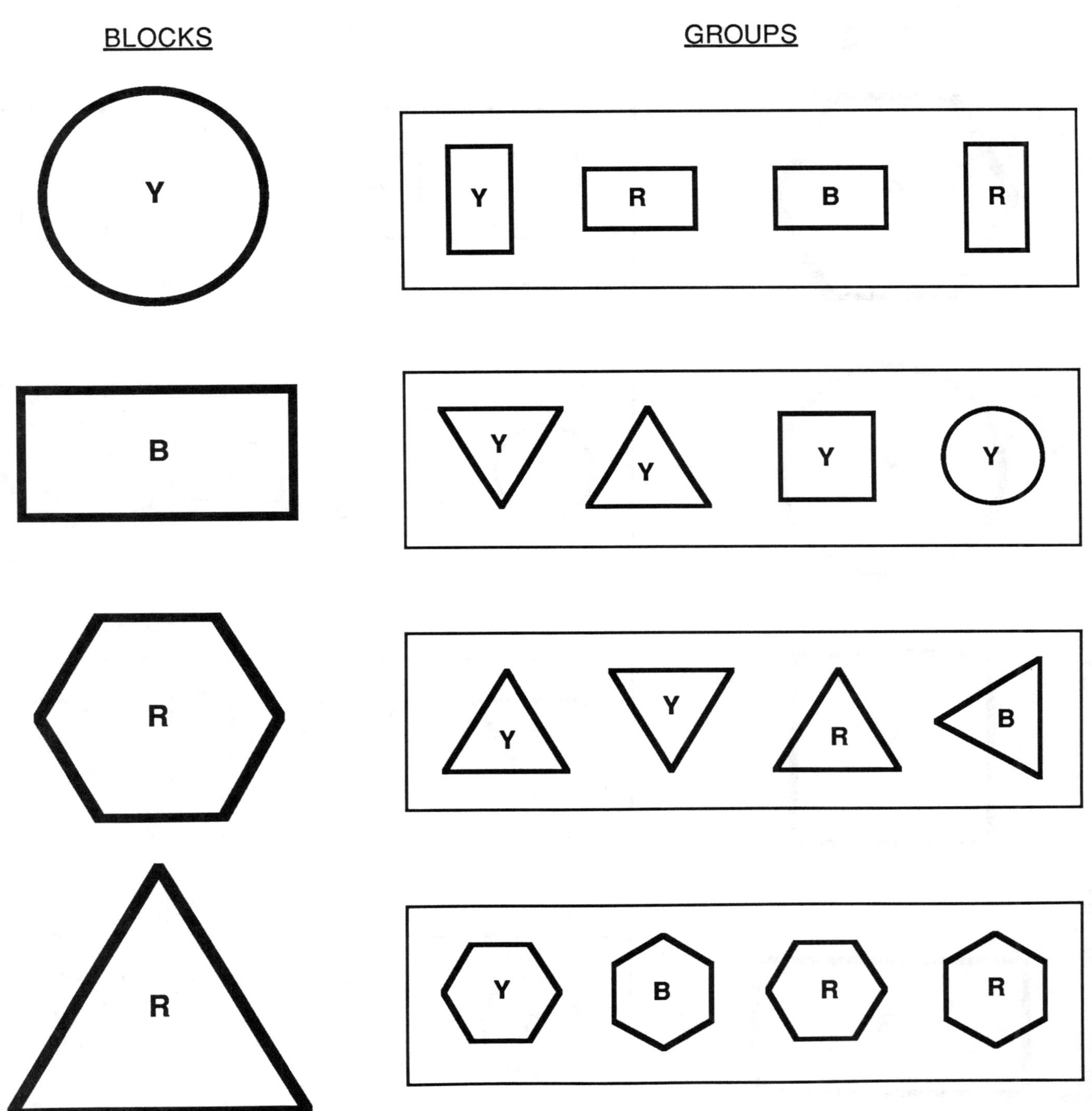

## DESCRIBING A GROUP—WHAT BELONGS?

Make a red (R), yellow (Y), or blue (B) INTERLOCKING CUBE construction to cover each figure in the first column.
Draw a line from each figure to the group in which it belongs.
The pictures of the figures in each group are smaller than your constructions.

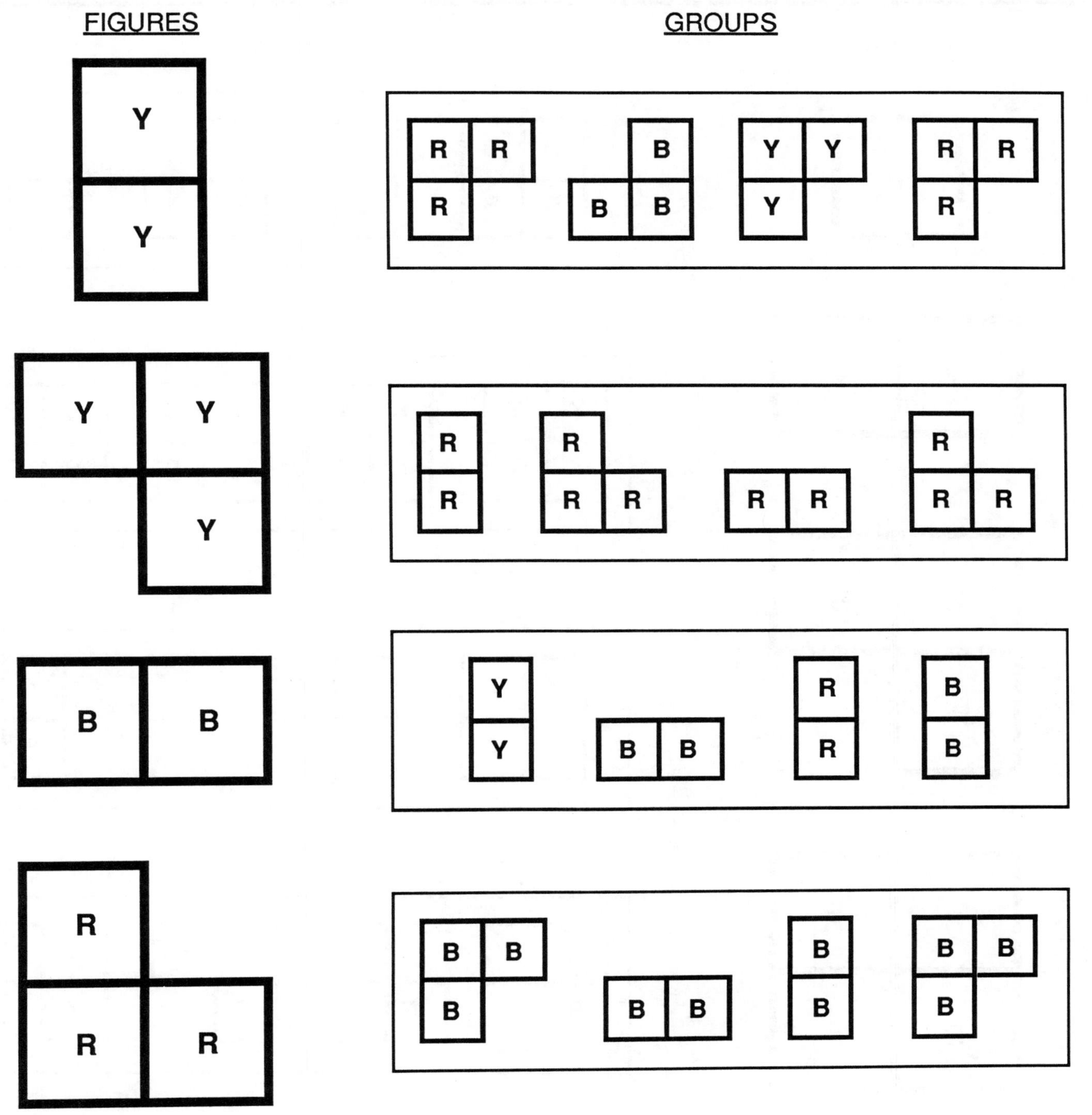

## DESCRIBING A GROUP—WHAT BELONGS?

Make a red (R), yellow (Y), or blue (B) INTERLOCKING CUBE construction to cover each figure in the first column.
Draw a line from each figure to the group in which it belongs.
The pictures of the figures in each group are smaller than your constructions.

---

FIGURES GROUPS

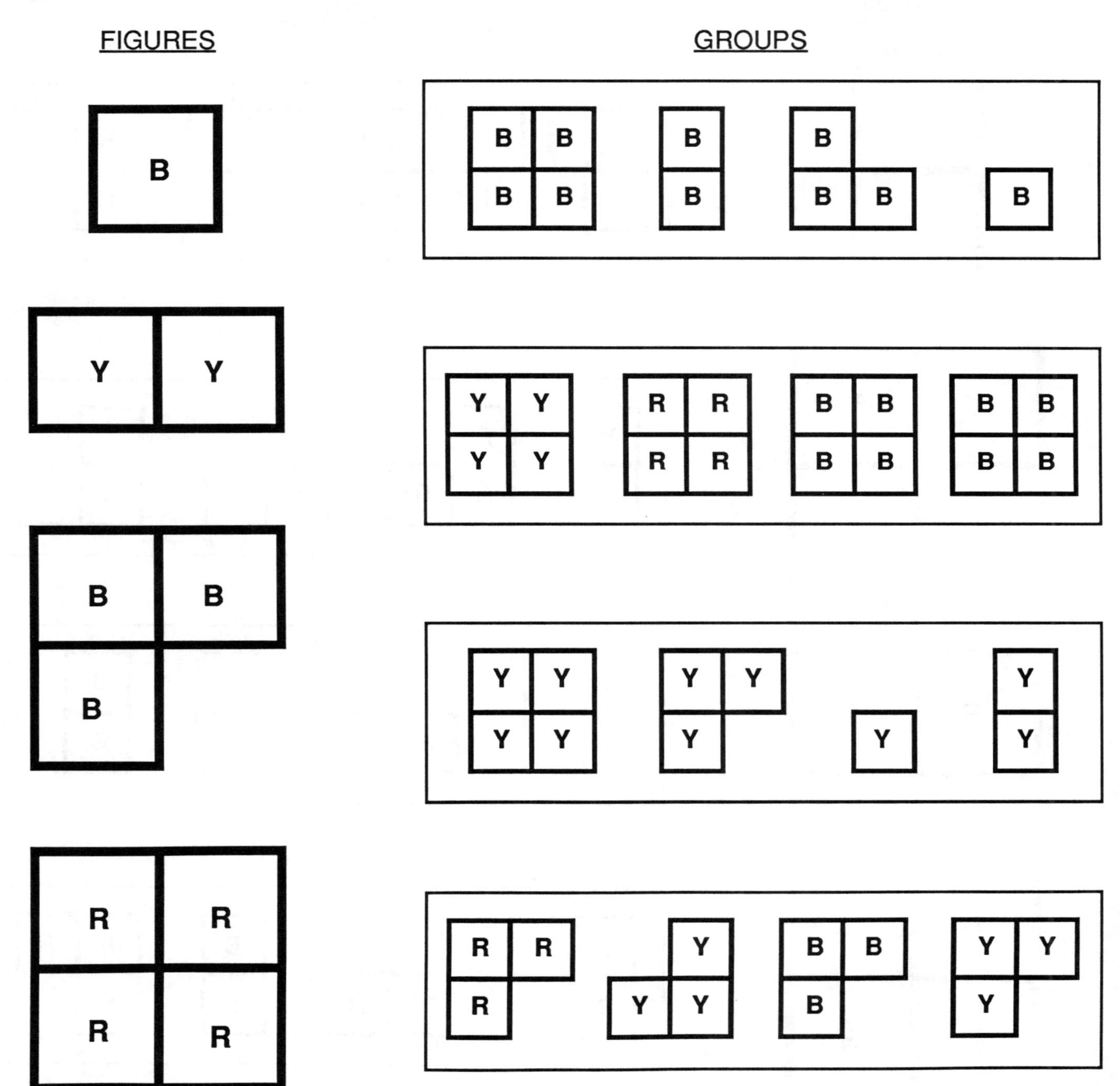

## SEPARATING GROUPS BY COLOR

Place a red (R) or yellow (Y) ATTRIBUTE BLOCK on each shape below.
Move the red blocks into the first small box and the yellow blocks into the second.
Trace the blocks and color the pictures to match.

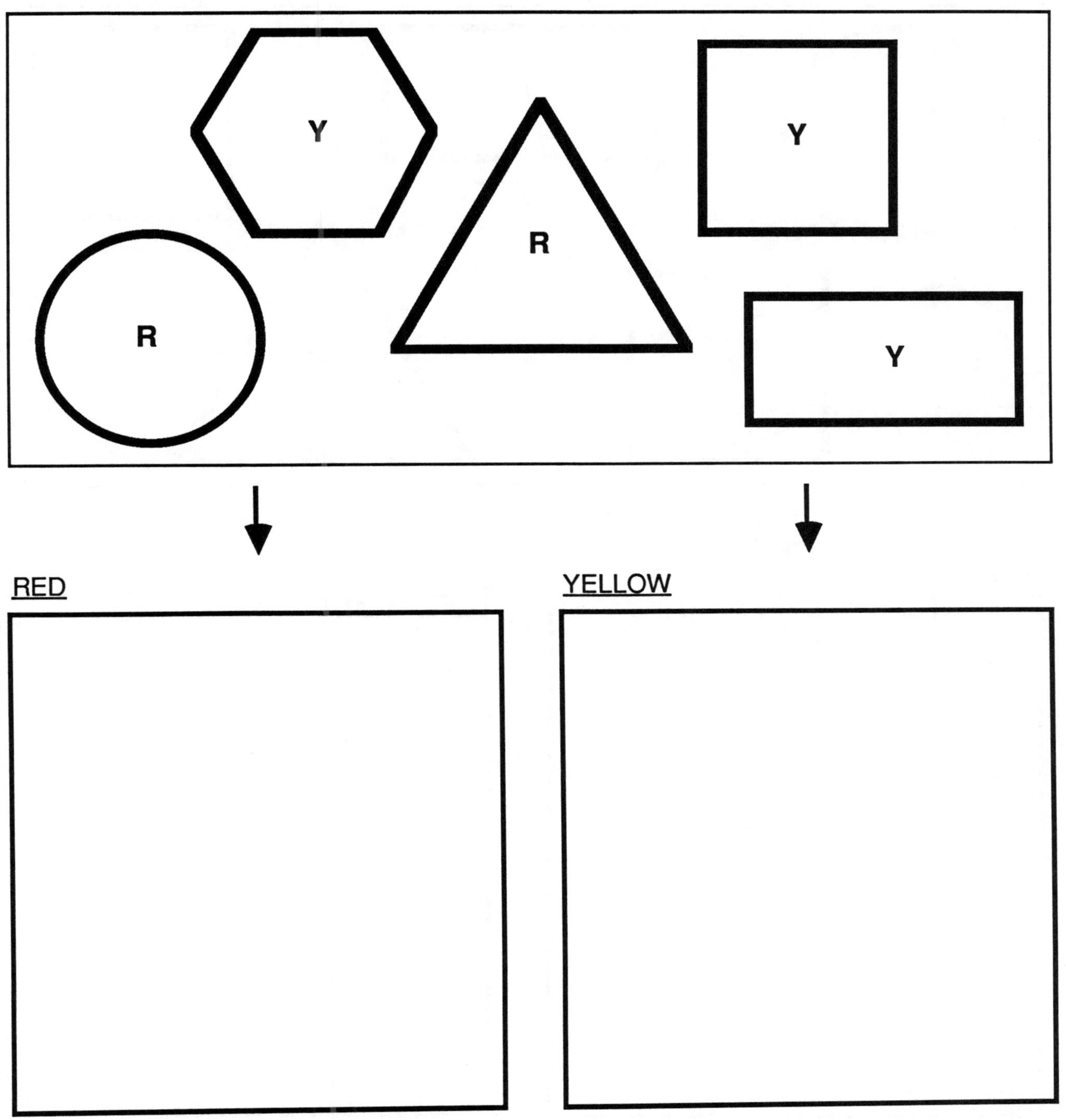

# SEPARATING GROUPS BY COLOR

Place a red (R) or blue (B) ATTRIBUTE BLOCK on each shape below.
Move the red blocks into the first small box and the blue blocks into the second.
Trace the blocks and color the pictures to match.

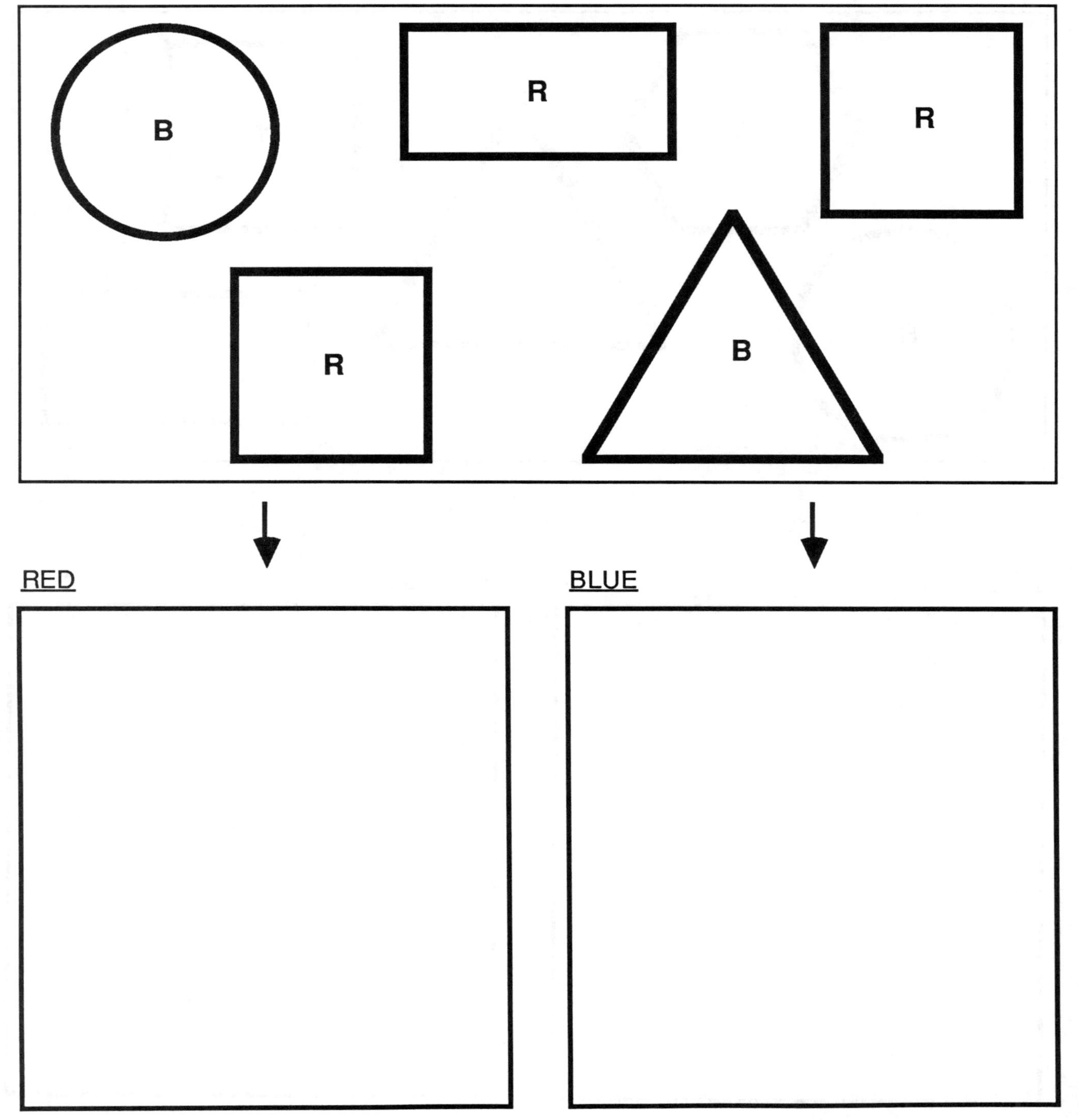

## SEPARATING GROUPS BY SHAPE

Place ATTRIBUTE BLOCKS on the shapes in the top box. Use any colors you wish.
Move the rectangles into the first small box and the squares into the second.
Trace the blocks and color the pictures to match.

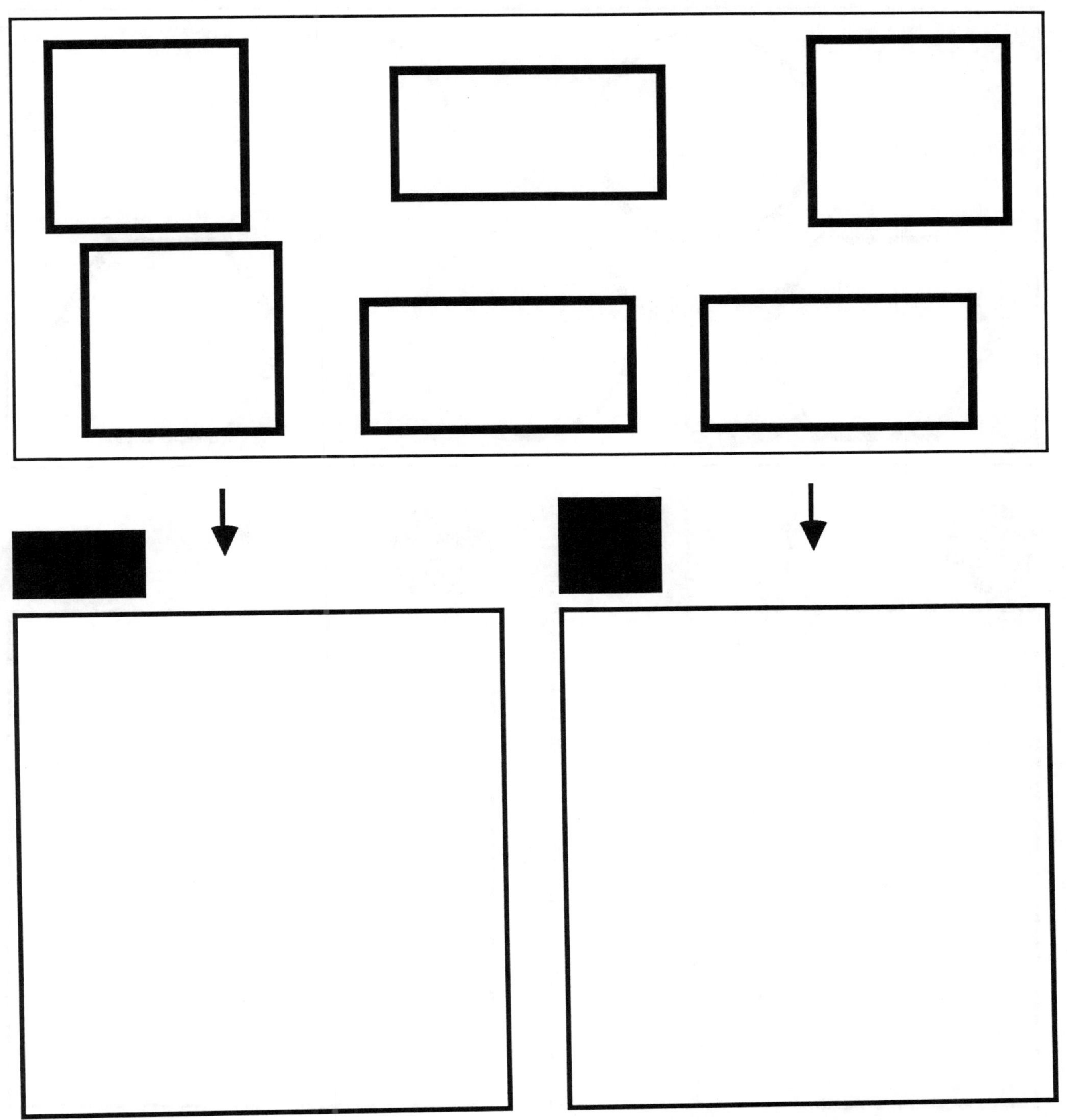

## SEPARATING GROUPS BY SHAPE

Place ATTRIBUTE BLOCKS on the shapes in the top box. Use any colors you wish.
Move the circles into the first small box and the hexagons into the second.
Trace the blocks and color the pictures to match.

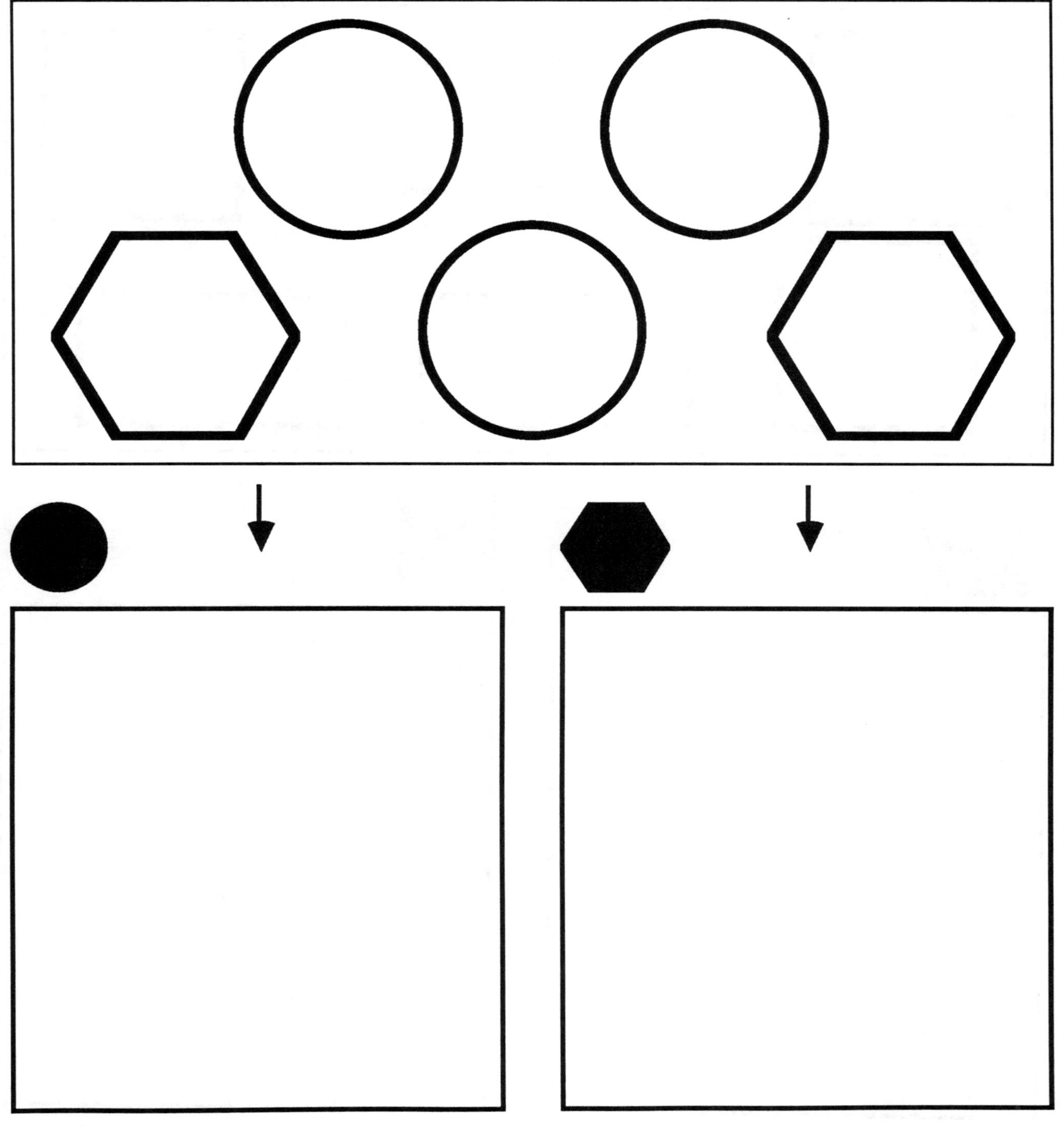

## SEPARATING GROUPS BY SHAPE

Place PATTERN BLOCKS on the shapes in the top box.
Move the squares into the first small box and the diamonds into the second.
Trace the blocks and color the pictures to match.

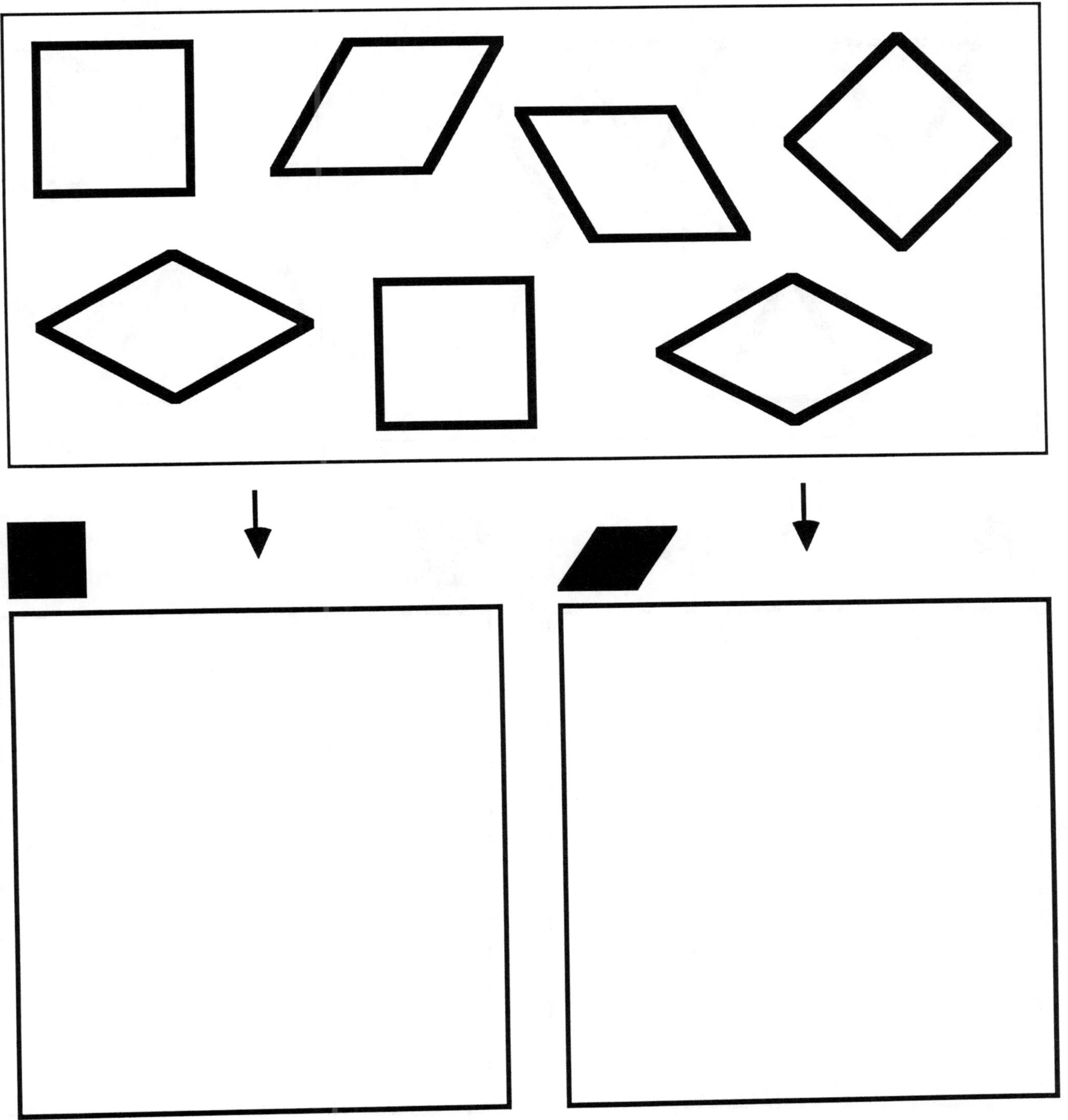

## SEPARATING GROUPS BY SHAPE

Place PATTERN BLOCKS on the shapes in the top box.
Move all triangles into the first small box and all hexagons into the second
Trace the blocks and color the pictures to match.

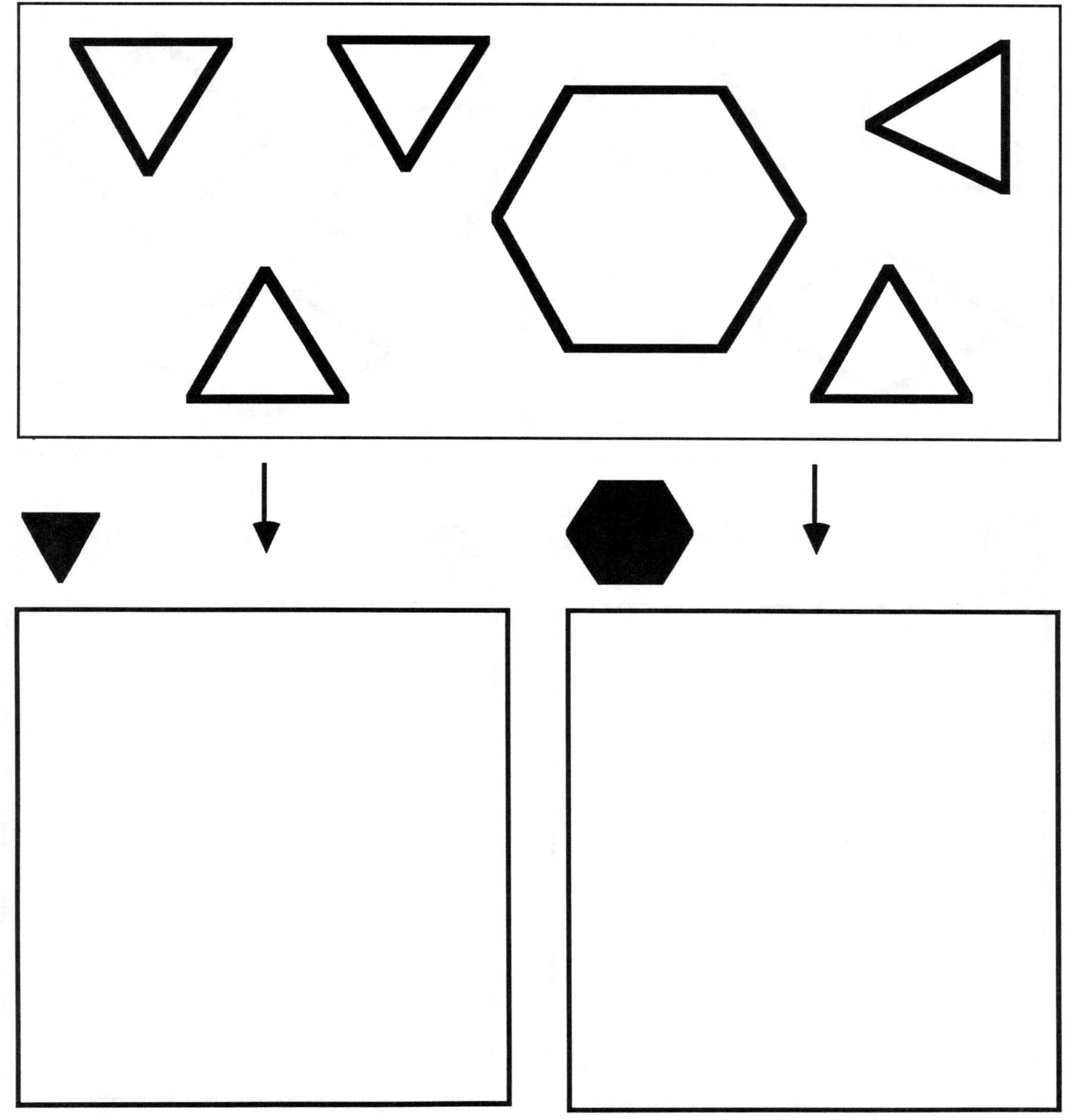

# SEPARATING GROUPS BY SHAPE

Place PATTERN BLOCKS on the shapes in the top box.
Move all blocks with 3 sides into the first box and all blocks with 4 sides into the second
Trace the blocks and color the pictures to match.

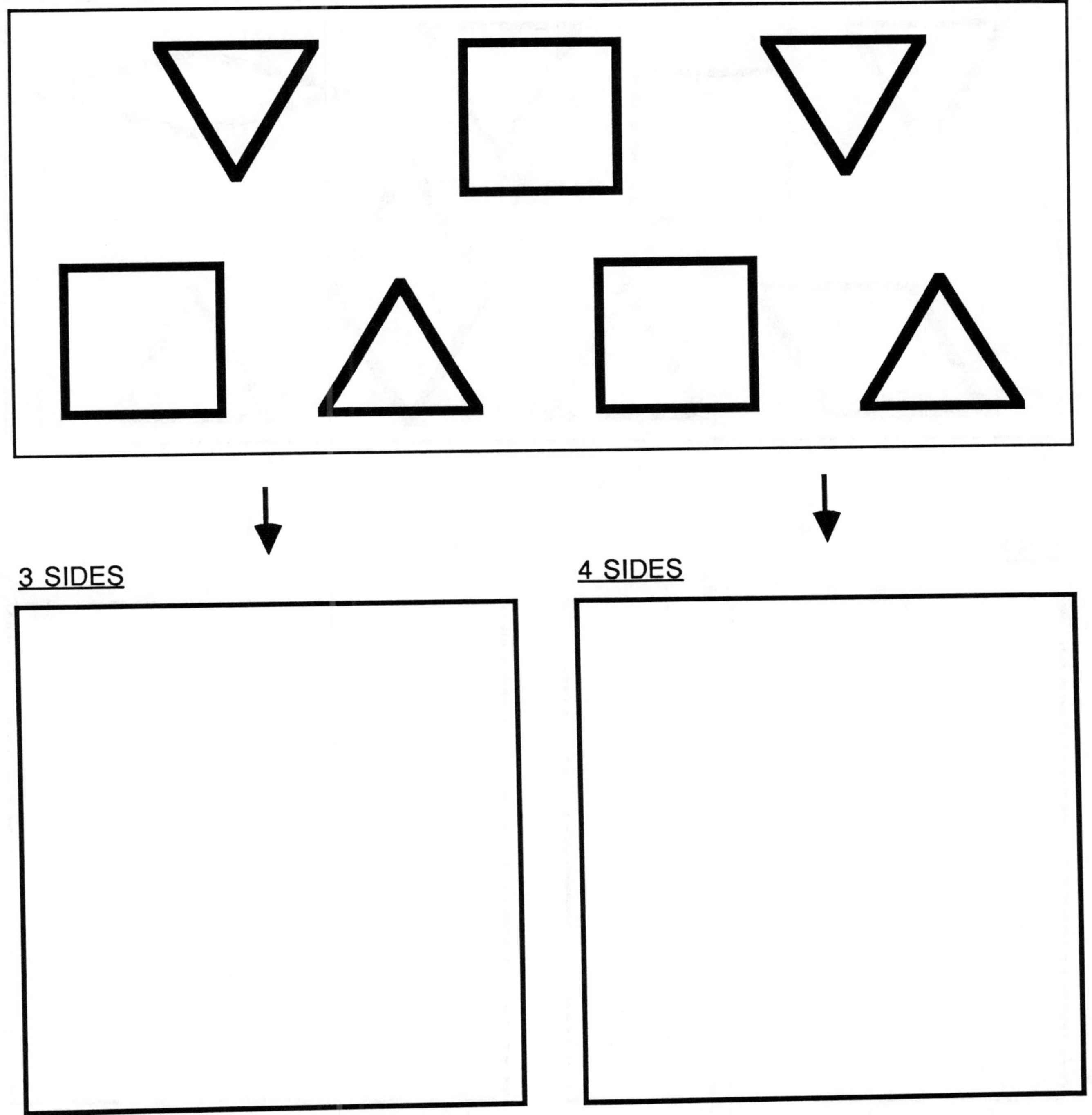

## SEPARATING GROUPS BY SHAPE

Place PATTERN BLOCKS on the shapes in the top box.
Move all blocks with 3 sides into the first box and all blocks with 4 sides into the second
Trace the blocks and color the pictures to match.

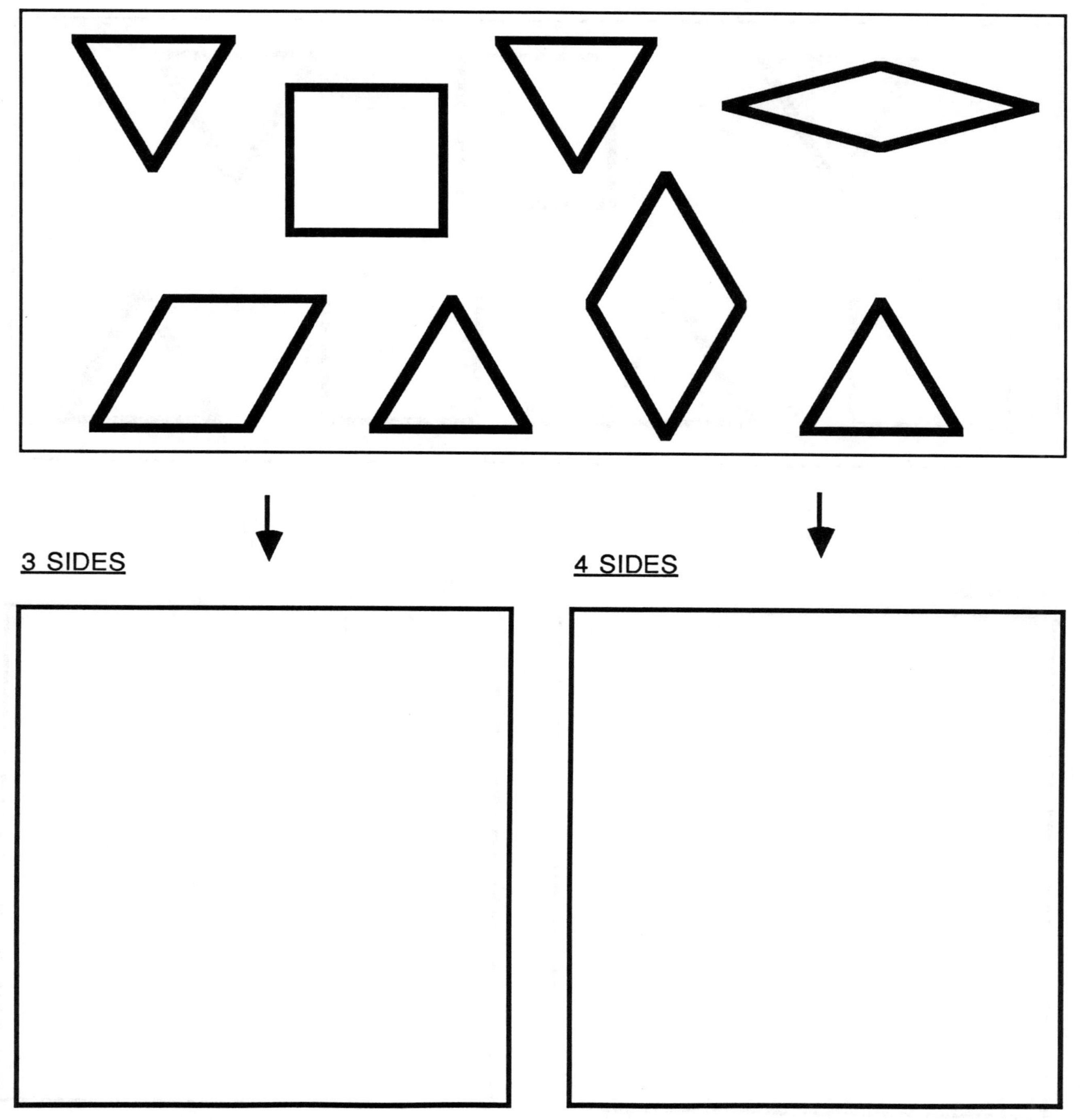

## SEPARATING GROUPS BY SIZE

Use INTERLOCKING CUBES of any color to construct and cover each figure in the top box. Move all 1-cube figures into the first small box and all 2-cube figures into the second Trace the figures and color the pictures to match the cubes.

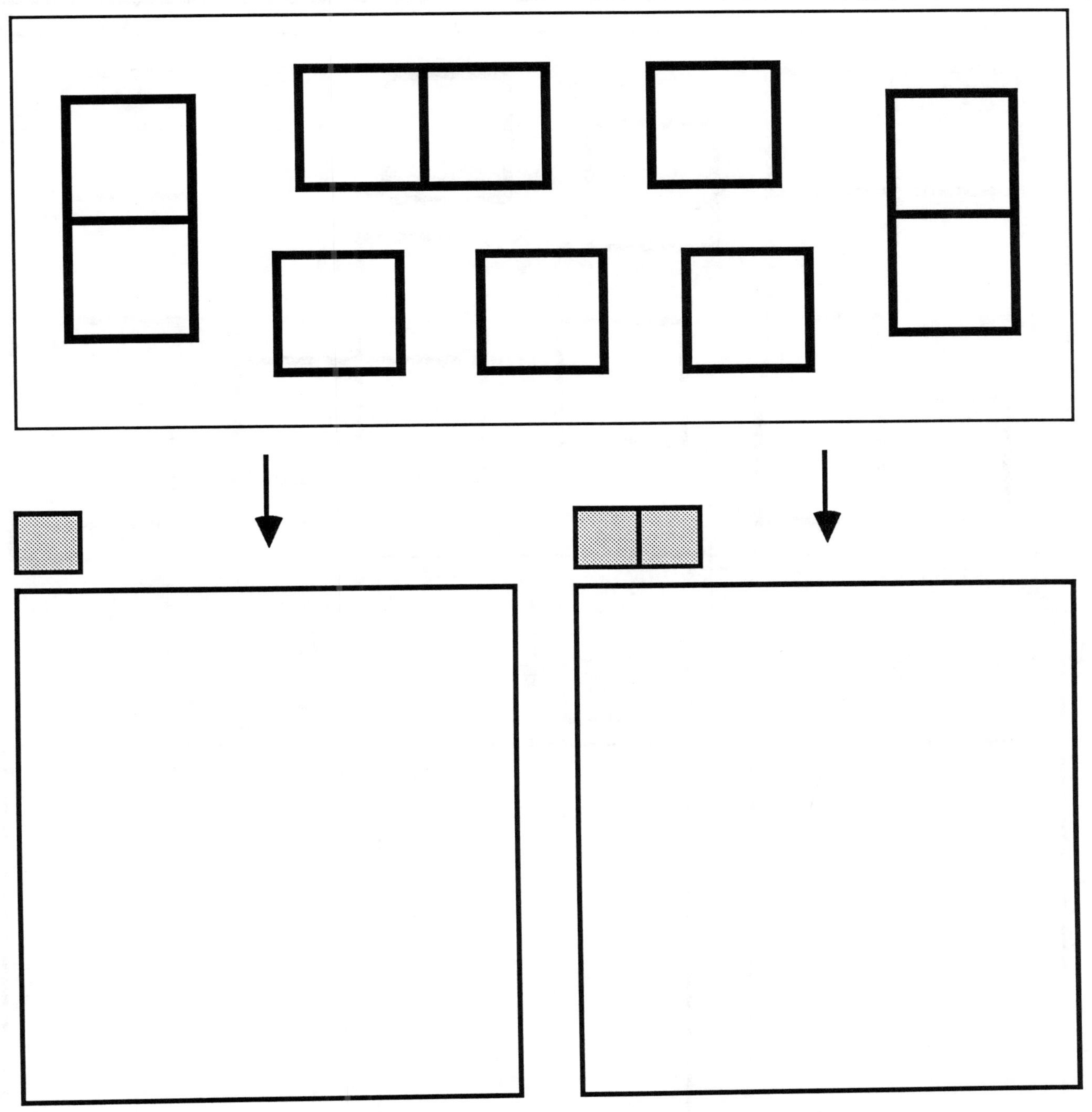

## SEPARATING GROUPS BY SIZE

Use INTERLOCKING CUBES of any color to construct and cover each figure in the top box.
Move all 1-cube figures into the first small box, all 2-cube figures into the second box, and all 3-cube figures into the third box
Trace the figures and color the pictures to match the cubes.

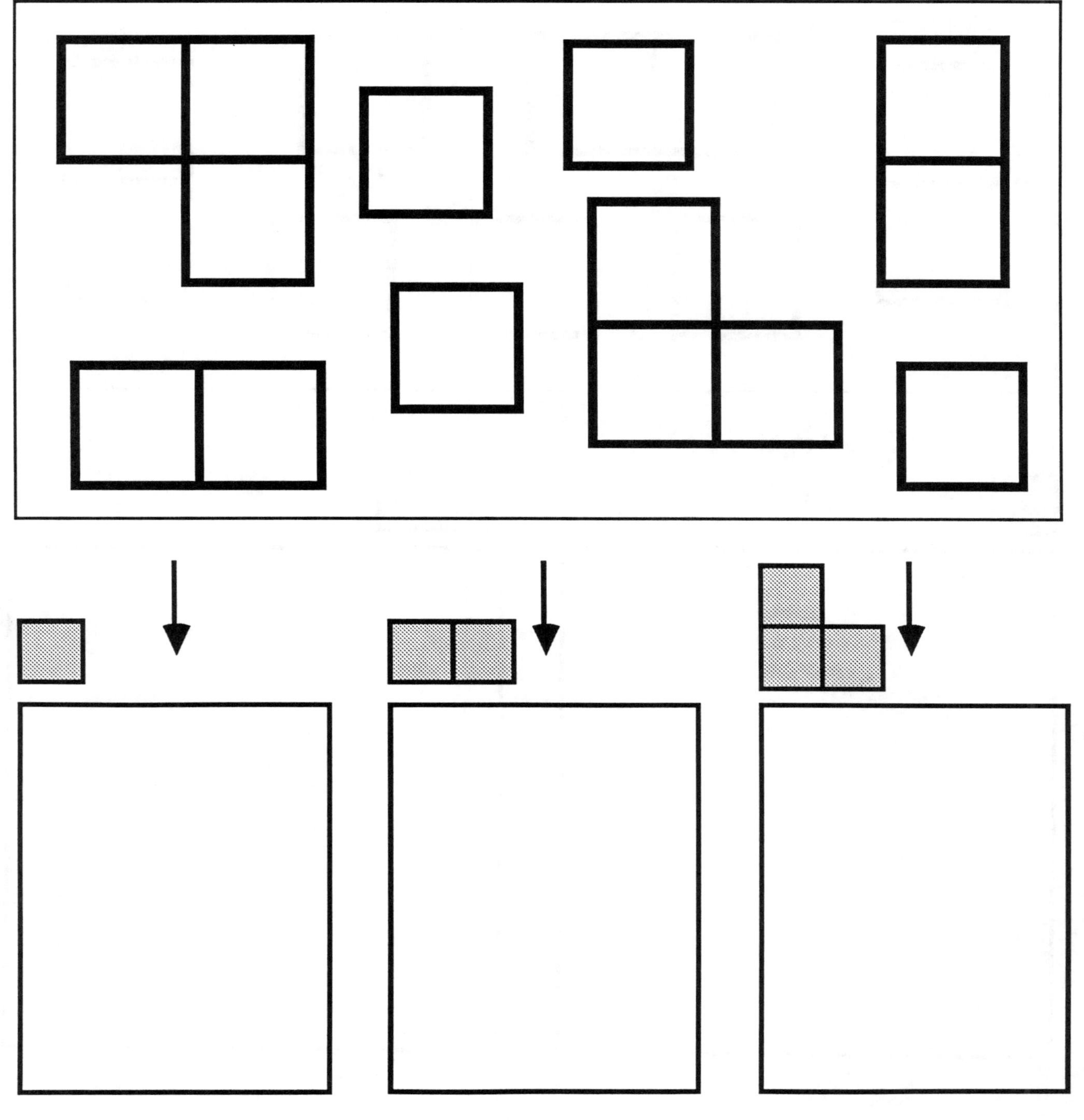

## FORMING A GROUP—SHAPE AND COLOR

Use a set of small ATTRIBUTE BLOCKS.
In the box, place all the blocks that have four sides and are red.
Trace the blocks and color the pictures to match.

## FORMING A GROUP—COLOR AND THICKNESS

Use a set of small ATTRIBUTE BLOCKS.
In the box, place all the blocks that are thin shapes and blue.
Trace the blocks and color the pictures to match.

## FORMING A GROUP—SHAPE AND COLOR

Use a set of small ATTRIBUTE BLOCKS.
In the box, place all the blocks that are round shapes but are NOT blue.
Trace the blocks and color the pictures to match.

## FORMING A GROUP—SHAPE AND THICKNESS

Use a set of small ATTRIBUTE BLOCKS.
In the box, place all the blocks that are thin shapes but are NOT round.
Trace the blocks and color the pictures to match.

# FORMING A GROUP—SHAPE

Place PATTERN BLOCKS on the shapes below.

In the box, place all the blocks with four sides.
Trace the blocks and color the pictures to match.

## FORMING A GROUP—SHAPE

Place PATTERN BLOCKS on the shapes below.

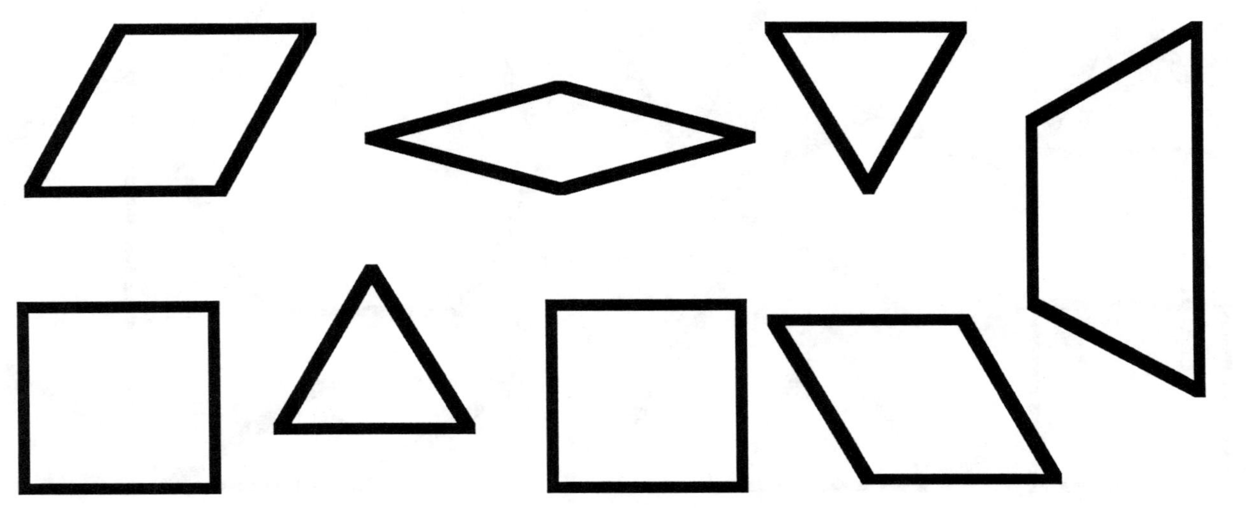

In the box, place all the blocks that are either squares or triangles.
Trace the blocks and color the pictures to match.

## GROUPS WITH COMMON ELEMENTS

Place PATTERN BLOCKS on the shapes below.
In each example, draw a line to connect any block in the first box to a block with the same shape in the second box.
Remove all the blocks and color the pictures of the blocks that matched.

---

**A**

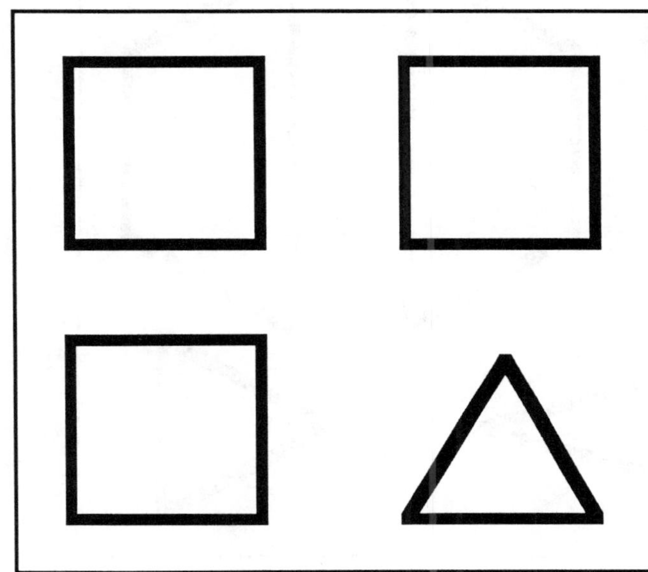
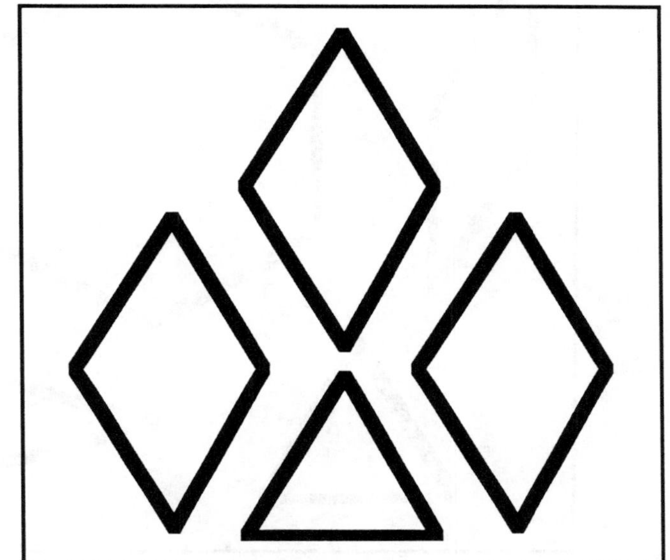

---

**B**

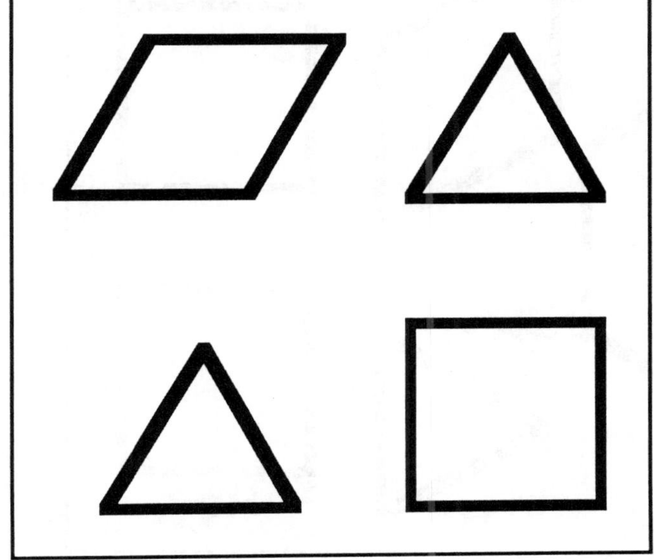
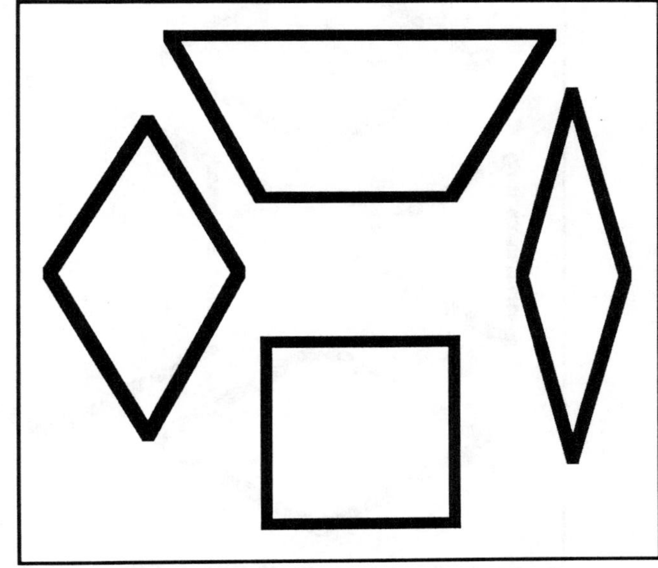

## GROUPS WITH COMMON ELEMENTS

Place PATTERN BLOCKS on the shapes below.
Draw a line to connect any block in the top box to a block with the same shape in the other box.
Remove all the blocks and color the pictures of the blocks that matched.

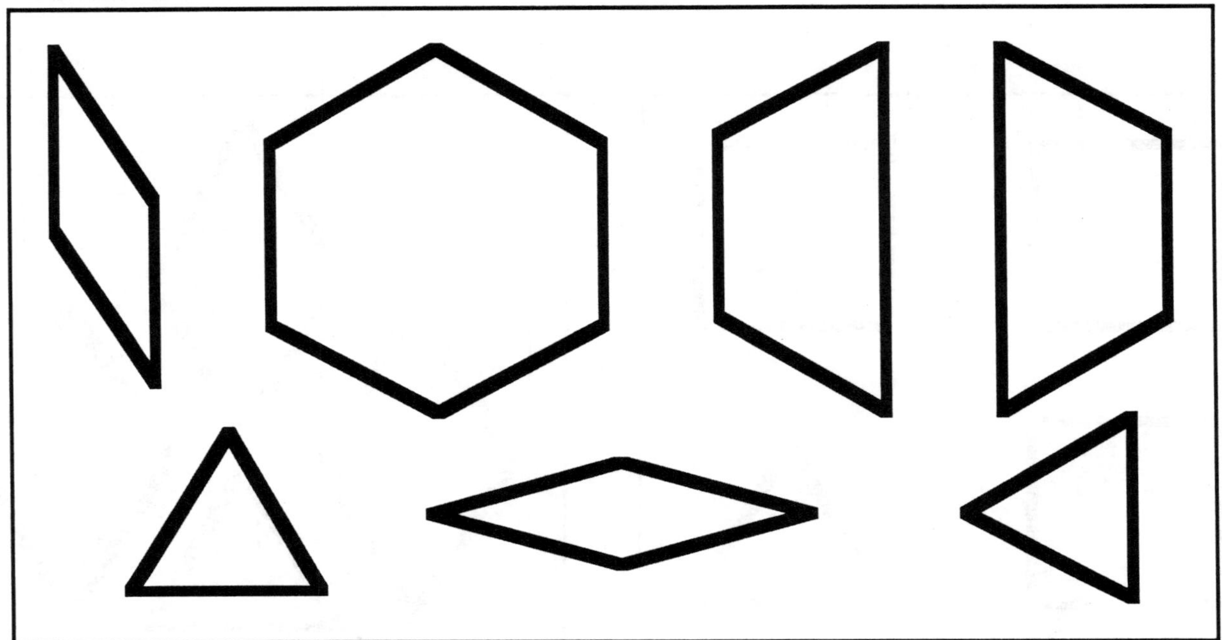

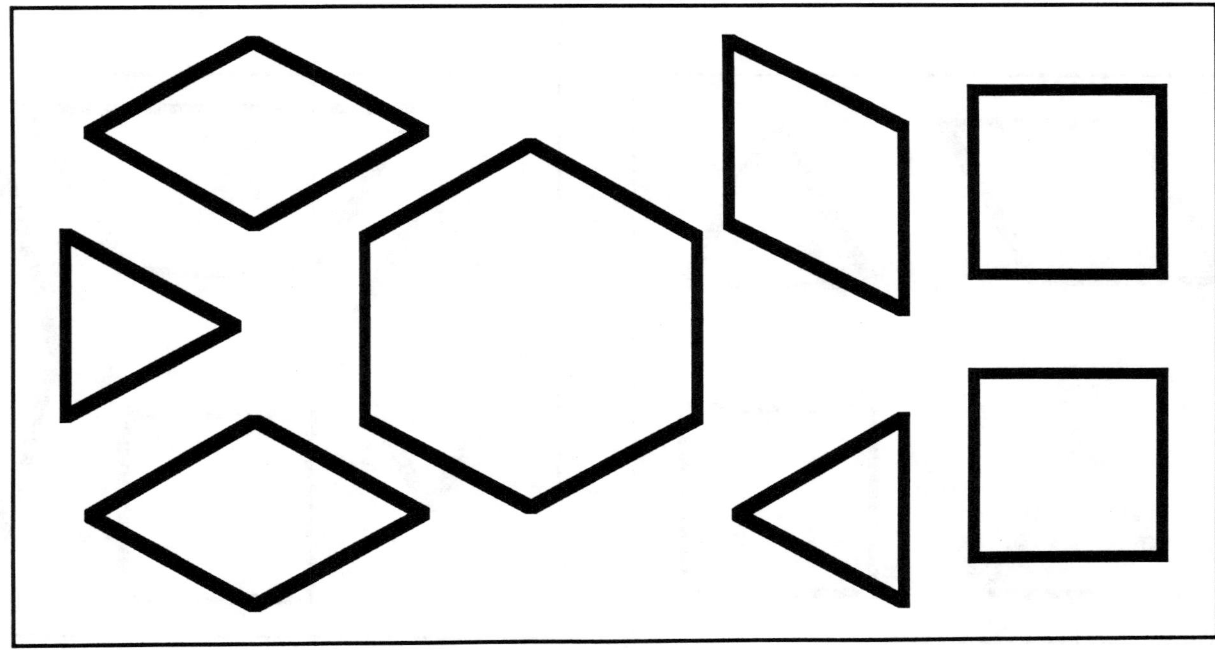

## GROUPS WITH COMMON ELEMENTS

Use INTERLOCKING CUBES to construct and cover the figures in each box.
Use one color of cubes for the white squares and another color for the shaded squares.
Draw a line to connect any figure in the first box to a figure with the same shape and color in the second box.
Remove all the figures and color the pictures to match the cubes.

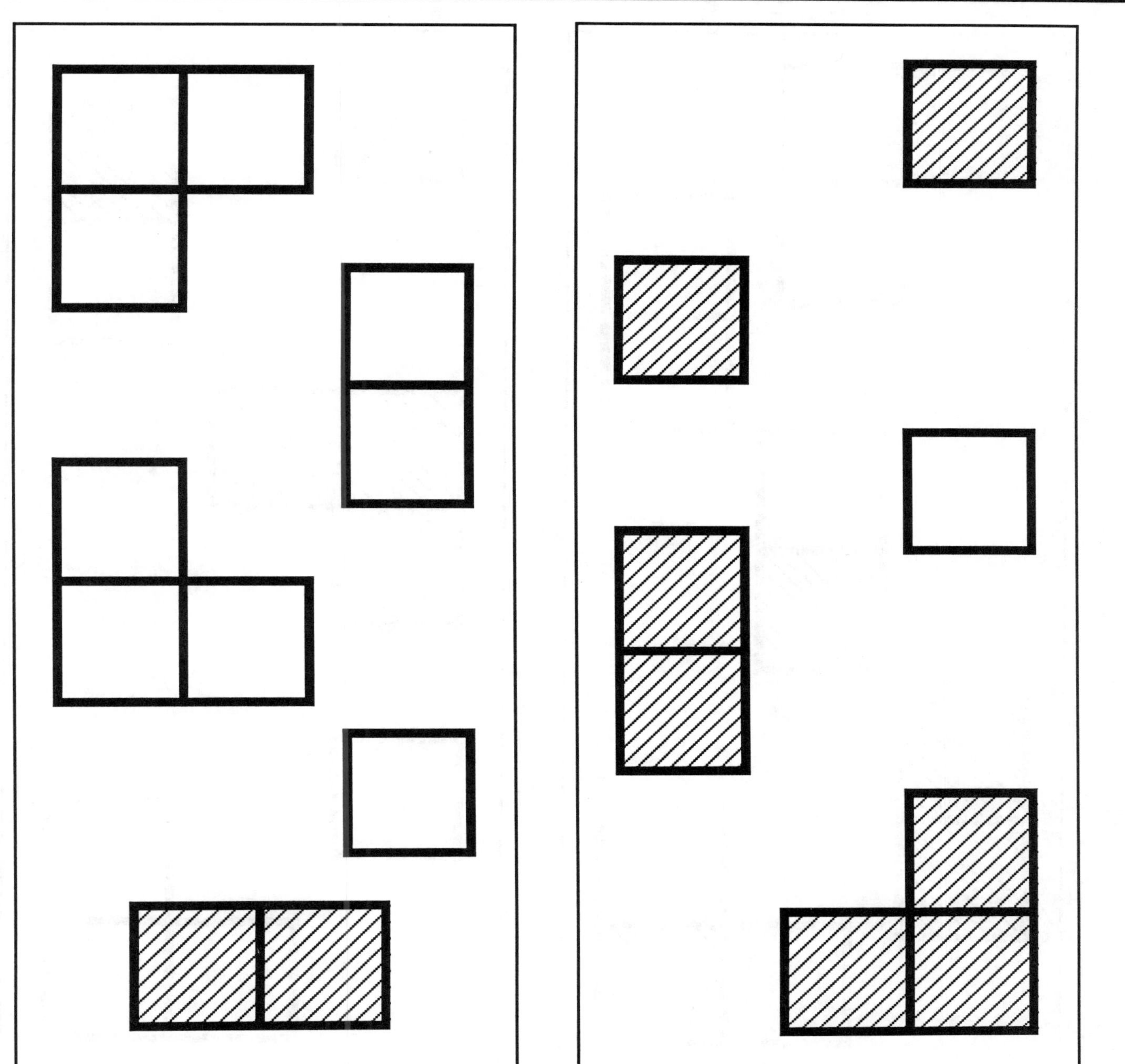

## GROUPS WITH COMMON ELEMENTS

Use INTERLOCKING CUBES to construct and cover the figures in each box.
Use one color of cubes for the white squares and another color for the shaded squares.
Draw a line to connect any figure in the first box to a figure with the same shape and color in the second box.
Remove all the figures and color the pictures to match the cubes.

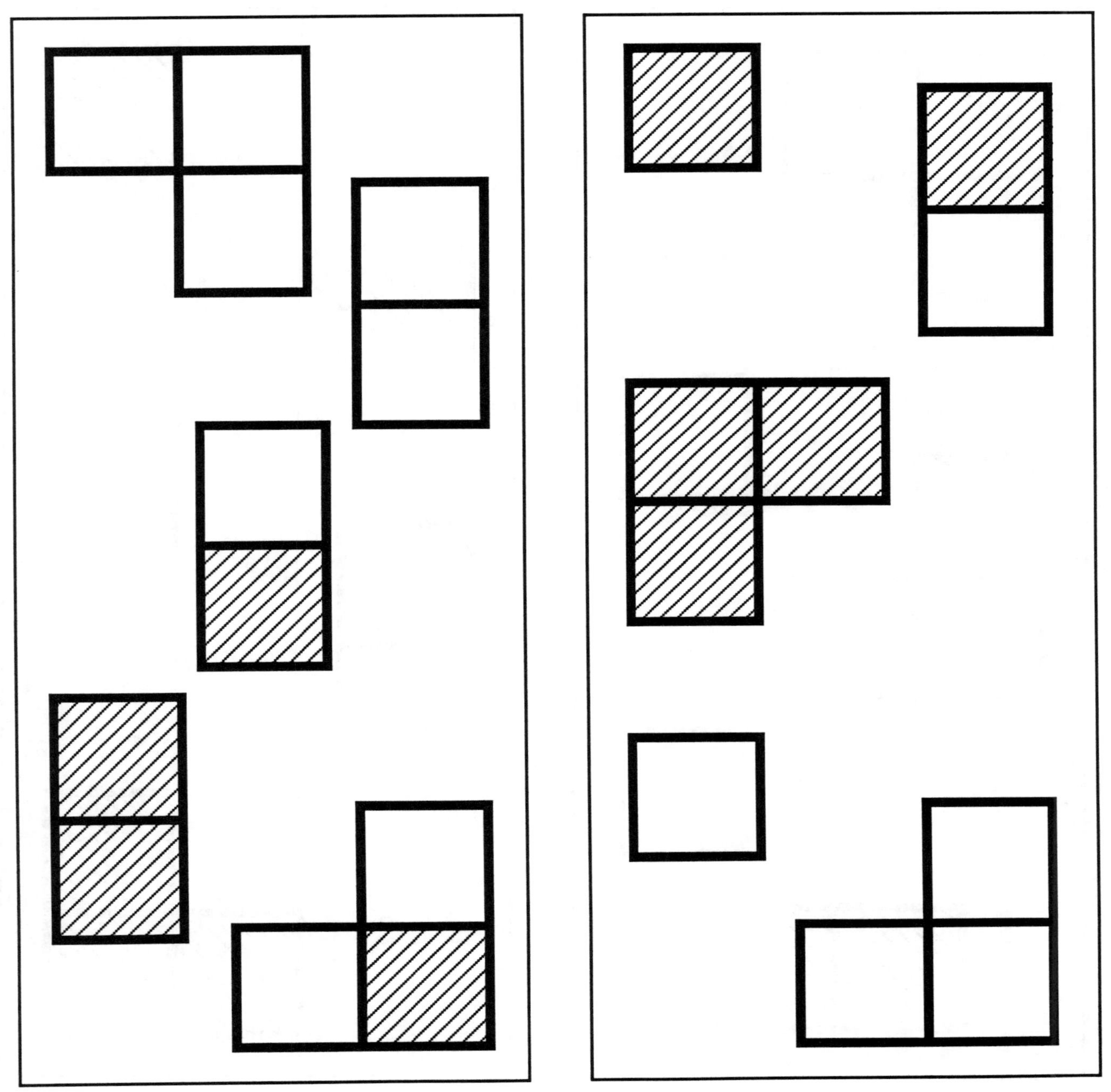

## GROUPS WITH COMMON ELEMENTS

Place a red (R), yellow (Y), or blue (B) ATTRIBUTE BLOCK on each shape below.
Draw a line to connect any block in the first box to a block with the same shape and same color in the second box.
Remove the blocks and color the pictures to match.

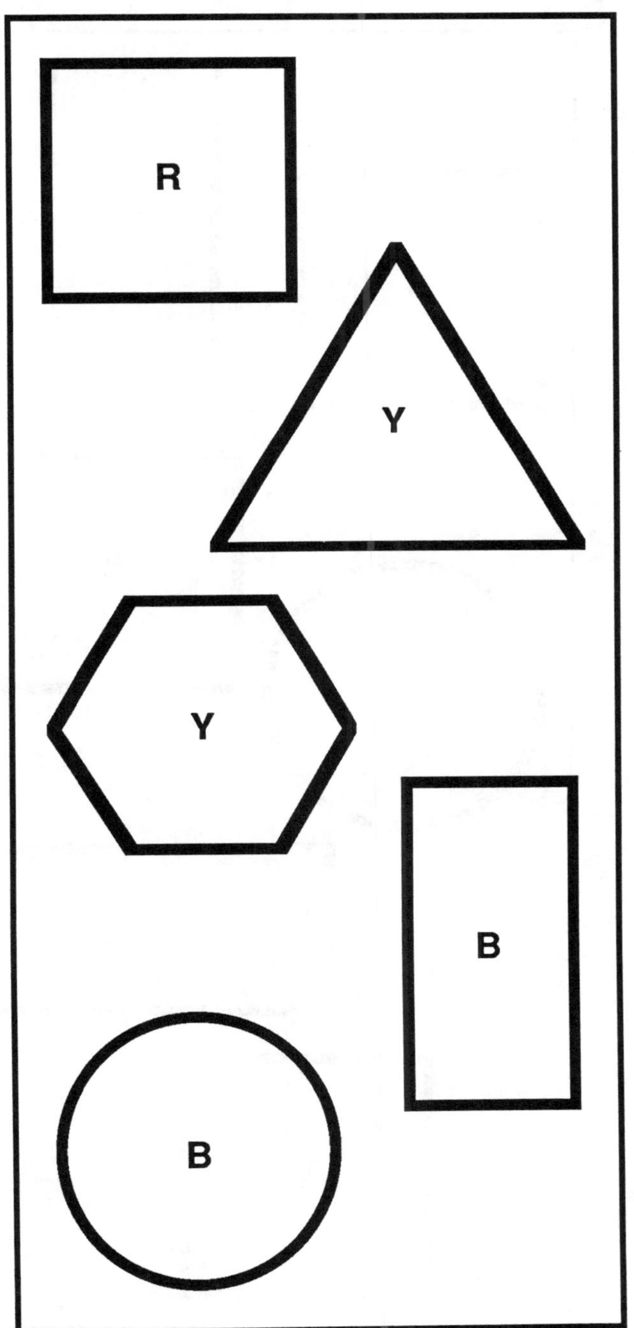


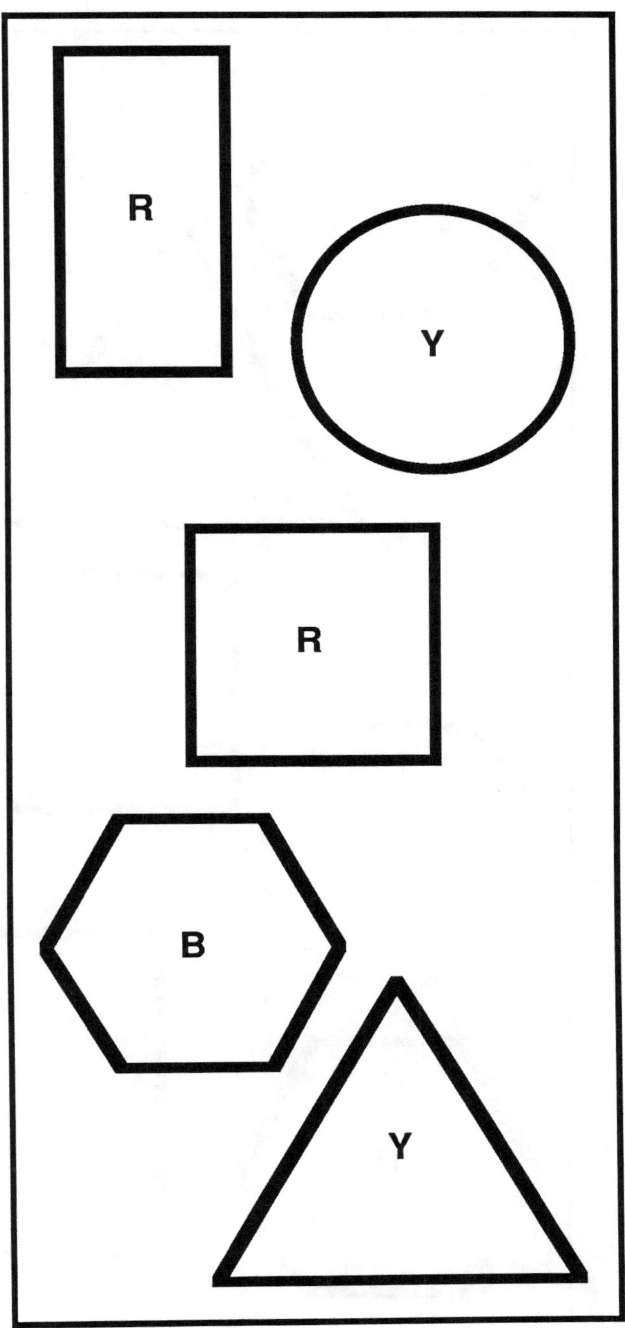

## GROUPS WITH COMMON ELEMENTS

Place a red (R), yellow (Y), or blue (B) ATTRIBUTE BLOCK on each shape below.
Draw a line to connect any block in the first box to a block with the same shape and same color in the second box.
Remove the blocks and color the pictures to match.

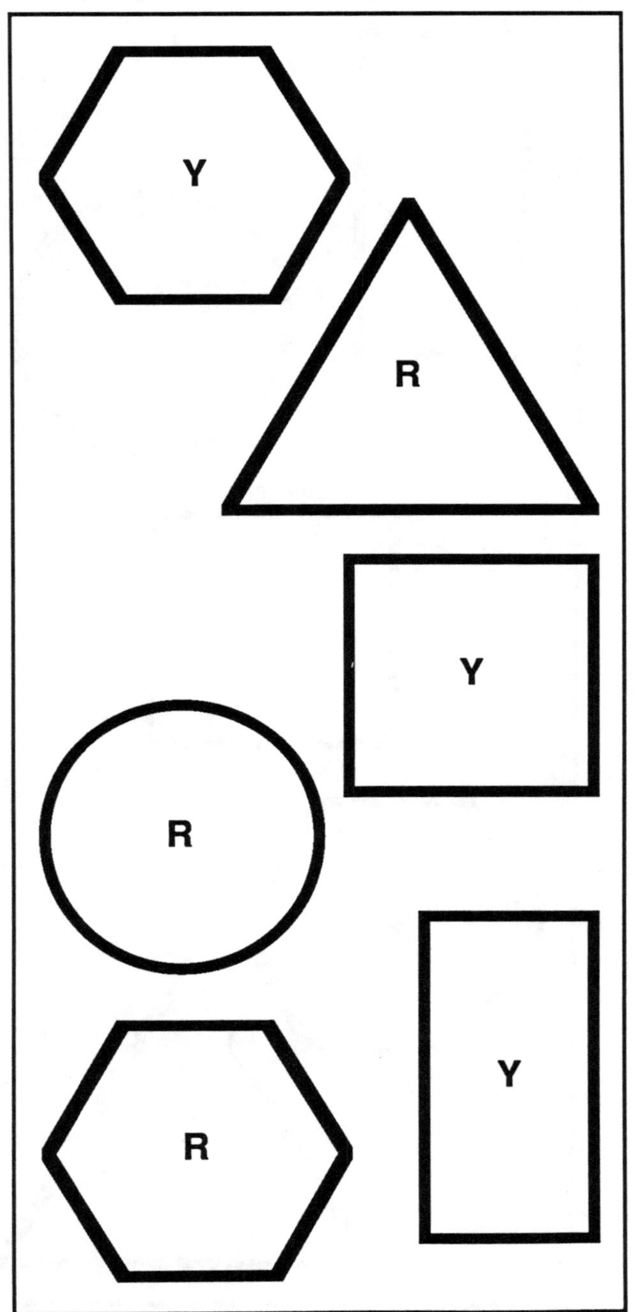


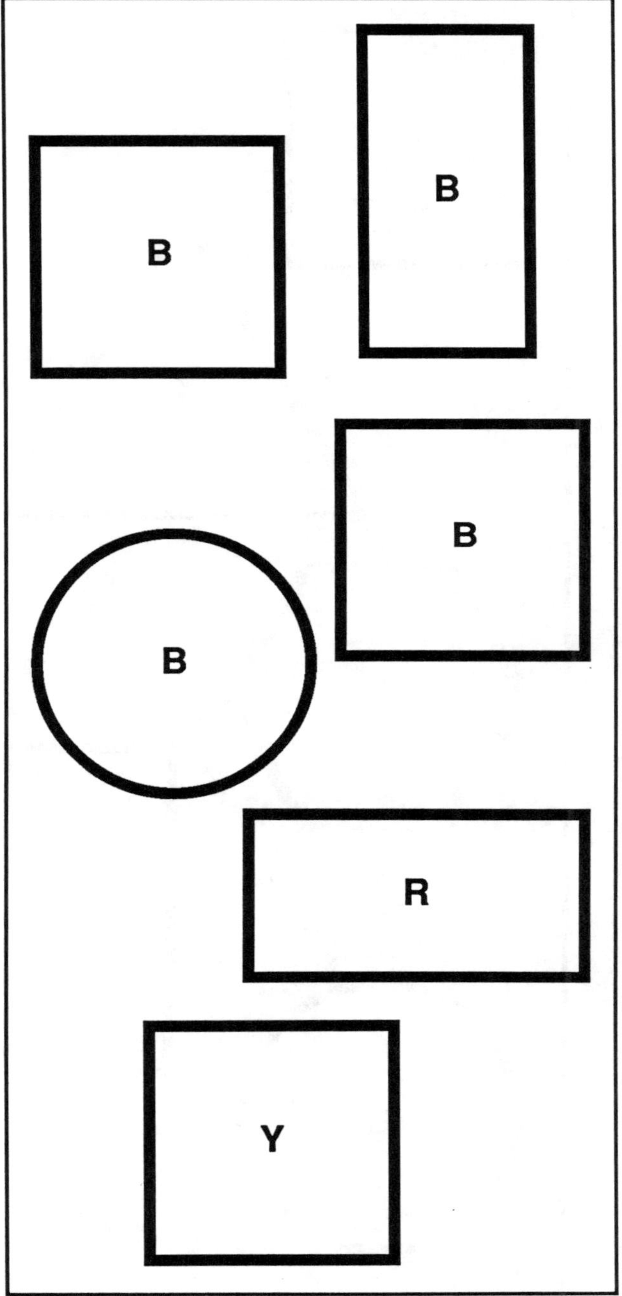

# DEFINING A GROUP

I am thinking of a group of small ATTRIBUTE BLOCKS.

R
R
R
R

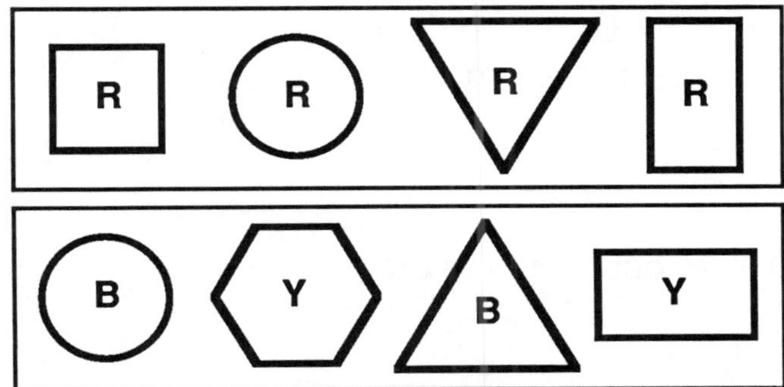

DO belong to the group.

B
Y
B
Y

DO NOT belong to the group.

---

Color the shapes below that DO belong to the group.

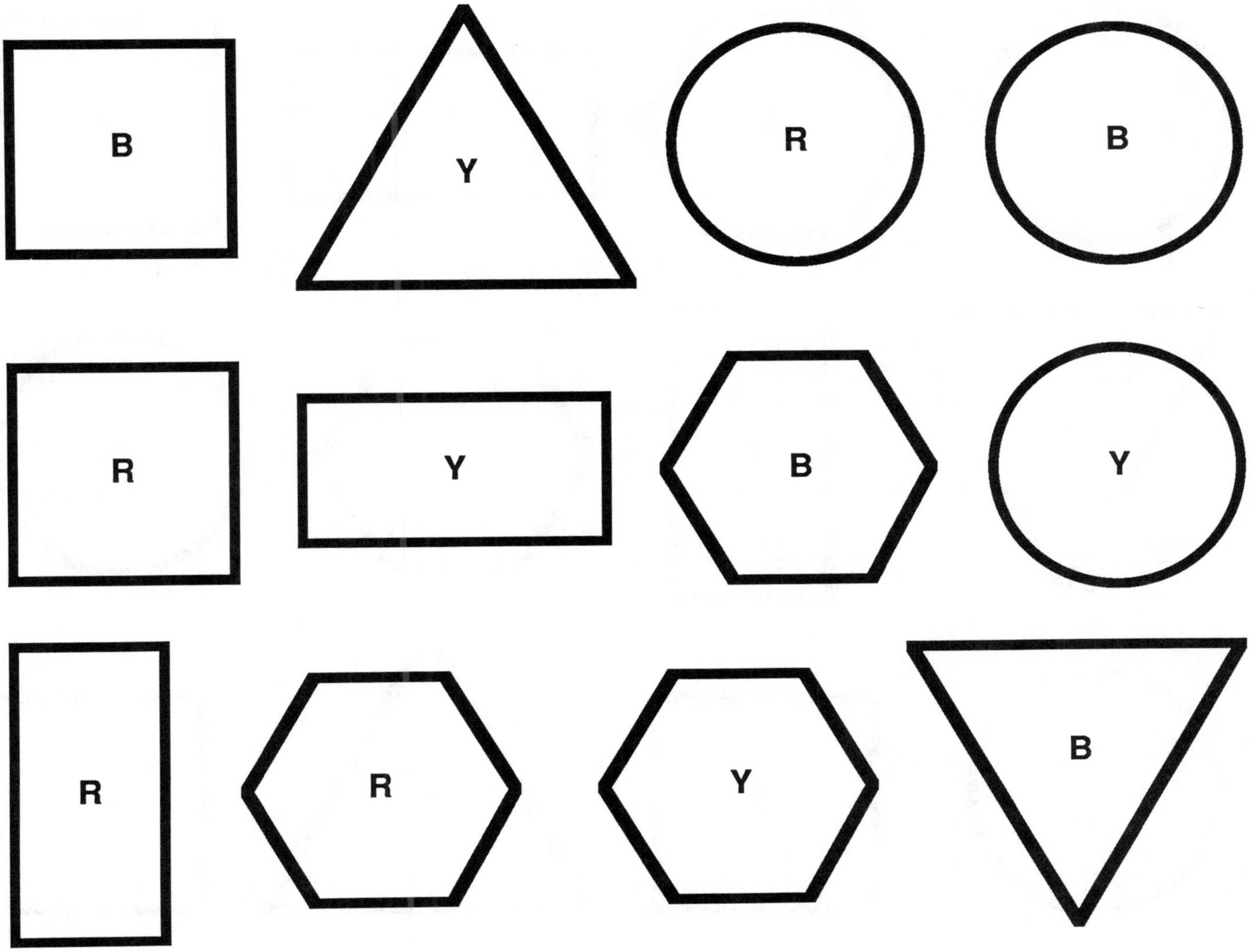

B
Y
R
B
R
Y
B
Y
R
R
Y
B

# DEFINING A GROUP

I am thinking of a group of small ATTRIBUTE BLOCKS.

B
Y
R

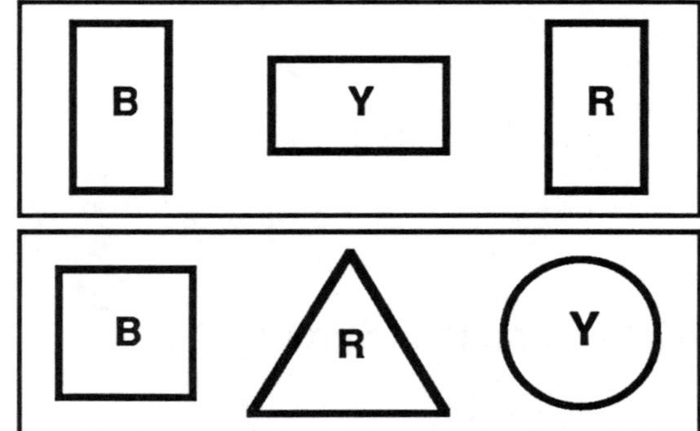

DO belong to the group.

B
R
Y

DO NOT belong to the group.

---

Color the shapes below that DO belong to the group.

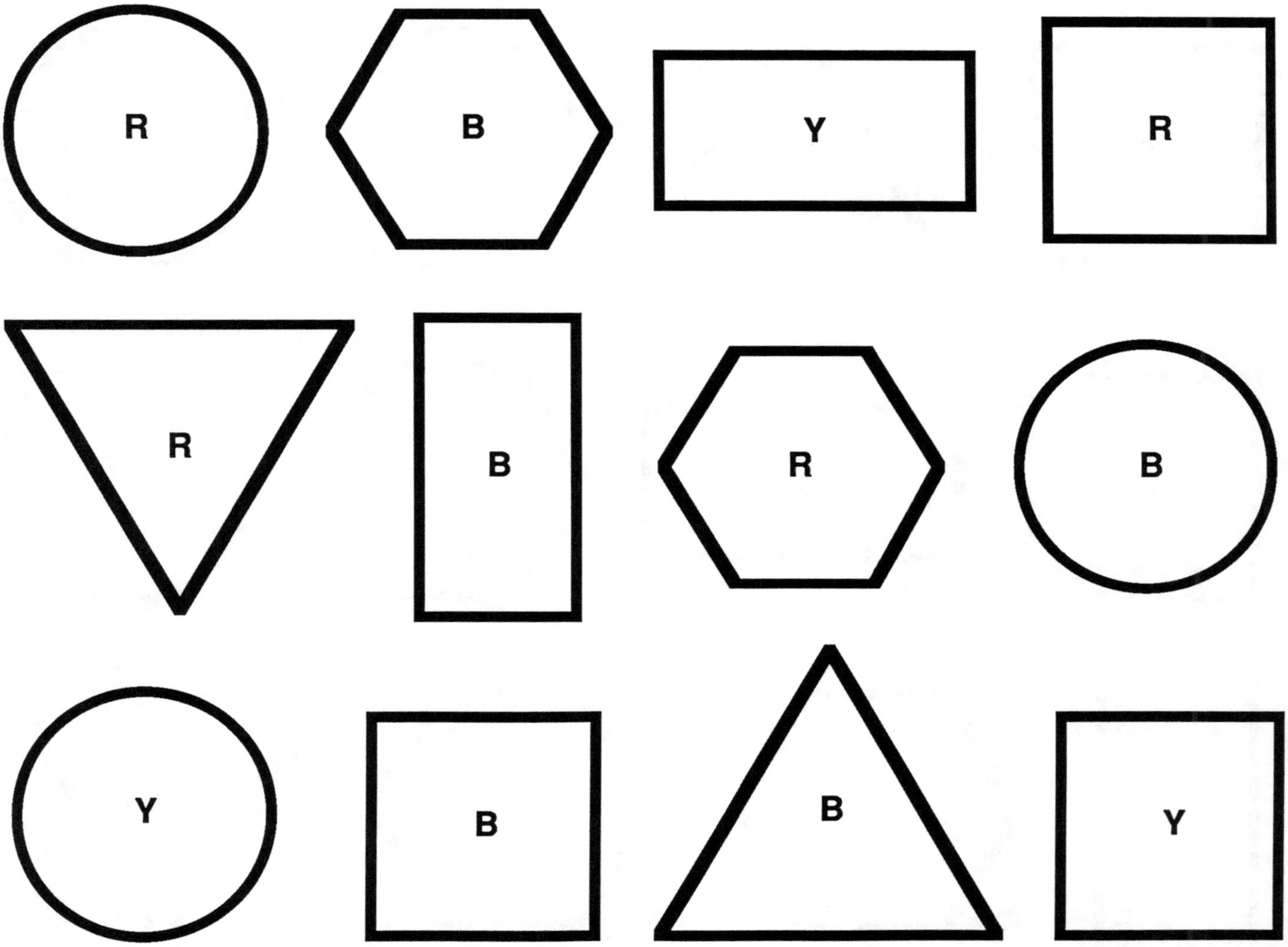

R
B
Y
R
R
B
R
B
Y
B
B
Y

## COMMON PROPERTIES

In the picture below, the SHAPES in each ROW are the same (2 triangles and 2 circles).
The COLORS of the shapes in each COLUMN are the same (2 red shapes and 2 blue shapes).

**A**

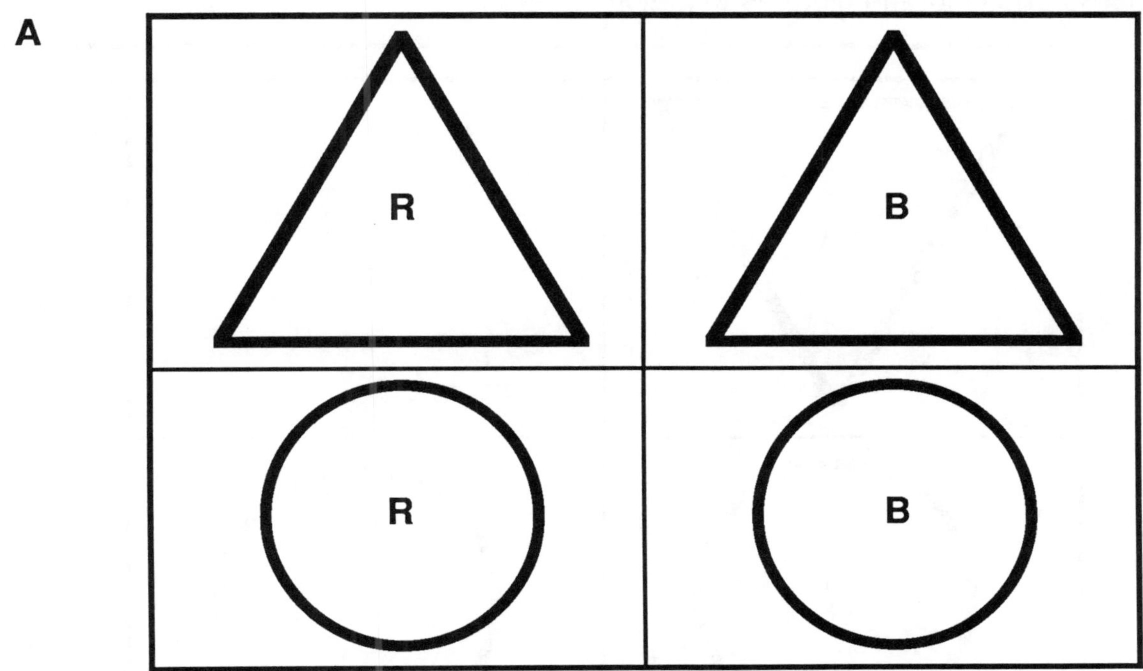


---

Place a red (R) or yellow (Y) ATTRIBUTE BLOCK on each shape below.
Choose the block with the correct shape and color, and place it in the blank box.
Trace the block and color the pictures to match.

**B**

| | |
|---|---|
| Y | R |
| ? | R |

## COMMON PROPERTIES

Place a yellow (Y) or blue (B) ATTRIBUTE BLOCK on each shape below.
In each exercise, place a block that is the correct shape and color in the blank box.
Trace the blocks and color the pictures to match.

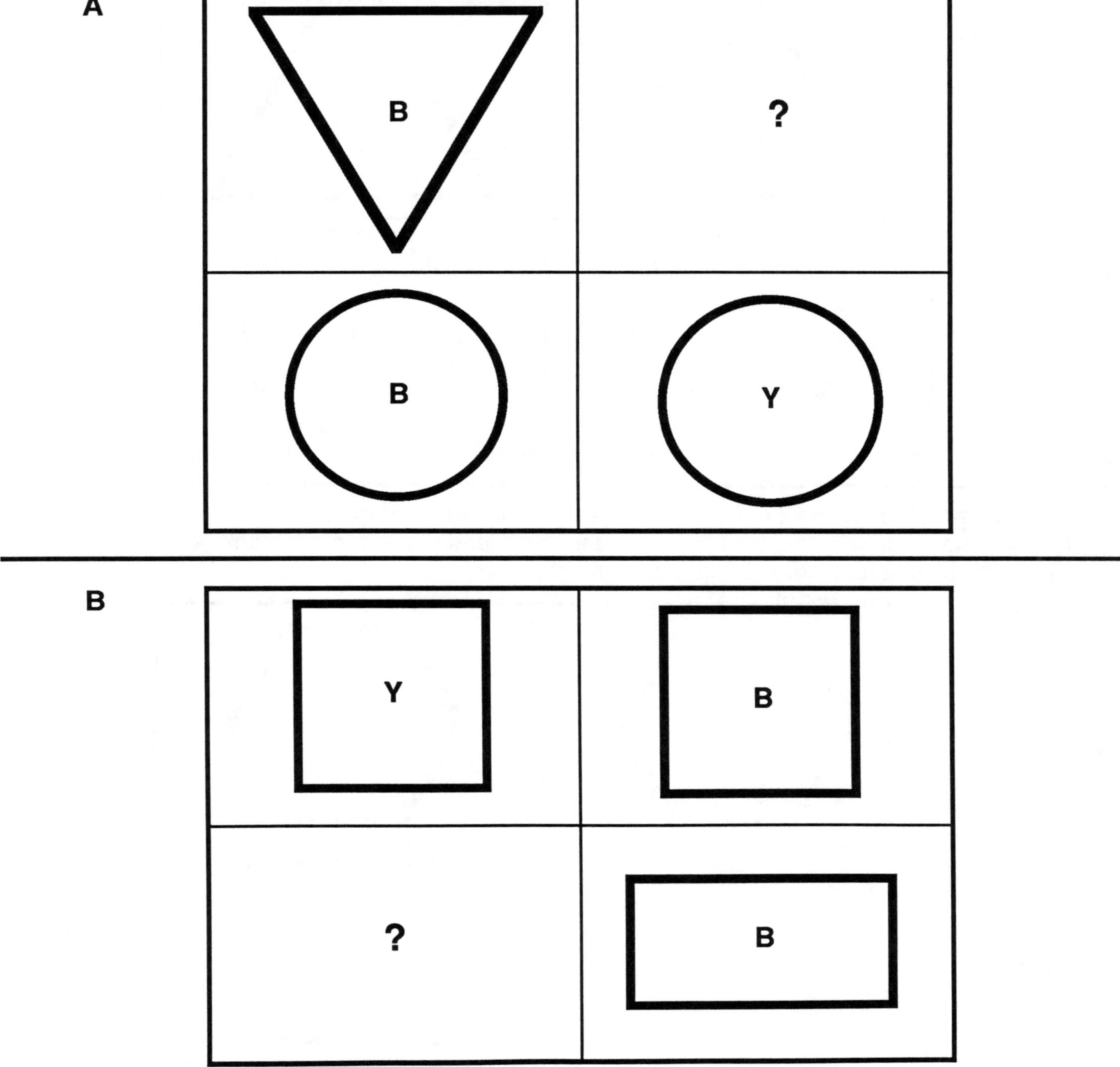

## COMMON PROPERTIES

Place a red (R), yellow (Y), or blue (B) ATTRIBUTE BLOCK on each shape below.
In each exercise, place a block that is the correct shape and color in the blank box.
Trace the blocks and color the pictures to match.

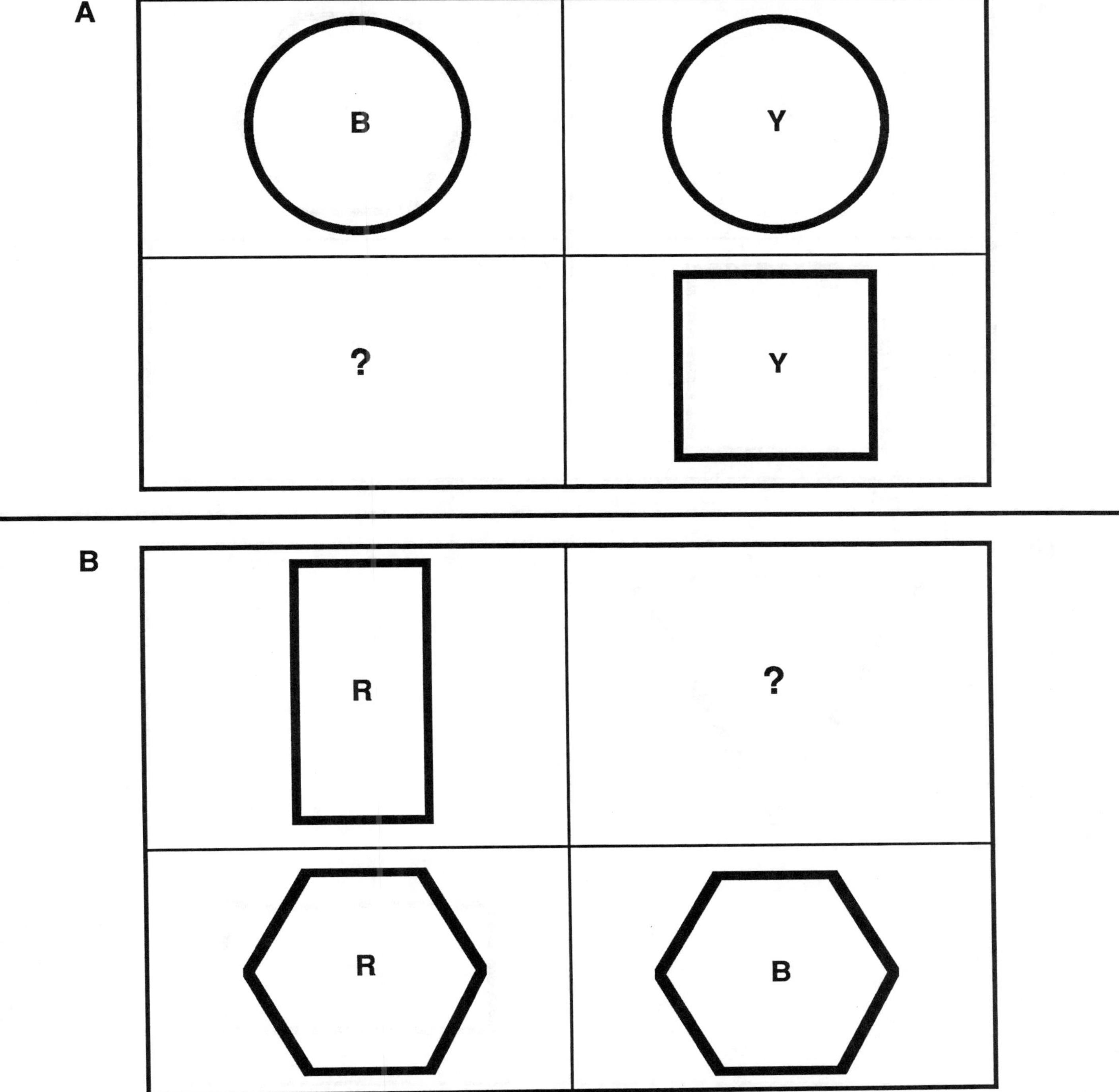

## COMMON PROPERTIES

Place a red (R), yellow (Y), or blue (B) ATTRIBUTE BLOCK on each shape below.
In each exercise, place the blocks that are the correct shape and color in the blank boxes.
Trace the blocks and color the pictures to match.

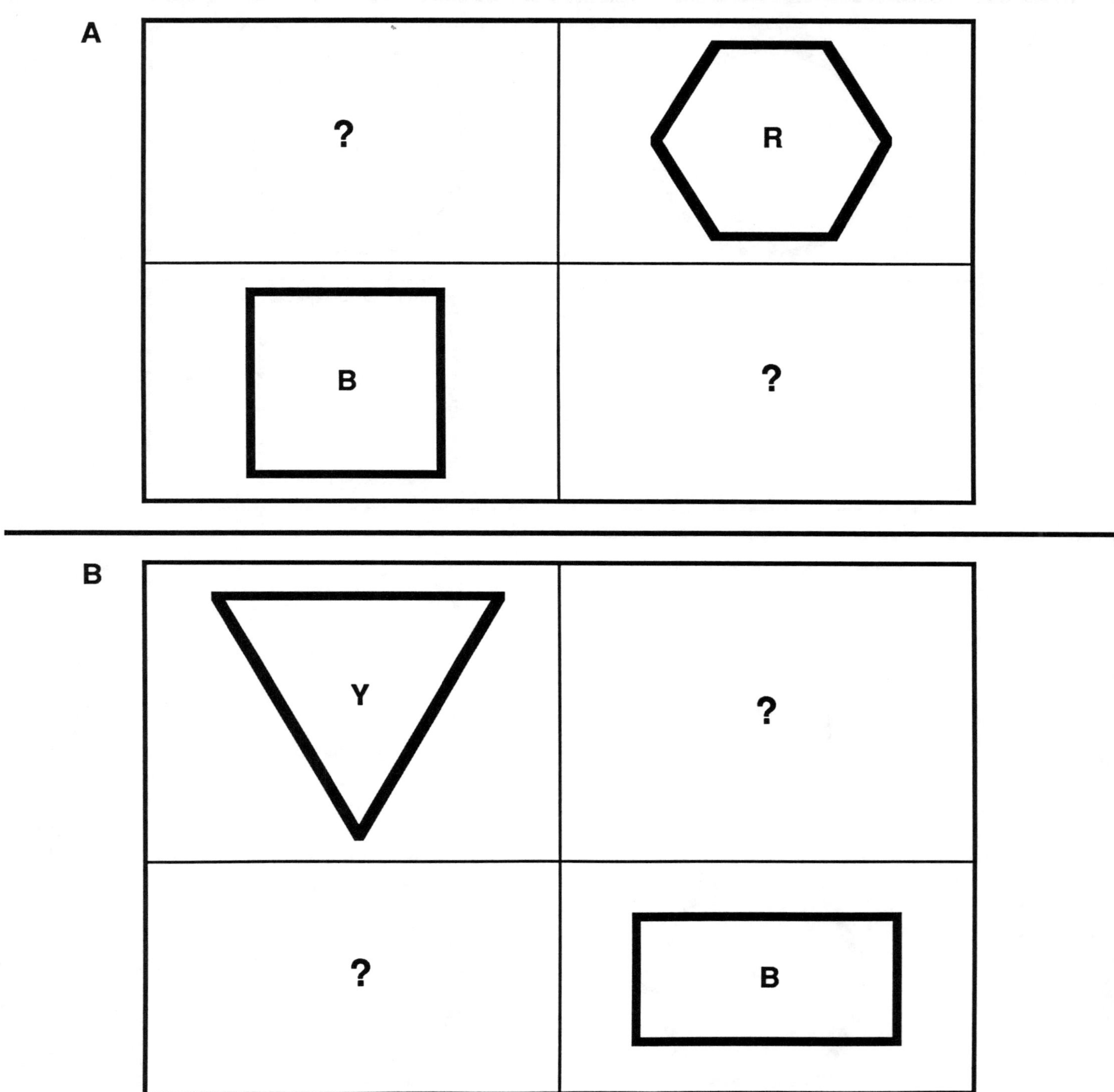

## SHAPE AND COLOR

Place a red (R), yellow (Y), or blue (B) ATTRIBUTE BLOCK on each shape on the page.

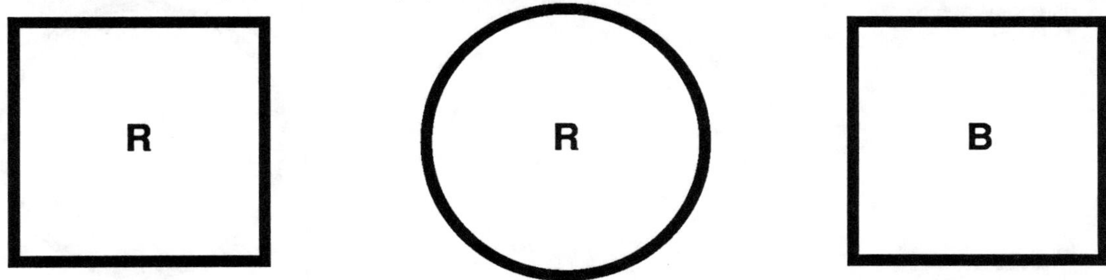


The first two blocks in each row below are related by shape and color.
Choose the block from above that is related to the third block in the same way.
Place it in the dotted box.
Trace the blocks and color the pictures to match.

A R B | R

B Y Y | R

C B R | B

## SHAPE AND COLOR

Place a red (R), yellow (Y), or blue (B) ATTRIBUTE BLOCK on each shape on the page.

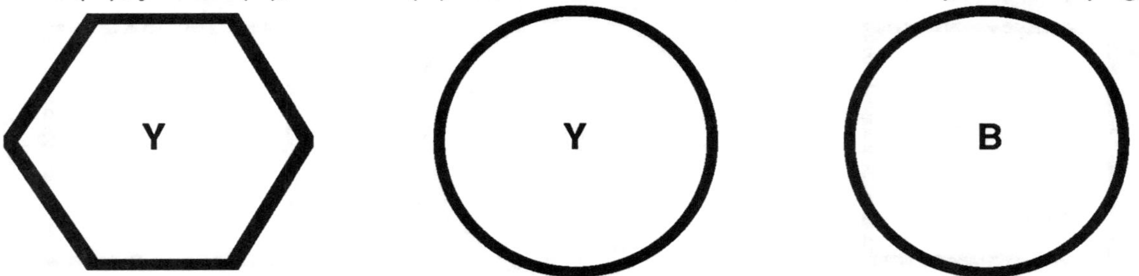


The first two blocks in each row below are related by shape and color.
Choose the block from above that is related to the third block in the same way.
Place it in the dotted box.
Trace the blocks and color the pictures to match.

**A** R R | B

**B** R Y | R

**C** B B | Y

## SHAPE AND COLOR

Place a red (R), yellow (Y), or blue (B) ATTRIBUTE BLOCK on each shape below.
The first two blocks in each row are related by shape and color.
Choose a block that is related to the third block in the same way and place it in the dotted box.
Trace the blocks and color the pictures to match.

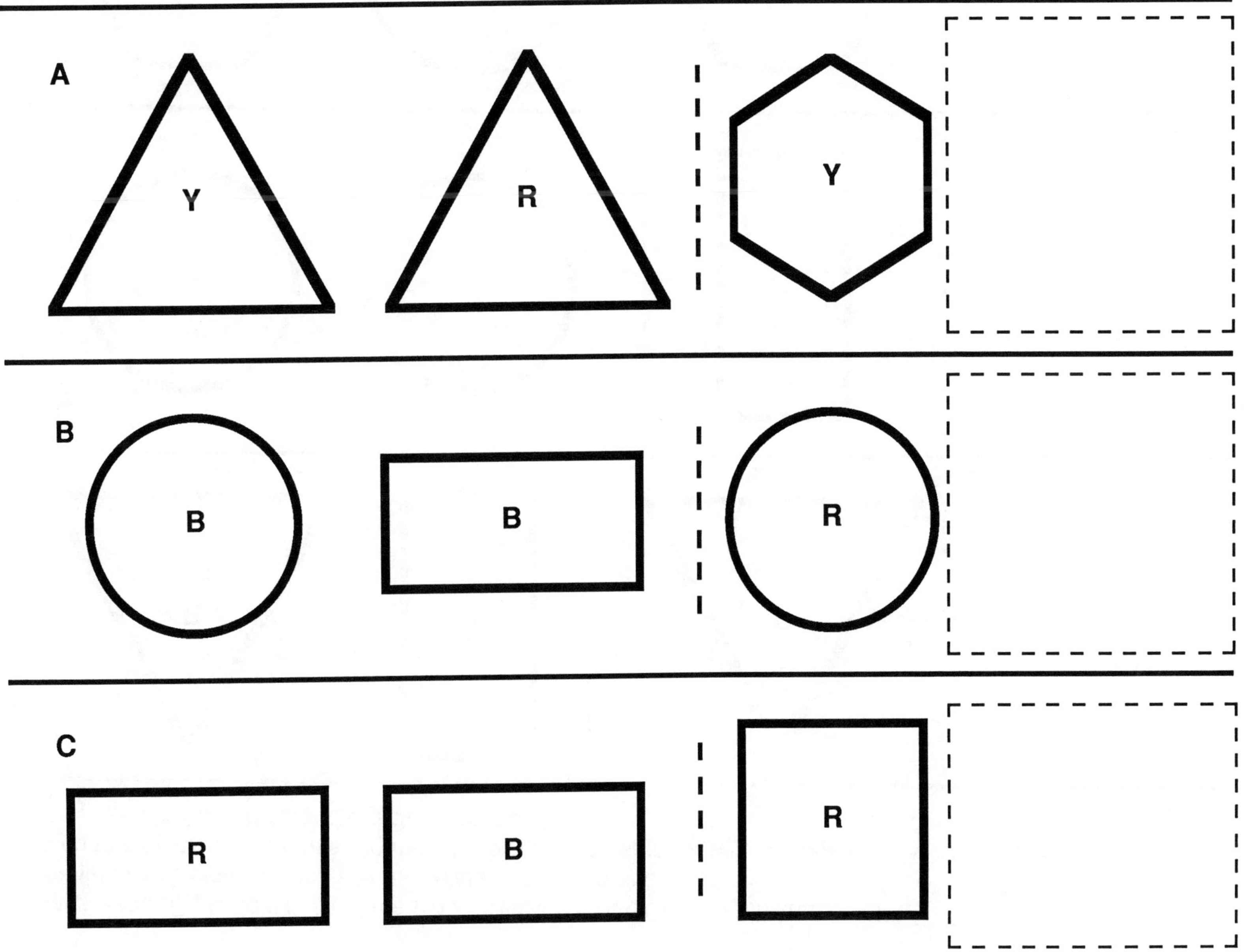

# SHAPE AND COLOR

Place a red (R), yellow (Y), or blue (B) ATTRIBUTE BLOCK on each shape below.
The first two blocks in each row are related by shape and color.
Choose a block that is related to the third block in the same way and place it in the dotted box.
Trace the blocks and color the pictures to match.

A R R B

B Y R Y

C Y Y B

# SHAPE AND SIZE

Place a red (R) or yellow (Y) ATTRIBUTE BLOCK on each shape below.
The first two blocks in each row are related by shape and size.
Choose a block that is related to the third block in the same way and place it in the dotted box.
Trace the blocks and color the pictures to match.

A

Y

Y

Y

B

R

R

R

# SHAPE AND SIZE

Place the correct red (R) or blue (B) ATTRIBUTE BLOCK on each shape below.
The first two blocks in each row are related by shape and size.
Choose a block that is related to the third block in the same way and place it in the dotted box.
Trace the blocks and color the pictures to match.

A

R

R

R

B

B

B

B

## SHAPE, COLOR, AND SIZE

Place a red (R), yellow (Y), or blue (B) ATTRIBUTE BLOCK on each shape below.
The first two blocks in each row are related by shape, color, and size.
Choose a block that is related to the third block in the same way and place it in the dotted box.
Trace the blocks and color the pictures to match.

A

B

Y

B

B

R

B

R

# SHAPE, COLOR, AND SIZE

Place a red (R), yellow (Y), or blue (B) ATTRIBUTE BLOCK on each shape below.
The first two blocks in each row are related by shape, color, and size.
Choose a block that is related to the third block in the same way and place it in the dotted box.
Trace the blocks and color the pictures to match.

A

Y

R

Y

B

B

Y

B

## SHAPE AND POSITION

Place a PATTERN BLOCK on each shape on the page.

The first two blocks in each row below are related by shape and position.
Choose a block from above that is related to the third block in the same way.
Place it in the dotted box.
Trace the blocks and color the pictures to match.

**A**

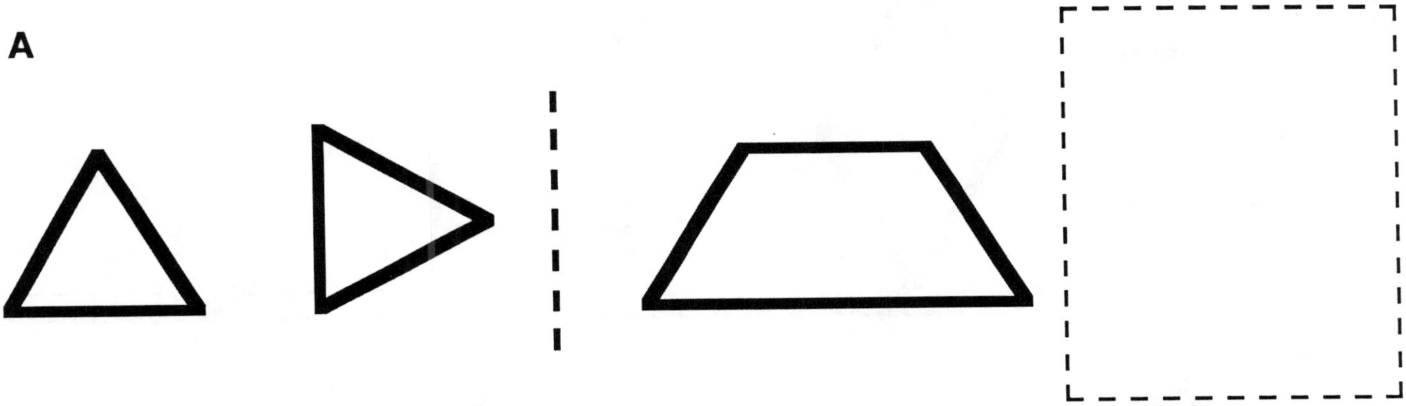

**B**

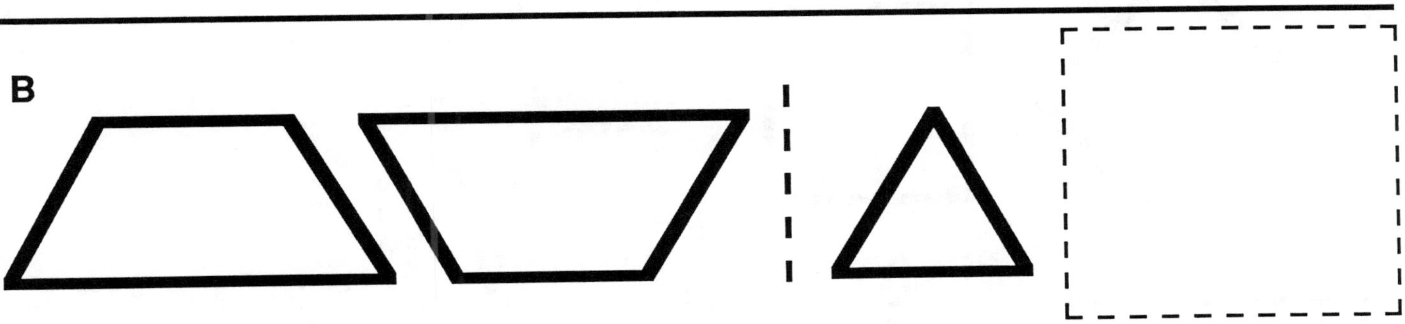

**C**

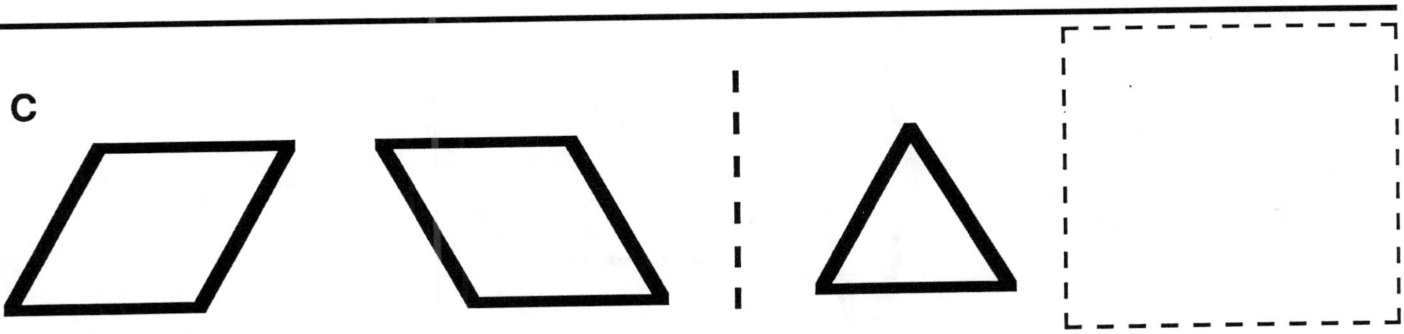

## SHAPE AND POSITION

Place a PATTERN BLOCK on each shape on the page.

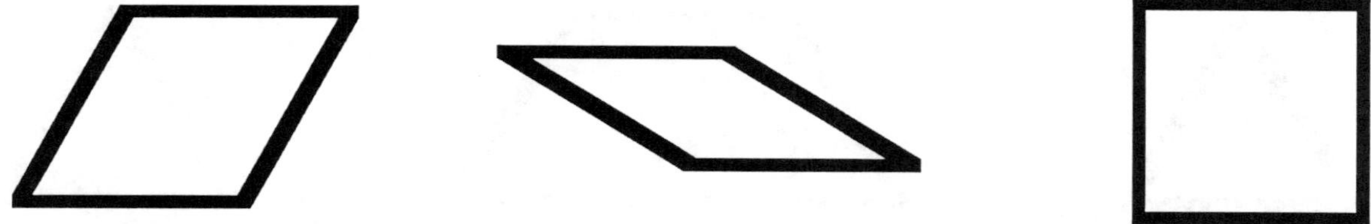

The first two blocks in each row below are related by shape and position.
Choose a block from above that is related to the third block in the same way.
Place it in the dotted box.
Trace the blocks and color the pictures to match.

**A**

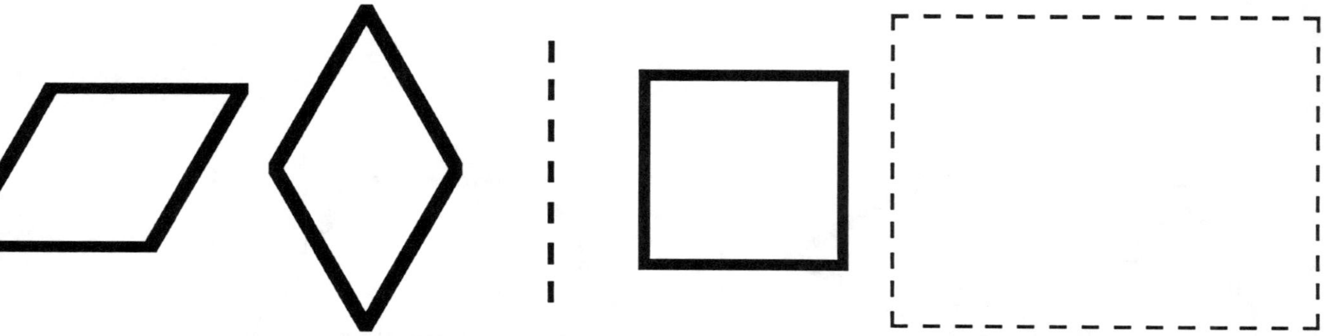

**B**

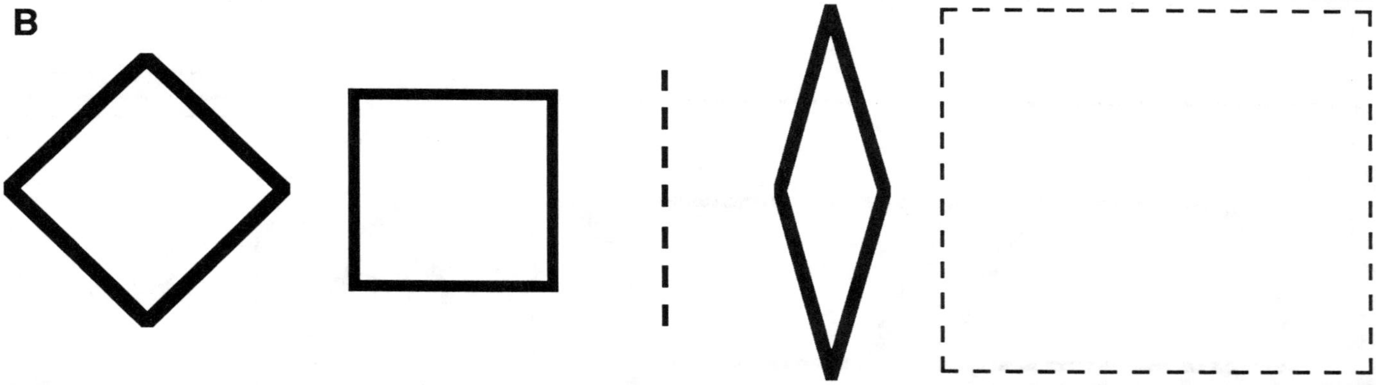

**C**

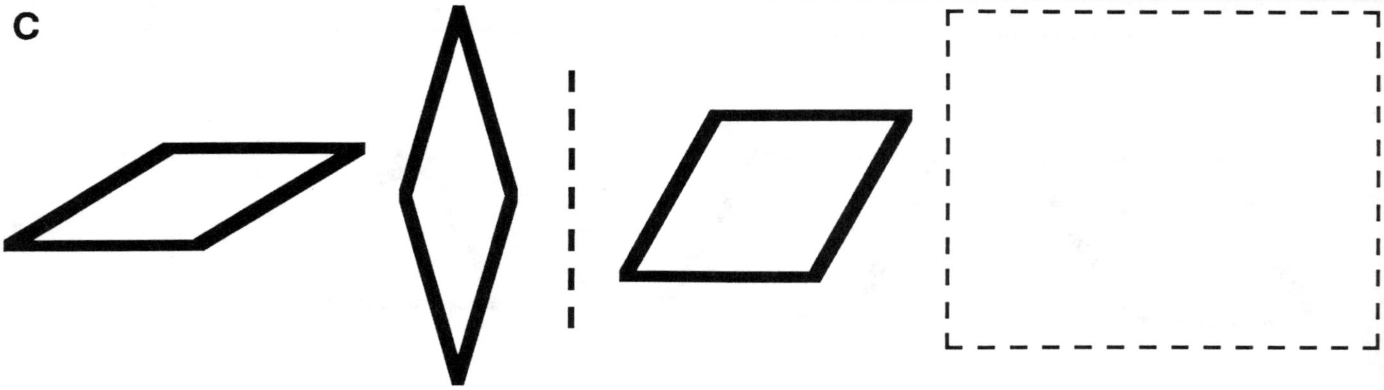

# SHAPE AND POSITION

Place a PATTERN BLOCK on each shape below.
The first two blocks in each row are related by shape and position.
Choose the block that is related to the third block in the same way and place it in the dotted box.
Trace the blocks and color the pictures to match.

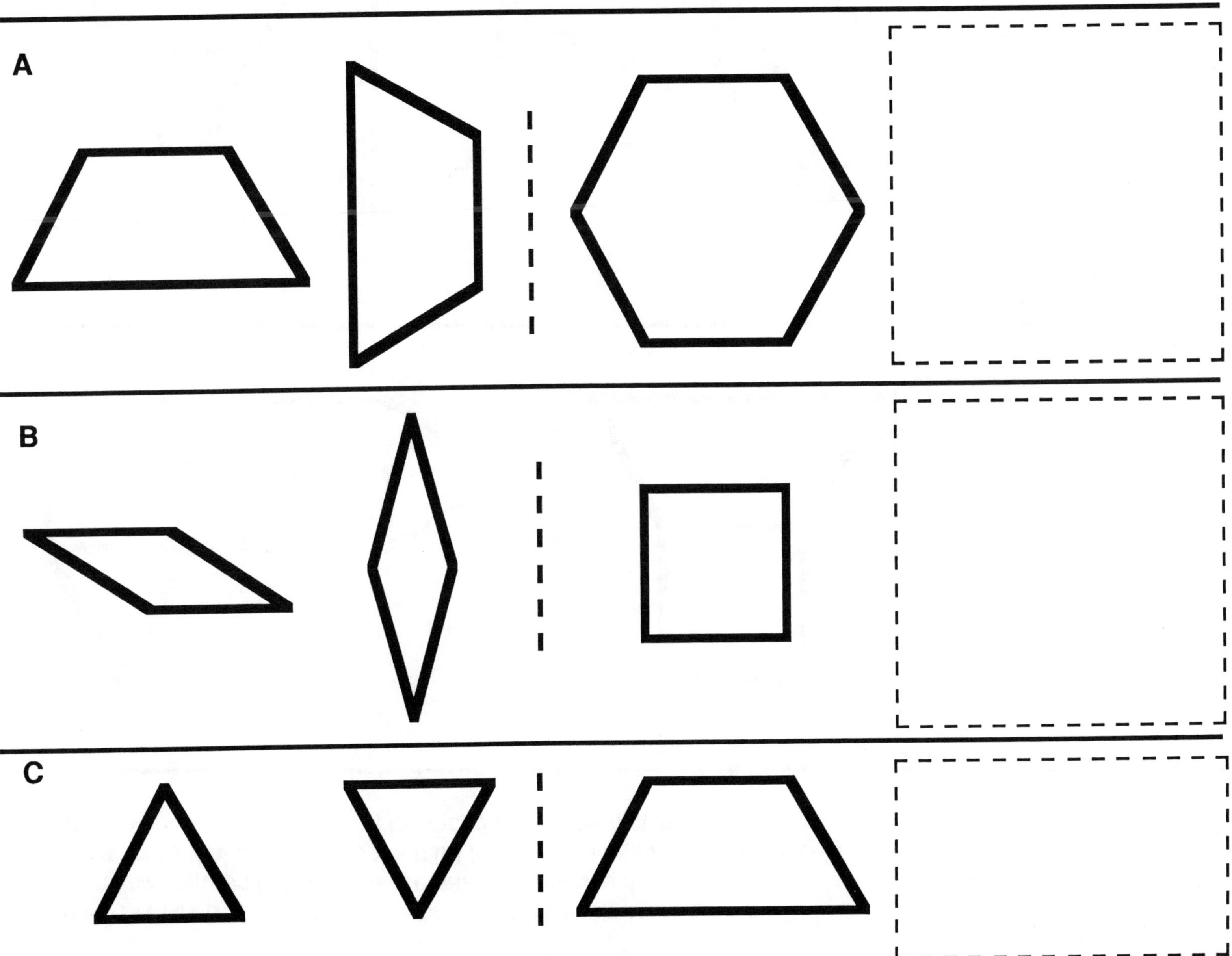

## SHAPE AND POSITION

Use PATTERN BLOCKS to construct and cover each figure below.
The first two figures in each row are related by shape and position.
Make a figure that is related to the third figure in the same way and place it in the dotted box.
Trace the figures and color the pictures to match the blocks.

A

B

## SHAPE

Use PATTERN BLOCKS to construct and cover each figure below.
The first two figures in each row are related by shape.
Make a figure that is related to the third figure in the same way and place it in the dotted box.
Trace the figures and color the pictures to match the blocks.

**A**

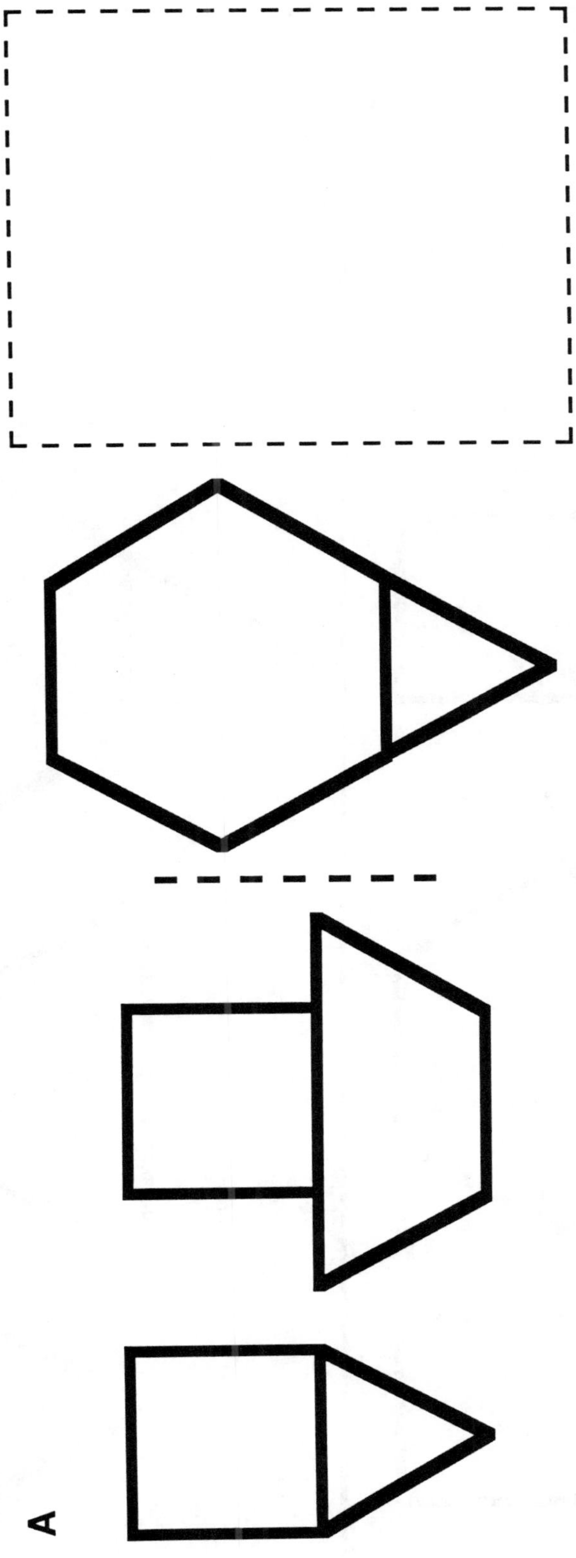

**B**

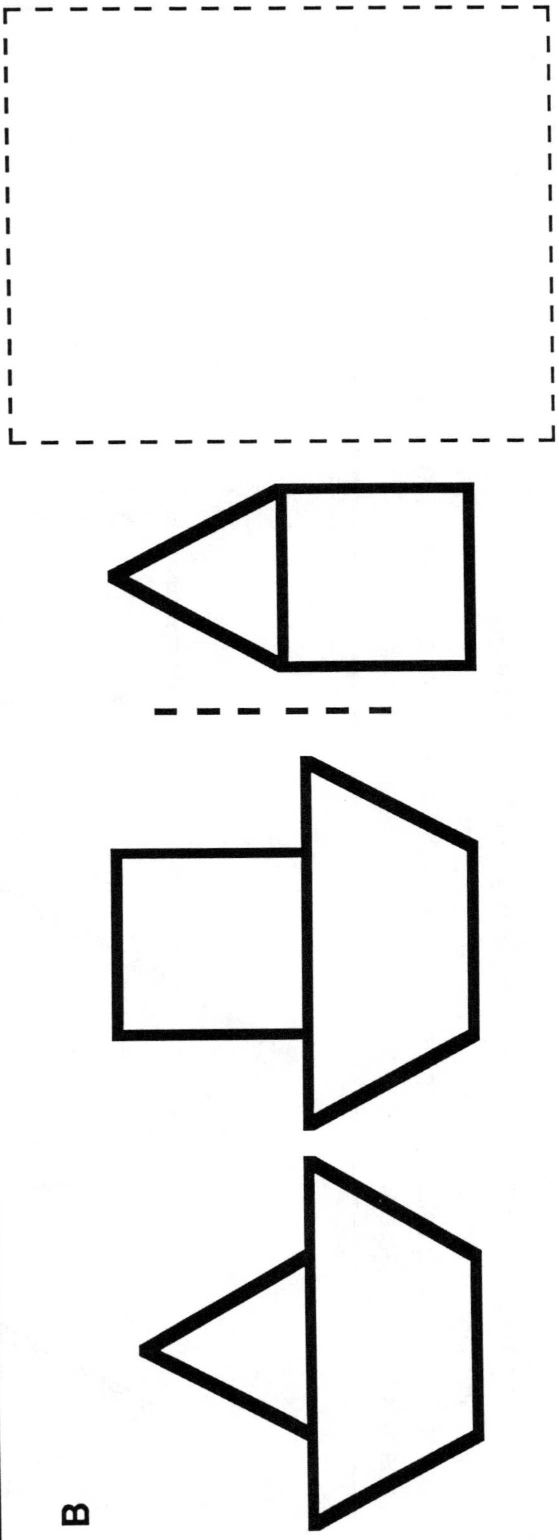

# SHAPE

Use PATTERN BLOCKS to construct and cover each figure below.
The first two figures in each row are related by shape.
Make a figure that is related to the third figure in the same way and place it in the dotted box.
Trace the figures and color the pictures to match the blocks.

A

B

## PATTERNS

Use two different colors of INTERLOCKING CUBES to construct these six figures.

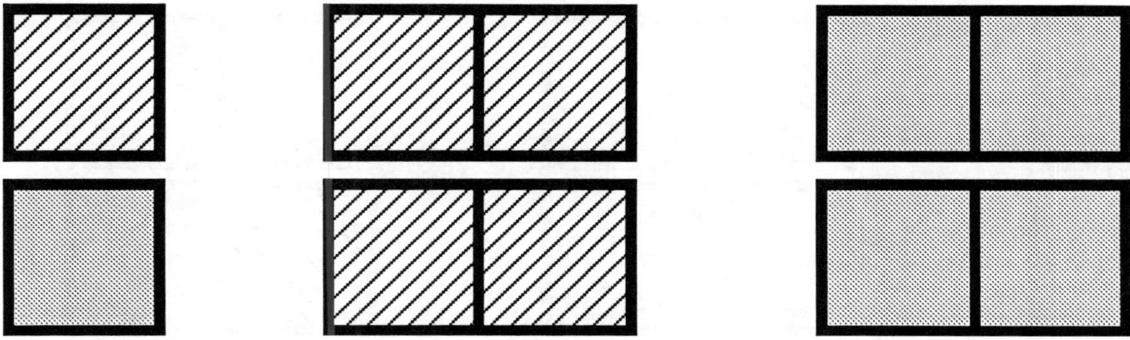

Place the constructed figures on the pictures below.
The first two figures in each row are related by color, shape, and position.
In the dotted box, place the figure from above that is related to the third figure in the same way.
Trace the figures and color the pictures to match the cubes.

**A**

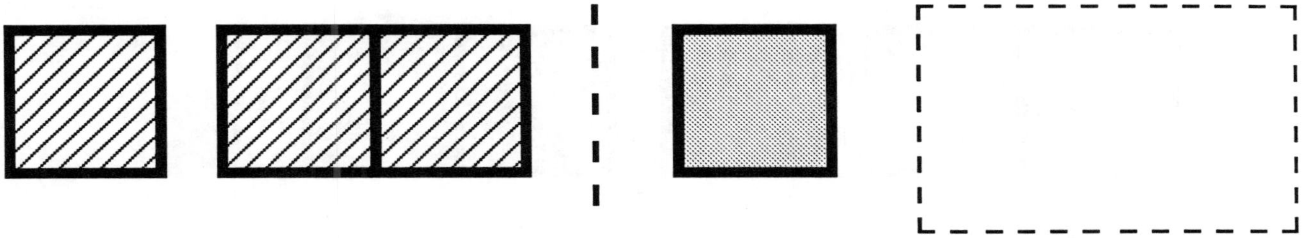

**B**

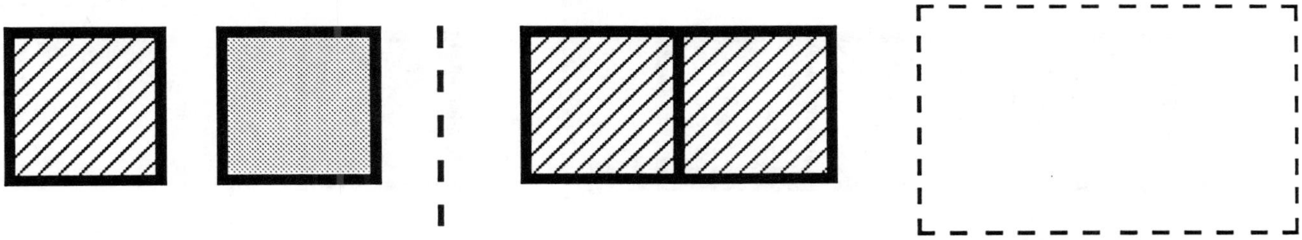

**C**

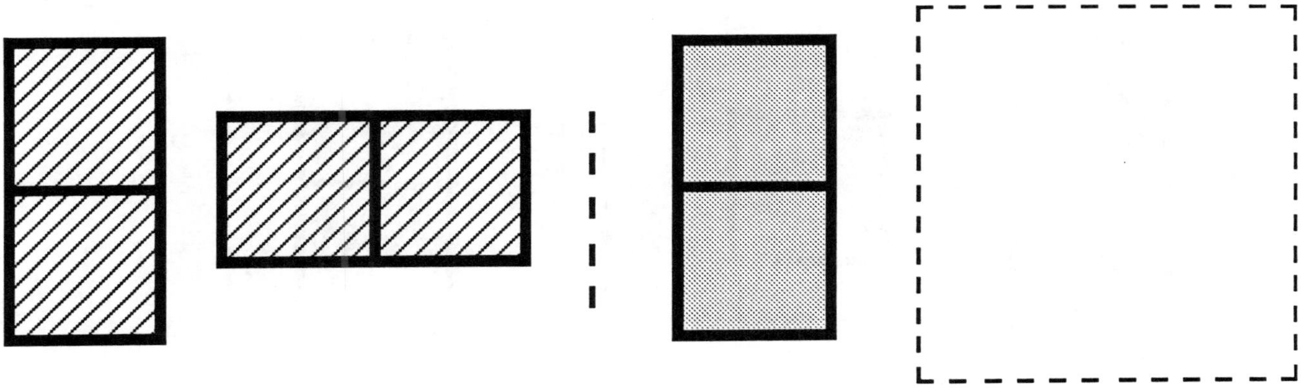

# PATTERNS

Use two different colors of INTERLOCKING CUBES to construct these six figures.

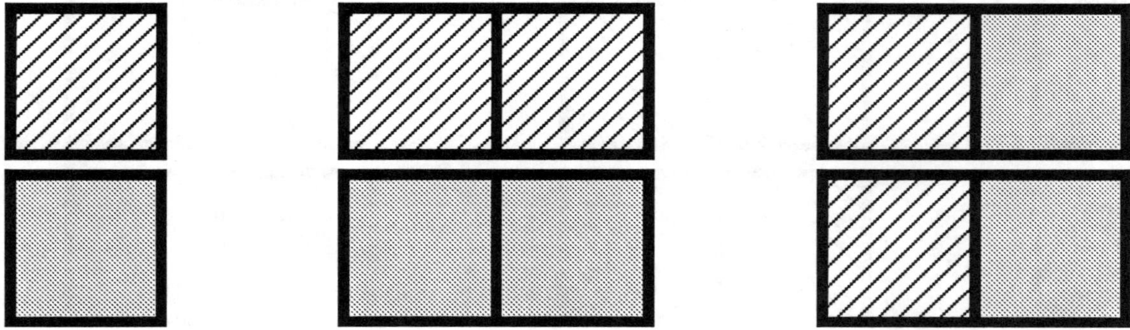

Place the constructed figures on the pictures below.
The first two figures in each row are related by color, shape, and position.
In the dotted box, place the figure from above that is related to the third figure in the same way.
Trace the figures and color the pictures to match the cubes.

**A**

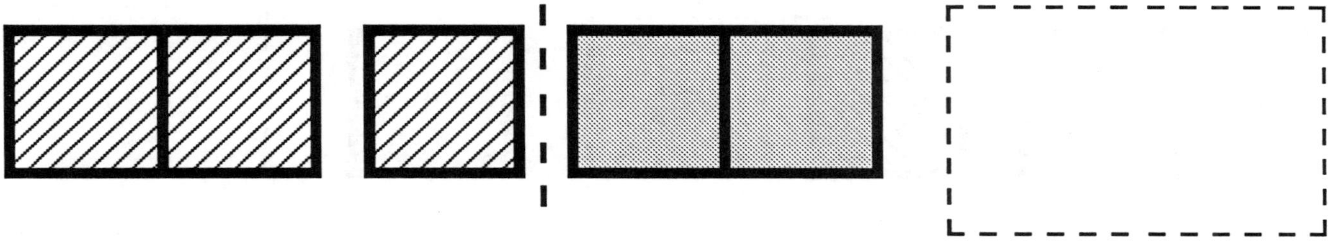

**B**

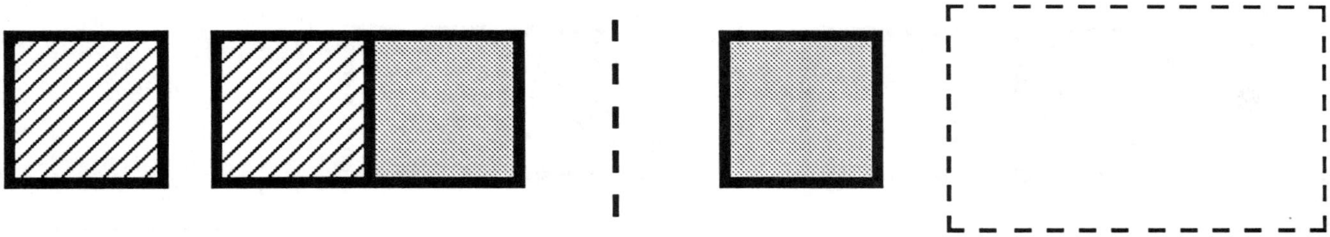

**C**

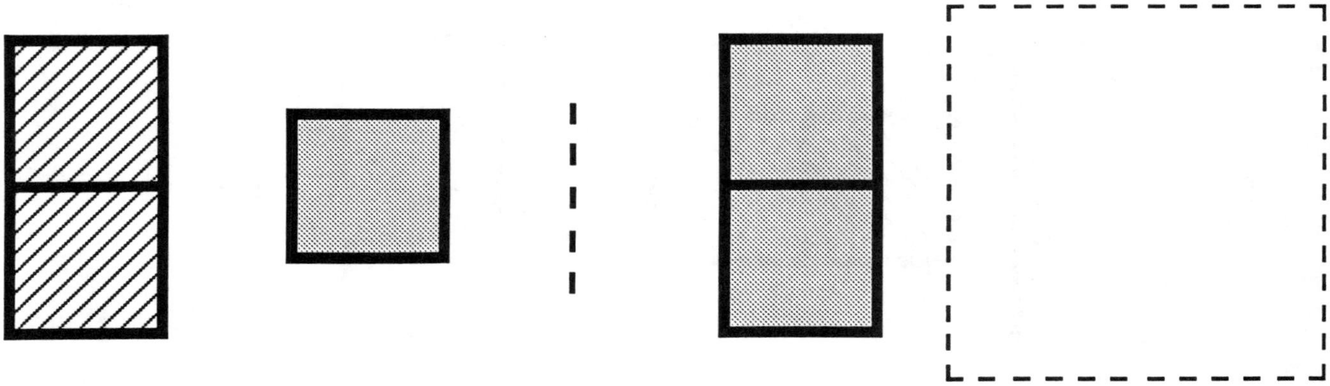

## SHAPE AND PATTERN

Use two different colors of INTERLOCKING CUBES to make and cover each figure below.
The first two figures in each row are related by shape and pattern.
In each blank box, construct a figure that is related to the third figure in the same way.
Color the pictures to match the cubes.

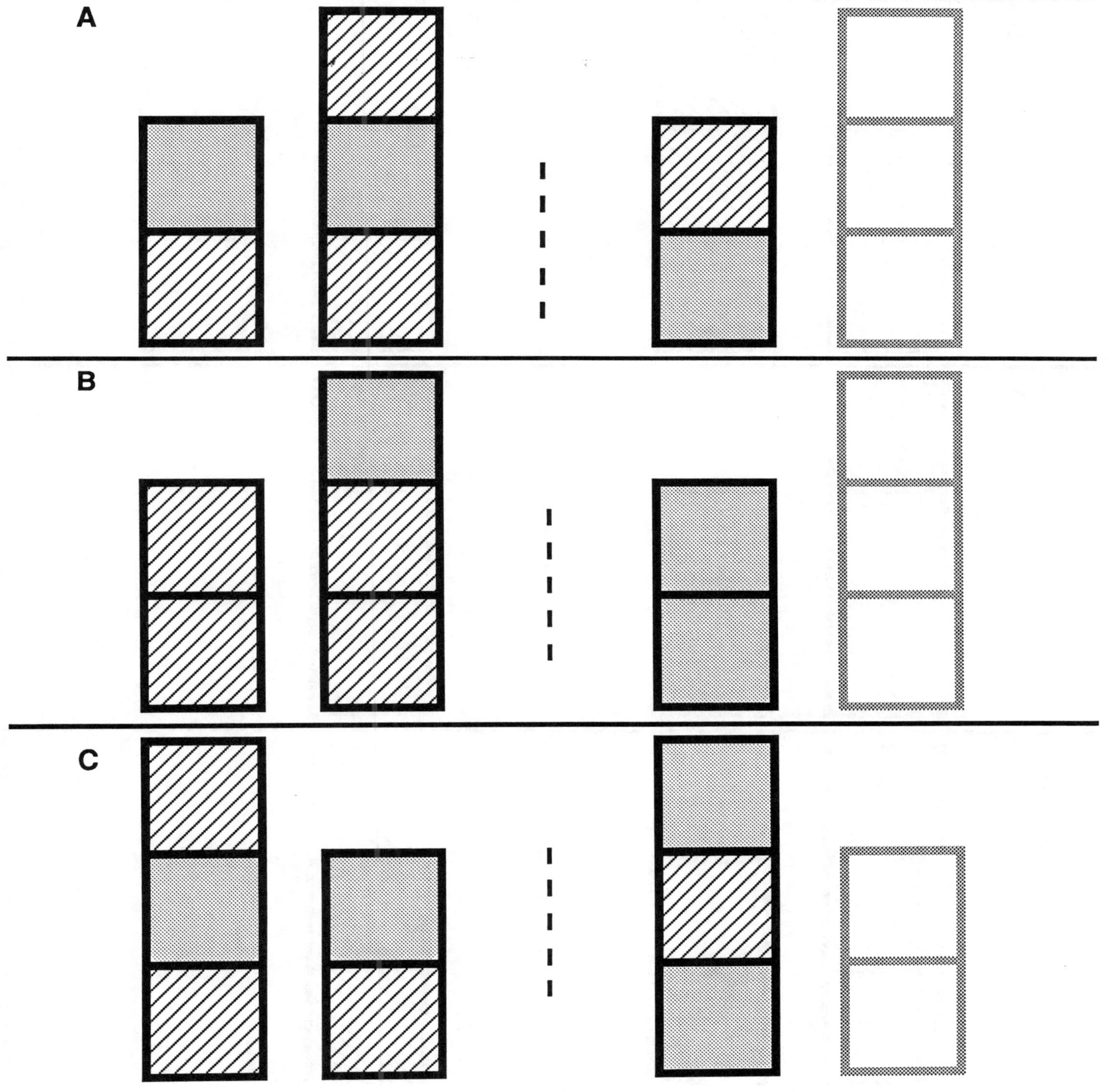

## SHAPE AND PATTERN

Use two different colors of INTERLOCKING CUBES to make and cover each figure below.
The first two figures in each row are related by shape and pattern.
In each blank box, construct a figure that is related to the third figure in the same way.
Color the pictures to match the cubes.

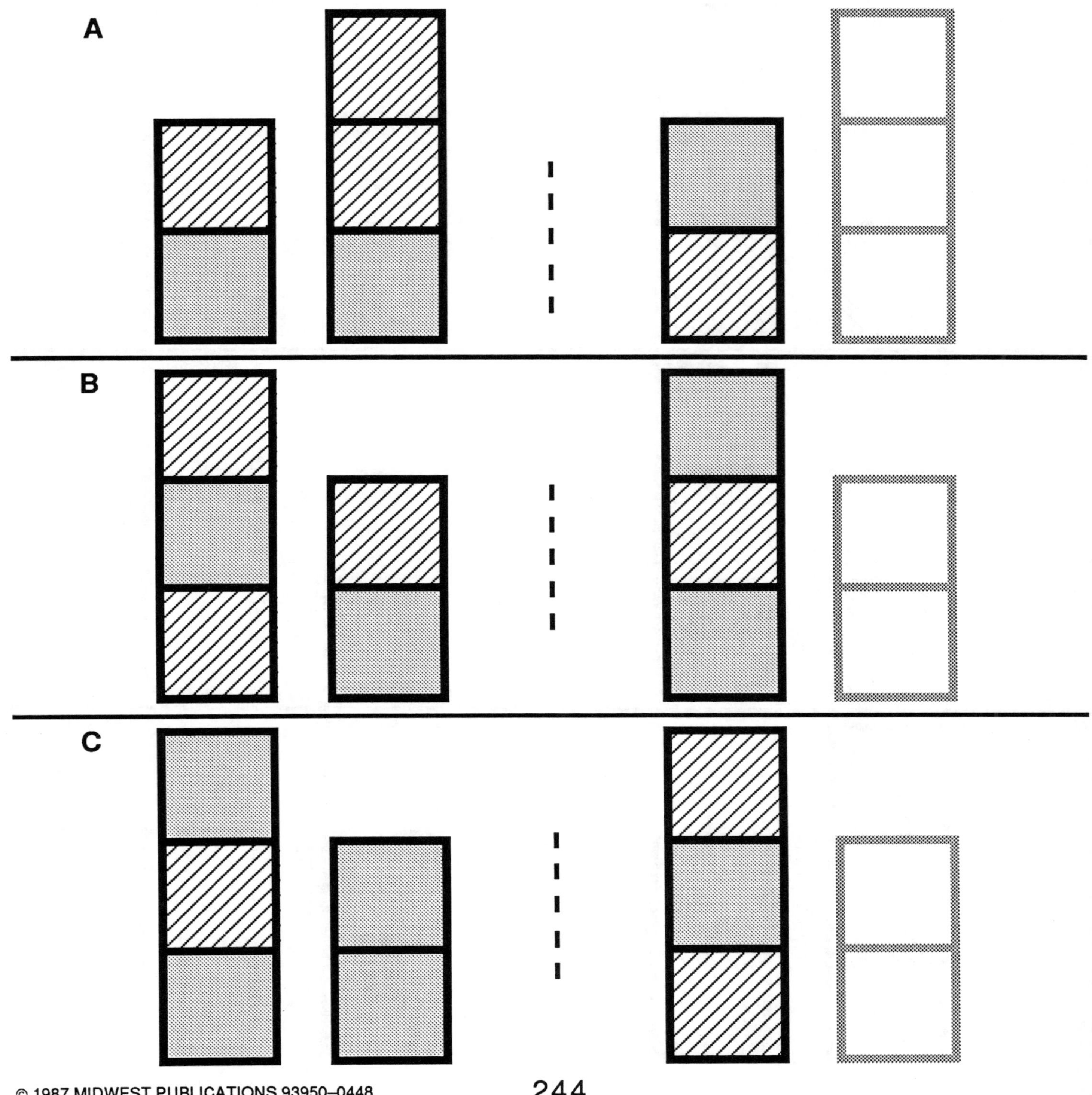

## SHAPE AND PATTERN

Use two different colors of INTERLOCKING CUBES to make and cover each figure below.
The first two figures in each row are related by shape and pattern.
In each blank box, construct a figure that is related to the third figure in the same way.
Color the pictures to match the cubes.

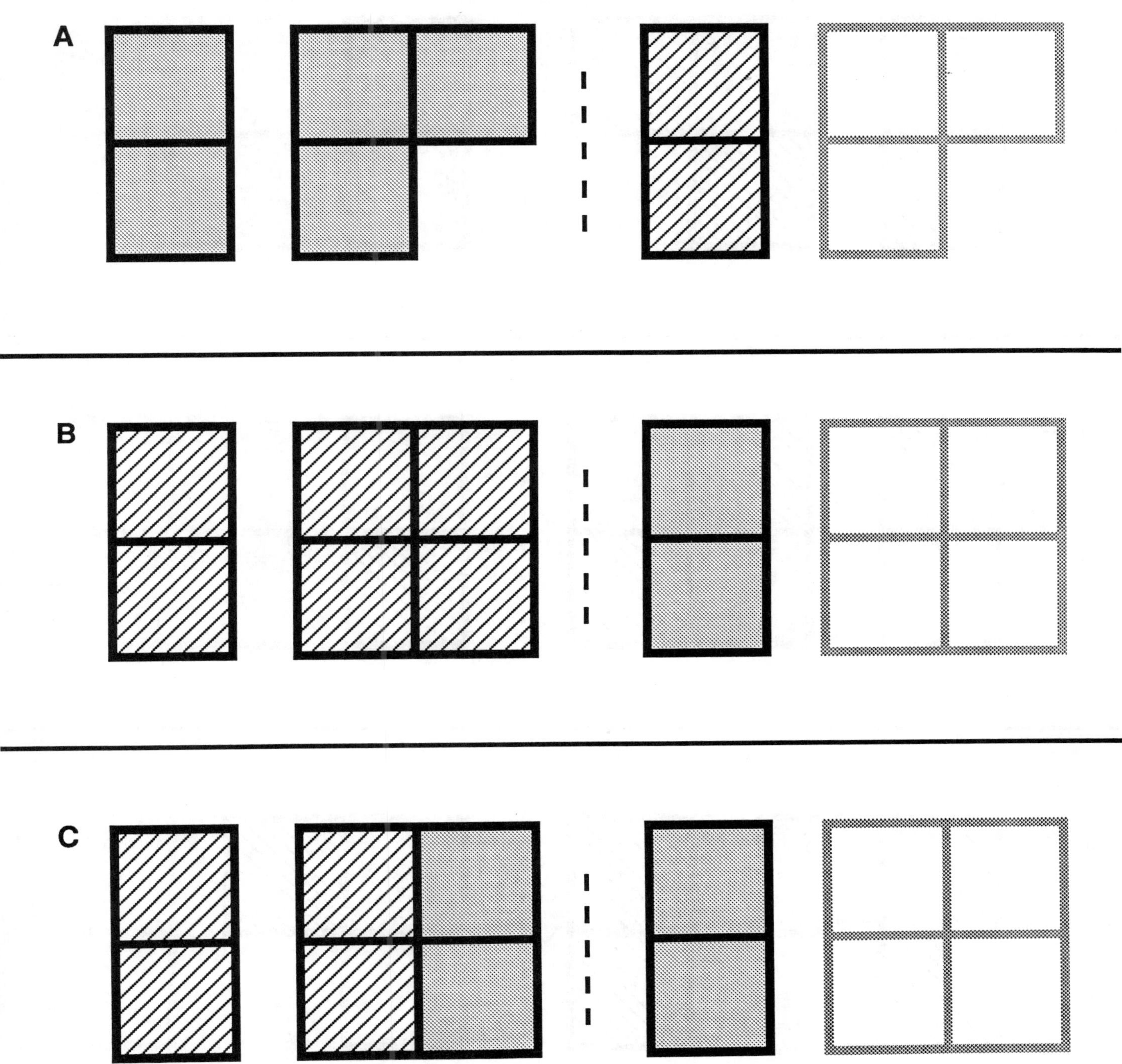

## SHAPE AND PATTERN

Use two different colors of INTERLOCKING CUBES to make and cover each figure below.
The first two figures in each row are related by shape and pattern.
In each blank box, construct a figure that is related to the third figure in the same way.
Color the pictures to match the cubes.

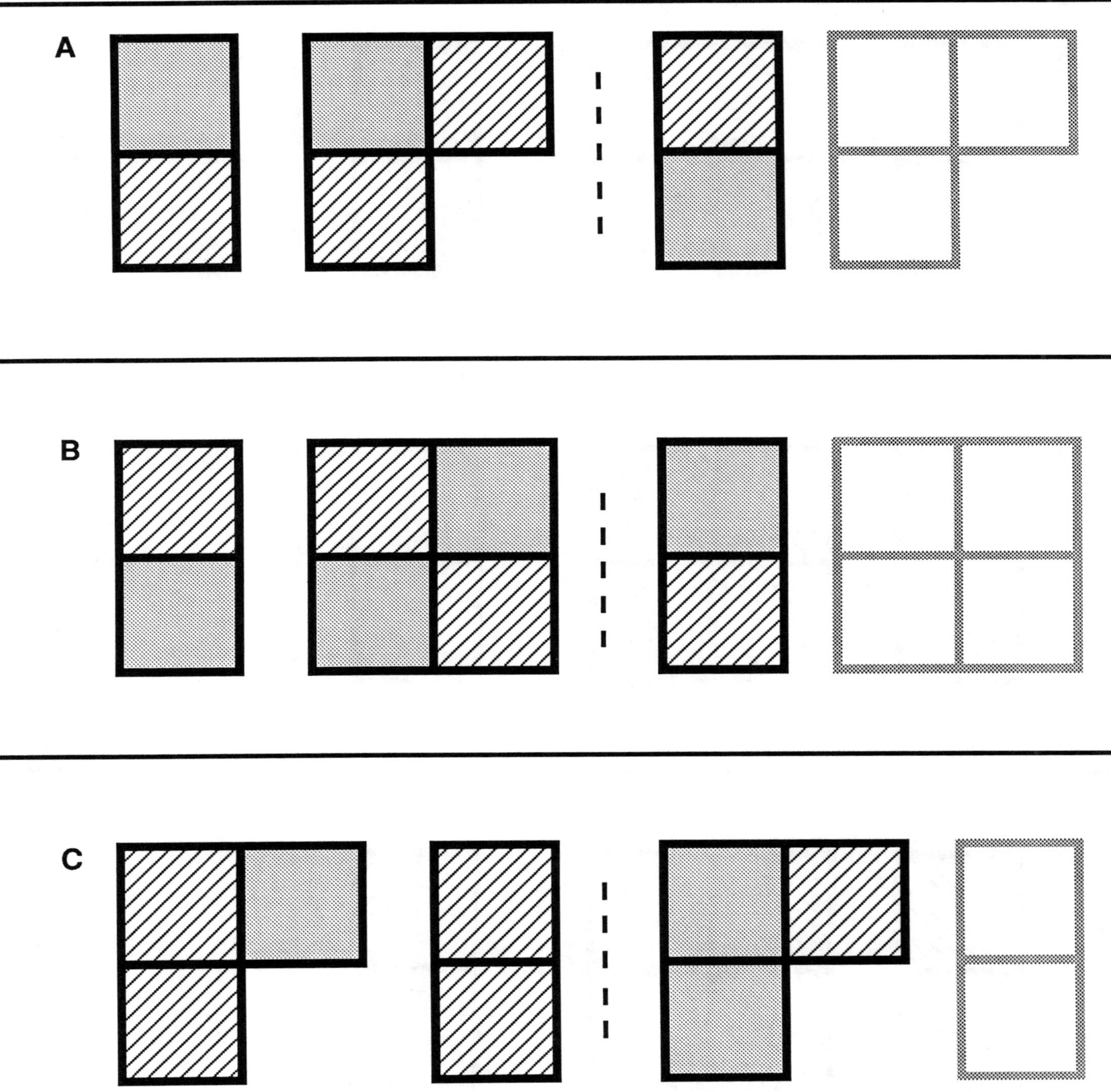